A PORTION - VOLUME THREE

Renewal of the Mind!

According to Romans 12:2

Minister Paulette Denise

A Portion Volume Three
Renewal Of The Mind!
© 2014

Scripture quotations are from:

Scripture quotations marked (AMP) are taken from the Amplified Bible, Old Testament, copyright © 1965, 1987 by the Zondervan Corporation. The Amplified Bible, New Testament, copyright © 1954, 1958, 1962, 1964, 1965, 1987 by the Lockman Foundation.

Scripture quotations noted (KJV) are taken from the Holy Bible, King James Version.

Scripture quotations marked (NIV) are taken from the Holy Bible, New International Version. Copyright © 1973, 1978, 1984, 2010 by Biblica.

Scripture quotations marked (MSG) are taken from The Message. Copyright © 1993, 1994, 1995, 1996, 2000, 2001, 2002 by Eugene H. Peterson.

Scripture quotations marked (NLT) are taken from the Holy Bible. New Living Translation copyright © 1996, 2004 by Tyndale Charitable Trust.

All Rights Reserved. No part of this publication may be reproduced or transmitted in any form or by any means, electronic or mechanical, including photocopy, recording, or any information storage and retrieval system, except for brief quotations in reviews, without the written permission of the author.

Cover design by Short Lady Graphic Designs, Connie Preston
Logo design by Design Byrd, Tracey D. Byrd

Printed in the United States of America

ISBN 978-0-9831341-1-4
Copyright © 2014 by Paulette Denise, A Portion Ministries

A Portion Volume Three
Renewal Of The Mind!
© 2014

Dedication and Acknowledgements:

This entire project is dedicated to the Lord Jesus Christ, the lover of my soul that has empowered me throughout my personal Renewal Of The Mind! process. To my daughters and grandsons (Rakiya "Rocky" Miles, Erica Sims, Jeremiah Sims, Brantley Rollins); to my mother Connie Preston (AKA Short Lady), my dad Robert Preston, my sister (Jacquelin Adams), my brother (Shannon "Mr. Dynisty" Martin) – thank you for being patient through my transformation process.

To Pastor Lorenzo Ewing and my Fellowship of Love Church family. I am grateful to God for the safe place to be planted, as the Obadiah cave and the continual provisions of bread and water (1 Kings 18:4) – and for a foundation of Proclaiming, Discipling, Serving, and Loving – (PDSL).

Also, the combined pouring and ministry outlets of:
    Apostle Ida B. Ullrich – Woman Rise Up Ministries
    Cassandra Scott Ministries – Created2Produce – Turning Point Faith Ministries
    Stacy Johnson-Harrell & Unified Praise Dance Company – Visual Arts Production

I also want to thank Short Lady Designs (Connie Preston, my mother) for her tireless work with the cover of this project, and the last minute changes. Also, to Design Byrd (Minister Tracey Denitra Byrd) for walking alongside me through this project, and providing the logos of life.

Preface:

Hallelujah! This part of the battle is over! You now hold in your hands the finished product of a major battle of purpose. This must be some powerful material, because it has been fought and contested every step along the way. I was 95% done with the project, and the driver that the document was on became corrupted! And the backup was over 1 month old without many major edits. But glory to God, I had the hardcopy of the final project and was able to rebuild the entire document – started over from a blank document, to this completed document! I didn't just view it as an attack from the enemy, but the Lord testing me to see if this material is live or Memorex. Well, it is live! It is within me, and was an honor to pull it all back together again! Prayerfully, I found all glitches. Persistence pays off. My determined purpose is to be pleasing unto the Lord, I pray He is well pleased with this test. I pray that you are blessed and learn more of the Renewal Of The Mind! process.

A Portion Volume Three
Renewal Of The Mind!
© 2014

Table of Contents

Chapter 1 – Introduction 6
1.1 Introduction of Volume III Project 6
1.2 The Journey Begins 7
1.3 Theme: Romans 12:1-3 11
1.4 Two Trees 12
1.5 Examination Time 18
1.6 Three-Part Being 26
1.7 Language of Soul (heart) 28
1.8 Changed Nature – Changed Name 35
1.9 From Worldly Conformity, To Kingdom Conformity 37

Chapter 2 – Battlefield 47
2.1 This Is Not A Battle, This Is War! 47
2.2 Grace 55
2.3 Contend 62
2.4 Identifying The Enemy 68
2.5 Thought Life 71
2.6 Contention 87
2.7 Thorn In The Flesh 90
2.8 Heart And Soul 96
2.9 Future Glory 109
2.10 Deception 114

Chapter 3 – Repent 123
3.1 Worldliness 128
3.2 Rest 136

3.3 Obedience 138
3.4 Receive 144
3.5 Salted in Fire 152
3.6 A Closer Look at the Book of Romans 163
3.7 Trailblazers 168
3.8 Soul Ties 173

Chapter 4 – Kingdom Mindsets 177
4.1 Pride 177
4.2 Memories 184
4.3 Healing 192
4.4 Like Psalm 23 206
4.5 Thirsts 211
4.6 Worship 213
4.7 The Role of Affliction 222

Chapter 5 – Kingdom Finances 226
5.1 Rich Verses Wealthy 226
5.2 Stewardship 237
5.3 Original Design 253
5.4 Content 257
5.5 Riches of Grace 260

Chapter 6 – Conclusion 263
6.1 After all of this… 263
6.2 Think on these things 264
6.3 Kingdom Ready, Thy Kingdom Come – Volume Four 265

Notes 266
References 286
Other Books By Paulette Denise 287
About The Author 288

Chapter 1 – Introduction

1.1 Introduction of Volume III Project

This is the third volume of God speaking to the nations through His yielded servant Paulette Denise. Speak Lord speak.

What you hold in your hands is a compilation and condensation of over 2 ½ years and countless hours of bible study, plus the numerous hours of meditation, with additional working the studies into fluid thoughts, paragraphs, etc. – not to mention editing and formatting. This is a "tortoise and hare" project of a little at a time, all the time – this project is rich and didactic, to be used as a study manual (supplement) with the word of God, to assist in the Renewal of the Mind! process.

With that said, this is not a literary project. Please take off your worldly glasses of perfection that look at punctuation and grammar because you will find a lot of grammatical errors. The comma (,) the semicolon (;) and the dash (–) are overused and misused. There should not be any misspelled words, however there are some "made-up" words. There will be broken and incomplete sentences.

At times it will appear to jump from thought to thought, and those sections are usually separated by a (☙) mark.

Just a note: the name satan/ devil/ lucifer are intentionally left in lower case, there is no reason to give him the honor of capitalizing his name – this is not a typo.

Yes, I now have a Bachelor's degree in Business Management, however, this project is more of a personal conversation, like a journal of me talking to God and sharing with His people. Also, there will be heavy scripture quotes, after all, we renew our mind with the word of God so there is no way around it. As a matter of fact, I was mentally assaulted by the enemy of the Renewal of the Mind! process saying that "no one will want to read this book, it is just a bunch of scripture quotes." Of course I did not listen to him and kept on, being obedient to the *assignment* from the Lord. I pray that you are blessed and truly transformed in your thinking by the end of this project, and continue to refer back to this project during your time here on earth as a kingdom ambassador.

Know that it is not Paulette that is writing. There is a lot of meat, a lot of scripture references, looking up definitions and original meaning of text (Greek, Hebrew, Aramaic, but I usually will not note that, just the meaning) – but this is the only way that I can write the book because it is not human knowledge, not the knowledge of Paulette, but the knowledge of the way the Spirit of the Lord has revealed His word to me. I am not a bible scholar or a theologian, but a yielded vessel that spends time in God's presence. I operate as a scribe chronicling revelation for my generation, and those to come. My call and *assignment* with A Portion Ministries is to lay it all out as such, and to be able to give tools to the next generation. I am leaving an inheritance for my children, and my children's children, but at the same time, I am leaving an inheritance for His children and His children's children — those are the children of God, those that would believe God, trust God, and grow in God. Feel free to use the "notes" section at the end of the book to chronicle your journey, and take notes along the journey.

Throughout the project, I will break forth into prayer. I have **changed the font of the prayers** to make it evident that this is a **"prayer-break"** sprinkled throughout the entire book. An essential element to Renewal of the Mind! is prayer — actually praying the word of God, incorporating it into our thought process. What better way to illustrate this, than to include these prayers of praying back the principles/ thoughts/ words of God.

Prayer: The Holy Spirit is the One that is writing this book; through me, a broken yielded vessel, yielded as a ready writer that You O Lord bring the word out of me and get all the glory, honor, and praise. Amen.

One day I had a thought to query and get a better understanding of the saying "a mind is a terrible thing to waste." In my research I found that this was an ad slogan for the United Negro College Fund in 1972, written by Forest Long of the Young & Rubicam Advertising Agency as a response to the *assignment* to put together this college campaign for the United Negro College Fund. The slogan raised millions of dollars, and in the advertising arenas, this is one of the major slogans that people use when teaching about marketing and advertising. For the kingdom, we are supposed to be epistles read of men, to be examples of what Christ-likeness looks like — so yes, a mind is a terrible thing to waste, don't let it be wasted, stuck in conformity to worldliness. Go ahead and transform it — lose your mind and receive the mind of Christ.

1.2 The Journey Begins

Defining "renewal": it is broken into 2 words, "re" and "newal." Re means *to do it again*, like rejoice, have joy all over again. Reapply, meaning you have applied once, and now you do it again, reapply. So to renew means that it was once new and now we have to go back and make it new again, to the way that God created us to be when He created us and breathed the breath of life into man and man became a living soul that already knew how to access the mind of Christ, and the Spirit of God — in Whose image we were created in.

Defining the word "new," I found *perfect, whole, new, intact.* So at one time, we were perfect, whole, new, and intact. So now renew, by the rebirth of being born again, we renew our mind — renew the soulish realm — renew the conscience, mind, will, emotions, intellect, imaginations, memories back to perfection, back to wholeness, back to being intact, back to the original intent of man in Genesis.

The "al" at the end of renewal means that it is continual; action; a process. You do not renew your mind just one time; it is over and over, renewal; a process. Every word of this project has meaning, Renewal of the Mind! — do it over and over again — as long as you are living in the land of the living this will be needed.

The title that the Lord gave me for this project is **A Portion — Volume III — Renewal Of The Mind!** Note that the exclamation is part of the title and we will see why in a moment.

In school, we may not have looked at punctuation as thorough as we should have (well, I didn't). I know that the exclamation mark meant "I mean it for real though," or something said with emphasis. Looking at the definition of exclamation mark from the Merriam-Webster online dictionary, the first definition is *used especially after an interjection or exclamation to indicate forceful utterance or strong feeling*. So from this definition, the Lord is saying He wants a Renewal of the Mind! with forceful utterance or strong feeling — *not lackadaisical or half-heartedly*. The force is not against God, but against the forces of this world that will try to keep you from renewing your mind and doing what needs to be done.

The next definition is *a distinctive indication of major significance, interest, or contrast*. So again, we can say the major significance of Renewal of the Mind! is that we need to know what the kingdom says, and have the kingdom interests in mind. The contrast is between kingdom and worldly. The theme text for this project is Romans 12:1-3, in verse 2 we see that we cannot be conformed to worldly thinking, but transformed by the renewing of the mind. Again, not lackadaisical or half-heartedly, but with forceful utterance and strong feeling.

I also found that the exclamation mark *is used as a screamer, a gasper, a startler — something to get your attention* and say "I have to do this, God will not do it for me, I have to."

One of the common usages of the exclamation mark is to say "wow!" Anyone that knows me, knows that I like to say "wow", it is part of my personality — therefore including the exclamation mark in the title is wow!

More of the definition is that *it is intended to be astonishing or show astonishment*. Our astonishment is when we see what the kingdom has for us; or, when we see the foolishness of the world that we were believing. Another note found was: *Casually, exclamation marks may be repeated for additional emphasis ("That's great!!!"), but this practice is generally considered unacceptable in formal writing*. The thought I had here was that we use the (!) so casually that it has lost its impact when we intended for it to be impactful. Yet God is saying Renewal of the Mind! will never lose its impact. God wants us to know He is serious about it!

Wow, here is another fact I found about the exclamation mark: *Warning signs are often an exclamation point enclosed within a triangle.* So it is a warning, that this must be done. We are living in the last days, gone are the days of just "churching" — we MUST renew our mind and be connected to the Head, to truly be a part of the body of Christ.

Another warning is that the exclamation mark is *used to emphasize a precautionary statement.* So beforehand, be cautioned that you will have to renew your mind because the enemy will try to tell you that you don't. He will tell you stuff like "If God wants you to think like that, then He will change your thoughts" — but no, He has given us a free will, and our will is part of our thoughts, and we have to choose to change our thoughts.

Romans chapter 12 is titled *Christian Conduct.* The Volume III project is about how we are to conduct ourselves as dual citizens in the earth realm, and of the higher realm of heaven.

The decisive part, your mind has to be made up that the body must be dead. Dead, but living. You may say how can this be? It is dead to speaking to my mind, and dead to me following what it says. The only reason that it lives is because I need a dirt suit for my spirit and my soul (my regenerated mind) to live in.

> Romans 12:1 I appeal to you therefore, brethren, and beg of you in view of [all] the mercies of God, to make a decisive dedication of your bodies [presenting all your members and faculties] as a living sacrifice, holy (devoted, consecrated) and well pleasing to God, which is your reasonable (rational, intelligent) service and spiritual worship.

Reasonable service in KJV, but AMP says reasonable, rational, and intelligent service — this is in the soulish realm. You have to choose to do this, it has to be your will (made up mind) that you will not listen to the flesh anymore. It cannot just be an idea in your head, but you have to be convinced; and let the body know that its place is: dead daily. The body will continue to come back hollering, but if it is dead, you do not take your cues from dead stuff. As in Galatians, we once lived after the flesh, but not anymore.

Know that we cannot get to true spiritual worship without getting the mind together as to what is going on with this dirt suit (the appetites and the lust of flesh).

"Entire renewal" — you cannot just do bits and pieces. The beauty of how God does it is that He does not just change everything at once, we could not handle that. Our minds (the un-regenerated heart part of the soulish realm), as in Jeremiah 17:9-10 are a mess, and must be renewed according to the word of God, transformed to think kingdom instead of worldliness.

> Jeremiah 17:9-10 The heart is deceitful above all things, and it is exceedingly perverse and corrupt and severely, mortally sick! Who can know it [perceive, understand, be acquainted with his own heart and mind]? 10I the Lord search the mind, I try the heart, even to give to every man according to his ways, according to the fruit of his doings.

> Romans 12:2 Do not be conformed to this world (this age), [fashioned after and adapted to its external, superficial customs], but be transformed (changed) by the [entire] renewal of your mind [by its new ideals and its new attitude], so that you may prove [for yourselves] what is the good and acceptable and perfect will of God, even the thing which is good and acceptable and perfect [in His sight for you].

Where did these new ideals and attitudes come from? They came from the mind of Christ that is in the spirit realm; that we have to renew our mind in the soulish realm to access it. These new ideals and new attitudes are what cause us to be able to make that reasonable, rational, intelligent service to God of presenting our body. It may take a long time to truly understand this, but God is gracious and merciful in the process.

Prove for yourself — not the devil, or your mother, or that person that said you would never be anything, not for the pastor, some committee board, or anyone else but prove for yourself. You must be convinced of who you are, who God is, and who you are in Him. The way to obtain this type of conviction is in the word of God.

As we transform our thinking with the word of God, and materials based on the word of God, we are getting to know for ourselves.

> Romans 12:3 For by the grace (unmerited favor of God) given to me I warn everyone among you not to estimate and think of himself more highly than he ought [not to have an exaggerated opinion of his own importance], but to rate his ability with sober judgment, each according to the degree of faith apportioned by God to him.

It says to judge yourself, not to be so concerned with what someone else has going on, but look at yourself. What do we have our mind stayed on? Is it Him? He said He would keep us in perfect peace; but what are we thinking on? These are some areas to check and judge ourselves. If something, a trial or situation that you are going through, causes you to not have peace, what is your idol? What are you thinking about? The situation? Or God? As long as you are thinking about God, you have perfect peace. When you lose your peace, you are not thinking on God, and anything that you think on more than God is an idol. You can even look at trouble as an idol. So you must be mindful how you look at things, that you praise Him in the midst of things.

1.3 Theme: Romans 12:1-3

> Romans 12:1-3 I appeal to you therefore, brethren, and beg of you in view of [all] the mercies of God, to make a decisive dedication of your bodies [presenting all your members and faculties] as a living sacrifice, holy (devoted, consecrated) and well pleasing to God, which is your reasonable (rational, intelligent) service and spiritual worship. 2 Do not be conformed to this world (this age), [fashioned after and adapted to its external, superficial customs], but be transformed (changed) by the [entire] renewal of your mind [by its new ideals and its new attitude], so that you may prove [for yourselves] what is the good and acceptable and perfect will of God, even the thing which is good and acceptable and perfect [in His sight for you]. 3For by the grace (unmerited favor of God) given to me I warn everyone among you not to estimate and think of himself more highly than he ought [not to have an exaggerated opinion of his own importance], but to rate his ability with sober judgment, each according to the degree of faith apportioned by God to him.

Yes, we need to renew our mind, but don't get puffed up and think of yourself more highly than you should. The sober judgment is that, it is not what we do, but what He has done, and does.

Let God transform you into a new person — your spirit man became new at the new birth, back in Romans 10 when you confessed and believed, the spirit man was made new and quickened when you confessed and made Jesus Lord of your soul — that is justification. Then the sanctification process began right then, and as you continue in this process, as you do as the NLT — *"don't copy the behavior and customs of this world"* — it may not be that you are copying it, but that is all you knew before new birth. So now you see that was not right. God transforms you by changing the way you think, and that is why the battlefield is in the mind. The enemy wants you "stinking thinking" about crazy stuff and having worldly thoughts such as "I would not take that from them!" When God is saying "Vengeance is mine" — they didn't do it to you, they did it to God, just keep doing what He told you to do.

This mind has to be transformed! And must be a tangible transformation, that the change is evident and visible. A quick testimony: I was on a prayer line and heard a seasoned minister say that he had "decided" to leave the ministry. This hurt and tore into my soul — my soul man began to cry and the Lord said to me "See Paulette, you are not the only one that gets to that point. This is the attack of the enemy, and this is why you have to write this book, and you have to finish this project. Because so many people are being assaulted in their mind, in their thinking." But in the church, we are so busy telling people "God is going to make it alright. Hold on baby, your turn is coming — change is going to come." Yet, what do I do while I am in the wait process? Or better yet, what are you thinking about while you are waiting? So we have to address the battlefield of the mind.

Back to the text: Let God transform you...then you will learn to know God's will. We want to know God's will right now! Even though our thinking is all stinking and contrary — then we want to give God an ultimatum "tell me what You want me to do, because if you don't, then I will just keep doing crazy" — well guess what? You will just keep on doing crazy if you do not take responsibility for your thought life.

Look at the progression. In verse one, you have to present your body as a living sacrifice. God is not going to do it for you. Then at verse two of the NLT *let God transform* you...then you will learn to know Gods will — it is not going to happen immediately. It is a process. It is a lifelong process. And the next part, verse three, it says don't think you have it all together...I personally have never thought I had it all together, this is actually one of the reasons that I have felt like I want to quit because people will put pressure on you to make you think, that you think, that you have it going on! Not so! I don't hold myself more highly than I ought. I don't do pedestals. I know how undone I was and am apart from Christ. For those that think that I think like that, they need to check their thinking, because my thinking knows my place of humility in Him. I don't think of myself more highly than I ought to, others do, and that is on them — I can't change anyone else's process or pattern, that is on them — I will not let them mess up my thinking.

Looking at the measurements in verse 3, I am not measuring myself by anybody else that has gone before me in ministry, my faith is in Him, and that is what I am measuring it by. How much of Him is in me? Am I taking the time to change my thinking? To allow God to change the way I think because He is making me so that I can know and learn the will of God for me. So that I can Romans 8:28 see how all things are working together for good... It is a process, it can be a painful process if you do not renew your mind/ memory/ intellect/ thinking. It will be painful if you do not renew those thoughts, or when something comes up and you are reminded of something and the thoughts that come up are painful. But as you go through the process of healing your thinking, it is no longer painful. It is like the major surgery I had in 2009, there was a healing process afterward. Yes, there was pain associated with the surgery, but it is wonderful to not have to go through the pain that made me have to have the surgery in the first place. I now think differently about the painful situation — and this is what we have to do about the painful situations in our lives.

Don't fight so hard to hold on to worldly thinking. Why not fight that hard to get the mind of Christ?

1.4 Two Trees

> Genesis 2:7-9 Then the Lord God formed man from the dust of the ground and breathed into his nostrils the breath or spirit of life, and man became a living being. ⁸And the Lord God planted a garden toward the east, in Eden [delight]; and there He put the man whom He had formed (framed, constituted). ⁹ And out of the ground the Lord God made to grow every tree that is pleasant to the sight or to be desired — good (suitable, pleasant) for food; the tree of life also in the center of the garden, and the tree of the knowledge of [the difference between] good and evil and blessing and calamity.

The God-conscience is what died when they ate of the tree of knowledge, and their sin-conscience was now alive to evil and calamity. Just a thought I have had, and heard someone teach on, "what would have happened if they had eaten of the tree of life?" But because of them transgressing the one commandment given and eating of the tree of knowledge, they were driven out of the garden as in Genesis 3, the sacrificial system was instituted, and a cherubim was set at the tree of Life that no one could get to it without the blood of Jesus. Now fast forward to a New Testament reference of what took place:

> Matthew 6:19-24 Do not gather and heap up and store up for yourselves treasures on earth, where moth and rust and worm consume and destroy, and where thieves break through and steal. ²⁰ But gather and heap up and store for yourselves treasures in heaven, where neither moth nor rust nor worm consume and destroy, and where thieves do not break through and steal; ²¹ For where your treasure is, there will your heart be also. ²² The eye is the lamp of the body. So if your eye is sound, your entire body will be full of light. ²³ But if your eye is unsound, your whole body will be full of darkness. If then the very light in you [your conscience] is darkened, how dense is that darkness! ²⁴ No one can serve two masters; for either he will hate the one and love the other, or he will stand by and be devoted to the one and despise and be against the other. You cannot serve God and mammon (deceitful riches, money, possessions, or whatever is trusted in).

Looking at verse 22 in several translations of the bible, we see that: the eye is the lamp of the body, the window into your body, the lamp that provides light for your body. So, what is the center? Where your treasure is, is where your heart is. So what are you putting your treasure on? Is it on seeking the King of the kingdom, or on people, stuff, circumstances or anything that we place before God (which are called idols, but we don't dare think of it that way)? Like the song by Israel Houghton "Jesus at the center of it all" — it is "in Him" that we access the tree of life — through Him do we see the difference between good and evil, blessing and calamity — we do not need to see this without Him. Jesus at the center of it all — He is the tree of life — He is the way, the truth, the life (John 14:6). He is the light of the world that drives out the darkness of the tree of knowledge that makes you want to hide — when they ate of that tree, they hid. We need some light to not hide. If you want your eye to have light, ask for it to be flooded as in Ephesians 1 — let's put it in context:

> Ephesians 1:16-20 I do not cease to give thanks for you, making mention of you in my prayers. ¹⁷ [For I always pray to] the God of our Lord Jesus Christ, the Father of glory, that He may grant you a spirit of wisdom and revelation [of insight into mysteries and secrets] in the [deep and intimate] knowledge of Him, ¹⁸ By having the eyes of your heart flooded with light, so that you can know and understand the hope to which He has called you, and how rich is His glorious inheritance in the saints (His set-apart ones), ¹⁹ And [so that you can know and understand] what is the immeasurable and unlimited and surpassing greatness of His power in and for us who believe, as demonstrated in the working of His mighty strength, ²⁰ Which He exerted in Christ when He raised Him from the dead and seated Him at His [own] right hand in the heavenly [places].

He is the light of the world that drives out darkness, and the eye is the lamp to the body; yet the body does not rule and control; it is just a dirt suit that the spirit man lives in; and my spirit man possesses my soul man, so I have to set my soul man on the things above, I need it to be flooded with light. As Paul said here in Ephesians, we need *a spirit of wisdom and revelation [of insight into mysteries and secrets] in the [deep and intimate] knowledge of Him* — this is connecting us to the tree of knowledge, according to the tree of Life, not apart from it. We have our eyes flooded with light so that we can know and understand Him. His immeasurable and unlimited and surpassing greatness, and the power that He has.

When we get flooded with light, that dense darkness referred to in Matthew 6 is not even an issue. And out of the abundance of the heart, the mouth will speak — and where your heart is, is where your treasure is — what are you speaking about? Your treasure can be identified by what is coming out of your mouth (through your heart).

My favorite scripture for help with the heart is found in Psalm 139:23-24 *Search me [thoroughly], O God, and know my heart! Try me and know my thoughts! And see if there is any wicked or hurtful way in me, and lead me in the way everlasting.* Asking to expose the "wicked or hurtful way" is asking to expose anything gained from knowledge apart from the tree of Life — from the other tree from the center of the garden. Another way of looking at the harmful wicked way, is to say any way that is deceitful, or not what God desires — ask to be led in God's way, no longer those ways. I found one of my journal entries from meditating on this text, and it reads:

> "Flood me with Your light, and lead me in Your way — let me not be deceived any longer as in Jeremiah 17:9-10 which shows the deceptive heart and why we need the flooding of light in our heart. So that we can no longer be deceived as in Genesis 3."

The eye is the lamp to the body; the body should never be in control. The way that we crucify the flesh (the body), is by making sure that our eyes are flooded with light.

> Jeremiah 17:5-10 Thus says the Lord: Cursed [with great evil] is the strong man who trusts in and relies on frail man, making weak [human] flesh his arm, and whose

mind and heart turn aside from the Lord. 6 For he shall be like a shrub or a person naked and destitute in the desert; and he shall not see any good come, but shall dwell in the parched places in the wilderness, in an uninhabited salt land. 7 [Most] blessed is the man who believes in, trusts in, and relies on the Lord, and whose hope and confidence the Lord is. 8 For he shall be like a tree planted by the waters that spreads out its roots by the river; and it shall not see and fear when heat comes; but its leaf shall be green. It shall not be anxious and full of care in the year of drought, nor shall it cease yielding fruit. 9 The heart is deceitful above all things, and it is exceedingly perverse and corrupt and severely, mortally sick! Who can know it [perceive, understand, be acquainted with his own heart and mind]? WI the Lord search the mind, I try the heart, even to give to every man according to his ways, according to the fruit of his doings.

Wow! He just keeps adding revelation of this text each time I read it! As I am putting this manuscript together, I went back and re-read this text about 4 times, it seems to switch from talking about the state of man apart from Christ/God in verses 4 – 6, to the man who has this promised hope (new heart) in verse 7 – 8, then it jumps back to the state of being without Him in verse 9 – 10. Just something to Selah — pause and calmly think on to allow the Lord to reveal more.

First He talked about the man that trusts in man, how that is just stupid and foolish — like a shrub. But then the one that trusts in Him, has confidence in Him, and relies on Him will be like a tree planted by water with good, deep roots that are not even concerned when the heat comes, because they know their roots go down, deep, the leaves are yet green, and they are yet yielding forth fruit. Reminds me of that tree in Revelation 22:1-2, this tree has leaves which are for the healing of the nations. But bringing this back to having the eyes of our heart flooded with light, we are asking for a search to make sure there is no darkness or evil in there — we are basically saying that our confidence is in God and we have the help of the Holy Spirit to do these things when we have the eyes of our heart flooded with light so that we can know and understand the mysteries of God! Oh my, the power that is available to us!

Now we are going to go back and look at this conversation in Genesis 3 where this deception first entered in, and caused sin to enter in, and has us where we are now. This is looking at why we have to renew our mind and be on guard against deception. We have to renew our mind that no matter how the enemy dresses up the deception, we can recognize it. We have to study the truth to be able to recognize the counterfeit — like in the banking world, they do not study counterfeit money to recognize the counterfeit, they study real money so they know when something is not real. When you know the real, the counterfeit cannot mess you up.

> Genesis 3:1-5 Now the serpent was more subtle and crafty than any living creature of the field which the Lord God had made. And he [satan] said to the woman, Can it really be that God has said, You shall not eat from every tree of the garden? 2 And

> the woman said to the serpent, We may eat the fruit from the trees of the garden, 3 Except the fruit from the tree which is in the middle of the garden. God has said, You shall not eat of it, neither shall you touch it, lest you die. 4 But the serpent said to the woman, You shall not surely die, 5 For God knows that in the day you eat of it your eyes will be opened, and you will be like God, knowing the difference between good and evil and blessing and calamity.

The deception that took place right here was that the enemy was playing on the Woman's nature of wanting to please God – wanting to be a God pleaser – but you cannot be a God pleaser outside of God's commands?! She was not supposed to mess with that tree, yet the enemy was telling her that she could get to God by messing with it – a total deception! That is also why religion is killing a lot of people right now, because we have things that sound good, and look like God, but are contrary to God's instructions – it is a subtle twist of words. The Lord is leading us on this journey of scripture, to be able to identify, and not get entangled with the subtle twistings of the instructions from God.

> Genesis 3:6-8 And when the woman saw that the tree was good (suitable, pleasant) for food and that it was delightful to look at, and a tree to be desired in order to make one wise, she took of its fruit and ate; and she gave some also to her husband, and he ate. 7 Then the eyes of them both were opened, and they knew that they were naked; and they sewed fig leaves together and made themselves apronlike girdles. 8 And they heard the sound of the Lord God walking in the garden in the cool of the day, and Adam and his wife hid themselves from the presence of the Lord God among the trees of the garden.

> Genesis 3:9-11 But the Lord God called to Adam and said to him, Where are you? 10 He said, I heard the sound of You [walking] in the garden, and I was afraid because I was naked; and I hid myself. 11 And He said, Who told you that you were naked? Have you eaten of the tree of which I commanded you that you should not eat?

God already knew the answer, He just wanted Adam to confess and admit – to tell the truth, the whole truth, and nothing but the truth; yet Adam began to make excuses. This is why when we get caught by deception, we need to stop trying to use deception to explain it away and get out of it! JUST TELL THE TRUTH!

> Genesis 3:12-13 And the man said, The woman whom You gave to be with me – she gave me [fruit] from the tree, and I ate. 13 And the Lord God said to the woman, What is this you have done? And the woman said, The serpent beguiled (cheated, outwitted, and deceived) me, and I ate.

She knew exactly what happened because her eyes were opened once she was disobedient and partook of the tree of knowledge, and she recognized that she was deceived. When your eyes are open to the knowledge of good and evil, verses the knowledge that we are talking about (the flood my heart with light type knowledge so that I can see it), all you will see is bad. No, we need our eyes flooded with light, someone needs to bring the light and turn some light on in dark places.

The Lord is speaking to the heart of His servant, Paulette Denise, to truly understand the Renewal of the Mind! process — being renewed to the state of which we were before the fall of mankind — before deception and sin entered in the world, so we must renew our minds to understand that deception.

This is a study of the meanings of the names from Eden — that we renew our minds back to God's original intent. We will look at this more in depth in the kingdom finances chapter. Eden was a paradise; one of the rivers was a flowing river; another was a river that gushes or spewed out sporadically (in times of drought, it would only gush once or twice a day, but in the rainy season, it would gush up to 8 times per day); then 2 of the rivers ended up being very industrious places to where people and businesses wanted to be by them. We are asking God to renew our minds so that we are these flowing gushing rivers, we are these abundant water sources. Water is symbolic of the Holy Spirit, of His presence.

Something I noticed regarding Genesis 2:9, stop focusing on what was lost, and focus on what we need to do to be restored back to the original intent. A lot of people emphasize the fact that woman should not have eaten of the forbidden tree, of the fruit of the knowledge of good and evil. She ate and awakened the wrong part of her conscience. Let us not emphasize what she did wrong, yes, it was wrong — we are not downplaying that, but as in John 10:10, do not emphasize that the enemy came to kill/ steal/ destroy, but the fact the Jesus came to bring abundant life — spend more time talking about the abundant life, instead of the fact that "the devil is busy". In doing this, it negates anything that the enemy tried to kill/ steal/ destroy. So let's not focus so much on the knowledge of good and evil — we see it, recognize it, and have identified it; now let's identify the tree of life and that is the only way that we can grow and have our minds renewed to get back to Eden. Let's not focus on good and evil, but focus on the tree of life — because no man is good except Jesus — He is the tree of life. Focus on Him, not the pastor, the preacher, the minister, religion, doctrines of men, but focus on Jesus — the tree of life.

1.5 Examination Time

Do we really want God to examine us, to test our heart and mind?

> Psalm 139:23-24 Search me [thoroughly], O God, and know my heart! Try me and know my thoughts! ²⁴ And see if there is any wicked or hurtful way in me, and lead me in the way everlasting.

Yes, I want You to test me and search my heart, to prove me. I am committed to God, and so when I get chastened by God, I will get disciplined and learn the lesson that He is teaching me (see Hebrews 5:8 and Proverbs 22:15). Like with the disciplining of a child, the goal is not to kill or hurt the child, but to teach them a lesson so that the behavior that is being exhibited will stop; and then to exhibit behavior that is suitable for a kingdom citizen. Don't make it worse than it has to be, don't be hard-headed and rebellious and fall out all over the place and get hit in areas that you don't need to get hit in. All we have to do is repent, submit to the chastening of the Lord, we know our actions were wrong... it stings now, and is painful now, but the memory of that painful thing will make us not do it anymore.

This next section is going to look throughout the book of Psalms to better understand what it means to renew our mind; looking at the soulish realm.

> Psalm 26:2 Examine me, O Lord, and prove me; test my heart and my mind.

This psalm is titled *the basis of judgment*, it is a good idea to judge myself according to Romans 12:3 NLT. I am looking at how I should be looking at myself, not looking at other's faith, but at me. My only responsibility to others is to sow seed, water seed, and turn the light on, God gives the increase. But I am responsible for Paulette's faith. Others can benefit from watching my faith walk, and in James it says not many should profess to be teachers because you are held to a higher standard, so I do have a responsibility of making sure that I am giving good seed, and turning on the bright/pure light of the gospel, not my own doctrines or theories, but turning on the right thing. That is my responsibility, but I can sow the same word to 5 people, and 2 people be transformed, but the other 3 not be changed. That is not my responsibility, but God's, and yours, the listener. Let him who has an ear, hear what the Spirit of the Lord is saying.

> Psalm 26:1 Vindicate me, O Lord, for I have walked in my integrity; I have [expectantly] trusted in, leaned on, and relied on the Lord without wavering and I shall not slide.

Can we say this about ourselves? That we have trusted Him? If we cannot, then we need to work on our trust walk. For the entire year of 2012, one of my meditation scriptures was

Proverbs 3, about learning to truly trust God. Not just the 3 verses about trust (verses 3-6), but the entire chapter. He says things like "whom the Lord loves, He chastens", so if you trust Him, you will be chastened, which is to discipline and correct you, some of your actions and thoughts. So when you are growing in your trusting of God, you may seem like you are always getting in trouble. It is not a bad thing, you are just growing in your trust of God. Again, can we honestly say this Psalm 26:1? Without wavering or sliding? The enemy is trying to get you to say "aww see, I can't do this." Some of the thoughts the enemy launched against my mind while dealing with a situation of financial integrity were not lies, but would not have been in good integrity. So I had to make a decision to throw down those thoughts. And the mind-assault did not stop there, he launched another set of thoughts that were not lies or sin, but just not integral, I threw those down also. Then another attack, through someone close to me, they meant well, but I knew it was contrary to the integrity God called me to walk in, so I cancelled it again. I had to have my mind steadfast on the fact that I would walk in integrity, no matter who is doing what, I must do what God has shown me — this was a personal conviction in the chastening process; causing me to truly believe God as the Provider for me and my family — that was what the test was all about, my faith in God as Provider.

Your provisions will be alright, but it may take some time, and/or may not look like what you think is working. See 1 Kings 17, Elijah was at the widow's house for 3 years! They both had to watch what they were thinking, they couldn't get 1 1/2 years into it and think "God I am tired of eating bread and water" — that was all they had, that was God's provision, and He was watching their thinking.

Bread and water — the Bread symbolizes Jesus, the Manna from heaven; the water is symbolic of the Holy Spirit; and they were being provided by God — we have to be content with the Triune God: Jesus, Holy Spirit, and Father God. he is truly our provider. Do not murmur and complain like the children of Israel — or try to add to His provisions. God provides bread and water when He is sustaining His children, see the account of the prophets Obadiah hid in the cave — He fed them with bread and water (1 Kings 18:4).

Back to 1 Kings 17, look at the miracle, for 3 years, the hand of God was there — and as long as she was obedient to do what the Spirit of God told her to do, then her, her son, and the man of God were eating — for 3 years! But what if she had gotten tired of it at 2 years? Somebody better tell us as baby believers, that when we are transforming our minds, that it may not happen overnight, it may take some time. Yet the microwave society that we live in tells us that "I want it now!" No! We better learn to operate in integrity. Some of the issues on my credit report come from not operating in integrity — not that I was trying to get over on someone, but I let others use my name knowing I could not cover the expense if they couldn't. When the book of Proverbs tells us if we sign our name for someone else's debt, then the bill collectors will come after us for it — that is wisdom and integrity, I lacked it in the past, I have learned my lesson. Use wisdom, there will always be the needy around you, there will always be something going on around you. You are not called to be the savior, Jesus is. Give them Jesus. We are going to learn how to operate in integrity.

The younger generation needs this type of wisdom and teaching, to know how to live life and walk right with God; people must be taught these things — such as do not do anything to mess up your name financially and in integrity.

> Psalm 25:19-21 Consider my enemies, for they abound; they hate me with cruel hatred. [20] O keep me, Lord, and deliver me; let me not be ashamed or disappointed, for my trust and my refuge are in You. [21] Let integrity and uprightness preserve me, for I wait for and expect You.

God will deal with your enemies because you are living a life of integrity. If it seems He is not moving on your behalf, it could be that you are not living a life of integrity, and He is not obligated to move on disobedience. You will have to repent for doing things outside of the will of God once knowledge has come to you. This is why you have to present your body as a living sacrifice — you have to repent — kill some stuff — change your way of thinking about things so that you do not commit them again. So everything we have done before today, we can repent of and ask God to give us wisdom to not walk like that in the future — so that we can go on and read verse 2 of Psalm 26.

> Psalm 26:2 Vindicate me, O Lord, for I have walked in my integrity; I have [expectantly] trusted in, leaned on, and relied on the Lord without wavering and I shall not slide.

Before we can even deal with judgment, I have to do deal with me — walk in integrity and trust and be examined tested, and proved. This Psalm 26:2 in the Amplified bible says test my heart AND mind. This shows that there is a difference between heart and mind. The heart is born again, and has the mind of Christ, but in the soulish realm, the heart that is of the mind must be renewed. We are babes in Christ, foolishness is bound in the heart, and so God has to bring the rod of discipline and correction. It is not a huge hand coming down from heaven and knocking us across the head, it is things that happen in our life that will drive us to Him. To quote one of my journals during a major life trial: "It is trying times like these that draw me closer and deeper to God. Trying times of sanity, like this, always draw me closer to God and deeper in Him. Because when I know that something is after my sanity, I will not amplify the enemy in this, he is the one trying to get me to go crazy, but God has given me the sound mind. So I will get closer to God, because I will keep my mind on Him...think more about Him than all the hell that is going on around me". That is why when people tell me "It does not take all of that," my response is "it does not take all of that for you, but for me...."

> Psalm 26:3 For Your loving-kindness is before my eyes, and I have walked in Your truth [faithfully].

This is past tense, that means that had to have been happening already. If it has not, then we need to ask God to change me.

> Psalm 26:4-7 I do not sit with false persons, nor fellowship with pretenders; ⁵ I hate the company of evildoers and will not sit with the wicked. ⁶ I will wash my hands in innocence, and go about Your altar, O Lord, ⁷ That I may make the voice of thanksgiving heard and may tell of all Your wondrous works.

What are you telling? Are you telling of his wondrous works, or "girl the devil is busy"? Make the voice of thanksgiving heard — not murmuring, complaining and gossiping! Praise God through it all and for it all.

> Psalm 26:8 Lord, I love the habitation of Your house, and the place where Your glory dwells.

This is Old Testament, but now His dwelling place is in our heart. His presence is with us always, but do you love that habitation? Have you cleaned the house so that He can come in and dwell with you? Or does your house look like hoarders — has too much stuff in there, too much baggage — too much mental issues?

> Psalm 26:9-11 Gather me not with sinners and sweep me not away [with them], nor my life with bloodthirsty men, ¹⁰ In whose hands is wickedness, and their right hands are full of bribes. ¹¹ But as for me, I will walk in my integrity; redeem me and be merciful and gracious to me. ¹² My foot stands on an even place; in the congregations will I bless the Lord.

The psalmist was basically saying: "With all of this going on around me, I will serve the Lord as for me and my house..."And it said "my integrity" — not my mother's, the pastor's, or anyone else. No matter how bad your past was, turn it around and walk in integrity. You cannot undo the past, all you can do is repent. The Amplified gives the definition of repent is *to abhor your past sins and change your heart and mind, with actions following, actions worthy of repentance* — then walk in integrity. The verse goes on to say "be merciful and gracious to me" he knows that he cannot do it on his own, that he needs a redeemer.

Psalm 73 — I first learned this text from Lauryn Hill quoting it in a song on the Mis-education of Lauryn Hill. She has a line in one of the songs that says "with all that is going on, I remain calm reading the 73rd Psalm." This made me go read it for myself to see what she was talking about. In my own studies, I found that the title of Psalm 73 is *God delivers the righteous*. The key is at verse 7, but we will begin looking at verse 1.

> Psalm 73:1-3 Truly God is [only] good to Israel, even to those who are upright and pure in heart. ² But as for me, my feet were almost gone, my steps had well-nigh

slipped. ³ For I was envious of the foolish and arrogant when I saw the prosperity of the wicked.

See at verse 3, you are not the only one that has these types of thoughts — looking at people seeming like they are prosperous. Don't get caught up looking at what is going on around you.

This is why we have to renew our mind, because this person that he is talking about is the foolish, the arrogant, the wicked that has all of this money and no problems. Yet we are the righteous that have blessings, yet it seems that we never have enough money and are constantly under attack. So the enemy will get you to contrast and look at the foolery of the world and begin to trip. But do not even get caught up in that, as we see in verse 7, they have these imaginations of the mind that overflow with folly.

> Psalm 73:7 Their eyes stand out with fatness, they have more than heart could wish; and the imaginations of their minds overflow [with follies].

In 2 Corinthians 10, we are told to pull down any imaginations and any high thing that will exalt itself above the knowledge of God. Quick fast money is an imagination that needs to be torn down. The enemy keeps bombarding God's people with quick fast money. Don't trip that he does that to us, he did it with Jesus in the wilderness; tempted Jesus to worship him. You pull those imaginations down with the word of God — Jesus dealt with the enemy in the wilderness with the word of God, with "it is written." In order to pull down a false stronghold, you have to know the real stronghold, that it is God.

> Psalm 73:10 Therefore His people return here, and waters of a full cup [offered by the wicked] are [blindly] drained by them.

We want to make sure that we are not a people drinking the offering of a full cup from the enemy because we are blinded by the god of this world blinding believers and non-believers alike.

> Psalm 73:11-12 And they say, How does God know? Is there knowledge in the Most High? ¹² Behold, these are the ungodly, who always prosper and are at ease in the world; they increase in riches.

We are dual citizens, we have another world we are preparing for. So don't be at ease in this world. That is why you have to take your mind off of worldly thinking.

> Psalm 73:13-14 Surely then in vain have I cleansed my heart and washed my hands in innocency. ¹⁴ For all the day long have I been smitten and plagued, and chastened every morning.

Chastened every morning — God is not mad at you, but training you. Keep in mind that His mercies are new every morning too. Focus on that!

> Psalm 73:15-16 Had I spoken thus [and given expression to my feelings], I would have been untrue and have dealt treacherously against the generation of Your children. 16 But when I considered how to understand this, it was too great an effort for me and too painful

Consider. That is where your thoughts are. You put your mind on Him, you do your part and He will do His.

> Psalm 73:17-23 Until I went into the sanctuary of God; then I understood [for I considered] their end. 18 [After all] You do set the [wicked] in slippery places; You cast them down to ruin and destruction. 19 How they become a desolation in a moment! They are utterly consumed with terrors! 20 As a dream [which seems real] until one awakens, so, 0 Lord, when You arouse Yourself [to take note of the wicked], You will despise their outward show. 21 For my heart was grieved, embittered, and in a state of ferment, and I was pricked in my heart [as with the sharp fang of an adder]. 22 So foolish, stupid, and brutish was I, and ignorant; I was like a beast before You. 23 Nevertheless I am continually with You; You do hold my right hand.

He was saying he looked at the wicked and had crazy thoughts, but verse 23 says nevertheless — thank God for His nevertheless' in our life! The right hand is a symbol of power — so He held my hand and gave me His power.

> Psalm 73:24 You will guide me with Your counsel, and afterward receive me to honor and glory.

The Holy Spirit is our Council.

> Psalm 73:25 Whom have I in heaven but You? And I have no delight or desire on earth besides You.

We have to get to where we stop looking at what is going on in this earth realm, and our delight is in Him.

> Psalm 73:26 My flesh and my heart may fail, but God is the Rock and firm Strength of my heart and my Portion forever.

Flesh and heart — the body and soulish realm will fail — but not God. He is my PORTION forever. We must renew our minds to understand this. We are not just reading a book, but the actual living/breathing word of God that has the power to empower us to live as dual citizens. And so we need the help of the Holy Spirit to show us things — as He sharpens our ear to hear Him.

> Psalm 73:27 For behold, those who are far from You shall perish; You will destroy all who are false to You and like [spiritual] harlots depart from You.

Spiritual harlots coming in the church trying to pimp folks to get off into worldly thinking.

> Psalm 73:28 But it is good for me to draw near to God; I have put my trust in the Lord God and made Him my refuge, that I may tell of all Your works.

Yes, these trying times draw us deeper in God. See verse 28, what are you telling of? Out of the abundance of the heart, the mouth speaks. There is a co-relation between your mind (what you are thinking), and your tongue (what you are speaking out of your mouth).

Part of renewing our mind is setting a guard before our mouth. This is so important as a new born baby, if someone would teach me how to get my mouth right, because it will get me in trouble — help me be disciplined to not allow my mouth to get me in trouble. That I deal with it as a baby, be taught and learn the process of setting a guard before my mouth.

> Psalm 39:1 I said, I will take heed and guard my ways, that I may sin not with my tongue; I will muzzle my mouth as with a bridle while the wicked are before me.

Watch what you are saying with the wicked in your presence; because they will take the words of your mouth and trip you up with them. Because out of the abundance of the heart, the mouth speaks. So if you are speaking foolishness in your heart, then they know what is in your heart and they will pull and play on that. This is also why we must be purged of pride — another reason for Romans 12:3. When the enemy hears pride coming out of your mouth, he will bait you to fall. Remember, the enemy does not come as a nasty red monster with horns, but disguised as an angel of light, and dresses things up so cunningly to try to get you to fall.

> Psalm 141:3 Set a guard, O Lord, before my mouth; keep watch at the door of my lips.

Here I am asking God to guard my mouth — to keep me from saying something stupid. Just close your lips, press them together real hard so foolishness does not fall out. You are asking Him to search your heart and get all of the foolishness out, that is a daily thing (see Psalm 139:23-24).

> Proverbs 13:3 He who guards his mouth keeps his life, but he who opens wide his lips comes to ruin.

We need wisdom from God; He is the one that sets a guard before my mouth anyway. He is the one that is keeping my mouth so that I do not come to ruin. And He is disciplining me to bite my tongue and let the Lord do my battles.

> Proverbs 21:23 He who guards his mouth and his tongue keeps himself from troubles.

No, you do not have to give someone a piece of your mind. That may be the piece that will kill someone.

Prayer: Thank You for showing us how to truly and actively present our bodies as living sacrifices; how to remove conformity to worldly thinking by being transformed by the renewing of our mind according to Your word. The times that we can't see or hear You, it is not that You aren't there, You just want to see us walk out what You have already given us. Yes Your servants are listening and we hear You and are walking in what You have said. Thank You for teaching us to be a people of integrity, that walk upright. To be stable in the midst of what seems like hellish situations. Help us Lord that we not fret like in Psalm 73 and 37, in the midst of evil doers.

We know that we will have to stand in judgment for the rebellion and hardness of heart that we persist to keep doing. Thank You for being the long-suffering God with us as You allow us to stay in this realm and get things right with You – as we are making preparations for eternity. As we are renewing our mind, help us to be eternity mindful, knowing that the things we say impact eternity. Words are containers that shape and frame our world and our lives, help us to be mindful of the words that come out of our mouth. Thank You for setting a guard before our mouth, and then we are mindful to listen to that guard that is convicting us and telling us words of peacefulness and kindness and love, when to speak, and when to hold our tongue – when to shut up, and when to cry loud and spare not. When to stand still and let You fight our battles, because You are in control of time. We now realize that what we think is taking too long, is Your timing. Thank You that in the midst of it all, You cause us to be calm and have peace in Your presence as we are letting You show us our purpose, as we are learning our will for and in You.

Let Your kingdom of heaven be advanced. We decrease that You increase – we give You access. We wash in the word daily, we are being transformed by the word daily. Have Your glory in our lives, in our marriages, with our children, in our homes, in ministry, in our finances – have Your way. Transform us God, conform us to kingdom thinking, not worldliness. Amen.

1.6 Three-Part Being

Man is a spirit, we possess a soul, and we live in a body. The spirit was created in Genesis 1:26-28, created in the image of God, male and female He created man and gave them dominion. The soulish side, we see in Genesis 2:7 after God created the dirt suit for man and breathed into his nostrils the breath of life, and man became a living soul. Prior to the fall, the soul and the spirit had constant communion; regular communication between the 2 realms. So in Genesis chapter 1, He created the spirit of man, in Genesis chapter 2 He created the body for man and breathed the soul into it — that is the tri-part being.

Man lives in an earth suit. The real me is not the body. What you see looking back at you in the mirror, that is not the real you. The dirt suit (body) can be attacked by sickness and disease, that is why we have to take authority over it — He gave us authority over the earth (over the dirt). The flesh cannot understand the spirit, and is an enemy to the spirit (especially after the fall in Genesis 3). The flesh does not mind sinning, because it knows it is going back to the dirt (ashes to ashes and dust to dust).

When sin occurred in Genesis 3, they surely died — yet it was not the body. It was not their dirt suit that died, but the ability to have access between the spirit and soulish realm. The fact that man was a living being, that knew how to access the spiritual realm, died! So the spirit of man must be born again, which we refer to as new birth.

Genesis 1:26-28 and Ezekiel 36... the mind of Christ in the spirit realm, we receive this at new birth, but must now renew the mind in the soulish realm to receive from the spirit realm. The new heart of Ezekiel 36 that already has God's laws in it, this comes when we are born again by accepting Jesus Christ as Lord and Savior. Yet our ability to access this new heart and mind of Christ only goes as far as we have renewed our mind. We do not know what it is like to regularly hear from God, but Adam and Eve knew what it was like to hear from God, but sin made them hide from Him. We have gotten that hiding part down real good — we think we are hiding from God, you can hide from the church, the pastor, the preacher, the brethren, but you cannot hide from God. God knew where they were, and He knew what they had done.

We renew our mind back to Eden, before there ever was a separation between spirit and soul. What better to do this with than the word of God, which in Hebrews 4:12 shows that it can divide, or shall we say decipher, between the soul and spirit.

The soulish realm is where the mind, will, emotion, imagination, intellect, reasoning, thoughts, personality; conscious, memory are. The bible says that we do not walk by sight, and sight is part of where our emotions are — when you see things, they make you scared or excited, that is where your emotions are. But don't be moved by what you see, you have to see what is unseen — which is the spiritual realm.

> Romans 10:9-10 Because if you acknowledge and confess with your lips that Jesus is Lord and in your heart believe (adhere to, trust in, and rely on the truth) that God raised Him from the dead, you will be saved. ¹⁰ For with the heart a person believes (adheres to, trusts in, and relies on Christ) and so is justified (declared righteous, acceptable to God), and with the mouth he confesses (declares openly and speaks out freely his faith) and confirms [his] salvation.

So your spirit is born again, and you must renew your mind (the heart part here in this text) to be able to receive from the spirit. The heart appears in both the spirit and the soul realm, we will discuss this principle further in another section. Your mind being renewed builds a strong heart. Because Romans 10:9-10 says if you believe in your heart, that is the soulish realm, that has to believe — and what are beliefs? Beliefs are thoughts — that you use your intellect and your reasoning to have faith in God. So you have to be constantly renewing your mind, that your faith in God can grow. That is how that little mustard seed grows and matures into a tree. The Holy Spirit will teach and show you the matters of the heart, whether in the spirit or soul realm. The Holy Spirit, Spirit of Truth will help us renew our mind — yet the devil does not want us to renew our mind because he knows that as long as he can keep us stuck on stupid with stinking thinking with dead/ decaying thoughts, he can play games with us. But not so! The Lord is exposing it!

The soul causes us to be unique. The mind must be renewed according to the word of God; through sanctification which is the process of transformation. It was the soulish realm that lived on apart from God, and that is how the thoughts got all crazy.

> Proverbs 15:13 A glad heart makes a cheerful countenance, but by sorrow of heart the spirit is broken.

This "heart" here is in the soulish realm. The heartache must be healed to heal the wounded soul. As the text says, by sorrow of heart, when we have heaviness in our heart that needs to be renewed to bring about the cheerful countenance and that we not walk around with our feelings on our shoulder. The wound in the soul, the soulish part is being sorrowful and needs to be healed, renew our thinking.

> Proverbs 15:26 The thoughts of the wicked are shamefully vile and exceedingly offensive to the Lord, but the words of the pure are pleasing words to Him.

The thoughts of the wicked — we have to renew our mind to make sure we are not having wicked thoughts. And if/when the wicked thoughts come in, He has empowered us on how to pull and tear them down. God watches our thoughts, but the words of the pure are pleasing. So He is watching our heart to see what our words are going to be, this is why our hearts cry should be "set a guard before my mouth," that no displeasing words come out. This should be our conviction, that says I can only change the words coming out of my mouth by renewing my mind, changing it to think properly, to think kingdom and God-pleasing thoughts, Christ-like thoughts. Know that out of the abundance of the heart, the mouth speaks; so God wants us to deal with the abundant things that are going on in our heart.

On a personal note, the warfare that I have endured to write this manuscript has been indescribable. The enemy is upset and does not want this teaching in print to expose his tactics, therefore I have been repeatedly assaulted in the mind. But it did not stop anything! I have learned to persevere and press forward in all circumstances! I have learned that I do not have time to try to explain everything to everyone, I have to just press on, and in the end they will see. As a warrior, I have to just do what I do, and they will see in due time. Okay, let me get back to writing.

And you have a choice, do you want to let your imaginations run wild, or do you want to renew your mind (2 Corinthians 10:5-7), do not let vain imaginations exalt themselves above the knowledge of God. So how do I know if my thoughts are going past the knowledge of God? Well, I have to have a knowledge of God myself to know when the thoughts are renegade. It is our understanding that enlarges.

1.7 Language of Soul (heart)

We are looking at the language of soul — seeing the different references to it throughout the bible.

> Psalm 119:81 AMP: My soul languishes and grows faint for Your salvation, but I hope in Your word.

> Psalm 119:81 MSG: I'm homesick—longing for your salvation; I'm waiting for your word of hope.

We need to know that salvation is past, present, and future. Justification, sanctification, and glorification. My soul languishes for you — I am justified in You, but while I am walking through this sanctification process, sometimes I get home sick! Ready to be with Him now!

When your soul cries out, and gets homesick, and wants to leave the earth realm — you really have to work on transforming yourself. As Paul said "I would rather be with God, but it is more better that I stay here..." and be the mouthpiece for God.

This stanza of Psalm 119 is titled *longing for comfort* — sometimes your soul longs for comfort, this is a good way to renew your mind when your soul is longing.

> Psalm119:82-88 My eyes fail, watching for [the fulfillment of] Your promise. I say, When will You comfort me? 83 For I have become like a bottle [a wineskin blackened and shriveled] in the smoke [in which it hangs], yet do I not forget Your statutes. 84 How many are the days of Your servant [which he must endure]? When will You judge those who pursue and persecute me? 85 The godless and arrogant have dug pitfalls for me, men who do not conform to Your law. 86 All Your commandments are faithful and sure. [The godless] pursue and persecute me with falsehood; help me [Lord]! 87 They had almost consumed me upon earth, but I forsook not Your precepts. 88 According to Your steadfast love give life to me; then I will keep the testimony of Your mouth [hearing, receiving, loving, and obeying it].

How can you keep the testimony of God's mouth...unless you spend time in the word. That is the renewal process; that is the transformation process. You will always have enemies coming after you, but you have to remember that God is your refuge. When people are judging you, and you are being falsely accused and attacked for no reason...blessed are those who suffer for righteousness sake. But you have to have your mind transformed to that. If you are still in worldly thinking, and people accuse you, you are ready to fight!

Looking at the whole heart — it ALL has to be renewed. We renew our mind with His laws, precepts, ordinances, testimonies, etc. as in Psalm 119.

> Psalm 119:10 AMP: With my whole heart have I sought You, inquiring for and of You and yearning for You; Oh, let me not wander or step aside [either in ignorance or willfully] from Your commandments.

> Psalm 119:10 MSG: I'm single-minded in pursuit of you; don't let me miss the road signs you've posted.

This stanza is titled *purity, the fruit of the law*. This was a cry out to God: don't let me be ignorant or willfully disobey. Similar to Psalm 139 when the psalmist cried out to God to search my heart O Lord and see if there is any evil way in me. If there are any ways in me that will make me miss Your commandments, and step aside of them, help me see it! As the Message bible says, He is posting road signs for our heart and soul. He has given us a new heart that has the law of God in it, that has the mind of Christ, but we must renew the soulish realm of the heart to receive from it. And the whole thing, not just bits and pieces — the whole heart. We try to pick and choose what we will get in line with, but it must be the whole.

Psalm 119:25-32 is titled *prayer for understanding the law* — so we need prayer to understand the law (which Jesus fulfills), don't think we just get it, or fully understand on our own.

> Psalm 119:25 My earthly life cleaves to the dust; revive and stimulate me according to Your word!

This is definitely referring to soulish talk!

> Psalm 119:26-32 I have declared my ways and opened my griefs to You, and You listened to me; teach me Your statutes. [27] Make me understand the way of Your precepts; so shall I meditate on and talk of Your wondrous works. [28] My life dissolves and weeps itself away for heaviness; raise me up and strengthen me according to [the promises of] Your word. [29] Remove from me the way of falsehood and unfaithfulness [to You], and graciously impart Your law to me. [30] I have chosen the way of truth and faithfulness; Your ordinances have I set before me. [31] I cleave to Your testimonies; O Lord, put me not to shame! [32] I will [not merely walk, but] run the way of Your commandments, when You give me a heart that is willing.

Not merely walk, but run. And the Message bible adds "show me how".

> Psalm 119:34 Give me understanding, that I may keep Your law; yes, I will observe it with my whole heart.

The understanding comes from God — like in Ephesians 1:17-19. As He is flooding us with light, this is how we get the understanding and this is how we do it with the whole heart, not just bits and pieces.

If there is something that you are having a hard time accepting, then ask God to give you revelation (the flood of light) so that you can see clearer what He wants you to see. Repentance is not just saying I'm sorry, but is changing your mind with actions following.

As Jesus said, produce fruit worthy of repentance. I can see by your actions following that you have changed your mind/ thinking. Deeds worthy of repentance.

Here are a few other examples of the whole heart:

> Psalm 119:2 AMP: Blessed (happy, fortunate, to be envied) are they who keep His testimonies, and who seek, inquire for and of Him and crave Him with the whole heart.

You have to do your best — seek Him while He may be found.

> Psalm 119:58 I entreated Your favor with my whole heart; be merciful and gracious to me according to Your promise.

This stanza is titled the *Lord our PORTION* (Psalm 119:57-64). We are seeing something that we have to do. It is in the spirit realm, change the course of your mind. You have to say this stanza with your whole heart.

> Psalm 119:80 Let my heart be sound (sincere and wholehearted and blameless) in Your statutes, that I may not be put to shame.

We have to be reminded that our confidence is in the Lord, in Him and His ability (see Psalm 119:73-80). It is in faithfulness that He afflicts...ouch!

When sinful thoughts come our way (willful or ignorant), our responsibility is to throw it down. Like with weight loss, you have to find smart ways to eat, to be in the calorie burning portion (all calories are not created equal). So too with the word, we can't be always getting the word/ information/ etc. and never metabolizing it to benefit from it — and end up spiritually obese. Always eating, but never walking the word, never really running the Christian race, it is by title only, not lifestyle.

Dealing with changing your thinking, you can't just think it. You have to get your thought life under control, change the channel in your thought life! We must check it in the thought life, and not let it run wild. If we would do this, then we would not have so many torn marriages and would have more patience in dealing with our children or difficult people.

Prayer: Lord we repent for allowing our minds to stay on channels that it shouldn't be on too long. Thank You Lord for putting parental controls in our thinking. That You would block out stuff that we do not have any business thinking on. That when our mind goes to a particular thing, the screen in our thinking would come up and say "this channel is blocked and restricted, for it is contrary to the laws, the precepts, the ordinances, the testimonies, and the fear of God"! AMEN!

Preparing us to be ready for such a time as this, vessels meet for the Master's use that have been washed and cleansed with the word of God.

Here is an entry from one of my personal journals:

> An acceleration in the spirit. I said in the past, that I had learned more in one year, than in the previous 12 years, I can now honestly say that as we are hungering and

thirsting after Him, and build our foundations in Him, then we begin to see more and more, and know more. And the years and years of reading, diligently reading and committing this stuff into our spirit man, not just into memory, but renewing our mind according to the word of God — it gives us a foundation that He can reveal more in less time. The less is more principle — He can give us more in less time because the foundation has already been established. Know that preparation time is never wasted time. I would have never gotten into the year of acceleration, had I not done the 12 years of gradual understanding. It was after the gradual, that He gave accelerated — and it carries on with even more acceleration — immeasurable. Anybody that is desiring to know more of God, there will be an acceleration in the spirit, but it only comes after you have proven yourself. Study to show yourself approved, a workman rightly dividing the word of God (2 Timothy 2:15). In this text, Paul was addressing a lot of things, false doctrine was one of them, and he was telling young Timothy to study to be approved by God, not man or religion or tradition. Approved by the living God, by the Holy Spirit that lives within. And why do we study to show ourselves approved? We study to renew our mind! Not to brag about reading through the entire bible, or memorizing favorite texts, but to renew our mind to what it means — get your heart attached to it.

My heart has to be yielded to God, it cannot be about me. Pride cannot exist — we must be meek and humble. Renew. Not just memorize it, or commit it to memory — it is still a living word.

> Isaiah 40:31 NKJV But those who wait on the Lord shall renew their strength; they shall mount up with wings like eagles, they shall run and not be weary, they shall walk and not faint.

As a baby believer, I got excited when I heard this. I was quick to say "Lord I'm waiting on You." And when it seemed like He didn't come through, I thought God had fallen off the throne. I had to renew my mind to what "wait" means. It does not mean to sit around twiddling your thumbs — but is like a waiter at a restaurant — you are waiting on consumers. That means you are providing a service, but your wages come from above, not the people sitting at the table. So you have to make sure that you have renewed your mind to deal with every kind of person that may come sit at your table (the rude, nasty, polite, all types) you must renew your mind to deal with it all.

> Isaiah 40:31 MSG But those who wait upon GOD get fresh strength. They spread their wings and soar like eagles, they run and don't get tired, they walk and don't lag behind.

Get fresh strength. We expect, look for, and wait in Him — how do you do this? In the word.

The renew is not about muscles, we don't need those in this battle; it is about spiritual strength. And in the spirit realm, it is in the soulish realm that needs the strength — your mind, will, emotions, reasoning, intellect, thoughts, memories, conscious — that is what is being renewed.

> Isaiah 40:27-29 MSG: Why would you ever complain, O Jacob, or, whine, Israel, saying, "GOD has lost track of me. He doesn't care what happens to me"? Don't you know anything? Haven't you been listening? GOD doesn't come and go. God lasts. He's Creator of all you can see or imagine. He doesn't get tired out, doesn't pause to catch his breath. And He knows everything, inside and out. He energizes those who get tired, gives fresh strength to dropouts.

He called out both natures, Jacob & Israel, both were complaining. We will see this principle better in the next section. The Message bible makes it clear.

He knows when we begin to get weak, that is why He called him by both natures. The weak nature is Jacob, but He called Jacob to renew his mind to be the Israel He called him to be. God gives us that strength, we see this in verse 31. The Greek & Hebrew of the word "renew" here in Isaiah 40:31 means *to change, substitute, alter, change for better, renew, show newness*. This is what you need to do in your mind, change, substitute, alter, change for better, renew, show newness in your mind.

> Genesis 41:14 Then Pharaoh sent and called Joseph, and they brought him hastily out of the dungeon. But Joseph [first] shaved himself, changed his clothes, and made himself presentable; then he came into Pharaoh's presence.

The word "changed" here is the same as renew in Isaiah 40:31. This was after all that Joseph had endured, now in prison, but being called to the King to interpret a dream, before Joseph went into the King's presence. Side note — we have to get like this, that when God calls us to come into His presence, we have to make some changes. Joseph cleaned up from his current state. Sometimes God has us in a wait (hold) pattern where we are not presentable, but our heart (the mind) is being changed, cleansed and renewed. The change has to be on the inside before it can come outwardly. But Joseph knew he could not go into the presence of the King looking like that — so he changed his clothes. We need to change the clothes of our mind! How dare we think that we can boldly go into the holy of Holies with these messed up minds, thinking on all types of things that we should not be thinking on. We need to change our clothes, because we are going into the presence of the King.

Sometimes thoughts have to be killed (brutally crucified).

> Judges 5:26 She put her [left] hand to the tent pin, and her right hand to the workmen's hammer. And with the wooden hammer she smote Sisera, she smote his head, yes, she struck and pierced his temple.

Strike that run-a-way thought through the temple. The same word here for stricken is the word renew in Isaiah 40:31. Some stuff in our thinking we need to flat out kill, like Jael, get the spike and hammer (which is the word of God) and get that stuff out of our thinking because it does not need to live. The decree was for them to all die, Sisera tried to run-a-way, but God said not so. Let's look at what we are to do with those thoughts:

> 2 Corinthians 10:5 [Inasmuch as we] refute arguments and theories and reasonings and every proud and lofty thing that sets itself up against the [true] knowledge of God; and we lead every thought and purpose away captive into the obedience of Christ (the Messiah, the Anointed One)

A stronghold is a house made of mental thoughts at a young age for future occupation, either godly or evil. So as a child, if a person is constantly built up and given thoughts that they are a mighty man of God, as they grow up and life happens, the house or thought life of "I am a mighty man of God" will rise up. Now the demonic stronghold that must be killed is stuff like "You will never be nothing — nobody wants to hear from you, a woman, single, not raised in the church, with no credentials behind your name" — all of these were strongholds that the enemy spoke to me from the day I got saved and fought with my call. I was fighting, because those childish strongholds were holding me. Stuff like the fact that I was 25 years old before I realized I was not ugly — from the enemy calling me awkward and weird and strange and funny.

> 2 Corinthians 10:4-5 For the weapons of our warfare are not physical [weapons of flesh and blood], but they are mighty before God for the overthrow and destruction of strongholds, 5 [Inasmuch as we] refute arguments and theories and reasonings and every proud and lofty thing that sets itself up against the [true] knowledge of God; and we lead every thought and purpose away captive into the obedience of Christ (the Messiah, the Anointed One)

You drive a spike through the thinking of thoughts that are not lining up with who Christ has called you to be. You take the spikes that were nailed in my Savior's hands and feet to drive them into that wrong thinking that would make you think that you can't be as obedient as He was, even unto death. That is a Renewal of the Mind!

Know this: The more you know, the more you see you don't know, and the more you don't know, the more you'll need to know. You'll never get it all, He is inexhaustible. Just know that one day that you have not renewed your mind in some degree; you are backslidden. This will give you the fire/ drive/ hunger/ thirst to press and renew the mind daily in some way, shape, or form. And what you know, you need to really know.

1.8 Changed Nature – Changed Name

There are several examples in scripture where the Lord changes the name of His servants. We will look at just a few.

> Matthew 16:17-18 Then Jesus answered him, Blessed (happy, fortunate, and to be envied) are you, **Simon Bar-Jonah.** For flesh and blood [men] have not revealed this to you, but My Father Who is in heaven. [18] And I tell you, you are **Peter** [Greek, Petros — a large piece of rock], and on this rock [Greek, petra— a huge rock like Gibraltar] I will build My church, and the gates of Hades (the powers of the infernal region) shall not overpower it [or be strong to its detriment or hold out against it].

Name change. If you will notice, the Lord addressed him first by the lower nature (Simon Bar-Jonah), then by the nature that had destiny in the kingdom (Peter). We see purpose is added at the recognition of the 2 natures — or at the entrance of revelatory power.

Hear O Jacob, hear O Israel...God speaking to both natures, the previous nature, and the current nature. Showing how all things can work together for the good. That even if in the beginning of your life, you may have been a trickster, a swindler, a supplanter, a deceiver — and then God comes in and changes your name. He said "You have contended with Me, so I change your name to Israel, contender with God." Looking back at Isaiah 40:27, we see what is needed to renew. Not muscular strength, but spiritual strength. Really it is not on the spirit realm, but the soulish realm that is being renewed and strengthened (mind, will, emotion, intellect, reasoning, memories, thoughts, conscience, etc.). Here in the text, God was questioning both natures because Jacob (the old nature) was murmuring and complaining, and Israel (the new nature) just fell in with it — had not renewed his mind. As the Message bible puts it "why would you ever complain saying God does not care and doesn't care what happens to me?" God knows when we begin to get weak, and knows what is going on, that is why He called him by both natures, Jacob and Israel. The weak nature speaking up, Jacob. But He has called him to renew his mind, Israel, the strong nature that he is called to be.

It took some time, and some failures (falling forward) for Abram to truly renew his mind to what the name Abraham meant. His name was Abram first (high, exalted father, Genesis 17:5), then when God gave him the promise to be the father of many nations and of faith, He changed his name to Abraham (father of a multitude, Genesis 17:5). God had given him the promise as Abram, he messed up and made Ishmael (seed of flesh, the old nature, trying to help God) — trying to fulfill a spiritual promise through fleshly acts. How many times have we done this? It took some time for Abram, and some failures (falling forward) to truly renew his mind to be Abraham.

The same with Jacob the trickster being changed to Israel — so the same with us today. Personally the Paulette Denise walk — "because no man has a hand in forming Christ in me" has been a Renewal of the Mind! process for sure. But to borrow a quote from an article by Ray Stedman:

> "Jacob was the rascal, the schemer, the man who thought he could live on his own, by his wits and by his own efforts. He went out trying to deceive everybody and ended up being deceived. Jacob is a beautiful picture of sanctification, that marvelous work of God in which we in our folly, attempting to live life in the energy of the flesh, are led into the very situations that drive us into a corner where at last, like Jacob wrestling with the angel, we discover God speaking to us and we give up. And when we give up our trying, we begin to live. That is what Jacob did when he gave up at the Brook of Peniel, knowing Esau was waiting with a band of armed men ready to take his life. He wrestled with the angel of God at the brook; it was there that God broke Jacob. And as a broken man, limping the rest of his life, he became Israel, prince of God. What a lesson that is. Some of us are going through this very experience right now. What an encouragement to us!"

All I can say is amen!!!! The old nature led Jacob into deceiving people, then he was deceived by Laban (his uncle) several times concerning marriage and wages (Genesis 31:7). Even as Jacob was returning to his home town, his previous trickster stuff was there to haunt him from when he tricked his brother (Esau) out of his birth right. Finally, sick and tired of being sick and tired, Jacob wrestled with letting go of the old and received the limp of Life (see Genesis 32). I can truly say I walk with a limp — no, it is not physical for the natural eye to see, but anyone with spiritual eyes can see that I am dependent on the Lord to take each step. Totally transformed nature.

He could have picked any other name for Jacob, but he named Jacob the deceiver. What did satan do to get man to sin in the first place? He deceived the woman, and through her deception, passing it on to Adam, sin was birthed. So Jacob being one of deception, he was going to always walk in sin; his nature had to be changed, and it started with his name being changed.

1.9 From Worldly Conformity, To Kingdom Conformity

> Romans 12:1 NKJV And do not be conformed to this world, but be transformed by the renewing of your mind, that you may prove what is that good and acceptable and perfect will of God.

The object is not to be conformed to the world, but to be conformed to the kingdom by the renewing of our mind. Before we go further in this project, let's take a few minutes to look at some definitions in this verse gleaned from www.blueletter.org:

"Conform" is defined as *to conform one's self (i.e. one's mind and character) to another's pattern, (fashion one's self according to)*.

"World" is defined as *forever, an unbroken age; period of time.*

We need to be conformed to eternity, not this present period of time. A few other texts that can be looked at to see this principle are: Matthew 13:22; John 6:51, John 8:35, Mark 4:19.

"Transform" is defined as *to change into another form, to transfigure.*

The root word for transform comes from the word we get metamorphosis, and we will look at it further in a moment. But from this definition of transform, we can see the principle further at

> 2 Corinthians 3:18 NJKV But we all, with unveiled face, beholding as in a mirror the glory of the Lord, are being transformed into the same image from glory to glory, just as by the Spirit of the Lord.

This shows that the transformations take place progressively *from glory to glory*. It is a process to be transformed; from the initial glory of accepting the Lord Jesus Christ, and then into continual glory, and glory, and glory — or as the Amplified bible says *ever increasing from one degree of glory to another.*

"Renewal" is defined as *renovation, complete change for the better...effected by the Holy Spirit.*

An example of this renewal is seen in Titus 3:5, and brings a complete change for the better. In essence, the text so far is saying: to not be patterned by this world (time period), but by eternity. Then to be changed for the better (transformed/transfigured) by the Holy Spirit — we do not do this apart from Him.

"Mind" is defined as *comprising alike the faculties of perceiving and understanding and those of feeling, judging, determining.*

A text to better understand what is being said here with "mind" is in Luke 25:24, when it was said of Jesus that He opened their understanding — He will do this for us so that we can receive from the mind of Christ. And we always quote Philippians 4:7, this "passing of understanding" is in the mind, the peace that comes as we renew our mind, hence the battle for the mind to remain conformed to worldliness instead of godliness, god-likeness, through Christ-likeness.

"Prove" is defined as *to recognize as genuine after examination, to approve, deem worthy — to see whether a thing is genuine or not (as with metal).*

An example of negative proof (or neglecting to prove for yourself) is at Romans 1:28, where the people did not retain God in their knowledge. And shows what can happen if you do NOT prove for your self — you end up with a reprobate mind, which is the opposite of a renewed mind. No, we want a renewed mind that is all the way better by the help of the Holy Spirit. Also, in 1 Corinthians 3:13 is a good example of rightly proving the word of God.

"Good" is defined as *excellent, distinguished; upright, honorable.*

"Perfect" is defined as *wanting nothing necessary to completeness...consummate human integrity and virtue; full grown, adult, of full age, mature.*

"Will" is defined as *of what God wishes to be done by us; commands, precepts. Choice, inclination, desire, pleasure.*

"Metamorphosis" in the Merriam-Webster online dictionary is defined as: *a major change in the appearance or character of someone or something...that happens as the animal or insect becomes an adult. Marked and more or less abrupt developmental change in the form or structure of an animal.* Synonyms and related words: *changeover, conversion, transfiguration, shift, transition, adjustment, alteration, modification, reconstruction, redo, reformation, remodeling, remaking, reworking, disfigurement, replacement, substitution.*

"Change" — from the root mean meaning *to exchange, crooked.* A few of the definitions: *to make radically different; transform; to give a different position, course, or direction to. To put fresh clothes or covering on.*

I know this has been a lot of definitions, but the Spirit of the Lord is showing us a deeper understanding of conformity verses transformity.

I will paraphrase and condense the 5 stages of a butterfly, or the metamorphosis process:

    1) Egg stage — the adult butterfly lays the eggs
    2) The larva stage — the feeding stage. The only time that it eats; has astonishing growth because it continually eats.

3) Caterpillar stage — molts 4 or 5 times; which means it sheds its exoskeleton because it is continually enlarging — as it is becoming radically new.
4) Pupa stage — or the cocoon stage (the chrysalis stage). Does not eat at all. Just before it is ready to emerge into the next stage, the cocoon becomes transparent.
5) Adult butterfly stage — emerges as a butter fly. The wings are wet and must be allowed to dry out. Their diet is completely liquid. The primary purpose of the adult butterfly is to mate and reproduce (mating is done by sight and pheromones). A side note: the adult butterfly does not provide care for the young.

These are the transformation stages. We are renewing our mind in so many areas: to justification, sanctification, glorification. To Jesus Christ and the help of the Holy Spirit. Putting this back into context of the metamorphosis process: we are exposed to the word of God (the egg stage); then we go into the larva where we are eating, we are studying, we are soaking up as much as we can; then we become a caterpillar, where there is constant growth and molting — basically maxing out and going to the next dimension because of the enlarging; then the pupa stage — a quietness — that shifts to transparency (sharing how we learned the Gospel); then to the emerging adult butterfly. The side note that the adult butterfly doesn't care for its young, is related to the fact that God wants us to be self-sufficient in Christ's sufficiency (as in Philippians 4), He is the One that is providing for us.

1 John 2:27 has given me confidence in my relationship with God. It is nice to have a pastor, or teacher, or mentor or someone to show you how to do what you do in the word. But when I first learned this text some 14 years ago, the Spirit of the Lord was letting me know that He could give revelation to me straight. I then made a vow to Him that if He allowed me to, I would never make anyone go through this alone — hence the mentoring PORTION of A Portion Ministries, the Elijah to Elisha mentoring. This is not a principle that I just picked up yesterday and am practicing on people, but something that I have lived personally and now am able to share with others.

This section in 1 John 2:27 is titled: *Obedience and love — Love in action — the test of belief.*

> 1 John 2:24-27 As for you, keep in your hearts what you have heard from the beginning. If what you heard from the first dwells and remains in you, then you will dwell in the Son and in the Father [always]. 25 And this is what He Himself has promised us — the life, the eternal [life]. 26 I write this to you with reference to those who would deceive you [seduce and lead you astray]. 27 But as for you, the anointing (the sacred appointment, the unction) which you received from Him abides [permanently] in you; [so] then you have no need that anyone should instruct you. But just as His anointing teaches you concerning everything and is true and is no falsehood, so you must abide in (live in, never depart from) Him [being rooted in Him, knit to Him], just as [His anointing] has taught you [to do].

I meditated on verse 27 for a long time, so whenever the enemy would attack my thinking that I was not qualified for the task God had given me, I would put myself in remembrance of this text and know that it was the deceiver trying to speak to me. What did the deceiver do in the Garden of Eden? Since we are talking about Renewal of the Mind!, we must remember what happened for the mind to get messed up and need to be renewed in the first place. What happened was, DECEPTION. When deception was not checked, sin was birthed.

> 1 John 2:28 And now, little children, abide (live, remain permanently) in Him, so that when He is made visible, we may have and enjoy perfect confidence (boldness, assurance) and not be ashamed and shrink from Him at His coming.

Because we are restored, and our mind has been renewed, we will not be found hiding and in shame. Back in Genesis when they ate of the tree of the knowledge of good and evil, they were shameful and knew they were naked, so they hid themselves. But because of the unction (which is access back to the tree of Life) we no longer hide from God. We can be open, honest, and transparent with Him about any and everything that is going on in and around us. Not only that, but this will also give us a boldness, an assurance, a confidence — a perfect confidence as the Amplified says. We must have our mind renewed to what it is to be a little child of God.

> 1 John 2:29 If you know (perceive and are sure) that He [Christ] is [absolutely] righteous [conforming to the Father's will in purpose, thought, and action], you may also know (be sure) that everyone who does righteously [and is therefore in like manner conformed to the divine will] is born (begotten) of Him [God].

"If you know" — that is in your thought life — you have to renew your mind to KNOW that Christ is absolutely righteous, and that in Christ is the right standing we need. You cannot get it anywhere else outside of Christ. You cannot get it in church, religion, traditions, by kissing up to people — but can only be achieved in Christ — we must renew our minds to know that.

> 1 John 3:1 See what [an incredible] quality of love the Father has given (shown, bestowed on) us, that we should [be permitted to] be named and called and counted the children of God! And so we are! The reason that the world does not know (recognize, acknowledge) us is that it does not know (recognize, acknowledge) Him.

The world's mind cannot even see Him. So if your mind is in worldliness, you cannot see Him. This is why we must Romans 12:2 our minds — take it off of worldliness and put it on kingdom. We do this through eating the word of God — metabolizing the word of God. Eat it, get an understanding of it, process it so that you can now benefit from the metabolization of it in your system, the word of God.

> 1 John 3:2-3 Beloved, we are [even here and] now God's children; it is not yet disclosed (made clear) what we shall be [hereafter], but we know that when He comes and is manifested, we shall [as God's children] resemble and be like Him, for we shall see Him just as He [really] is. ³ And everyone who has this hope [resting] on Him cleanses (purifies) himself just as He is pure (chaste, undefiled, guiltless).

When our hope is in Him, through the renewed mind — we therefore wash in the water of the word to cleanse us and make us pure, chaste, undefiled and guiltless. Remember that Romans 8:1 says there is no condemnation to those who are in Christ Jesus. The enemy will bring guilt, will try and condemn us. But God, through the Holy Spirit, brings conviction, that we repent — change our thinking with actions following. This is all through the washing of the water of the word. Some people stop reading the word, or coming to church, especially to churches that are preaching the unadulterated word of God, because they feel like the pastor is always beating up on them; it is not the pastor beating up on them, but it is the Spirit of the Lord that is trying to get them to wash in the water of the word. Change. Renew. Repent.

> 1 John 4:4 Everyone who commits (practices) sin is guilty of lawlessness; for [that is what] sin is, lawlessness (the breaking, violating of God's law by transgression or neglect— being unrestrained and unregulated by His commands and His will).

So if you are unrestrained and unregulated, that means if you slip and fall, because the righteous man does stumble, or may even fall into sin (as in Galatians 6), but not practicing it. "Transgression or neglect", we cannot neglect God's law. God's law is love. This is why when we get a better understanding of the love of God, which 1 John is all about the love of God, but when we get this better understanding of the law, we will see that Jesus fulfills the law.

> 1 John 4:5 You know that He appeared in visible form and became Man to take away [upon Himself] sins, and in Him there is no sin [essentially and forever].

"You know" — talking about our thinking and knowing again.

> 1 John 4:6-7 No one who abides in Him [who lives and remains in communion with and in obedience to Him— deliberately, knowingly, and habitually] commits (practices) sin. No one who [habitually] sins has either seen or known Him [recognized, perceived, or understood Him, or has had an experiential acquaintance with Him]. ⁷ Boys (lads), let no one deceive and lead you astray. He who practices righteousness [who is upright, conforming to the divine will in purpose, thought, and action, living a consistently conscientious life] is righteous, even as He is righteous.

Habitually sinning — you continue in sin because you do not have experiential acquaintance with God, yet it is His righteousness, not our own. I did not die for the sins of the world, Jesus did, and it is through His righteousness that I am in right standing with God, not through my own righteousness. So even though I am falling short in some areas, I still have partaken of His righteousness and I ask Him to strengthen me in those areas in which my mind has not been renewed enough to keep my flesh from doing what it is doing. Whatever your IT is, whether it is smoking, cussing, partying, fornicating, murmuring, complaining, etc. — whatever IT is, just because I am dealing with "IT's" does not mean that I am not in the righteousness of Him by accepting Jesus Christ as Lord and Savior. Now we are to work out our own salvation with fear and trembling (Philippians 2:12). There are some issues that are to be cleansed, and we do that through the water of the word. That is why the enemy fights us so hard to not be serious about renewing our mind — he tries to get us when we see our mistakes and our shortcomings, that we get so hard on ourselves that we stop pressing toward/ running after/ and seeking God. The enemy's whole role and purpose is that we never realize that it is not even in my own strength that I will come out of this any way, it is in Jesus' strength. And as long as the enemy can have us focused on us, instead of Jesus, then we are not a threat to him. WE HAVE TO RENEW OUR THINKING!

> 1 John 3:8-12 [But] he who commits sin [who practices evildoing] is of the devil [takes his character from the evil one], for the devil has sinned (violated the divine law) from the beginning. The reason the Son of God was made manifest (visible) was to undo (destroy, loosen, and dissolve) the works the devil [has done]. 9 No one born (begotten) of God [deliberately, knowingly, and habitually] practices sin, for God's nature abides in him [His principle of life, the divine sperm, remains permanently within him]; and he cannot practice sinning because he is born (begotten) of God. 10 By this it is made clear who take their nature from God and are His children and who take their nature from the devil and are his children: no one who does not practice righteousness [who does not conform to God's will in purpose, thought, and action] is of God; neither is anyone who does not love his brother (his fellow believer in Christ). 11 For this is the message (the announcement) which you have heard from the first, that we should love one another, 12 [And] j not be like Cain who [took his nature and got his motivation] from the evil one and slew his brother. And why did he slay him? Because his deeds (activities, works) were wicked and malicious and his brother's were righteous (virtuous).

Because he was in line with the law of love that says to bring a blood offering — self — living sacrifice.

> 1 John 3:13-16 Do not be surprised and wonder, brethren, that the world detests and pursues you with hatred. 14 We know that we have passed over out of death into Life by the fact that we love the brethren (our fellow Christians). He who does not love abides (remains, is held and kept continually) in [spiritual] death. 15 Anyone who hates (abominates, detests) his brother [in Christ] is [at heart] a murderer, and you know that no murderer has eternal life abiding (persevering) within him. 16 By this we come to know (progressively to recognize, to perceive, to

understand) the [essential] love: that He laid down His [own] life for us; and we ought to lay [our] lives down for [those who are our] brothers [in Him].

"You know" — talking about our thinking and knowing again.

We always quote John 3:16, that is God's love, that God's love gave His Son. Now in 1 John 3:16, because of God's love and the love of the Son, then we ought to love the brethren and lay down our life for the brethren.

> 1 John 3:17-20 But if anyone has this world's goods (resources for sustaining life) and sees his brother and fellow believer in need, yet closes his heart of compassion against him, how can the love of God live and remain in him? [18] Little children, let us not love [merely] in theory or in speech but in deed and in truth (in practice and in sincerity). [19] By this we shall come to know (perceive, recognize, and understand) that we are of the Truth, and can reassure (quiet, conciliate, and pacify) our hearts in His presence, [20] Whenever our hearts in [tormenting] self-accusation make us feel guilty and condemn us. [For we are in God's hands.] For He is above and greater than our consciences (our hearts), and He knows (perceives and understands) everything [nothing is hidden from Him].

Re-read verse 20 a few times to truly walk in freedom, free hearts. We know this by the love of God, that my love of God causes me to be there for the brethren.

> 1 John 3:21 And, beloved, if our consciences (our hearts) do not accuse us [if they do not make us feel guilty and condemn us], we have confidence (complete assurance and boldness) before God,

Our consciences, the mind/ soulish realm. The conscience is part of the heart-mind that needs to be renewed according to the word of God. So if it does not accuse us, our boldness before God comes. We must change our hearts to know that there is no condemnation in Christ Jesus (Romans 8:1).

> 1 John 3:22 And we receive from Him whatever we ask, because we [watchfully] obey His orders [observe His suggestions and injunctions, follow His plan for us] and [habitually] practice what is pleasing to Him.

I had some habitually dis-pleasing situations going on in my life and He had to cut some stuff up and off.

> 1 John 3:23-24 And this is His order (His command, His injunction): that we should believe in (put our faith and trust in and adhere to and rely on) the name of His Son Jesus Christ (the Messiah), and that we should love one another, just as He has commanded us. [24] All who keep His commandments [who obey His orders and follow His plan, live and continue to live, to stay and] abide in Him, and He in

them. [They let Christ be a home to them and they are the home of Christ.] And by this we know and understand and have the proof that He [really] lives and makes His home in us: by the [Holy] Spirit Whom He has given us.

Now look closer at the battle that is going on between your father the devil, and your Father God. See Romans 7, beginning at verse 7, which is titled the *Christian's Struggle*. We have to realize that only being found in Him is where the victory is.

> Romans 7:7-8 What then do we conclude? Is the Law identical with sin? Certainly not! Nevertheless, if it had not been for the Law, I should not have recognized sin or have known its meaning. [For instance] I would not have known about covetousness [would have had no consciousness of sin or sense of guilt] if the Law had not [repeatedly] said, You shall not covet and have an evil desire [for one thing and another]. ⁸ But sin, finding opportunity in the commandment [to express itself], got a hold on me and aroused and stimulated all kinds of forbidden desires (lust, covetousness). For without the Law sin is dead [the sense of it is inactive and a lifeless thing].

Sin — was getting in the thought life, working through the members with lust, covetousness, etc. The law plays to the un-regenerated side of the soulish realm of man. Because when we take the time to regenerate and renew our mind with the word of God, we will not only keep the law, but fulfill it. This is also why we must grow in understanding love.

> Romans 7:9 Once I was alive, but quite apart from and unconscious of the Law. But when the commandment came, sin lived again and I died (was sentenced by the Law to death).

The body did not drop dead, but the ability for the soulish realm to access the spirit realm did. The law killed the living spirit, caused a separation — sin coming on the scene is what caused death. And because of that death, the law had to be given. It was a type and a shadow of the coming Savior Jesus Christ Who fulfills the law.

> Romans 7:10-13 And the very legal ordinance which was designed and intended to bring life actually proved [to mean to me] death. ¹¹ For sin, seizing the opportunity and getting a hold on me [by taking its incentive] from the commandment, beguiled and entrapped and cheated me, and using it [as a weapon], killed me. ¹² The Law therefore is holy, and [each] commandment is holy and just and good. ¹³ Did that which is good then prove fatal [bringing death] to me? Certainly not! It was sin, working death in me by using this good thing [as a weapon], in order that through the commandment sin might be shown up clearly to be sin, that the extreme malignity and immeasurable sinfulness of sin might plainly appear.

Look at verse 13 in the Message bible, *sin simply did what it is famous of doing, used the good as a cover to tempt me.* This is why we cannot live by the knowledge of the tree of good and evil. Relationship with God is not through law, but through the narrow gate, the door, Jesus Christ. So the sin nature is warring in your body, no doubt. But Jesus overcame sin. Lord help renew our mind that we can see that You have strengthened us to make it through this part of the toil.

> Romans 7:14-15 We know that the Law is spiritual; but I am a creature of the flesh [carnal, unspiritual], having been sold into slavery under [the control of] sin. 15 For I do not understand my own actions [I am baffled, bewildered]. I do not practice or accomplish what I wish, but I do the very thing that I loathe [which my moral instinct condemns].

There is a battle going on in my mind. My mind is telling me "Don't do that!" but I keep doing what my mind told me not to do. It is a battle going on!

> Romans 7:16-20 Now if I do [habitually] what is contrary to my desire, [that means that] I acknowledge and agree that the Law is good (morally excellent) and that I take sides with it. 17 However, it is no longer I who do the deed, but the sin [principle] which is at home in me and has possession of me. 18 For I know that nothing good dwells within me, that is, in my flesh. I can will what is right, but I cannot perform it. [I have the intention and urge to do what is right, but no power to carry it out.] 19 For I fail to practice the good deeds I desire to do, but the evil deeds that I do not desire to do are what I am [ever] doing. 20 Now if I do what I do not desire to do, it is no longer I doing it [it is not myself that acts], but the sin [principle] which dwells within me [fixed and operating in my soul].

This is why we have to deal with and renew the mind in the soul — that it does not take it's cues from the sin nature. So renew, cut it off and put it back to the way it was in the garden, and not do foolishness. This is a process, it does not happen overnight.

In this Christian race, hit hurdles do not end the race; they just mean that you are hurt while you are running.

> Romans 7:21-22 So I find it to be a law (rule of action of my being) that when I want to do what is right and good, evil is ever present with me and I am subject to its insistent demands. 22 For I endorse and delight in the Law of God in my inmost self [with my new nature].

The spirit man is born again, and the mind of Christ in the spirit realm is trying to tell the mind in the soulish realm not to do that behavior. The new nature knows that renewal is needed to not keep going through this over and over again. Rejoice with the new nature, yet verse 23 discerns the battle within.

Romans 7:23-25 But I discern in my bodily members [in the sensitive appetites and wills of the flesh] a different law (rule of action) at war against the law of my mind (my reason) and making me a prisoner to the law of sin that dwells in my bodily organs [in the sensitive appetites and wills of the flesh]. 24 O unhappy and pitiable and wretched man that I am! Who will release and deliver me from [the shackles of] this body of death? 25 O thank God! [He will!] through Jesus Christ (the Anointed One) our Lord! So then indeed I, of myself with the mind and heart, serve the Law of God, but with the flesh the law of sin.

MSG 23 Parts of me covertly rebel, and just when I least expect it, they take charge. 24 I've tried everything and nothing helps. I'm at the end of my rope. Is there no one who can do anything for me? Isn't that the real question? 25 The answer, thank God, is that Jesus Christ can and does. He acted to set things right in this life of contradictions where I want to serve God with all my heart and mind, but am pulled by the influence of sin to do something totally different.

We are on this path to renew our mind. Do not say that you are not strong enough, or not able to, because 1 John 2:27 says that you have the unction, the Holy Spirit that is your teacher there leading you and guiding you. As you continue in this process and this struggle that you are in, as we see in Romans 7, gets nullified/ killed/ deadened/ and becomes not so much of a struggle as you see Jesus, as in Romans 7:25, so that we end up in Romans 8:1 with no condemnation. Romans 8 is all about living in the Spirit, read it in context when you get a moment.

Chapter 2 – Battlefield

2.1 This Is Not A Battle, This Is War!

Prayer: Thank You Lord for setting us on this journey, to weekly, daily, seek after You and to have our minds transformed by Your word. Thank You for moving us from conformity to worldly thinking by transforming our mind, to conformity to heavenly (kingdom) thinking. Place our minds on that which is above – on the kingdom. Let us not try to have a dual allegiance to You and to mammon – we serve You God. Because we seek the kingdom first, all of the other stuff is added unto us – it is chasing us down. Your word says miracles signs and wonders shall follow them that believe, so we are not seeking You for miracles signs and wonders, but we seek You for Your kingdom – to know You even the more and those things just follow. We are not moved by naysayers, by people that mis-understand what is going on – we know that You are in control – and that our life is in the palm of Your hand. We know that You are at the center of our lives. We seek after You, we press into You to know You the more.

Holy Spirit we give You access as our teacher according to I John 2:27, come into this time of study, give us revelation, illumination, insight, wisdom into understanding this is not a battle, this is war! By Your spirit, flood the eyes of our hearts so that we can know You more and more – and know the mysteries and have an understanding of what You have called us to do. So that we can know and understand the immeasurable and the unlimited and the surpassing greatness of Your power that is working within us. Thank You God that we know that we are simply vessels that carry Your glory and we are doing our part to purge and cleanse anything that is not like You... We seek You daily for the fresh Manna, the newness in You, fresh and new that You would add on to all that You have already placed within us. That You would enlarge us and increase us in our understanding of who You are and who we are in You. That You would get the glory from Your servants have Your way as we go forward looking at Renewal of the Mind! – this is not a battle, this is war!

We thank You for giving us spiritual eyes to see, know, and understand the battles and the war that we are in. Battle after battle; win some, lose some; but we still fight from a place of victory. We are in the war, and the war is for our minds and for our focus to stay on You – as Your word has told us that You keep us in perfect peace whose mind is stayed on You – so in this war that involves several battles, the enemy is trying to get us to take our mind off of You, but we thank You for Your word in Romans 8 that says nothing can separate us from You. No matter what comes our way: war, weapons, peril, no matter what comes our way – NOTHING can separate us from Your love – You love us that much! Amen!

I could pray on and on — because prayer is simply communicating with God. We pray the word of God back to Him and He shows us things we have not seen in the past.

"War" is defined in the American Heritage Dictionary as a *state of open and declared armed hostile conflict between states of nations; a state of hostility, conflict, or antagonism; is a struggle or a competition between opposing forces or for a particular end.*

There is a conflict, the war of the ages, the war between the 2 trees is a war between dark and light. This is not a battle, this is war — and this struggle is going to go on until the 2nd coming of the Lord Jesus Christ — that is how long this war is going on. Really, it has been going since before the fall of mankind, since before the foundations of the world, back since God created heaven and lucifer got lifted up in pride and was cast out of heaven — this is where the war began — the war is between being prideful and being humble. The enemy tries to trick us and cloak us with deception so that we do not realize that we are operating in pride.

> James 4:1-10 What leads to strife (discord and feuds) and how do conflicts (quarrels and fightings) originate among you? Do they not arise from your sensual desires that are ever warring in your bodily members? 2 You are jealous and covet [what others have] and your desires go unfulfilled; [so] you become murderers. [To hate is to murder as far as your hearts are concerned.] You burn with envy and anger and are not able to obtain [the gratification, the contentment, and the happiness that you seek], so you fight and war. You do not have, because you do not ask. [Or] you do ask [God for them] and yet fail to receive, because you ask with wrong purpose and evil, selfish motives. Your intention is [when you get what you desire] to spend it in sensual pleasures. 4 You [are like] unfaithful wives [having illicit love affairs with the world and breaking your marriage vow to God]! Do you not know that being the world's friend is being God's enemy? So whoever chooses to be a friend of the world takes his stand as an enemy of God. 5 Or do you suppose that the Scripture is speaking to no purpose that says, The Spirit Whom He has caused to dwell in us yearns over us and He yearns for the Spirit [to be welcome] with a jealous love? 6 But He gives us more and more grace (power of the Holy Spirit, to meet this evil tendency and all others fully). That is why He says, God sets Himself against the proud and haughty, but gives grace [continually] to the lowly (those who are humble enough to receive it). 7 So be subject to God. Resist the devil [stand firm against him], and he will flee from you. 8 Come close to God and He will come close to you. [Recognize that you are] sinners, get your soiled hands clean; [realize that you have been disloyal] wavering individuals with divided interests, and purify your hearts [of your spiritual adultery]. 9 [As you draw near to God] be deeply penitent and grieve, even weep [over your disloyalty]. Let your laughter be turned to grief and your mirth to dejection and heartfelt shame [for your sins]. 10 Humble

yourselves [feeling very insignificant] in the presence of the Lord, and He will exalt you [He will lift you up and make your lives significant].

I know this is a large quote, but is needed to fully identify this war and the battles. Verse 1 of James 4 shows us an example of the many battles that will be fought in this war; strife, envy, murdering in the heart, etc. — all of this comes as a root of deception, of pride. It is that you want something that someone else has — the enemy is lying to you, and tries to belittle you to feel like less than, when really, God said He would supply all of your needs according to His riches in glory — so if it is not manifested, lets seek God — that my needs be met. Our one need is life and breath, everything else is a bonus — it is possible, but we must have a renewed mind and thinking concerning our needs being met. We are such a self-centered generation, operating more out of the knowledge of good and evil, blessings and cursings — where we are more concerned about being blessed, not truly understanding what it means to be blessed. Based on 2 Chronicles 4:10, this "bless" means to be endowed with power, which is what we see here in James 4:6 when it says that He gives us more and more grace. That is true blessing — the blessing is grace — is the Holy Spirit within that helps us to not fall prey to the deception of the enemy to get mixed up in pride, no matter how it is cloaked.

This is another look at the war that has been going on between pride and humility — where the enemy tries to deceive us to operate in pride, not true humility (many operate in false humility, which is cloaked in religion and tradition). I learned that shyness is a form of pride because we are more concerned about ourselves than the *assignment* God has placed before us — shy is just an excuse and a deception of pride.

Back to the fact that we are in a war that has been going on for thousands of years. We are in a war that we really do not know anything about; this is why we must renew our mind to understand the war tactics that are going on.

The chapter is titled the Battlefield, sub-titled "This is not a battle, this is war!" So we need to understand that there is a battlefield — but this is not a battle, this is war. The conflict is not even the soldiers that are in the battle, but is what is going on in the heavenlies, as in Ephesians 6.

> Ephesians 6:10-11 In conclusion, be strong in the Lord [be empowered through your union with Him]; draw your strength from Him [that strength which His boundless might provides]. ¹¹ Put on God's whole armor [the armor of a heavy-armed soldier which God supplies], that you may be able successfully to stand up against [all] the strategies and the deceits of the devil.

You recognize the enemy's deceits by putting on the whole armor of God. We must transform and renew our mind with understanding the whole armor of God. Let's keep looking to identify the battlefield.

> Ephesians 6:12-14 For we are not wrestling with flesh and blood [contending only with physical opponents], but against the despotisms, against the powers, against [the master spirits who are] the world rulers of this present darkness, against the spirit forces of wickedness in the heavenly (supernatural) sphere. 13 Therefore put on God's complete armor, that you may be able to resist and stand your ground on the evil day [of danger], and, having done all [the crisis demands], to stand [firmly in your place]. 14 Stand therefore [hold your ground], having tightened the belt of truth around your loins and having put on the breastplate of integrity and of moral rectitude and right standing with God.

Verse 12 shows that the battle is against dark and light. The first piece of the armor is the belt of truth, the word of God (which according to Psalm 119 is a lamp and a light) — the whole truth and nothing but the truth. Give me the ugly truth over a pretty lie any day! Then the breastplate of righteousness. We have our chest stuck out as the righteousness of God in Christ, recognizing that our self-righteousness is as filthy rags (as it says in Isaiah 65); the only righteousness that we have is imputed and is found by being "in Him." That is why we must renew our mind with what it means to be "in Him" — of what it means to be in right standing with God — of having integrity with God.

> Ephesians 6:15 And having shod your feet in preparation [to face the enemy with the firm-footed stability, the promptness, and the readiness produced by the good news] of the Gospel of peace.

We have to understand the gospel presentation; who Jesus is; redemption; justification; sanctification; reconciliation and so much more. Understand that salvation has many parts: it was done on Calvary, really, before the foundations of the world, but it was enacted at Calvary when Jesus was crucified on the Cross and died as a substitute for us — that was justification. Just as if I'd never sinned — even though I was shaped and born into iniquity and sin — but through accepting Jesus Christ as savior, and His grace in growing and knowing Him more and more through the help of the Holy Spirit... all of this is understanding the gospel, as the verse said *having our feet in preparation* — this is why we must learn scripturally how we know we are saved, learn scripturally how to have a foundation in salvation — this is how our feet are firm in the gospel; ready for the walk by faith and the race set before us. That we can understand scripturally and know the "it is written" of the word to respond to the enemy who deceivingly twists the word (adding boo-boo to the brownies and trying to slip it to you unawares); you must know scripturally for yourself so that you can see someone putting boo-boo in the brownies (that means adding something in there deceivingly that is not needed, disgusting and harmful to our health).

> Ephesians 6:16 Lift up over all the [covering] shield of saving faith, upon which you can quench all the flaming missiles of the wicked [one].

Yet another piece of the armor, this shield of saving faith — it is as we get an understanding of faith. Faith is not acquiring material things, as the world has amplified, but faith is leaning your entire personality in complete trust and confidence in God through Jesus Christ. When we lift this up, it does not matter what the devil throws at us: like telling you that "you cannot read, or that no one wants to hear what you have to say because you are not educated or you are a woman", no matter what he tries to throw at you and tell you that you do not have, or make you feel disqualified for doing what God is calling you to do — my confidence is in Him, not me anyway!

Another aspect of this shield of faith is that it is the faithfulness of God that we lift up. He is the epitome of faith — He is faithfully faithful! We must keep this *lifted* up to extinguish ALL of the missiles and harassments of the enemy.

> Ephesians 6:17 And take the helmet of salvation and the sword that the Spirit wields, which is the Word of God.

My salvation is in Him — the cross is victory — I am fighting FROM a place of victory; and as all of these battles come, I will just stand still and see the salvation of the Lord as in 2 Chronicles 20:20. Stand still knowing that He has this. It says the sword that the Spirit wields, so He will reveal things to us, the things of the word of God, He will reveal them.

> Ephesians 6:18 Pray at all times (on every occasion, in every season) in the Spirit, with all [manner of] prayer and entreaty. To that end keep alert and watch with strong purpose and perseverance, interceding in behalf of all the saints (God's consecrated people).

This little side journey in the section on definitions of battle and war, was identifying us the battlefield and the equipment that must be worn on this battlefield. This is not a battle, this war, and we must know how to operate in it.

Defining "battle": a *combat between two persons; a general encounter between armies, ships of war, or aircraft.*

Armies — they will come at you by foot, by water, and above your head. So you will have crazy thoughts coming at you from every direction.

More of the definition of battle: *it is an extended contest, struggle, or controversy; to contend with full strength, vigor, skill, or resources; to struggle.*

You must contend with full strength, not half-heartedly, or halfway fighting the devil and crazy thoughts. You contend by being a person of integrity (when you say you will do something, do it) — you cannot be half-hearted in a battle. I am a veteran of the United States Air Force, and one of the first things we learned in basic training was how to perform dorm guard; meaning that someone was always on watch in the dorm at all times. Even through the night when everyone would be asleep, there would be an airman up at the door, watching at all times, contending with full strength — woke and alert. They were training us that when we got into true battle we would know how to contend and be watchful — they would also train us how to sound the alarm if danger did arise, in order to let everyone know something was going on. Why can we do this type of training in the natural military, but then when it comes to the body of Christ we want to have a fit and don't expect the same type of training and equipping? God calls us to wake up in the middle of the night (well morning) and get up with Him, but we want to make excuses of why we can't. No! We must keep our eyes open, we are on duty!

Jacob contended with God and his name was changed to Israel because he contended with God. Jacob was doing things in his own strength, then saw that he needed God's strength, so he wrestled in His presence until God blessed him. We can say, endow me with power and the Holy Spirit grace to contend with these evil powers that I am facing and have been trying to face on my own, but I see that I cannot do it like this. Then God changed Jacobs name to Israel (meaning contended with God). Contending — it took some effort. And God had to let Jacob know that He recognized his strong contending, but wanted to let him know that He was stronger than him, so God touched Jacob in the hallow of his thigh, and he then walked with a limp for the rest of his life. I interpreted this to symbolize for me, that He touched me in my own strength, because in my own strength I can do nothing. As long as we are relying on Him, we will walk with a cane in our thinking, which is the word of God — we walk with the sword, with His rod and His staff leading us as our Great Shepherd.

This is not a battle, this is war! You will have encounters with this hierarchy as in Ephesians 6:12, not contending only with physical opponents, but there is a spiritual war going on. Despotisms — we are in a war, we must get educated.

We must learn what this hierarchy is in Ephesians 6:12. What they are trying to do is cloak you with deception — and they have been at it for thousands of years, and we have only been at it a few years. Yet what we have that this hierarchy does not have, is the help of the Holy Spirit, Who has been around since before them all, and He is showing us their entire strategy (their war plans). But we must do our part: present your body as a living sacrifice; do not be conformed to this world because if you think like this world, you will be deceived. Transform your mind by the renewing with the word!

This is not a battle, this is war! Again, a battle is an extended contest, do not think that it is over just one time, there will be many battles to win the war. Now we fight FROM the place of victory, from the "it is finished", but we still must walk it out.

It is an encounter which depicts the hierarchy in Ephesians 6, but also, at salvation you were drafted into a war — yet this battle is not yours, but the Lord's. We must learn, as in Matthew 11:28-30, some things do not just come automatic. Salvation (justification) is automatic once you believe, but the sanctification process has some requirements of us — things we must do. You are not working for your salvation, that is a done deal, but you are growing in grace, growing in knowing who God is and who you are in Him.

> Matthew 11:28-30 Come to Me, all you who labor and are heavy-laden and overburdened, and I will cause you to rest. [I will ease and relieve and refresh your souls.] ²⁹ Take My yoke upon you and learn of Me, for I am gentle (meek) and humble (lowly) in heart, and you will find rest (relief and ease and refreshment and recreation and blessed quiet) for your souls. ³⁰ For My yoke is wholesome (useful, good — not harsh, hard, sharp, or pressing, but comfortable, gracious, and pleasant), and My burden is light and easy to be borne.

When you learn of Him, you will be able to resist the devil. If you do not, then you will have a hard time resisting the devil, but will dance right along with him. This is not a battle, this is war! — we stand still and see the salvation of the Lord by learning of Him — and His yoke does all the work. It is His anointing that destroys the yoke; when we are yoked up with His anointing, the yoke of the enemy will not be an issue for you.

We are exposing the tactics, plans, strategies of the enemy on the battleground of the mind — which is the soulish realm: the mind, will, emotion, imagination, intellect, reasoning, thoughts, personality; conscious, memory. This is the battlefield — and if the enemy can mess up your thinking, he can have you living raggedy. But the Lord is exposing and revealing the plans, tactics, strategies of the enemy.

The Lord once spoke to me about "lizard wisdom" in an open vision one day. Afterward I sought the word of the Lord regarding this, He led me to Proverbs 30:28 *The lizard you can seize with your hands, yet it is in kings' palaces.* He said He was giving lizard wisdom, and that we serve the King of kings — the ranking officer in these battles, in this war. Yet He would give the wisdom from the enemy's counsel — similar to what happened when the Lord kept revealing the enemy's plan to the Elisha in 2 Kings 6:8-12. The Lord reveals the enemy's plan so that we know how to defeat them in their tactics and strategies. We will discuss this "lizard wisdom" revelation more in a moment.

Prayer: Thank You for truly training us to renew our mind – to not be conformed to worldly thinking, to be transformed by the renewing of our mind according to Your word, that we would be conformed to kingdom thinking. According to 1 John 2:27 that teaches us all things, to truly be our Helper and revealer of Truth. Give us spiritual eyes to see, and spiritual ears to hear and understand what You are saying to us the body of Christ, the church, the called out ones, the ecclesia, those that are called for such a time as this, those that are drafted and enlisted in this war. Thank You for doing what only You can do in our understanding as You give us revelation, illumination, knowledge, insight, wisdom as we go forward looking at "this is not a battle, this is war" – help us to understand the battles that we go through, and that we are fighting from a place of victory in this war. Amen.

In fighting these battles, we need the wisdom of God, not our wisdom. Back to the open vision (the lizard wisdom referred to earlier) in October 2010 that I did not recognize was from the Lord at first – kind of like Eli and Samuel when God first called Samuel (1 Samuel 3), they didn't recognize it was God at first, but once I realized that my eyes were not playing tricks on me, and the Lord was trying to reveal His mysteries to me (as in 1 Corinthians 2:10), I said like Eli told Samuel to say "Here I am, Your servant is listening." I will not give the details of the vision, but the fact that the Holy Spirit led me to the following text:

> Proverbs 30:24-28 There are four things which are little on the earth, but they are exceedingly wise: 25 The ants are a people not strong, yet they lay up their food in the summer; 26 The conies are but a feeble folk, yet they make their houses in the rocks; 27 The locusts have no king, yet they go forth all of them by bands; 28 The lizard you can seize with your hands, yet it is in kings' palaces.

The Lord is unleashing wisdom, these things here in this text (lizards, ants, conies, locusts) are small, yet they have wisdom. I am "On Assignment" to hear the plans/ tactics/ strategies of the enemy and to sound the alarm to the saints, the other believers, the other called out ones, to the body of Christ.

These lizards, ants, conies, locusts are despised and minor, yet exceedingly wise. At times, we may appear to be despised, minor, and a nobody, but when we spend time with God, and He gives us His wisdom, it will cause us to be exceedingly wise. God takes the foolish things of this world (worldly thinking) to confound the wise (of this world). So He will make you the wise of His world, and mess this world up.

Yet, we must purge flesh (fleshly thinking, and being led by the dictates of the flesh) and grow out of immaturity (we must mature in the things of God) in order to receive and operate in this promised wisdom.

As a people, we repent for not moving out and releasing this wisdom. We must go/ speak/ say/ do because we must release the word/wisdom; that we be obedient to the spirit of the

Lord. Know that preparation time is never wasted time — God is preparing the army for such a time as this. As we discussed about military basic training — God is training us, trying to get some basic skills in us where we can just operate as needed. While in basic training, they taught us a lot of stuff. They taught us how to dress, how to keep the areas clean around us to standard — one reason was for hygiene, the other reason is that in the midst of a battle, you do not have time to waste fumbling around, things must be ready. I remember we had to iron our underwear. One of the airman complained to a Drill Instructor about why did we have to iron our underwear (she was the only one who verbalized what we were all thinking); the Drill Instructor informed her (in a very cinematic way) that it was to teach us how to operate without having to think about what we were doing — because when in battle, we don't have time to think about it, it needs to be second nature. It is crazy that this took place back in October 1988, but I still remember to this day, in 2013, how to do this regulatory ironing of the underwear (of course I NEVER iron them now, but I know how). The Drill Instructor's principle to this lesson was for us to learn what to do as told, and do it the same way every time, without much thought — this was the lesson to learn, and is the lesson that we learn spiritually. I remember when I enlisted in the military, basic training was 6 weeks — I thought that was forever, but 6 weeks is only 40 days — is a training time, a testing time. It may seem to be a long time, but it is not — and after basic training, I went into another training; a technical training environment. Everyone is taught the same thing in basic training, then go on to technical training or a specialty training. So some of us have the basics down, we know not to trust in self — but the Lord; we understand that faith is not for stuff — but is the leaning of our entire personality in complete trust and confidence in the saving grace of Christ Jesus, these are the basics, now it is time to get into some technical training.

2.2 Grace

The role of grace in the process of renewing our mind — we must truly understand grace. We live in the Age of Grace, where God's grace is poured out — He has extended salvation through grace, to both the Gentiles as well as the Jews.

> Titus 2:11-13 For the grace of God (His unmerited favor and blessing) has come forward (appeared) for the deliverance from sin and the eternal salvation for all mankind. 12 It has trained us to reject and renounce all ungodliness (irreligion) and worldly (passionate) desires, to live discreet (temperate, self-controlled), upright, devout (spiritually whole) lives in this present world, 13 Awaiting and looking for the [fulfillment, the realization of our] blessed hope, even the glorious appearing of our great God and Savior Christ Jesus (the Messiah, the Anointed One).

So when we get a better understanding of the grace of God, it trains us to reject worldly thinking — all ungodliness. We are supposed to be godly, we are to be Christ-like, to be holy for He is holy. It is when we understand grace, that we begin to see things that are ungodly, even in our own behavior, and we reject it/ renounce it. Meaning, we once may have been in agreement with it, but now, as we renounce it, we no longer agree with it. We are taking our mind off of worldly thinking.

In Jeremiah 1:10, we see a process of uprooting.

> Jeremiah 1:10 See, I have this day appointed you to the oversight of the nations and of the kingdoms to root out and pull down, to destroy and to overthrow, to build and to plant.

There are 4 things that we do that are according to Jeremiah 1:10 and Titus 2, to tear out anything that is ungodly worldly passionate desires:

1) Root out,
2) Pull down,
3) Destroy,
4) Overthrow — all these things.
   Then follow it up by building and planting discretion, temperance, self-control, uprightness, devoutness, spiritually wholeness.

The grace of God allows us to do this, to reject and renounce worldliness and to walk in spirit filled living. We must renew our minds and understand that we cannot do it on our own, apart from God.

As a person helping shepherd God's people, we have a responsibility to tell them of this to build up their courage. And discipline them if they are out of line; discipline with the word of God.

> 2 Timothy 3:16-17 Every Scripture is God-breathed (given by His inspiration) and profitable for instruction, for reproof and conviction of sin, for correction of error and discipline in obedience, [and] for training in righteousness (in holy living, in conformity to God's will in thought, purpose, and action), 17 So that the man of God may be complete and proficient, well fitted and thoroughly equipped for every good work.

We must do what Titus 2 is instructing us to do, discipline God's people to encourage them, we do it according to the word of God. This 2 Timothy 3 goes on to show us what we should be teaching: what believers should do, should stop doing, should increase in doing — scripture is there to teach us, give instruction, give reproof, give doctrine in right living. The grace of God is here for each and every one of us.

The book of Titus was written from Paul to the young Pastor Titus (at Crete) — Paul was giving him instructions on how to handle the people — how to disciple and train them. We do this according to the word of God, put this all in context and go back and read Titus 2 from the beginning, he was giving instructions to several people groups. We have to change our thinking about all these topics he was addressing, such as steal no more; when you change your thinking, you will not be trying to get your needs met the wrong way (stealing); but you will discover that God will supply all of your needs according to His riches in glory, not according to this worldly standard. God is trying to get our attention, we are thinking too much on worldly things — we need to think on *these* things — the things above, whatever is pure and holy (as in Philippians 3:1-21).

Now we will look at Philippians 3, which is titled *the example of Paul*, I will add, Paul's example of being an upright Christian, or his example of renewing the mind. Again, we are talking about being transformed by the word and not being conformed to the world.

> Philippians 3:1 For the rest, my brethren, delight yourselves in the Lord and continue to rejoice that you are in Him. To keep writing to you [over and over] of the same things is not irksome to me, and it is [a precaution] for your safety.

Part of training and teaching others; it is not burdensome to keep going over the same thing. The goal is progress. It gets burdensome like 1 Corinthians 3, when Paul said of the believers there that they should know the basics already, and they were rebuked because they were not handling the things of God properly, but here in Philippi, there is no rebuke, he doesn't mind repeating it.

> Philippians 3:2 Look out for those dogs [Judaizers, legalists], look out for those mischief-makers, look out for those who mutilate the flesh.

This explains why Paul does not mind repeating himself, because religious people will try to get them off. This is why I personally teach people that their trust is not in religion, or tradition, or the doctrines of men, not in the arm of man, but it is in Jesus Christ.

> Philippians 3:3-4 For we [Christians] are the true circumcision, who worship God in spirit and by the Spirit of God and exult and glory and pride ourselves in Jesus Christ, and put no confidence or dependence [on what we are] in the flesh and on outward privileges and physical advantages and external appearances— 4 Though for myself I have [at least grounds] to rely on the flesh. If any other man considers that he has or seems to have reason to rely on the flesh and his physical and outward advantages, I have still more!

Paul was saying if anybody could boast about religion, he could, he had his credentials in religion — but he did not rely on it, as in verse 7, it was all a combined loss for the sake of Christ. When you get Christ, all the worldly knowledge that you have is nothing compared to the knowledge that comes from Christ Jesus.

> Philippians 3:5-8 Circumcised when I was eight days old, of the race of Israel, of the tribe of Benjamin, a Hebrew [and the son] of Hebrews; as to the observance of the

> Law I was of [the party of] the Pharisees, ⁶ As to my zeal, I was a persecutor of the church, and by the Law's standard of righteousness (supposed justice, uprightness, and right standing with God) I was proven to be blameless and no fault was found with me. ⁷ But whatever former things I had that might have been gains to me, I have come to consider as [one combined] loss for Christ's sake. ⁸ Yes, furthermore, I count everything as loss compared to the possession of the priceless privilege (the overwhelming preciousness, the surpassing worth, and supreme advantage) of knowing Christ Jesus my Lord and of progressively becoming more deeply and intimately acquainted with Him [of perceiving and recognizing and understanding Him more fully and clearly]. For His sake I have lost everything and consider it all to be mere rubbish (refuse, dregs), in order that I may win (gain) Christ (the Anointed One)

He was basically saying that he used to rely on that stuff in his thinking, but now he was not. He even added that he was *progressively becoming more deeply and intimately acquainted with Him, [of perceiving and recognizing and understanding Him more fully and clearly]*. This is when we ask God to flood the eyes of our heart with light so that we can know, perceive, and understand the depths of Him. This is what happens when we become more intimate with Him, as we grow and know who God is and who we are in Him.

> Philippians 3:9 And that I may [actually] be found and known as in Him, not having any [self-achieved] righteousness that can be called my own, based on my obedience to the Law's demands (ritualistic uprightness and supposed right standing with God thus acquired), but possessing that [genuine righteousness] which comes through faith in Christ (the Anointed One), the [truly] right standing with God, which comes from God by [saving] faith.

Again, we do not rely on going to church every Sunday, or ritualistic acts — but on being found as the righteousness of God in Christ Jesus.

> Philippians 3:10 [For my determined purpose is] that I may know Him [that I may progressively become more deeply and intimately acquainted with Him, perceiving and recognizing and understanding the wonders of His Person more strongly and more clearly], and that I may in that same way come to know the power outflowing from His resurrection [which it exerts over believers], and that I may so share His sufferings as to be continually transformed [in spirit into His likeness even] to His death, [in the hope]

Determined purpose — a made up mind — thinking — this is where the battlefield is. This is not a battle, this is war! So in order to win the battles, you have to have a made up mind, a determined purpose. As this verse says, get a better understanding of the wonders of His person. We also must change our thinking about resurrection and about suffering. Nobody wants to go through anything — if we are told we have to suffer, we don't want to go through.

This verse 10 is a daily thing, a moving thing, it says *progressively becoming* — should be added onto. My determined purpose — I have set my mind to do this, to understand Him. We can meditate on this verse 10 and see so much! Selah! There is a lot being said, many layers of understanding to obtain.

Looking at the words from Philippians 3:10, *to know Him and the power* ... this word "power" means: *strength power, ability; inherent power, power residing in a thing by virtue of its nature, or which a person or thing exerts and puts forth; power for performing miracles; moral power and excellence of soul; the power and influence which belong to riches and wealth; power and resources arising from numbers; power consisting in or resting upon armies, forces, hosts.*

The power that we are looking for is the power that comes through resurrection. It is through the resurrection of Jesus Christ that we now have victory over the forces of the enemy. We now have victory, power, and influence which belong to wealth — it is the Lord that gives you the power to get wealth — and it is for the kingdom, not for selfish ambitions; this is why we must renew our mind to the role of riches and wealth — as we will cover in another chapter.

Now looking at the word "resurrection" here means: *a raising up, a rising (e.g. from a seat); a rising from the dead.* He raised up from the seat of humanity and is now seated at the right hand of God; back in His divinity, back in His deity as Christ — and He will be coming back again a second time — so we need to know Him through the power of what happened when He got up those 3 days later. That is why we must preach the blood, we must preach the gospel presentation that He came through immaculate conception, He lived, was crucified, laid in a tomb, and was raised, miracles/ signs/ wonders that followed Him (not that He performed them, but they followed Him because of who He was). We must have relationship with God, not just association — a lot of people are only associated to Him based on the miracles/ signs/ wonders He performs, not because of true relationship — relationship goes deeper than that, you have to know the person behind the miracles/ signs/ wonders — and that is what I need to get to know — the power of the resurrection, I need to know the Person that I am found in — and grow progressively.

The resurrection and the fellowship — this word "fellowship" means: *fellowship, association, community, communion, joint participation, intercourse; intimacy.*

The resurrection and the fellowship of His suffering — this word "suffering" means *that which one suffers or has suffered; externally, a suffering, misfortune, calamity, evil, affliction. Of the sufferings of Christ. Also the afflictions which Christians must undergo in behalf of the same cause which Christ patiently endured. Of an inward state, an affliction, passion; an enduring, undergoing, suffering.*

We are really getting an understanding of what it means to know Him through the power of His resurrection and the fellowship of His suffering. This suffering is saying that there are some afflictions and some things that are going to happen, we need to patiently endure

— let patience have its perfect work in us. The root word for suffering means: *whatever befalls one, whether it be sad or joyous; specifically a calamity, mishap, evil, affliction. A feeling which the mind suffers; an affliction of the mind, emotion, passion; in the New Testament in a bad sense, depraved passion, vile passions.* So we are renewing the mind so that it does not suffer the way the world suffers, we are suffering in the power if His resurrection. We need to make sure that we are renewing the mind, that it does not give way to the depravity and the vileness. As in Romans 1 when they rejected the truth and would not acknowledge Him as the truth, He gave them over to a depraved mind — and they began to suffer.

"Being made conformable" — means *to be conformed to, receive the same form as.* And the root word goes deeper and means *having the same form as another, similar, conformed to;* and I found a footnote relating this to when Jesus took on the *"form" of a bondservant and came in the likeness of man* in Philippians 2.

That we are not to be conformable to the world, but to the death of Jesus Christ and the power of resurrection. It is as we are conformed to having strong moral excellence, and to not being in a depraved mind with vile passions.

The word "death" means *the death of the body; that separation (whether natural or violent) of the soul and the body by which the life on earth is ended. In the widest sense, death comprising all the miseries arising from sin, as well physical death as the loss of a life consecrated to God and blessed in him on earth, to be followed by wretchedness in hell.*

Ignorance and sin can keep you locked in darkness — it is like a death. We need to be fleeing from sin, we need to not let temptation or lust in our minds allow us to sin. That is why we need to renew our mind to not sin; to not operate out of the vile passions.

In Philippians 3:10, knowing God in the power of His resurrection suffering — we need to renew our mind and know that every single day it is through the resurrection of Jesus, that sin no longer has dominion over me. When the sin nature begins to rise and try to trip you into doing foolishness (rebellion against the law of God, the principles of godly living) — it is then that you must not let your mind be conformed to worldly thinking, but to go to where you are being transformed to know that through the resurrection power of Jesus Christ, whatever your "IT" is, you have power over it.

God's grace is out of proportion to the fall of man.

Putting this in context, we are looking at the Renewal of the Mind! of Romans 12:2, we are also relating that this is not a battle, this is war! — now we are looking at the roots of rejection. This text here is saying that even though we reject God, He never utterly rejects us. All we have to do is cry out; His grace will come in and deliver. But do not think there are no consequences attached, people are/were dying — a whole generation of Israelites had to die off in the wilderness and did not enter into the Promised Land — so why would we pervert grace, knowing that it could kill off a generation?! We will not pervert grace. We will grow in understanding grace, and the role of it in our life — as here in Titus 2:11, it helps and empowers us to reject ungodliness and live upright lives in this present world. We are dual citizens, we live in this world, we are in it, but not of it. Do not be conformed to this present world, but to kingdom — by renewing our mind according to the word of God. When we grow in knowing the grace of God, then we will not yield to worldliness and foolishness.

> Philippians 3:11-16 That if possible I may attain to the [spiritual and moral] resurrection [that lifts me] out from among the dead [even while in the body]. 12 Not that I have now attained [this ideal], or have already been made perfect, but I press on to lay hold of (grasp) and make my own, that for which Christ Jesus (the Messiah) has laid hold of me and made me His own. 13 I do not consider, brethren, that I have captured and made it my own [yet]; but one thing I do [it is my one aspiration]: forgetting what lies behind and straining forward to what lies ahead, 14 I press on toward the goal to win the [supreme and heavenly] prize to which God in Christ Jesus is calling us upward. 15 So let those [of us] who are spiritually mature and full-grown have this mind and hold these convictions; and if in any respect you have a different attitude of mind, God will make that clear to you also. 16 Only let us hold true to what we have already attained and walk and order our lives by that.

We are renewing our mind to be mature and full grown, as with the lizard wisdom of Proverbs 30:28, we have to move out of immaturity, and move into maturity to receive full grown wisdom.

As we are submitted unto God, if our mind is not right, if we are not thinking right, God will make that clear to us — we just have to accept it, and have an ear to hear.

Verse 16 is why we have so many spiritually obese people; they have been exposed to this spiritual food, but are not digesting it and metabolizing it; just eating it and being lazy, not walking it out or living their life by it. No, we must get spiritually fit and walk it out.

> Philippians 3:17-21 Brethren, together follow my example and observe those who live after the pattern we have set for you. 18 For there are many, of whom I have often told you and now tell you even with tears, who walk (live) as enemies of the cross of Christ (the Anointed One). 19 They are doomed and their fate is eternal misery (perdition); their god is their stomach (their appetites, their sensuality) and they glory in their shame, siding with earthly things and being of their party. 20 But we are citizens of the state (commonwealth, homeland) which is in heaven, and from it also we earnestly and patiently await [the coming of] the Lord Jesus Christ (the Messiah) [as] Savior, 21 Who will transform and fashion anew the body of our

humiliation to conform to and be like the body of His glory and majesty, by exerting that power which enables Him even to subject everything to Himself.

2.3 Contend

Now we are returning to Ephesians 6. Wrestling is hand to hand combat — thanks be unto God who teaches my hands to war (Psalm 18:34).

For this PORTION of study, I used www.blueletter.org to better define the meaning of these words.

"Contend" in the Amplified is "wrestle" in the KJV, and is defined as a *contest between two in which each endeavors to throw the other, and which is decided when the victor is able to hold his opponent down with his hand on his neck; the term is transferred to the Christian's struggle with the power of evil.* As we look at this word deeper, we will see that it is dealing with our thinking.

> John 6:52 Then the Jews angrily contended with one another, saying, How is He able to give us His flesh to eat?

This section was titled *many of the disciples turn away* — Jesus knew that He did not have everyone's heart — so He found out who was for real, or was just there for the miracles, signs, and wonders. He began to say some tough sayings; they began to argue amongst themselves instead of going to Him for a better understanding, but they began to contend among themselves.

When contention happens among man, it will cause struggle and suffering — but be of good cheer because through it all, you are being transformed to be more and more Christ-like.

> Acts 11:2 So when Peter went up to Jerusalem, the circumcision party [certain Jewish Christians] found fault with him [separating themselves from him in a hostile spirit, opposing and disputing and contending with him].

This is another example of religious people contending the incorrect way. Know that when you are walking in what God has called you to be, there will be some people that get a hostile, opposing, disputing spirit against you. This is not a battle this is war! — they will contend against you, but God will respond and bring vengeance (it belongs to Him).

> Acts 23:9 Then a great uproar ensued, and some of the scribes of the Pharisees' party stood up and thoroughly fought the case, [contending fiercely] and declaring, We find nothing evil or wrong in this man. But if a spirit or an angel [really] spoke to him—? Let us not fight against God!

> 2 Timothy 2:24 And the servant of the Lord must not be quarrelsome (fighting and contending). Instead, he must be kindly to everyone and mild-tempered [preserving the bond of peace]; he must be a skilled and suitable teacher, patient and forbearing and willing to suffer wrong.

We have to be on the watch for this fighting spirit because it disguises itself in several ways. I myself did not (and do not) like confrontation, I never like to argue or fight, but I would get upset and have a fighting spirit within. We cannot do this.

Contention is also listed several times in the epistles when the writers are warning against operating in the flesh. The best example is seen in Galatians 5:19-23; which using this verse, we tie back into the process of Jeremiah 1:10

1) Root out,
2) Pull down,
3) Destroy,
4) Overthrow the works of the flesh

And plant and build the fruit of the spirit, which are a result of, as the Amplified bible puts it: *But the fruit ... which His presence within accomplishes] are love joy peace...* We root out contention and the other worldly things, and build/plant love, joy, peace, patience, kindness, etc.

To sum it up, looking at this 2 Timothy 2:24 text, contention against the plan of God cannot be found in someone desiring to be a leader in the body of Christ. We must accept the word of God, and understand that He contends on our behalf, and we contend with spiritual principles, not worldly principles (not religious, traditional, legalistic principles).

> Jude 1:3 Beloved, my whole concern was to write to you in regard to our common salvation. [But] I found it necessary and was impelled to write you and urgently appeal to and exhort [you] to contend for the faith which was once for all handed down to the saints [the faith which is that sum of Christian belief which was delivered verbally to the holy people of God].

We are to fight for the faith, stand up for it in the face of others. Another definition of contend is *to agonize* — so this is what we should be doing for the faith.

We have a common salvation, and in that we get a better understanding of faith. But we must also understand what faith is. Here in the book of Jude, he was addressing apostasy and false teachers. These Pharisees thought they had it going on, but they were apostate — they were not accepting Jesus as the Christ, the awaited Messiah — remember, it was the religious people that crucified Him. And this next verse shows us that we do not contend in our own power, but we call on God.

> Jude 1:9 But when [even] the archangel Michael, contending with the devil, judicially argued (disputed) about the body of Moses, he dared not [presume to] bring an abusive condemnation against him, but [simply] said, The Lord rebuke you!

We must learn that it is not us that rebukes satan, but the Lord in you that rebukes him — the Greater One in you, the Lord of lords, and the King of kings, the Lord of the armies of God, He is in control, He is a fighting God. We do not contend on our own, we do not wrestle with worldly principles, we must wrestle using kingdom principles.

Contend — God contending on our behalf —

> Psalm 35:1, 27-28 Contend, O Lord, with those who contend with me; fight against those who fight against me... 27 Let those who favor my righteous cause and have pleasure in my uprightness shout for joy and be glad and say continually, Let the Lord be magnified, Who takes pleasure in the prosperity of His servant. 28 And my tongue shall talk of Your righteousness, rightness, and justice, and of [my reasons for] Your praise all the day long.

We want the Lord to be on our side, contending for us. As the definition of contend, we want Him to agonize for us; to fight for us, to stand up for us. This Psalm 35 shows in verse 1 that God will contend for us, and at verse 27-28 we see that we must contend for Him in praise.

> Psalm 103:8-10 The Lord is merciful and gracious, slow to anger and plenteous in mercy and loving-kindness. 9 He will not always chide or be contending, neither will He keep His anger forever or hold a grudge. 10 He has not dealt with us after our sins nor rewarded us according to our iniquities.

One of the benefits of God is that even though things are going on, He will not hold a grudge. We may get into trouble, but verse 8 tells of His mercifulness and grace that is available to us, His erring children. He contends for us even when we get caught up in drama.

> Proverbs 3:30 Contend not with a man for no reason — when he has done you no wrong.

For no reason — but if there is a reason, keep in mind Matthew 5:9, blessed are the makers and maintainers of peace, so seek wisdom how to deal with the issue at hand in a way that will be pleasing to God and maintain peace.

> Proverbs 28:4 Those who forsake the law [of God and man] praise the wicked, but those who keep the law [of God and man] contend with them.

As keepers of the law, we are contending with those who forsake the law. Either the law is kept, or the law is forsaken, there are no grey areas; and we can only keep the law "in Him" — because Jesus fulfills the law, and by ourselves and with this fleshly nature, we can't.

> Ecclesiastes 6:10 Whatever [man] is, he has been named that long ago, and it is known that it is man [Adam]; nor can he contend with Him who is mightier than he [whether God or death].

It does not make sense to contend with God; especially because we are mere men — created beings — so why would we contend with Him?

A theme that I have found as I have studied through these scriptures concerning the word contend, is that of judgment.

> Isaiah 3:8 For Jerusalem is ruined and Judah is fallen, because their speech and their deeds are against the Lord, to provoke the eyes of His glory and defy His glorious presence.

> Isaiah 3:13 The Lord stands up to contend, and stands to judge the peoples and His people.

Sometimes God is contending for you and judging based off of your speech and your deeds.

> Isaiah 49:25 For thus says the Lord: Even the captives of the mighty will be taken away, and the prey of the terrible will be delivered; for I will contend with him who contends with you, and I will give safety to your children and ease them.

We must learn that we have to stay on God's side. Here in Isaiah chapters 48 – 50, there is a lot being said about contending against God, and Him contending on behalf of His people; and about being obedient unto the Lord.

> Jeremiah 2:9 Therefore I will still contend with you [by inflicting further judgments on you], says the Lord, and with your children's children will I contend.

I know that I do not want God contending with me or my children. This was in a section titled *Israel's faithlessness* – so this lets us know that faithlessness can bring the contending of God against us in a non-favorable manner.

> Jeremiah 12:1-4 Uncompromisingly righteous and rigidly just are You, O Lord, when I complain against and contend with You. Yet let me plead and reason the

case with You: Why does the way of the wicked prosper? Why are all they at ease and thriving who deal very treacherously and deceitfully? ² You have planted them, yes, they have taken root; they grow, yes, they bring forth fruit. You are near in their mouths but far from their hearts. ³ But You, O Lord, know and understand me and my devotion to You; You see me and try my heart toward You. [O Lord] pull [these rebellious ones] out like sheep for the slaughter and devote and prepare them for the day of slaughter. ⁴ How long must the land mourn and the grass and herbs of the whole country wither? Through the wickedness of those who dwell in it, the beasts and the birds are consumed and are swept away [by the drought], because men [mocked] me, saying, He shall not [live to] see our final end.

Verse 1-4 is Jeremiah's prayer; then beginning at verse 5 is the Lord's answer. I hear so many scriptures combined in this prayer. At verse 2, Jeremiah calls out the people that give lip service with no heart involvement (Matthew 15:8). Then at verse 3, when Jeremiah told the Lord that He sees and knows Jeremiah's ways, this reminds me of my favorite text — Psalm 139:23-24, and add on Psalm 139:1-3; the Lord is aware of Jeremiah's lifestyle because they are intimate as the Lord continually examines Jeremiah's heart; and as Jeremiah delights himself in the Lord, the Lord is giving him the desires of His heart for His people. Also of Habakkuk asking "how long O Lord", and in Psalm 37 and then Psalm 73, when the psalmist is wondering why it looks like people are getting away with living contrary. All of this was the prayer, but don't stop there, you must read the answer, it starts off with a rebuke in verse 5! Prayer is a 2-way thing, a dialogue, not a monologue, we must listen for the Lord's responses and know that He has the best interest of His people in mind.

Jeremiah 12:5-13 [But the Lord rebukes Jeremiah's impatience, saying] If you have raced with men on foot and they have tired you out, then how can you compete with horses? And if [you take to flight] in a land of peace where you feel secure, then what will you do [when you tread the tangled maze of jungle haunted by lions] in the swelling and flooding of the Jordan? ⁶ For even your brethren and the house of your father — even they have dealt treacherously with you; yes, even they are [like a pack of hounds] in full cry after you. Believe them not, though they speak fair words and promise good things to you. ⁷ I have forsaken My house, I have cast off My heritage; I have given the dearly beloved of My life into the hands of her enemies. ⁸ My heritage has become to Me like a lion in the forest; she has uttered her voice against Me; therefore I have [treated her as if I] hated her. ⁹ Is My heritage to Me like a speckled bird of prey? Are the birds of prey against her round about? Go, assemble all the wild beasts of the field; bring them to devour. ¹⁰ Many shepherds [of an invading host] have destroyed My vineyard, they have trampled **My portion** underfoot; they have made **My pleasant portion** a desolate wilderness. ¹¹ They have made it a desolation, and desolate it mourns before Me; the whole land has been made desolate, but no man lays it to heart. ¹² Destroyers have come upon all the bare heights in the desert, for the sword of the Lord devours from one end of the land even to the other; no flesh has peace or can find the means to escape. ¹³ They have sown wheat but have reaped thorns; they have worn themselves out but without profit. And they shall be ashamed of your [lack of] harvests and revenues because of the fierce and glowing anger of the Lord.

Then the Lord switches His direction and gives counsel.

> Jeremiah 12:14-17 Thus says the Lord against all My evil neighbor [nations] who touch the inheritance which I have caused My people Israel to inherit: Behold, I will pluck them up from their land and I will pluck up the house of Judah from among them. 15 And after I have plucked them up, I will return and have compassion on them and will bring them back again, every man to his heritage and every man to his land. 16 And if these [neighbor nations] will diligently learn the ways of My people, to swear by My name, saying, As the Lord lives—even as they taught My people to swear by Baal—then will they be built up in the midst of My people. 17 But if any nation will not hear and obey, I will utterly pluck up and destroy that nation, says the Lord.

We definitely do not want to be found contending against God. Because of their contentions against God, this prophecy against Babylon takes place (see Jeremiah 50:24).

> Philippians 1:20-26 This is in keeping with my own eager desire and persistent expectation and hope, that I shall not disgrace myself nor be put to shame in anything; but that with the utmost freedom of speech and unfailing courage, now as always heretofore, Christ (the Messiah) will be magnified and get glory and praise in this body of mine and be boldly exalted in my person, whether through (by) life or through (by) death. 21 For me to live is Christ [His life in me], and to die is gain [the gain of the glory of eternity]. 22 If, however, it is to be life in the flesh and I am to live on here, that means fruitful service for me; so I can say nothing as to my personal preference [I cannot choose], 23 But I am hard pressed between the two. My yearning desire is to depart (to be free of this world, to set forth) and be with Christ, for that is far, far better; 24 But to remain in my body is more needful and essential for your sake. 25 Since I am convinced of this, I know that I shall remain and stay by you all, to promote your progress and joy in believing, 26 So that in me you may have abundant cause for exultation and glorying in Christ Jesus, through my coming to you again.

Here in this text, Paul was saying that he would rather be with God and free of this world — but also notices that it would be good for him to stay here with the church for God's glory — and that he was not sure which way to go, but what he was sure of was that while he was here in the earth realm, he would be found doing what the Lord called him to do. That is a personal testimony for myself, having experienced the Presence of God (a live encounter with Him), and would rather be done with this world and be with Him now, but there is yet purpose for me here, and I must fulfill it. The sufferings that we go through are producing fruit for His kingdom, I choose to stay here.

We must change our thinking, even about death, I live for the purpose of bringing Him glory. So if I live one day that I have not brought Him glory, either by advancing myself spiritually, or advancing someone else spiritually then why am I living? What am I here for? What is my purpose?

> Philippians 1:27-30 Only be sure as citizens so to conduct yourselves [that] your manner of life [will be] worthy of the good news (the Gospel) of Christ, so that whether I [do] come and see you or am absent, I may hear this of you: that you are standing firm in united spirit and purpose, striving side by side and contending with a single mind for the faith of the glad tidings (the Gospel). 28 And do not [for a moment] be frightened or intimidated in anything by your opponents and adversaries, for such [constancy and fearlessness] will be a clear sign (proof and seal) to them of [their impending] destruction, but [a sure token and evidence] of your deliverance and salvation, and that from God. 29 For you have been granted [the privilege] for Christ's sake not only to believe in (adhere to, rely on, and trust in) Him, but also to suffer in His behalf. 30 So you are engaged in the same conflict which you saw me [wage] and which you now hear to be mine [still].

We need to be contending in faith with one another with a single mind, for the faith of Jesus, of the gospel. We must have our own gospel presentation, live it, and be able to share it. Verse 28 shows that the enemy has no power to torment us, but we torment him and his forces with our confidence in God, and our confidence/ boldness/ wisdom in Him is an evidence to us that we are His. Question: are we living this? We need to change our thinking! We must contend with a kingdom mindset, with the mind of Christ. We must *learn of Him* to not be weak at the knees in the face of the enemy.

2.4 Identifying The Enemy

Looking back in Ephesians 6:12, defining who the enemy is, looking a little deeper at what these words mean. In the message bible, this section is titled *a fight to the finish* — this is not a battle, this is war!

> Ephesians 6:10-12 MSG And that about wraps it up. God is strong, and he wants you strong. So take everything the Master has set out for you, well-made weapons of the best materials. And put them to use so you will be able to stand up to everything the devil throws your way. This is no afternoon athletic contest that we'll walk away from and forget about in a couple of hours. This is for keeps, a life-or-death fight to the finish against the devil and all his angels.

"Principalities" is defined *as: the person or thing that commences, the first person or thing in a series, the leader; the first place, principality, rule, magistracy of angels and demons*. So these are ranks of demonic forces that we are battling and wrestling with — this is not a battle, this is war! They are defeated, we already have the victory over them, it is as we learn to operate with the whole armor that this is evident/manifest.

This word "powers" in Greek is exousia, I know this from several classes taken at bible college, and hearing several other sermons on it, even studied it out for myself (as a Berean), but this time around, I see the exousia of the enemy juxtaposed with the exousia of the Lord. From memory, the word exousia comes from the root word where we get the word dynamite. Now looking at the definition I found it to *mean the power of choice, liberty of doing as one pleases; leave or permission*. So we are battling with the power of choice — choose ye this day who you will serve, as for me and my house, we will serve the Lord — and I set before you life and death, choose life. There is a choice, and then He gives you the answer, but you still have your own free will. The battle is dealing with the free will of man. Another definition of powers is *physical and mental power; the ability or strength with which one is endued, which he either possesses or exercises. The power of authority (influence) and of right (privilege)*.

Understand that when we say we wrestle not against flesh and blood, we are wrestling against people's choice to listen to the enemy or listen to God; to listen to tradition and religion or listen to the voice of God — the word of God.

"Rulers" is defined *as: the lord of the world, the prince of this age; the devil and his demons*. This word rulers is plural, meaning many. We saw in Genesis 3 how the enemy came through the serpent; deceived woman; mankind sinned — but how did the enemy get there? We see that in Ezekiel 28 and Isaiah 14; in one of these accounts, it says that when lucifer rebelled, he and 1/3 of the angels were cast out of heaven — this is the hierarchy — the plural, like principlalitieS, rulerS, powerS. The enemy has powers, but God is all powerful! As the definition says, these rulers are the lord (lower case, of this world, the prince of this age) — as Jesus said *the god of this world comes and he finds nothing in common with Me* — we need to get to this place where this can be said of us. We need to change our thinking to not think like the god of this world, but like God (Elohim). Renewal of the Mind! process.

"Of darkness" is defined *as: of darkened eyesight or blindness; metaphorically of ignorance respecting divine things and human duties, and the accompanying ungodliness and immorality, together with their consequent misery in hell; persons in whom darkness becomes visible and holds sway*. The enemy wants to get us spiritually blind and walking in this darkness.

"World" is defined as: *forever, an unbroken age, perpetuity of time, eternity; the worlds, universe; period of time, age*. So this world has a time on it, it is referring to the god of this world, not the God who created the world, who lives outside of time. We are battling in this period of time, in this age of grace is where this battle is taking place.

"Spiritual" is defined *as: relating to the human spirit, or rational soul, as part of the man which is akin to God and serves as instrument or organ; that which possesses the nature of the rational soul. Belonging to a spirit, or a being higher than man but inferior to God belonging to the Divine Spirit; of God the Holy Spirit; one who is filled with and governed by the Spirit of God pertaining to the wind or breath; windy, exposed to the wind, blowing.*

Relating to the human or the rational spirit — your spirit man is born again, that is in the spirit realm, created in His image. But there is also the rational spirit that is in the soulish realm, the part that is supposed to receive from the mind of Christ, but we must renew it to be able to receive. As in Hebrews 4:12 *the word of God is sharper than any two-edged sword... penetrating to the dividing line of the breath of life (soul) and [the immortal] spirit* — we could not see the spirit of man and the soul of man without the word of God exposing them to us. We are shining light on this, in the area where the enemy is trying to keep people in darkness; ignorant to what is going on between the soulish and the spirit realm. When mankind died in the garden, it was not the body that died, the soul of man did not die, but his access to the spirit of God died — and mankind now must be born again through accepting Jesus Christ by grace through faith — we are in the age of grace.

So spiritual can be of God or of the enemy, but here in the text of Ephesians 6:12, it refers to spiritual wickedness.

"Wickedness" is defined as: *depravity, iniquity, wickedness; malice; evil purposes and desires.* The enemy has some evil purposes and desires for us spiritually. He does not want us to be restored back to the way it was before woman was deceived and man sinned. That is why we are in the process of renewing our mind — so that we are no longer trying to exalt ourselves above God; that comes from the enemy and is deception — we cannot be above the Creator (the deception whispered in Genesis 3, and still echoing today through worldliness).

"High places" is defined as: *existing in heaven; things that take place in heaven; the heavenly regions. Heaven itself, the abode of God and angels. The lower heavens, of the stars. The heavens, of the clouds; the heavenly temple or sanctuary. Of heavenly origin or nature.*

There are battles going on, and we have a lower heaven and a high heaven — the heavens of the clouds. The battle is not just in what you can see in the natural realm, that is why these weapons of our warfare are not carnal, but they are mighty through God for the pulling down of strongholds. Strongholds are houses of mental thoughts that are made at a young age for future occupation (of godly forces, or demonic forces). And like in Jeremiah 1:10, we are tearing down some stuff, uprooting some stuff that is wrong and bad, the doctrines of man/ tradition/ religion; all tradition and religion are not bad, but they must be rooted and grounded in the tree of Life and knowing God and must be lived out in its actual purpose, not the tree of the knowledge of good and evil — trying to be good and acceptable to God through tradition and religion instead of through the imputed righteousness of Jesus Christ — so present your body as a reasonable sacrifice and renew your soulish mind to receive from the born again mind of Christ in the spirit realm.

2.5 Thought Life

Lets' look at several references seeing that the mind is the battlefield, looking at our thought life and this Renewal of the Mind! process:

> Matthew 3:2 And saying, Repent (think differently; change your mind, regretting your sins and changing your conduct), for the kingdom of heaven is at hand.

> Mark 1:15 And saying, The [appointed period of] time is fulfilled (completed), and the kingdom of God is at hand; repent (have a change of mind which issues in regret for past sins and in change of conduct for the better) and believe (trust in, rely on, and adhere to) the good news (the Gospel).

Change your mind, have regret for past sin, and not just a regret, but change your conduct, the way in which you act. That is the Renewal of the Mind!, worldly thinking is sinful thinking, we must change our mind and our thinking. This is the first level of what must take place in the mind, to have a different view of sin and sinful behavior that brings about godly change in our life (Christ-likeness transformation).

We heartily amend our ways with abhorrence of past sins with our mind — we do not just keep thinking the same way. According to Mark 1:4, in order to be forgiven of sins, we have to change the way we think about sins, we must abhor them, with actions following. According to Luke 5:32, Jesus came to get people to change their mind about sin, to empower people to have Renewal of the Mind! — to help people really do Romans 12:1-3. You cannot be thinking worldly, it is difficult to crucify the flesh, change worldly thinking, and walk in the spirit — you must be transformed by the mind of Christ that was born again in your spirit.

Luke 13:3 and 5, both verses say the same thing, I had to double check and make sure this was not a typo: *I tell you, No; but unless you repent (change your mind for the better and heartily amend your ways, with abhorrence of your past sins), you will all likewise perish and be lost eternally* — a repeat of what repent means, and how without it we can be lost eternally. This is to repent initially to accept Jesus Christ — this is where the forgiveness of sins and the ability to have the rightful wages of sin (which is death) paid for and the access to the power to the help of the Promised Holy Spirit. We see this even further in Luke 16:30 when the rich man in hell was asking for someone to go warn his family, to keep them from coming to hell, to help them make a choice — but the Lord would not, that is part of free will. We utilize our free will to choose Christ, then we must go on and allow the Holy Spirit to help us renew our mind through the several areas that we must apply repentance and abhorrence of past errors and misdeeds.

> John 12:39-41 Therefore they could not believe [they were unable to believe]. For Isaiah has also said, ⁴⁰ He has blinded their eyes and hardened and benumbed their [callous, degenerated] hearts [He has made their minds dull], to keep them from seeing with their eyes and understanding with their hearts and minds and repenting and turning to Me to heal them. ⁴¹ Isaiah said this because he saw His glory and spoke of **Him**.

Notice this is a capital "Him" — why did God do that? It was because they had already hardened their hearts, it was because of the hardness of heart. This is why we must keep our hearts pliable before God with the washing of the word.

> Matthew 15:19 For out of the heart come evil thoughts (reasonings and disputings and designs) such as murder, adultery, sexual vice, theft, false witnessing, slander, and irreverent speech.

He was basically telling them if their thoughts are on worldliness, then worldly is what they would be. We should not have evil thoughts in the heart (which is the process of Renewal of the Mind!).

> Matthew 18:6 But whoever causes one of these little ones who believe in and acknowledge and cleave to Me to stumble and sin [that is, who entices him or hinders him in right conduct or thought], it would be better (more expedient and profitable or advantageous) for him to have a great millstone fastened around his neck and to be sunk in the depth of the sea.

We should be helping people think right, and get out of stinking thinking. If you are adding on to their wrong thinking, and their sinning, you have a problem! God will send the spiritual mobsters after you (I say spiritual mobster because television portrays mobsters tying a weight around someone and throwing them in a sea/lake).

Next we will look at an example of some people that had gone through the mind renewal process, and some that had not.

> Matthew 25:2 Five of them were foolish (thoughtless, without forethought) and five were wise (sensible, intelligent, and prudent).

The first 5 continued in the Renewal of the Mind! process, and matured in the things of God, they were prepared. Yet the other 5 were thoughtless and without forethought — but that is why we have the Holy Spirit in us to give us forethought.

We can see again that foolishness is another sign of the lack of the Renewal of the Mind!

> Mark 7:22 Coveting (a greedy desire to have more wealth), dangerous and destructive wickedness, deceit; unrestrained (indecent) conduct; an evil eye (envy), slander (evil speaking, malicious misrepresentation, abusiveness), pride (the sin of an uplifted heart against God and man), foolishness (folly, lack of sense, recklessness, thoughtlessness).

We must purge all of this out of us according to this text. This is another text that we can combine with my favorite daily text of Psalm 139:23-24, ask the Lord, actually give Him permission to expose any of these things listed here in Mark 7:22 that hide out in our heart — ask Him to search us and lead us in His way.

And we must watch what our mind is on. The thoughtlessness mentioned at the end, not even thinking about the things of God, or as we saw earlier thinking on these things, Philippians 3 — and not thinking on them can hinder and hurt us. A saying of the world is "ignorance is bliss" — no, ignorance is ignorance — the word says *My people perish for a lack of knowledge* (Hosea 4:6), generations were hindered and in danger of being cut off because of the ignorance of who God is — modern day: Renewal of the Mind!

Another example of the importance of thoughts:

> Mark 12:30 And you shall love the Lord your God out of and with your whole heart and out of and with all your soul (your life) and out of and with all your mind (with your faculty of thought and your moral understanding) and out of and with all your strength. This is the first and principal commandment.

We can think that we are loving God with our all, but if we do not get our mind (our faculty of thought and moral understanding) lined up with the love of God, with the word of God — then Houston we have a problem!

ALL as with the Great Commandment in the gospels, see Mark 12:28-34. Present ALL of your faculties...renewing our mind... here Jesus saw that Peter answered intelligently, not with worldly intelligence, but with intelligence that comes from the kingdom. We must make sure that we are loving the Lord with our all. For some, this may be difficult because we never really understood love, or had a good example of what natural love looks like — we have to deal with at, and renew the mind.

> John 5:38-40 And you have not His word (His thought) living in your hearts, because you do not believe and adhere to and trust in and rely on Him Whom He has sent. [That is why you do not keep His message living in you, because you do not believe in the Messenger Whom He has sent.] ³⁹ You search and investigate and pore over the Scriptures diligently, because you suppose and trust that you have eternal life through them. And these [very Scriptures] testify about Me! ⁴⁰ And still you are not willing [but refuse] to come to Me, so that you might have life.

As in Isaiah 58:9-11 when He says *My thoughts are not your thoughts and My ways are not your ways* — His ways are for us to rely on His Son, believe in the plan of redemption, accept the grace that Jesus Christ came to bring us.

> John 5:45-47 Put out of your minds the thought and do not suppose [as some of you are supposing] that I will accuse you before the Father. There is one who accuses you—it is Moses, the very one on whom you have built your hopes [in whom you trust]. ⁴⁶ For if you believed and relied on Moses, you would believe and rely on Me, for he wrote about Me [personally]. ⁴⁷ But if you do not believe and trust his writings, how then will you believe and trust My teachings? [How shall you cleave to and rely on My words?]

Jesus is not accusing you of anything, He came to acquit you, not accuse you.

> Matthew 5:48 You, therefore, must be perfect [growing into complete maturity of godliness in mind and character, having reached the proper height of virtue and integrity], as your heavenly Father is perfect.

Perfection, we grow into complete maturity of godliness — it is a process. This is where we see as in Titus 2:11, we have grace to grow into this.

> Matthew 21:29 And he answered, I will not; but afterward he changed his mind and went.

Here the man had 2 sons, the first said he would not go, but thought about it, changed his mind with actions following, he went. The other son "said" that he would go, but never did it (lip service) — his thoughts were not right in the first place.

> Matthew 21:32 For John came to you walking in the way of an upright man in right standing with God, and you did not believe him, but the tax collectors and the harlots did believe him; and you, even when you saw that, did not afterward change your minds and believe him [adhere to, trust in, and rely on what he told you].

Their mind had its determined purpose in not believing that Jesus was the Messiah — bad doctrine and wrong expectations hindered them; but did not excuse them and their rejection.

> Matthew 26:37 And taking with Him Peter and the two sons of Zebedee, He began to show grief and distress of mind and was deeply depressed.

Even Christ had to deal with the distress of mind, but He stayed His course in God, and when He came out of that distress of mind, His declaration was *nevertheless, not My will but Your will be done God* — we must get our mind to where we really say this, for real!

> Matthew 27:3 When Judas, His betrayer, saw that [Jesus] was condemned, [Judas was afflicted in mind and troubled for his former folly; and] with remorse [with little more than a selfish dread of the consequences] he brought back the thirty pieces of silver to the chief priests and the elders.

It said with remorse — remorse is not repentance, but as defined here it is selfish dread of the consequences. Judas had a change of mind, but it was not true repentance and it was too late, he had already let his wrong thinking cause him to betray the Savior.

> Mark 5:15 And they came to Jesus and looked intently and searchingly at the man who had been a demoniac, sitting there, clothed and in his right mind, [the same man] who had had the legion [of demons]; and they were seized with alarm and struck with fear.

When they saw the man that had been out of his mind, restored to a right mind, they were scared? That is stinking thinking — they should not have been scared like God would do something to them, but they should have had a reverential fear of God, and acknowledged the power He had to do what nobody else could do — but their minds weren't right.

> Mark 8:33 But turning around [His back to Peter] and seeing His disciples, He rebuked Peter, saying, Get behind Me, satan! For you do not have a mind intent on promoting what God wills, but what pleases men [you are not on God's side, but that of men].

Peter, who after Pentecost preached a sermon and 5,000 people got saved in 1 day, then another day 3,000 people got saved — but that was after Jesus checked him on the fact that he did not have the mind of God. This post-Pentecost preaching shows that Peter *changed* his mind to line up with the purpose of God — he still wavered at Calvary, it was not until Pentecost, the outpouring of the Holy Spirit — the empowering grace, that we see this transformation. We have access to this very same power!

Another point I gleaned from the latter part of this Mark 8:33 when Jesus said *For you do not have a mind intent on promoting what God wills, but what pleases men [you are not on God's side, but that of men* — so when we address religion and tradition, there are things that are pleasing to us, but not to God.

> Luke 1:29 But when she saw him, she was greatly troubled and disturbed and confused at what he said and kept revolving in her mind what such a greeting might mean.

This was the virgin Mary, when the Angel first came to speak to her, she was in her thinking trying to figure out what was going on, then the Angel spoke further to give her peace, then she was in agreement with what was said as he further explained. She had a made up mind to be at peace, and do what was asked of her, for she said *be it unto me as you have said*. It did not take a lot for her mind to be made up, she knew she was dealing with a servant of God.

> Luke 12:29 And you, do not seek [by meditating and reasoning to inquire into] what you are to eat and what you are to drink; nor be of anxious (troubled) mind [unsettled, excited, worried, and in suspense]

Do not be troubled in your mind about where you will live and what you will eat; you are a citizen of the kingdom and all of that stuff will be taken care of — just seek first the kingdom (a repeat of Matthew 6:33). Get your mind on kingdom, not on stuff. Do not let your mind be unsettled and upset and worried about the stuff of this world — the cares of this world.

> Luke 21:14 Resolve and settle it in your minds not to meditate and prepare beforehand how you are to make your defense and how you will answer.

When you have the mind of Christ, and when you have renewed your mind, you do not have to come up with a plan of what you will say to the adversary — God will give you what to say.

> Luke 22:44 And being in an agony [of mind], He prayed [all the] more earnestly and intently, and His sweat became like great clots of blood dropping down upon the ground.

Jesus was in agony of mind, he was contending with God, wrestling with God, to make sure that the task He was about do was what He was supposed to do. Sometimes we will do this and have to give earnest and intent prayers unto God, seek the presence of God. Know that people will say they have your back and will be there with you, but they may not be able to be there with you because they just can't — look at Jesus here in Gethsemane — He kept going to the disciples and asking them to pray, and they kept falling to sleep.

> Luke 24:25 And [Jesus] said to them, O foolish ones [sluggish in mind, dull of perception] and slow of heart to believe (adhere to and trust in and rely on) everything that the prophets have spoken!

When you receive the word of the prophet, do not be dull of mind to hear it. Some of the scripture references in this section are prophetic thoughts like Isaiah 58:9-11 our thoughts are not His, and Jeremiah 1:10 with the call to be a mouthpiece, to uproot and to tear down, and to plant and to build up some things — this is the word of the prophet, do not be sluggish to hear it.

> Luke 24:45 Then He [thoroughly] opened up their minds to understand the Scriptures

He opened their mind, this is similar to Ephesians 1:17-19, when we ask God to flood the eyes of my heart and open my mind so that I can understand Your intent, Your mind, Your ways of doing things.

> John 12:40 He has blinded their eyes and hardened and benumbed their [callous, degenerated] hearts [He has made their minds dull], to keep them from seeing with their eyes and understanding with their hearts and minds and repenting and turning to Me to heal them.

This is God's doing — they have to turn and repent from the heart, not just fire insurance because they don't want to go to hell.

> Matthew 5:17 Do not think that I have come to do away with or undo the Law or the Prophets; I have come not to do away with or undo but to complete and fulfill them.

We have to change our thinking about the law and the prophets. There are people that are trying to make you live to the letter of the law and the prophets — but understand that you cannot do it apart from Jesus Christ — you can't fulfill this any other way but in Him. And He did not come to do away with them, some people think that because we are now under grace that we do not have to do the law. No — we can only do the law by grace through Jesus Christ — we do not throw out the law, He fulfills it.

> Matthew 6:7 And when you pray, do not heap up phrases (multiply words, repeating the same ones over and over) as the Gentiles do, for they think they will be heard for their much speaking.

What do you think is going to happen when you do vain repetitions in prayer? Nothing! We must think and know with confidence that when we are praying, God is hearing us, so we do not have to do vain repetitions and keep repeating His name like as if He does not hear us or is not listening. If we know that God is listening to us, then just make your request known and move on to the next request — unless it is that of thanksgiving.

> Matthew 9:4 But Jesus, knowing (seeing) their thoughts, said, Why do you think evil and harbor malice in your hearts?

Jesus could see they were not right. He can see into the hearts of man, we cannot — but sometimes He will give us a word of wisdom or a word of knowledge so that we can see that is what we are dealing with.

> Matthew 10:34 Do not think that I have come to bring peace upon the earth; I have not come to bring peace, but a sword.

The world is trying to say "can't we all get along" — no, we can't get along because some are pretenders that really do not believe in Him that came to bring His peace. As He said "My peace I leave with you" — not this world's peace — but the peace that passes all understanding, the world cannot understand this peace, it is only understood when you keep your mind stayed on Him, and learn of Him.

> Matthew 18:10 Beware that you do not despise or feel scornful toward or think little of one of these little ones, for I tell you that in heaven their angels always are in the presence of and look upon the face of My Father Who is in heaven.

So do not pre-judge people just because they appear "little" to you, this is not right.

> Mark 14:72 And at once for the second time a cock crowed. And Peter remembered how Jesus said to him, Before a cock crows twice, you will utterly deny Me [disclaiming all connection with Me] three times. And having put his thought upon it [and remembering], he broke down and wept aloud and lamented.

Jesus told him beforehand what would happen, and when it happened, he did not run crazy wondering what happened. No, he humbled himself, he broke down and lamented — so that when God gave him another chance, with the outpouring of the Holy Spirit, he did not run from that, but received it — he truly changed his thinking along the process.

> John 10:21 Others argued, These are not the thoughts and the language of one possessed. Can a demon-possessed person open blind eyes?

They were thinking wrong about Jesus, they said He was of the devil when He healed this person — their thoughts where wrong, and their thinking was carnal.

> Luke 16:15 But He said to them, You are the ones who declare yourselves just and upright before men, but God knows your hearts. For what is exalted and highly

thought of among men is detestable and abhorrent (an abomination) in the sight of God.

When we look at religion and how people are jockeying for titles and imploring false authority over God's people, we see that this stuff is exalted and highly thought of among men, but not to God.

> Luke 19:11 Now as they were listening to these things, He proceeded to tell a parable, because He was approaching Jerusalem and because they thought that the kingdom of God was going to be brought to light and shown forth immediately.

They misunderstood the kingdom, their thoughts were off — He was not coming to establish a kingdom like they thought — although He did come to erect a kingdom; just not the way they thought.

Prayer: Thank You for showing Your grace to us, and illuminating Your word to us that we can see the role of grace in renewing our mind. Thank You for showing us what wrestling is all about, that we can see that there will be those that contend with us, but we have to contend as the Contender of the world. We thank You for revealing to us what the hierarchy of the enemy is as in Ephesians 6:12, that we have a better understanding of these things – and You are helping us see them. You are giving us pure, unadulterated wisdom, where You are exposing the plans/ tactics/ strategies of the enemy to us Your people so that we can wage warfare – the good warfare – and so that we can fight this fight and say like Paul: I have fought a good fight, and have finished my race – whenever You say it is over. We have learned to be content in You. We understand and recognize Your timing, that You are in control. And now we ask You to expose to us what we need to see in this PORTION of the process of Renewal of the Mind! Amen!

> Romans 8:22-28 MSG All around us we observe a pregnant creation. The difficult times of pain throughout the world are simply birth pangs. But it's not only around us; it's within us. The Spirit of God is arousing us within. We're also feeling the birth pangs. These sterile and barren bodies of ours are yearning for full deliverance. <u>That is why waiting does not diminish us, any more than waiting diminishes a pregnant mother. We are enlarged in the waiting. We, of course, don't see what is enlarging us</u>. But the longer we wait, the larger we become, and the more joyful our expectancy.
>
> 26-28 Meanwhile, the moment we get tired in the waiting, God's Spirit is right alongside helping us along. If we don't know how or what to pray, it doesn't matter.

He does our praying in and for us, making prayer out of our wordless sighs, our aching groans. He knows us far better than we know ourselves, knows our pregnant condition, and keeps us present before God. That's why we can be so sure that every detail in our lives of love for God is worked into something good.

We always quote Romans 8:28, that all things are working together for the good – they may not all be good, but are working for the good. Yet now, we are putting it back into context. Pregnant creation, around us, and within us — we are impregnated in the image of God, with purpose. There is a waiting, but this is also why waiting does not diminish us, we are enlarged in the waiting. What are we waiting for? If we look at verse 23 in the Amplified, we can see this purpose clearer.

> Romans 8:23 And not only the creation, but we ourselves too, who have and enjoy the firstfruits of the [Holy] Spirit [a foretaste of the blissful things to come] groan inwardly as we wait for the redemption of our bodies [from sensuality and the grave, which will reveal] our adoption (our manifestation as God's sons).

This verse here is a summation of the Romans 7 struggle that is going on, our bodies are still struggling with sensuality because of the carnal nature that is still attached to us as our mind is being renewed.

> Romans 8:24-25 For in [this] hope we were saved. But hope [the object of] which is seen is not hope. For how can one hope for what he already sees? 25 But if we hope for what is still unseen by us, we wait for it with patience and composure.

We see that we must have patience and composure in the wait process, as we become larger. Even though we cannot see what is enlarging us, we must be patient.

We are enlarged with purpose — pregnant with purpose. Pregnancy in the spirit realm will cause you to be enlarged in the spirit realm. Society sometimes mis-understands people's pregnancy; what comes to mind is when I was pregnant, I looked so young, I was misjudged as being too young to be pregnant, yet I was married, and a veteran of the United States Air Force — but people not knowing or mis-understanding my pregnancy did not negate the fact that I was going to give birth to a child. People will misunderstand the enlargement — but it does not matter what people think as long as I know that I am to steward this that He is birthing out of me. Whatever we are pregnant with, whether it be ministry, marriage, raising children, writing projects — whatever — God is enlarging us in the waiting process.

Raw study of the word "thought":
Looking at the fact that this is not a battle, this is war. And the battlefield is in the mind, which includes thoughts – know that the weapons of our warfare are not carnal, but they are mighty through God for the pulling down of strongholds/ imaginations/ and every high thought that tries to exalt itself above the knowledge of God.

These next few texts show where we need to engage our weapon and be spiritually on guard. As a watchman, I sound the alarm that the enemy is coming with lies, and the way to recognize them, or not fall prey to them, is to know what the word says.

> John 11:13 However, Jesus had spoken of his death, but they thought that He referred to falling into a refreshing and natural sleep.

This was Jesus prophesying that He was going to be crucified – He was exposing and explaining kingdom to them, but their thoughts were still on the world, because they were trying to put it together in a worldly thought, instead of a kingdom thought. Their thoughts truly were not His thoughts as in Isaiah 55:8 – and the spirit of the Lord allowed this to be recorded in the canon of scripture so that we can see that we must mature, and that our thoughts be in line with His thoughts/ plans/ purposes for His people. Do not try to make it fit according to what you see (or saw) in the world – you need the help of the Holy Spirit.

> John 13:2 So [it was] during supper, satan having already put the thought of betraying Jesus in the heart of Judas Iscariot, Simon's son.

We see that satan put the thought there, but how? Judas Iscariot had a problem with filthy lucre, looking at money the wrong way (he was trying to serve God and mammon – which cannot be done), this allowed an opening for the enemy to talk to him and "put the thought" there due to his mind not being transformed to kingdom finances, so the "thought" of the this betrayal was accepted. A side note is that we must recognize when the adversary is opposing us and operating through weak minded people whose thoughts are not right – they did it to Jesus!? Like Judas, their thoughts are already on the wrong thing, this is just the occasion to operate in foolishness. The enemy "put the thought" into his thinking – but he had a right to reject it, but he just accepted it because his guards were down; he was out of order in some other areas. This is why it is a MUST that we be constantly growing in knowing who God is and who we are in Him so that when the enemy comes twisting stuff up, we don't accept it – we don't get deceived and end up in sin. The deception was in his thought life – additional silver blinded Judas to purpose – yet was used in the overall purpose of God. He betrayed Jesus because he did not have "Jesus at the center of it all" – no, money was at the center of it all.

> John 13:27-29 Then after [he had taken] the bit of food, satan entered into and took possession of [Judas]. Jesus said to him, What you are going to do, do more swiftly

than you seem to intend and make quick work of it. ²⁸ But nobody reclining at the table knew why He spoke to him or what He meant by telling him this. ²⁹ Some thought that, since Judas had the money box (the purse), Jesus was telling him, Buy what we need for the Festival, or that he should give something to the poor.

They tried to make sense of what Jesus was saying, assuming that since Judas took care of the money, Jesus was talking about going to buy something needed, but Jesus was actually prophesying the betrayal that was needed for Him to fulfill purpose as prophesied centuries ago. It made worldly sense what they assumed in verse 29, but when you understand that He came to die and would be betrayed, as talked about in the Old Testament — as we get off of worldly thoughts, we will begin to see the spiritual things manifest in front of us.

The soulish realm is our mind, will, emotion, intellect, reasoning, imaginations, memories, thoughts, conscience — all of this needs to be renewed according to the word of God — it is the inner self:

Raw study of the words "inner self":

> Psalm 6:3 My [inner] self [as well as my body] is also exceedingly disturbed and troubled. But You, O Lord, how long [until You return and speak peace to me]?

We see the soulish realm and the physical (body) realm here.

> Psalm 16:9 Therefore my heart is glad and my glory [my inner self] rejoices; my body too shall rest and confidently dwell in safety.

When we get in God's presence, it will bring the knowing that the joy of the Lord is my strength. This verse shows the tri-part being again: my heart is glad, that is the spirit. My glory (inner self), that is the soul. My body.

> Psalm 31:9 Have mercy and be gracious unto me, O Lord, for I am in trouble; with grief my eye is weakened, also my inner self and my body.

Because of grief, we will have a hard time keeping our inner self on Him — hope deferred makes one sick. We cry out for mercy and grace as in Titus 2:11, now grace allows us to see what we should be rejecting and renouncing to stay devoted to God.

> Titus 2:11-12 For the grace of God (His unmerited favor and blessing) has come forward (appeared) for the deliverance from sin and the eternal salvation for all

> mankind. [12] It has trained us to reflect and renounce all ungodliness (irreligion) and worldly (passionate) desires, to live discreet (temperate, self-controlled), upright, devout (spiritually whole) lives in this present world.

> Psalm 41:4 I said, Lord, be merciful and gracious to me; heal my inner self, for I have sinned against You.

We have to ask for His extended mercy and grace, and admit and be open with God, that He brings in the inner healing — this is similar to Psalm 51:4-13 — we must go through all of this, the inner-self must be healed. Personally, I recognize bitterness as sin and a deceiver that will hide in our heart to sabotage the Renewal of the Mind! process. When we recognize that sin is in the camp, ask for healing, do not let it fester because a little spike or root of bitterness can cause major problems. Another reason why we cry out to God with my favorite text of Psalm 139:23-24 for the Lord's help searching our heart and to have the eyes of our heart flooded with light as in Ephesians 1:17-19. I specifically call out the name of bitterness because it is the root of so many issues that block and hinder the "inner self" from being made whole.

> Psalm 42:2 My inner self thirsts for God, for the living God. When shall I come and behold the face of God?

Our inner-self has to be thirsty for Him, as we see in Revelation 22:17, it needs to be painfully aware that there are things that can refresh/ strengthen/ restore/ support my soul — these things only come in the presence of God — the things referred to here are His mercy and graciousness towards me His beloved.

> Psalm 42:5 Why are you cast down, O my inner self? And why should you moan over me and be disquieted within me? Hope in God and wait expectantly for Him, for I shall yet praise Him, my Help and my God.

He was talking to himself here — sometimes we have to do this. It is even repeated in Psalm 42 more than once (see verse 5 and 11).

So when there is a battle going on inside of you, you have to talk to yourself, as in Joshua 1, this book of the law shall not depart out of your mouth, you shall meditate in it day and night, and then shall you make your way prosperous and then have great success, as He said in Jeremiah 29:11 that He has plans to prosper you and to bring you to a good end, and then in Psalm 1 it talks about being upright in the inner-self.

We have to get our minds renewed to understand and control the inner self-talk; it must be according to the word. The enemy is trying to insert thoughts just like he did to Judas, but the trick this time around is "you ain't nobody. No one will want to listen to you. You are the smallest, the least." — but do not give in to this, people can look over me all they want, but when God looks upon me, having a pure heart is what He is concerned with. Renew your mind, not just a cliché, but truly renew it ask God to flood your heart with understanding. There are a lot of people that are reading their bible, but they still have areas that are out of order, and displeasing to God — there must be some teaching and training to help us apply the word, to truly understand it and live it. We have the teacher of 1 John 2:27, the Holy Spirit, who teaches us all things. I am not fussing or judging, but being transparent and sharing what I myself had to go through to stop the displeasing behavior that was in my life — to truly renew my mind and live as an upright kingdom citizen. Not changing because of a list of rules, but because the conviction of the Holy Spirit that leads to repentance (abhorrence of past sins, and changed thinking and behavior).

Psalm 57 is titled *the mercy and the truth of God* — we are talking about how we need His mercy to deal with the inner-self and the Renewal of the Mind!; we also need His truth, we need to be growing in the knowledge of His truth as the Holy Spirit floods the eyes of our heart with light so that we can know more of His truth.

> Psalm 57:7-8 My heart is fixed, O God, my heart is steadfast and confident! I will sing and make melody. ⁸Awake, my glory (my inner self); awake, harp and lyre! I will awake right early [I will awaken the dawn]!

Renew your mind and understand — your heart must be fixed/ steadfast/ unmoveable.

Psalm 63 is another look at the thirsty soul:

> Psalm 63:1-6 O God, You are my God, earnestly will I seek You; my inner self thirsts for You, my flesh longs and is faint for You, in a dry and weary land where no water is. ² So I have looked upon You in the sanctuary to see Your power and Your glory. ³ Because Your loving-kindness is better than life, my lips shall praise You. ⁴ So will I bless You while I live; I will lift up my hands in Your name. ⁵ My whole being shall be satisfied as with marrow and fatness; and my mouth shall praise You with joyful lips ⁶ When I remember You upon my bed and meditate on You in the night watches.

The "sanctuary" is not talking about the church building, you are now the sanctuary and the temple of the living God. The Greater One is living in you; the One that came to give you Abundant Life. The one that is in this world, is the one that came to kill steal and destroy — but when you grow in knowing the Greater One that is within you, the enemy cannot steal anything, kill anything, or destroy anything! Renew your mind!

> Psalm 138:3 In the day when I called, You answered me; and You strengthened me with strength (might and inflexibility to temptation) in my inner self.

The battlefield is in your mind, and this text says He strengthens us — that strength is shown here as *inflexibility to temptation*. The enemy comes and tempts us with deception; when we accept the deception, it then gives birth to sin. But God will strengthen you so that you are inflexible to the temptation in your inner self — that battle that is going on — as in Romans 7, when I want to do good, I don't — but we must learn to talk to ourselves, like these examples instead of giving in to it, when you are trying to talk yourself into doing something wrong. It isn't really you doing it, but satan trying to put the thought in your mind, like he did with Judas — but we tie his hand by having a renewed mind, a determined mind to honor God.

> Psalm 139:14 I will confess and praise You for You are fearful and wonderful and for the awful wonder of my birth! Wonderful are Your works, and that my inner self knows right well.

Your spirit man has known Him since the womb, it just had to be born again. Just like you were born in the natural, the spirit man has to be born.

> Psalm 143:8 Cause me to hear Your loving-kindness in the morning, for on You do I lean and in You do I trust. Cause me to know the way wherein I should walk, for I lift up my inner self to You.

We see from looking at all of these psalms and references that our soul needs to be strengthened, refreshed, and supported. God does this through His mercy, loving kindness, graciousness. Our soul longs for Him, and we need to feed it Him, instead of all these other things that we try to fill the void with. Some people try to fill the void with relationships, with alcohol, some with cigarettes, some with sex, some with drugs, some with television, some with partying and just being around other people — but we must get to where we are comfortable in our own skin. We must realize and like the God in me the me — we must like the me that is transformed to be like the God in me — be comfortable in my own skin — deal with my inner self — and be cool with it.

> Psalm 143:10-12 Teach me to do Your will, for You are my God; let Your good Spirit lead me into a level country and into the land of uprightness. 11 Save my life, O Lord, for Your name's sake; in Your righteousness, bring my life out of trouble and free me from distress. 12 And in your mercy and loving-kindness, cut off my enemies and destroy all those who afflict my inner self, for I am Your servant.

Understand that it is not just wishing bad on someone (cut off my enemies), but the spirit that is motivating these people to vex me and to cause my inner self to be weighted down, deal with those! Destroy those spirits! This battle is in the heavenlies, as in Ephesians 6, it is not against flesh and blood, but against principalities, despotisms, powers, spiritual darkness in high places — that is where the battle is taking place. Deal with these Lord, these are the enemies of my soul — not the person standing before me (they are just a host for the spirit to operate through, that has access because of the un-renewed mind, or sin in that person). Like when Jesus called Peter out because his thoughts were on the worldly things, not what He had come here for, Jesus came to die — so for Peter to try to talk Him out of doing what God told Him to do, that is not thinking kingdom. Jesus didn't even deal with Peter, but went straight to the source and shut satan down. We have to get to where we can recognize and ask God to deal with the enemy, even when it is operating through someone whom I love (the thorn in my flesh — see the section in this chapter for further explanation). See in the Old Testament that thorns usually represent people, and the flesh represent people that are close to you.

> Proverbs 3:19-22 The Lord by skillful and godly Wisdom has founded the earth; by understanding He has established the heavens. By His knowledge the deeps were broken up, and the skies distill the dew. 21 My son, let them not escape from your sight, but keep sound and godly Wisdom and discretion, 22 And they will be life to your inner self, and a gracious ornament to your neck (your outer self).

Keep godly wisdom and discretion in front of your spiritual eyes (that have been flooded with light), so that the thoughts of dark cannot keep depositing thoughts. We are casting down imaginations, strongholds, high things — cast these things down so that we can see clearly when we look to the hills from which comes our help.

Lamentations is a continuation of the book of Jeremiah, written by him as well. The word lament is like a deep cry.

> Lamentations 3:24 The Lord is MY PORTION or share, says my living being (my inner self); therefore will I hope in Him and wait expectantly for Him.

My hope, faith, trust is in HIM — my confidence is in Jesus Christ.

> Habakkuk 3:16-18 I heard and my [whole inner self] trembled; my lips quivered at the sound. Rottenness enters into my bones and under me [down to my feet]; I tremble. I will wait quietly for the day of trouble and distress when there shall come up against [my] people him who is about to invade and oppress them. 17 Though the fig tree does not blossom and there is no fruit on the vines, [though] the product of the olive fails and the fields yield no food, though the flock is cut off from the fold and there are no cattle in the stalls, 18 Yet I will rejoice in the Lord; I will exult in the [victorious] God of my salvation! 19 The Lord God is my Strength, my personal bravery, and my invincible army; He makes my feet like hinds' feet and will make me to walk [not to stand still in terror, but to walk] and make [spiritual] progress upon my high places [of trouble, suffering, or responsibility]!

2.6 Contention

> Proverbs 10:12 Hatred stirs up contentions, but love covers all transgressions.

God is love — and of course love covers a multitude of sin, and contention amongst the brethren is sinful.

> Proverbs 13:10 By pride and insolence comes only contention, but with the well-advised is skillful and godly Wisdom.

When a person is operating in pride and selfishness (high-mindedness), all that will come out is contention. But godly Wisdom will bring peace.

> Proverbs 15:18 A hot-tempered man stirs up strife, but he who is slow to anger appeases contention.

> Proverbs 17:14 The beginning of strife is as when water first trickles [from a crack in a dam]; therefore stop contention before it becomes worse and quarreling breaks out.

So when you see the first trickle of contention, deal with it right then. The example that came to mind as I typed this is like what happened in New Orleans during Hurricane Katrina and Rita when the damn broke. They knew there were cracks and foundational problems, but failed to address them, so when these hurricanes came, it was exposed — we have several situations in our relationships (at home, at work, at church, etc.) that have cracks and trickles of contention that must be dealt with to keep from having major damage in the future; as with these natural hurricanes, thousands of people's lives were impacted and hundreds lost their life — we have several people attached to us that will be impacted by unchecked contentions.

> Proverbs 18:6 A [self-confident] fool's lips bring contention, and his mouth invites a beating.

As in the prophets, because of their speech and deeds judgment came, as this proverb says, it invites a beating (see Luke 12:42-48 for a better understanding of the 'beatings' of the Lord).

> Proverbs 18:19 A brother offended is harder to be won over than a strong city, and [their] contentions separate them like the bars of a castle.

Contentions can really cause problems with believers.

> Proverbs 19:13 A self-confident and foolish son is the [multiplied] calamity of his father, and the contentions of a wife are like a continual dripping [of water through a chink in the roof].

A major warning to wives — stop it and do not continue, you will get an outpour of calamity. The contentious wife is compared to a self-confident and foolish son — one of the reasons that we have the sons so out of control is that if their mother was a quarreling woman, the son may turn around and become the same way.

> Proverbs 22:10 Drive out the scoffer, and contention will go out; yes, strife and abuse will cease.

> Proverbs 22:10 MSG Kick out the troublemakers and things will quiet down; you need a break from bickering and griping.

Driving out what is causing this contention — and honestly, it is the spirit that is underlying with these people. So we must ask God for wisdom and insight as to how to deal with contention, because He will contend with those who contend with you, and will fight on your behalf — but you want mercy when it is coming from those whom you love and care about (really, all men).

> Proverbs 26:20 For lack of wood the fire goes out, and where there is no whisperer, contention ceases.

Keep your mouth off of stuff, let the fire die. If you must talk about it, talk to God in prayer and allow the water of His word to smoother any contentious spirit that wants to operate through us, which is half the battle.

> 1 Corinthians 1:11 For it has been made clear to me, my brethren, by those of Chloe's household, that there are contentions and wrangling and factions among you.

> 2 Corinthians 7:5 For even when we arrived in Macedonia, our bodies had no ease or rest, but we were oppressed in every way and afflicted at every turn—fighting and contentions without, dread and fears within [us].

In these last 2 references, we see Paul addressing the church at Corinth, he was showing that there would be external fighting and contention (going on among you), as well as internal (dread and fears) from within — we must deal with the external and the internal so that it does not overtake us.

> Ephesians 4:31 Let all bitterness and indignation and wrath (passion, rage, bad temper) and resentment (anger, animosity) and quarreling (brawling, clamor,

contention) and slander (evil-speaking, abusive or blasphemous language) be banished from you, with all malice (spite, ill will, or baseness of any kind).

Here contentions is named in this list of things that we must get out of us, that should not come out of our mouth. And again in James:

> James 3:14 But if you have bitter jealousy (envy) and contention (rivalry, selfish ambition) in your hearts, do not pride yourselves on it and thus be in defiance of and false to the Truth.

> James 3:16 For wherever there is jealousy (envy) and contention (rivalry and selfish ambition), there will also be confusion (unrest, disharmony, rebellion) and all sorts of evil and vile practices.

Prayer: Thank You for allowing us to see contention, thank You for allowing us to see the wait process. Give us peace in the midst as we wait on You and are enlarged in the waiting. We understand that we are not to be a people that operate in contention amongst the brethren, but be found in covenant with You, that You O God contend with those who contend with us, and You fight for us, not against us. Let our speech and deeds be pleasing in Your sight O Lord, as in Psalm 19:14 let the words of our mouth, and the meditation of our heart be acceptable in Your sight O Lord. It is You that we want to be pleasing. Thank You God for helping us renew our mind and understand the place of contention in our individual lives, that You get the glory, and the honor, and the praise out of Your servants. Amen!

> Jude 1:3 Beloved, my whole concern was to write to you in regard to our common salvation. [But] I found it necessary and was impelled to write you and urgently appeal to and exhort [you] to contend for the faith which was once for all handed down to the saints [the faith which is that sum of Christian belief which was delivered verbally to the holy people of God].

Defining what an exhortation is. "Exhort" means: *to call to one's side, call for, summon. To address, speak to, (call to, call upon). To admonish, exhort; to beg, entreat, beseech; to strive to appease by entreaty; to console, to encourage and strengthen by consolation, to comfort; to instruct, teach.*

So in the text he is saying I exhort you to earnestly contend for the faith — he is teaching us, instructing us, encouraging us, strengthening us by consolation, he is comforting us that we should get a better understanding of what it means to contend for the faith.

Not just contend, but to earnestly contend. The root of this term means: *to enter a contest: contend in the gymnastic games. To contend with adversaries, fight. Metaphorically, to contend, struggle, with difficulties and dangers. To endeavor with strenuous zeal, strive: to obtain something.* From that root word, I found even a deeper meaning of "contend" to be *a place of assembly to see games; any struggle or contest (for a prize); a battle.*

We are fighting from victory, not FOR victory, but FROM victory. Since we are fighting FROM victory, we must learn how to operate in each of these battles, because this is not a battle, this is war! We are not fighting against flesh and blood, but we are wrestling (hand to hand combat) against the hierarchy of the enemy.

Prayer: Thank You for calling us to renew our mind – to pause out of the busyness of life, and our day to day – to make sure that we set our sights on You. That we truly renew our minds according to Your word. Thank You for not leaving us without any help, we have the help of the Holy Spirit, our Teacher, our Helper, our Strengthener, our Advocate – who is here with us, leading us and guiding us into all Truth. Thank You for continually flooding the eyes of our heart so that we can know and understand what You've called us to do, and to know and understand the mysteries of Your kingdom. That You give us revelation, wisdom, knowledge, illumination into the things of God, that we may be able to walk out as the ambassadors that You have placed in the earth realm for such a time as this. Amen!

2.7 Thorn In The Flesh

This is not a battle, this is war! – we are renewing our mind to what this thorn really means; and seeing more of the role of grace.

> Romans 12:19 Beloved, never avenge yourselves, but leave the way open for [God's] wrath; for it is written, Vengeance is Mine, I will repay (requite), says the Lord.

There is no way that you can pray for your enemy if you have not renewed your mind. Because worldly thinking is "an eye for an eye" – it is not "bless them Lord". The blessing is that they will see God in His true character, and they will stop hurting someone (or something) that belongs to Him. But we can never get to the Renewal of the Mind! if flesh is always there screaming at us – so we must first crucify the flesh, and as Romans 12:2 of the NLT says *don't copy the behavior and customs of this world, but let God transform you into a new person by changing the way you think.* As in Isaiah 55, our thoughts are not His thoughts, so we must seek Him for His thoughts concerning us.

Second Corinthians 11 is addressing false teachers, then coming into chapter 12, it begins to discuss strength from weakness, this is all a set up for us to review the battles that Paul encountered based on the revelations that the Lord was revealing to him.

> 2 Corinthians 12:7-12 And to keep me from being puffed up and too much elated by the exceeding greatness (preeminence) of these revelations, there was given me a thorn (a splinter) in the flesh, a messenger of satan, to rack and buffet and harass me, to keep me from being excessively exalted. 8 Three times I called upon the Lord and besought [Him] about this and begged that it might depart from me; 9 But He said to me, My grace (My favor and loving-kindness and mercy) is enough for you [sufficient against any danger and enables you to bear the trouble manfully]; for My strength and power are made perfect (fulfilled and completed) and show themselves most effective in [your] weakness. Therefore, I will all the more gladly glory in my weaknesses and infirmities, that the strength and power of Christ (the Messiah) may rest (yes, may pitch a tent over and dwell) upon me! 10 So for the sake of Christ, I am well pleased and take pleasure in infirmities, insults, hardships, persecutions, perplexities and distresses; for when I am weak [in human strength], then am I [truly] strong (able, powerful in divine strength). 11 Now I have been [speaking like] a fool! But you forced me to it, for I ought to have been [saved the necessity and] commended by you. For I have not fallen short one bit or proved myself at all inferior to those superlative [false] apostles [of yours], even if I am nothing (a nobody). 12 Indeed, the signs that indicate a [genuine] apostle were performed among you fully and most patiently in miracles and wonders and mighty works.

"Should be exalted above measure" — www.blueletter.org says *to raise up over something. To be haughty. To carry one's self haughtily, behave insolently towards one*. The whole goal of renewing our mind is to renew our mind to the way God created us in Genesis before deception and sin entered. The fall of lucifer is recorded in Ezekiel and Isaiah (which will be discussed in further detail in the section on pride), but we see the fallen spiritual being here in Genesis 3:1, as it entered the serpent and spoke to the woman. This fallen spirit again tried to exalt himself above God in the garden, as in heaven. Coming back to 2 Corinthians 12:7, this was a reminder to not get lifted up in pride — which reminds me of the same caution by grace in Romans 12:3. We live in the age of Grace.

In 2 Thessalonians 2:4, the same word is used here for exalt. This text was in a section that was addressing apostasy. Understand that God is in control — the enemy is trying to trip up a lot of stuff and trick people with bad doctrine that tries to get us to operate in heresy, not realizing that we are trying to exalt ourselves above God. It is not that the person is trying to say that they are God, but they are placing other things before God, they think they know everything and you cannot tell them anything — yet we are warned to change our thinking, and operate based on the grace of God.

"Because of the revelations" — of the spiritual things that we now see because we have asked God according to Ephesians 1:17-19 to flood the eyes of our heart to know the spiritual mysteries, and as in 2 Corinthians 12:6 the unspeakable spoken. It is as we are asking for this, that the messenger from satan is attached, and we have to begin to look at it is a gift, and not a harassment (see Message translation).

So what is it that we are asking God to give us when we ask for revelation, illumination, knowledge, insight, wisdom into spiritual things? When we ask this, we are inadvertently asking for the thorn to go a little deeper, because it comes with the revelations to keep you from getting exalted (OUCH!). Do not let the thorns hinder or distract us from receiving the revelation.

The word "revelation" means: *laying bare, making naked. A disclosure of truth, instruction; concerning things before unknown; used of events by which things or states or persons hitherto withdrawn from view are made visible to all. Manifestation, appearance.* We are asking the Lord to manifest the things before unknown; He first manifests them in our spirit man, and it is the renewed mind that receives the disclosed truth. It is as we spend time in the word, the Lord lays bare or makes naked the original intent for mankind that had to be covered after deception and sin entered the world. Renewing back to the Garden of Eden state of communion and fellowship with God.

"Thorn" — the thorn was given to him in the flesh — this is figurative and symbolic, not literal flesh. The verse defines what the thorn is, it is *a messenger of satan, to rack and buffet and harass me, to keep me from being excessively exalted.*

"Messenger from satan" — this word messenger is the same word used for angel. As we discussed previously when the adversary was evicted out of heaven for pride, him and 1/3 of the angels were cast down with him (see Ezekiel 28 and Isaiah 14). Also, in Ephesians 6:12 we wrestle not against flesh and blood, but these things spiritually. It is as we receive revelation, as asked for, we also intensify this battle. Another glimpse of this battle and demonic-angelic activity can be seen in Job chapters 1 and 2, satan had to get permission from God before he tempted/tested Job, he came as a messenger with the *assignment* to get Job to curse God, and no longer rely on grace (God's character and power).

"Thorn in the flesh" — so I have a messenger from satan that is messing with my flesh (the dirt suit). "Flesh" has 4 definitions, but I will only share 2 of them: 1) *The flesh, denotes mere human nature, the earthly nature of man apart from divine influence, and therefore prone to sin and opposed to God.* 2) *The body of a man; used of natural or physical origin, generation or relationship; the sensuous nature of man; without any suggestion of depravity; the animal nature with cravings which incite to sin; the physical nature of man as subject to suffering.*

So we crucify our sensual nature to keep us from being prideful, not relying on the sensual nature which incites to sin. Substituting this definition back into the text: we have a messenger from satan that is in your human nature (the earthly nature of man, apart from divine influence), therefore prone to sin, and opposed to God. We can clearly see this battle taking place in Romans 7 between the carnal nature and the nature of the spirit of God. satan plays with the flesh side of us that is not crucified and submitted to the divine influence of God. Again, the thorn is not a physical ailment (sickness and disease) — when researching the definition of thorn in the flesh in the text at hand, it is again apparent that the definitions of flesh and thorn are figuratively speaking.

We are not to do anything in our own thinking or understanding (as in Proverbs 3:5-6), but the way around this is to renew our minds according to the word of God, and His ways and thoughts as in Romans 12:2 and Isaiah 55:8-11. This is why we must die to worldly thinking and be renewed to think the way in which God thinks.

Defining "satan": *adversary (one who opposes another in purpose or act). The prince of evil spirits, the inveterate adversary of God and Christ; he incites apostasy from God and to sin; circumventing men by his wiles; the worshippers of idols are said to be under his control; by God's assistance he is overcome.*

Looking at this definition, it shows why we cannot idolize people, places, and things. The only thing we can idolize is God. We cannot put our spouse, children, job, ministry, anything — ahead of God, or it becomes our idol — and in doing this, it now gives the enemy the opportunity to control. We have this adversary that has a right to play with the human nature that is not submitted to the influence of God, so we should do all we can do to get to know more about God so that the enemy loses his rights to play with us! We must get our mind right — and we do not have the capacity/ ability/ strength to do it on our own. This is why upon confession of the Lord Jesus Christ as your Savior, the Holy Spirit quickens your spirit, and He now lives in you as your teacher, your guide, as in 1 John 2:27, He will teach you all things you need to know pertaining to godliness. He is your help and your defense from this messenger of satan.

Paul even said he prayed 3 times that this messenger be removed, but the resolve and the solution is the grace of God, His sufficiency in trials and buffeting. Paul only says he prayed 3 times here in chapter 12, but if you look in 2 Corinthians 11, he gave an account of over 30 persecutions that he went through — instead of praying for it to be removed, he viewed it as a gift and used each of them to draw closer to God. I say "gift" because the Message translation says *was given to me the GIFT of a handicap to keep me in constant touch with my limitations.* When we recognize our weakness against the enemy, our limitations to wrestle carnally, in the flesh — then we tap into the true strength that is perfected in our weakness, our limitations — God has no limits, yet we must be submitted to Him, a yielded vessel that He can get the glory and show off to the forces of darkness just how Bad He is!

"To buffet" means *to strike with the fist, give one a blow with the fist. To maltreat, treat with violence.* This word was first mentioned in Matthew 26:67 and Mark 14:65, in reference to what they did to Jesus during the week of passion. Or as our example in 1 Peter 2:20 *[After all] what kind of glory [is there in it] if when you do wrong and are punished for it, you take it patiently? But if you bear patiently with suffering [which results] when you do right and that is undeserved, it is acceptable and pleasing to God.* The principle we see is that when we are buffeted by satan, it needs to be for righteousness sake not because we did something stupid and deserve to be buffeted by him — harassed by him. Jesus is our example — we need to learn to set a guard before our mouth that we never say a mumbling word, even when the enemy is acting stupid in our presence.

"Grace" means *love;* and is defined as *good will, loving-kindness, favor. Of the merciful kindness by which God, exerting his holy influence upon souls, turns them to Christ, keeps, strengthens, increases them in Christian faith, knowledge, affection, and kindles them to the exercise of the Christian virtues.* So this shows us how to deal with a messenger from satan violating us: through God's grace, good will, loving kindness and favor — not our own — these are good for you, they increase and strengthen you to live the Christian life — His grace is sufficient.

The word "grace" appears over 140 times in the New Testament. As I browsed through a few of them, I found a few principles to share:

- There may be some things that make you scared, but say like Mary "be it unto me as You have said" — one of the words for grace is favor — Mary found favor with God because of her faithfulness. (Luke 1:30)
- Jesus grew because the grace of God was upon Him at birth (Luke 2:40), and it continued to grow when He was again seen as a teen (Luke 2:52).
- In the book of Acts, we see the acts of the Holy Spirit, also known as the spirit of Grace (Acts 2:47).
- Because of the prayer for boldness, God gave them grace and power (Acts 4:29-33).
- We see favor and wisdom in the life of Joseph — he was despised, thrown into a pit, sold into slavery, falsely accused, imprisoned — yet we do not hear him complaining. He is imprisoned and the gift is still operating, the gift of grace — to where he goes on as the Prime Minister, to prepare a posterity for his people (Acts 7:10).
- His grace is sufficient: *to possess unfailing strength, to be strong, to suffice, to be enough, to defend, to ward off, to be satisfied, to be contented.* His grace will make us strong to ward off anything that is not right. We see this with the 10 virgins, (5 wise and 5 foolish) — the word in the text, when the wise told the foolish "less there be not enough," that is the word sufficient. So we must take the time to trim our lamp, get the oil (of the Holy Spirit) so that when the bridegroom comes we are ready. And you cannot give someone else your oil — you can help them get to the pump and make their own; help them to understand the pressing that produces the oil, and to truly know what they need to know — but we cannot give ours (Matthew 25:9).
- Be content with your wages — is basically saying be sufficient with your wages. The LOVE of money is the root of all evil; if you are not content with what you have, you can get over into the root of evil (Luke 3:14).

- It is in His grace that we learn contentment, as in Philippians 4. We must learn contentment.

The text said His strength is made perfect in our weakness. This word "perfect" means *to make perfect, complete. To carry through completely, to accomplish, finish, bring to an end.* His grace is accomplished and made perfect in our weakness. The word "weakness" is *a want of strength; infirmities.* So this verse is basically God saying, "When you want strength, I will give you strength." The word "weakness" also has the following definition: *weakness of the soul – want of strength; to understand a thing to do things great and glorious, to restrain corrupt desires, to bear trials and troubles.* When we need to understand spiritual things, we must plug into God's strength and God's understanding (not our own, that we are not supposed to lean to), when we receive His, then we will do great and glorious things, and will not give in to corrupt desires, and will be able to bear up under trials and tribulations because His strength is made perfect in our weakness. His strength is powerful, effective – His power is made perfect in our want or strength of soul, and our soul is strengthened in Him. "Glory in my infirmities" – is another way of saying I will glory in my weaknesses, and the text goes on to say, that the power of Christ may rest upon me. I defined this word "rest", and it means *to fix a tent or habitation on; to take possession of and live in the houses. Of the citizens; of the power of Christ descending upon one, working within him and giving him help.* So I do not mind being weak, because when I am weak, the power of God finds its habitation in me. When I am weak, the power of the resurrected Jesus Christ, comes and takes possession and dwells in me because I realize that I cannot do anything without Him. It is when I am weak, that Christ comes in and is strong – but I cannot get elevated in my thinking, or get the big head, or He will not come in.

Prayer: Yes, we thank You for the revelation, illumination, knowledge, insight, wisdom that You give to us – and we know that at the same time, there comes a persecution from the enemy, yet at the same time there comes more power from the resurrected Jesus Christ living within, that is empowering us with "Another" that He promised to send, the Holy Spirit, that is empowering and equipping us for such a time as this. He is taking of the things of God and of Jesus Christ, and revealing them to us, as kingdom citizens living here in the earthly realm. Thank You for allowing us to appreciate our weaknesses as the very gifts that come from You, that strengthen Your gift of grace in us. We will not amplify the gift of the thorn in the flesh, but we will amplify the gift of Your grace that is sufficient, more than enough, perfecting and accomplishing things in our lives. Thank You for renewing our minds to see and know how to view the persecution and buffeting that is coming our way; the messenger of satan that is coming to get on our last nerve. Move us out of self, and more into You God – get Your glory/ honor/ praise out of us Your servants.

We will be a people that purge ourselves and cleanse ourselves from worldly conformity, and will press into You even the more – as You continue to reveal to us the "unspeakable, spoken". Thank You for I Corinthians 2:9-10, it hasn't entered into the hearts of those...but You have revealed them to us by Your spirit. And as You reveal more of Your plans, and the buffeting accompanies it,

we will be more like Paul when he stopped praying about the buffeter after 3 times, but began to glory in it and boast in the persecutions endured. Thank You for transforming our thinking that we no longer pray "God move this" – but instead we would pray and say God thank You for Your strength, for the power of the resurrected Jesus Christ operating through me and in me in every situation. Thank You for Your grace being more than enough and for perfecting and completing things in my life, and in the lives of those You have me praying and interceding for. Amen.

2.8 Heart And Soul

The following will be examples of a bible query looking for "heart" and "soul" in the same text. When we see the tri-part being of man, we can better understand how to renew the soulish realm. Man is a spirit, possesses a soul, and lives in a body (a dirt suit). The spirit is created in the image of God (in Genesis 1:26-28); we are born spiritually dead, and awakened at the time of new birth (when we make a conscious decision to receive Jesus Christ) consciously responding to the gospel of Jesus Christ – to the plan of redemption that God made for mankind.

The soulish realm (the mind, will, emotion, imagination, intellect, reasoning, thoughts, personality, conscious, memory) must be renewed to thinking the way God thinks. Apart from Him, before we were born again, we thought on our own. Romans 1 tells that we always knew there was a God – we knew ABOUT God, but didn't KNOW God, an example from my youth was when I was a cheerleader in high school; the student body was over 5,000 multi-racial people; I was a cheerleader, seen publicly, but no one really KNEW me, they didn't know the intimate details of my life. They knew me externally, and for what I did, and by giftings, but they did not really know me. We are like that with God. We know He exists, we see His external attributes, but do we really KNOW Him? Do we know what makes His heart tick? Do we know His heart?

Back to the example of a cheerleader, everyone saw me smiling and doing what cheerleaders do, but no one knew that inside I was hurting and in turmoil. Lost. Unsaved. Going through some things that built mental images in my thinking that would later become strongholds to try and keep me from being who God called me to be. Once I was saved (after high school), I began to see how it all worked together – I began to see the hand of God in it all, as well as the hand of the enemy – but it was the hand of God that kept me alive over and over again. Not just me, but many others – how many times has the devil lied to you and told you he was going to kill you? There have been so many "I'm going to kill you" lies, and so many "this is going to take you out" lies – but who is in control? The One that you can't see, but you know is in control – He is the Lord God sovereign ruler.

We are still looking at "heart" and that we are a tri-part being (spirit, soul, body) — there is a part of the heart that is in both the spirit and the soul realm. The part that is in the spirit realm is the part that was born again; this is where the mind of Christ is. Yet we also have the heart part in the soulish realm which is where the seat of emotions is. So this next section of text will allow us to see when it is differentiating between the soulish realm of the heart, and the spirit realm. Bear with me as we are going down this trail of text:

> Deuteronomy 4:29 But if from there you will seek (inquire for and require as necessity) the Lord your God, you will **find** Him if you [truly] seek Him with **all your heart [and mind] and soul** and life.

Here we see this reference to the soulish realm, it must be renewed to want to seek Him. It must be renewed to inquire and require from Him. I noticed that the word "seek" is mentioned twice in this verse, but upon further study, I found that the 2 quotes are different words.

The first "seek" is H1245 and means *to seek require, desire, exact, request.*

The word "find" is H4872 and means *to attain, to secure, to acquire, to get the thing that you sought. To meet, to encounter, to find, to learn.*

The second "seek" is H1875 and means *to resort to, seek, seek with care, enquire, require. To frequent a place. To investigate, inquire. Require; demand; to practice, study, follow, seek with application.*

This does not mean to just look up and you will find Him. You must go deeper than that.

The word "heart" is H3824 and means *inner man, mind, will, heart, soul, understanding. Inner part, midst; midst (of things); heart (of man); soul, heart (of man); mind, knowledge, thinking, reflection, memory; inclination, resolution, determination (of will); conscience; heart (of moral character); as seat of appetites; as seat of emotions and passions; as seat of courage.*

We see that heart here is referring to the soulish realm, and those things must all be renewed to how God thinks. This is why we always pray according to Ephesians 1:17-19, that He would flood the eyes of our heart with light so that we can understand Him better, because Isaiah 55 tells us that His thoughts and ways are not ours — so we must renew our mind with His word.

We need the help of the Holy Spirit, the Light of the world — He is our Teacher, our Guide, our Leader. He does that because the word of God is a lamp unto our feet and light unto our path, so as we get in the word and get a better understanding with the help of the Holy Spirit (our Master Teacher), then we begin to find Him.

The word "soul" is H5315 and means *soul, self; life, creature, person, appetite, mind, living being, desire, emotion, passion. That which breathes, the breathing substance or being, soul, the inner being of man; living being (with life in the blood); the man himself, self; person or individual; seat of the appetites; seat of emotions and passions; activity of mind, of the will, of the character.*

Where it said "that which breathes" reminds me of the word pneuma, which is one of the words for the Holy Spirit — He is the very breath of God. In Genesis 1:26-28, they said "let Us create man in our image" — the spirit man was created here, but the body was created in Genesis chapter 2; it was in Chapter 2 that God breathed the breath of life and man became a living being — that is the soulish realm. It is right here that man was perfect, in constant communion with God (koininia), until the enemy came in and sowed seeds of deception and doubt, which then caused sin. We have to renew our mind to recognize when the enemy comes in twisting things up. This is why we must renew our mind to know the word. It is okay if you do not know the entire bible verbatim — but what you know, you must really know. You need to know who God is and who you are in Him. You have to know that you have the Holy Spirit according to 1 John 2:27 as your Teacher who teaches you all things, and brings things to your remembrance (Romans 8). Now in order for Him to bring things to your remembrance, that means you had to be exposed to it already, in order for Him to bring it back up. We cannot be a lazy people that never take the time to get in the word and renew our mind —we must be exposed to it so that the Holy Spirit has the building materials to bring back up to you when you come across a hard spot and need to build a bridge.

With all your heart — when God repeats Himself this many times, it is very important for us to pay attention. The following text was after the children of Israel were returning from exile, coming into the Promised Land, the land was divided for each tribe, the Eastern tribes went to help their brethren get situated in the land, and were now coming to their own lot of land.

> Joshua 22:3-6 You have not deserted your brethren [the other tribes] these many days to this day but have carefully kept the charge of the Lord your God. ⁴ But now the Lord your God has given rest to your brethren, as He promised them; so now go, return to your homes in the land of your possession, which Moses the servant of the Lord gave you on the [east] side of the Jordan. ⁵ But take diligent heed to do the commandment and the law which Moses the servant of the Lord charged you: to love the Lord your God and to walk in all His ways and to keep His commandments and to cling to and unite with Him and to serve Him with **all your heart and soul** [your very life]. ⁶ So Joshua blessed them and sent them away, and they went to their homes.

These 3 tribes were warrior tribes that went along with their brethren to help them conquer their land. Now the man of God is thanking them and reminding them to keep the commandments of God, and serve Him with "all" — basically to not put their mind on worldly things.

At the end of Joshua's life, he addresses Israel, they renew their covenant with God, then Joshua dies.

> Joshua 23:11-14 Be very watchful of yourselves, therefore, to love the Lord your God. 12 For if you turn back and adhere to the remnant of these nations left among you and make marriages with them, you marrying their women and they yours, 13 Know with certainty that the Lord your God will not continue to drive these nations from before you; but they shall be a snare and trap to you, and a scourge in your sides and thorns in your eyes, until you perish from off this good land which the Lord your God has given you. 14 And behold, this day I am going the way of all the earth. Know in **all your hearts and in all your souls** that not one thing has failed of all the good things which the Lord your God promised concerning you. All have come to pass for you; not one thing of them has failed.

Could you imagine a thorn in your eye? God was using some serious imagery to warn His people. But they were disobedient anyway, because we see in the book of Ezra, they had to divorce those whom they intermarried. And in verse 14, the Message bible says nothing is left undone — the devil will try to lie to you and scare you with the threat of killing you, but God has always preserved you and taken care of you, and brought you out. He may not have delivered the way you thought it would be, but He has kept you here in the land of the living.

> Joshua 23:15-16 But just as all good things which the Lord promised you have come to you, so will the Lord carry out [His] every [warning of] evil upon you, until He has destroyed you from off this good land which the Lord your God has given you. 16 If you transgress the covenant of the Lord your God, which He commanded you, if you serve other gods and bow down to them, then the anger of the Lord will be kindled against you, and you shall perish quickly from off the good land He has given you.

God wants our undivided attention, He does not want us listening to the lies of the enemy and of this world. The enemy lies to you, through other people around you — the voice of the enemy speaks through other people. When Peter tried to rebuke Jesus, Jesus' response was to rebuke satan — He didn't even respond to Peter, He knew it was the spirit of satan operating through Peter trying to sow seeds of discord and doubt, to get Him outside of His purpose. This is why we must press in to know God, so that He can reveal our purpose to us more and more. Every day that we grow in knowing who God is, and who we are in Him, we tie the enemy's hands to be able to play tricks with our mind.

> Psalm 19:7-14 The law of the Lord is perfect, restoring the [whole] person; the testimony of the Lord is sure, making wise the simple. 8 The precepts of the Lord are right, rejoicing the heart; the commandment of the Lord is pure and bright, enlightening the eyes. 9 The [reverent] fear of the Lord is clean, enduring forever; the ordinances of the Lord are true and righteous altogether. 10 More to be desired are they than gold, even than much fine gold; they are sweeter also than honey and drippings from the honeycomb. 11 Moreover, by them is Your servant warned (reminded, illuminated, and instructed); and in keeping them there is great reward. 12 Who can discern his lapses and errors? Clear me from hidden [and unconscious] faults. 13 Keep back Your servant also from presumptuous sins; let them not have dominion over me! Then shall I be blameless, and I shall be innocent and clear of great transgression. 14 Let the words of my mouth and the meditation of my heart be acceptable in Your sight, O Lord, my [firm, impenetrable] Rock and my Redeemer.

Jesus fulfills the law, so I am not telling you to be legalistic. His law is perfect, when you grow in knowing who He is and who you are in Him, it restores your whole person. Will you be made whole? Jesus said "your faith has made you whole." And what is faith? Faith is the leaning of your entire personality in complete trust and confidence in God, through Jesus Christ. It is your faith that makes you whole. Jesus is perfect. When you get in the law of Jesus, in Him, then you are restored to wholeness.

The testimony of the Lord is both the testimony of the gospel, and the testimony of HIS-story in your life (Psalm 19:7). We overcome by the blood of the Lamb and the word of our testimony. When you hear "He is no respecter of persons, if He did it for them, He will do it for you" — when you begin to hear the moving/ working/ doings of God, His personality, His character, His integrity — it will make the wise simple — as the text says making wise the simple.

The precepts (Psalm 19:8) — when you begin to understand the precepts of the Lord and how we should perceive things according to His precepts, His way of doing and being right — that is when you get the joy of the Lord as your strength. Then you can have peace in the midst of a chaotic situation because you understand the precepts of the Lord, such as even though I walk through the valley of the shadow of death, I fear no evil. It is when we get a better understanding of this that we benefit.

The commandment of the Lord (Psalm 19:8) — when we keep His commandments, which the number 1 commandment is "the Lord our God is one, and we are to love Him with all our heart, mind, soul, strength" — when we keep this it enlightens our eyes. Not your natural eyes, but your spiritual eyes like in Ephesians 1:17-19. So when we ask Him to flood the eyes of our heart, we need to get in the word and get a better understanding of God. God is love.

Fear of the Lord (Psalm 19:9) — we must really fear God, (not just scared of going to hell) but really recognize that He is the Lord God sovereign ruler, so we stand in awe and reverence of Him. This is a different type of fear — not the fear of punishment, but that He is so great, grandeur, and awesome — yet He lives within you, and is concerned about you. And because we know this, we will not pervert grace and live any kind of way.

The ordinances of the Lord (Psalm 19:9) — He is our righteousness. Our righteousness is imputed through the Lord Jesus Christ. Do you see why we must grow in knowing about all of these things? That is also when we can boldly say *let the words of my mouth and the meditation of my heart be acceptable*. Once we begin to understand that it grieves God for us to talk corrupt communication (as in Ephesians 4:27), when we understand this better, we will no longer fly off at the handle. But the enemy will always try to see what is still out of order in us, or what we are still ignorant to, so do not think that you ever arrive.

> 2 Kings 23:3 The king stood [on the platform] by the pillar and made a covenant before the Lord—to walk after the Lord and to keep His commandments, His testimonies, and His statutes with **all his heart and soul,** to confirm the words of this covenant that were written in this book. And all the people stood to join in the covenant.

Another renewal of the covenant — it seems like every time God renews the covenant He is saying "I need you to know that I am God, and I need you to know that you need to seek after Me, inquire of Me, require Me — as a vital necessity. With all of your emotions, your appetites, your desires, your passions — all directed to Me."

This is why when people say "you are only human, God understands" — I have to say no. I may be only human, I live in a human body, but the real me is not human — I am created in the image of God, and I am renewing my mind to receive from the mind of Christ, meaning that I do not give in to my fleshly appetites, human nature. God knows that I have them, and He has given ways for them to be legitimately fulfilled in ways that are pleasing unto Him. So for someone to try to get me to do something that is not pleasing unto God, woe unto him. I am not called to address all the wrongs and woes, but to stand up right — and when He tells me to address them, then I will.

Do not ask me to compromise truth. Truth is truth! A personal testimony of a particular trial I experienced: for some-teen years of my adult life, I operated in the opposite (contrary to truth) — I was exposed to the truth, and had been behaving contrary to the truth. The bottom line truth is that sex is for marriage — a husband and a wife that have a marriage covenant before the Lord (and earthly, have a legal marriage with a marriage license) — then sex is a wonderful thing. But God is not pleased any other way, whether it is heterosexual, or homosexual — because homosexual is still a sexual activity, and it is not the marriage that is pleasing before God.

◈

We MUST renew our mind. Part of the Renewal of the Mind! is remembering that we are in covenant with God. We must endure for it to be said of us, as was said of Josiah:

> 2 Kings 23:25 There was no king like him before or after [Josiah] who turned to the Lord with **all his heart and all his soul** and all his might, according to all the Law of Moses.

When the person in charge, in leadership, is serving God with his whole mind, soul, might — then the people will; but when the king is not serving God, the people will not serve God. This is why I do not have time to be at a church with a pastor that is playing pitty-pat with me; the pastor must be serving God and I can see the evidence, if I do not see it, I will not be planted there. I do understand ecclesiastical order, and the 5-fold ministry and that a pastor is needed — I am saying that I will not be submitted to mess! I will not be at a dead church, if the person that is operating as the pastor is not called for the task, and graced by God to do so, the people there will be perishing, because one of the roles of the pastor is to share vision and lead God's people as God is telling them (shepherds after God's heart). Foolishness and mis-representation of true leadership irritates me! The pastor must have a shepherd's heart — and shepherds smell like sheep.

> 2 Chronicles 34:24-33 Thus says the Lord: Behold, I will bring evil upon this place and upon its inhabitants, even all the curses that are written in the book which they have read before the king of Judah. ²⁵ Because they have forsaken Me and have burned incense to other gods, that they might provoke Me to anger with all the works of their hands, therefore My wrath shall be poured out upon this place and shall not be quenched. ²⁶ But say to King Josiah of Judah, who sent you to inquire of the Lord, Thus says the Lord, the God of Israel, concerning the words which you have heard: ²⁷ Because your heart was tender and penitent and you humbled yourself before God when you heard His words against this place and its inhabitants, and humbled yourself before Me and rent your clothes and wept before Me, I have heard you, says the Lord. ²⁸ Behold, I will gather you to your fathers, and you shall be gathered to your grave in peace, and your eyes shall not see all the evil that I will bring upon this place and its inhabitants. So they brought the king word again. ²⁹ Then King Josiah sent and gathered all the elders of Judah and Jerusalem. ³⁰ And [he] went up into the house of the Lord, as did all the men of Judah, the inhabitants of Jerusalem, the priests, the Levites, and all the people, great and small; and he [the king] read in their hearing all the words of the Book of the Covenant that was found in the Lord's house. ³¹ **Then the king stood in his place and made a covenant before the Lord—to walk after the Lord and to keep His**

commandments, His testimonies, and His statutes with <u>all his heart and with all his soul,</u> to perform the words of the covenant that are written in this book. ³² And he caused all who were present in Jerusalem and Benjamin to stand in confirmation of it. And the inhabitants of Jerusalem did according to the covenant of God, the God of their fathers. ³³ Josiah removed all the [idolatrous] abominations from all the territory that belonged to the Israelites, and made all who were in Israel serve the Lord their God. All his days they did not turn from following the Lord, the God of their fathers.

The book of the law was mis-placed because the keepers of it were in rebellion. This is a story of reformation — that the children of Israel were out of order by worshiping the false gods that their forefathers were told not to worship. Yet the king cried out to God and humbled himself, he knew he had messed up. The devil tries to make you think that you are too far gone and God doesn't want anything to do with you, but do not even listen to him, he is the father of lies — and that is a lie. No, cry out to God, and when He sees the state of your heart — that you really are repenting and that you truly abhor your past sins and want to make changes to not repeat them — it is then that the Lord sends in His anointing and breakthrough.

Prayer: Thank You for opening our eyes to truly see what it means to be in covenant with You. Help us to get a better understanding of Your precepts, Your statutes, Your commandments, Your ordinances, Your laws, the fear and the reverence of You O God. Help us to know better who You are and who we are in You. That the words of our mouth and the meditation of our heart be acceptable to You O God. Help us know how to seek after You with our all, how to seek, how to find, how to search, how to inquire, how to turn our very emotions, passions, desires over to You – and how to line it up according to Your word, that we would be pleasing in Your sight. Thank You for causing all things to work together for the good. The good, the bad, the ugly – it is all working together for the good – that You get the glory. That the people round-about may see Your doings through us Your vessels, Your chosen ones, Your people – and they may glorify and honor You – that Your kingdom be expanded even the more. Thank You for causing us to be a people that live repentant, with our minds stayed on You – giving You glory and honor. No, we do not understand it all, but we will not minimize what You have brought us through, and what we do understand. Thank You for helping us renew our mind, and that we stay humble in the process – not be lifted up in pride, or be deceived by the enemy with thoughts of deception of being haughty, or thoughts of deception of doubt/ fear/ uncertainty that You can use someone as simple as me. For Your word says that You make wise the simple. Thank You for Your wisdom that confounds those things of the world. Amen!

Prayer: As we sit and seek You Lord, daily, weekly, day after day, week after week, seeking You O God to help us understand the renewal of our mind; help us be restored back to the way in which You created man and woman to have regular constant communion and fellowship with You, to worship You, to commune with You. We did not have to worry about self, because we were dead to self; the self-awareness came alive when the tree of the knowledge of good and evil was partaken of – which was in direct rebellion against You – and the war has been on every since. Thank You God for giving us tools/ insight/ knowledge/ wisdom/ understanding/ revelation/ illumination into who You are, and who we are in You. We are not studying the enemy, or the battle, but we are studying the Lord of the battle – the Lord of hosts. We seek You to know how to fight each and every battle, that we would know how to stand still and see the salvation of You O Lord, that we would know how to stand and have our armor on – being ready to stand therefore and know how to deal with the wiles/ tricks/ schemes/ strategies of the enemy because we are well equipped soldiers; trained for such a time as this. Like Navy SEALS, trained to go behind enemy lines, on a mission for You, going in after the very target that seems to be hidden in darkness. Turn the light on, put some salt on it, and bring it out whole – that You get the glory/ honor/ praise. Give us insight/ knowledge/ wisdom/ understanding/ revelation/ illumination into understanding rejection and its roots – to deal with the things underground, that the symptoms that are popping up be killed and cauterized at the root. That You get the glory. Amen!

This is not a battle — this is war! We are drafted into this war at salvation, battle after battle we go through, win some lose some, but overall the war is already won, victory is already ours. We are fighting FROM victory, not FOR victory. God is examining us and trying to pull out His fruit and characteristics, such as integrity and uprightness in us as we go through various battles. We have learned that we have to make sure that we seek the Lord and His purpose for whatever it is that we are facing.

The war actually began in Genesis, before deception and sin entered. The following section are nuggets I gleaned from a book titled "Rejection — Its roots and its fruits" book by Dr. William G. Null. I will be looking at the scriptures referenced in a section defining rejection in the garden (pages 23-46) and putting them in context.

Yes, we read books that are based on scripture, this is really good, but we also need to go back and look at the scripture for ourselves. To let the Lord illuminate to us what it is that He wants us to see. I know for me personally, because I did not know any bible stories, and was a real skeptic, I would read books with my bible right alongside so I could make sure what was being quoted was what was in the bible — I later found out that was the leading of the Holy Spirit (my Teacher) and was a good discipline to establish at the beginning of my walk and true relationship with Jesus Christ.

Rejection began in the garden. The enemy deceived woman and made her think that God had rejected her; when really God had rejected the enemy, not mankind. Another nugget from what happened in the garden; man was named Adam when he was created, but woman did not have a name prior to the fall of mankind — she is always referred to as woman — she received her name after the inception of sin.

> Genesis 3:20 The man called his wife's name Eve [life spring], because she was the mother of all the living.

Mother of all the living — the instruction was to not eat of the tree, or they would die, the physical body did not die, but the spirit of man died to the ability to regularly commune with God. Mother of the living apart from constant fellowship and communion with God — the life spring of the knowledge of good and evil, it was birthed through her actions of disobedience.

In the KJV footnote, Eve means wind. It is amazing that wind is symbolic of the Holy Spirit (pneuma); and the wife is the "helper" also another name of the Holy Spirit.

> Colossians 2:1 For I want you to know how great is my solicitude for you [how severe an inward struggle I am engaged in for you] and for those [believers] at Laodicea, and for all who [like yourselves] have never seen my face and known me personally.

Laodicea is known as the lukewarm church in Revelation 3:14-22. In Colossians, they were spiritually quickened, receptive and listening, but by the time they are recorded in Revelation, they are no longer receptive.

> Revelation 3:17-20 For you say, I am rich; I have prospered and grown wealthy, and I am in need of nothing; and you do not realize and understand that you are wretched, pitiable, poor, blind, and naked. 18 Therefore I counsel you to purchase from Me gold refined and tested by fire, that you may be [truly] wealthy, and white clothes to clothe you and to keep the shame of your nudity from being seen, and salve to put on your eyes, that you may see. 19 Those whom I [dearly and tenderly] love, I tell their faults and convict and convince and reprove and chasten [I discipline and instruct them]. So be enthusiastic and in earnest and burning with zeal and repent [changing your mind and attitude]. 20 Behold, I stand at the door and knock; if anyone hears and listens to and heeds My voice and opens the door, I will come in to him and will eat with him, and he [will eat] with Me.

Revelation 3:17 is the state mankind was in back in Genesis after being deceived and sinning — blind and naked. First they were naked and unashamed, then they were ashamed and made manmade coverings. Revelation 3:20, is like in John 6 when Jesus said eat of my flesh and drink of my blood. Revelation 3:19, is like 1 Timothy 3:16, and Proverbs 3, whom the Lord loves, He chastens. He loves us, He just doesn't like us lukewarm — so we must be hot for God, zealous and pressing on.

Because of their riches and wealth, they became lukewarm. This is why we must renew our minds to the role and purpose of riches and wealth. It is so important for us to have the right understanding about riches and wealth — that it is for the kingdom, and not for us to blow frivolously.

> Colossians 2:2-3 [For my concern is] that their hearts may be braced (comforted, cheered, and encouraged) as they are knit together in love, that they may come to have all the abounding wealth and blessings of assured conviction of understanding, and that they may become progressively more intimately acquainted with and may know more definitely and accurately and thoroughly that mystic secret of God, [which is] Christ (the Anointed One). 3 In Him all the treasures of [divine] wisdom (comprehensive insight into the ways and purposes of God) and [all the riches of spiritual] knowledge and enlightenment are stored up and lie hidden.

This wisdom that we need is lying hidden in Him — in Jesus Christ. This is why we have to get a better understanding of Jesus Christ, because this is how we access the things of Christ, as an ambassador, I need to have access to these things.

> Colossians 2:4-5 I say this in order that no one may mislead and delude you by plausible and persuasive and attractive arguments and beguiling speech. 5 For though I am away from you in body, yet I am with you in spirit, delighted at the sight of your [standing shoulder to shoulder in such] orderly array and the firmness and the solid front and steadfastness of your faith in Christ [that leaning of the entire human personality on Him in absolute trust and confidence in His power, wisdom, and goodness].

According to verse 5, when people ask you if you have faith (the size of a mustard seed), that means if you are leaning your entire personality (not just a piece of it) on Him. If you are putting your absolute trust and confidence — just the size of a mustard seed — which means that I hear it, there are some things I do not fully understand, but I still believe it — that is your mustard seed. Some of us have grown to where that mustard seed has turned into a huge tree — that is because we are growing in knowing who He is and who we are in Him. Yet understand that your tree will never be fully matured in this earth realm — yes, we strive for maturity, and God is perfecting that which concerns you, but you never "ARRIVE" — and you will not get to the place of lukewarm if you continue to grow. Lukewarm — no fire there; just cold — to reject Him; and not hot to share Him; they are just comfortable — complacent — lukewarm. Riches and wealth does this to make you think that you are comfortable. You are never comfortable in this realm, in a spiritual sense. Yes, there may be some natural comfort, because money answers all things (Ecclesiastes

10:19) — so you do not go through such needs and wants. But our minds must be renewed according to the word of God with what we should be looking at. Not looking at money, but like in Colossians 2:2, all the riches of spiritual knowledge.

> Colossians 2:6-7 As you have therefore received Christ, [even] Jesus the Lord, [so] walk (regulate your lives and conduct yourselves) in union with and conformity to Him. 7 Have the roots [of your being] firmly and deeply planted [in Him, fixed and founded in Him], being continually built up in Him, becoming increasingly more confirmed and established in the faith, just as you were taught, and abounding and overflowing in it with thanksgiving.

See all of the "in Him's" that we see in these few verses. All things culminate in Him, as they all began in Him — as in John 1:1, in the beginning was the word = HIM.

> Colossians 2:8 See to it that no one carries you off as spoil or makes you yourselves captive by his so-called philosophy and intellectualism and vain deceit (idle fancies and plain nonsense), following human tradition (men's ideas of the material rather than the spiritual world), just crude notions following the rudimentary and elemental teachings of the universe and disregarding [the teachings of] Christ (the Messiah).

> Colossians 2:9 For in Him the whole fullness of Deity (the Godhead) continues to dwell in bodily form [giving complete expression of the divine nature].

Godhead — as in Genesis 1:26, we are created in His image.

> Colossians 2:10 And you are in Him, made full and having come to fullness of life [in Christ you too are filled with the Godhead—Father, Son and Holy Spirit—and reach full spiritual stature]. And He is the Head of all rule and authority [of every angelic principality and power].

Like In Ephesians 6, we wrestle not...here we see that Jesus is the Head of all rule and authority — He has it all, and we are found in Him — which gives us access to that power — but we must be able to fully renew our mind to be able to operate in it.

> Colossians 2:11-13 In Him also you were circumcised with a circumcision not made with hands, but in a [spiritual] circumcision [performed by] Christ by stripping off the body of the flesh (the whole corrupt, carnal nature with its passions and lusts). 12 [Thus you were circumcised when] you were buried with Him in [your] baptism, in which you were also raised with Him [to a new life] through [your] faith in the working of God [as displayed] when He raised Him up from the dead. 13 And you who were dead in trespasses and in the uncircumcision of your flesh (your sensuality, your sinful carnal nature), [God] brought to life together with [Christ], having [freely] forgiven us all our transgressions

Forgiven of ALL — that is past, present, and future. Now this is not a license to keep sinning and living crazy, but rather a license to live upright.

Spiritual warfare/recognizing the enemy operating through people: Discernment is recognizing whether the spirit is of God, or of the enemy — you are either for Me or against Me, is what God said... spiritual eyes to see into the spirit realm and know what is going on. Also, knowing the jurisdiction you are called/assigned to (the level of authority called/tested/ purified to walk in) — we are called to walk in integrity with God, but know that the enemy does not play fair and he will lie to you to try and get you back into bondage to things that you have been delivered from, that he tries to bring you back into. You must denounce it at the onset, do not play with it — if you slip and fall, get back up and stay in Him — as the text says now **_unto Him_** who is able to keep you — get back in Him, stay in Him, don't just play around in something you know you should not be doing.

> Colossians 2:20-23 If then you have died with Christ to material ways of looking at things and have escaped from the world's crude and elemental notions and teachings of externalism, why do you live as if you still belong to the world? [Why do you submit to rules and regulations? — such as] 21 Do not handle [this], Do not taste [that], Do not even touch [them], 22 Referring to things all of which perish with being used. To do this is to follow human precepts and doctrines. 23 Such [practices] have indeed the outward appearance [that popularly passes] for wisdom, in promoting self-imposed rigor of devotion and delight in self-humiliation and severity of discipline of the body, but they are of no value in checking the indulgence of the flesh (the lower nature). [Instead, they do not honor God but serve only to indulge the flesh.]

We see a lot of the worldly conformity that was taking place within these few verses — as in the Message bible, do not let the world squeeze you into its way of thinking.

In Nehemiah 9, this is when the children of Israel were returning from exile in 2 parts. Nehemiah 8 gives a genealogy of those returning with him; and we also see that the government funded the effort for them to return from captivity. Then we get to the prayer of Ezra in Nehemiah 9.

> Nehemiah 9:1-3 Now on the twenty-fourth day of this month, the Israelites were assembled with fasting and in sackcloth and with earth upon their heads. 2 And the Israelites separated themselves from all foreigners and stood and confessed their sins and the iniquities of their fathers. 3 And they stood in their place and read from

the Book of the Law of the Lord their God for a fourth of the day, and for another fourth of it they confessed and worshiped the Lord their God.

It was Ezra's job to read the word in their hearing, the Torah, the first 5 books of the bible. The children of Israel saw where they were not living right, and they repented. The day was referring to a 12 hour time period — so for a fourth of the day (3 hours) they sat and listened to the word being read, then for another fourth of the day (3 hours), they repented — what is wrong with us in modern day?! No one wants to hear the word, no one wants to repent. There was no preaching or music, but simply opened the scroll and begin to read — and it brought repentance.

If you read on in Nehemiah 9, you will see that the Levite leaders cried out to the Lord, then spoke to the people and told them to stand up and praise God (see verse 4-5). And at verse 16-17, you will see that they stiffened their neck and were a rebellious people, but God's grace was still there for them. The stiff-necked will of the people. Yet even though they were a stiff-necked people, God still led them by day and night, and provided for them food to eat and water to drink (see verse 18-20). Reading on, Ezra is praying, but he is recounting to God, and in front of the people, all that they did, how they kept being rebellious, and God kept be Provider. Ezra is laying it all on the table, telling how we the people are hard-headed/ stiff-necked/ rebellious, but God keeps forgiving and providing for us.

> Nehemiah 9:36-38 Behold, we are slaves this day, and as for the land that You gave to our fathers to eat the fruit and the good of it, behold, we are slaves in it. ³⁷ And its rich yield goes to the kings whom You have set over us because of our sins; they have power also over our bodies and over our livestock at their pleasure. And we are in great distress. ³⁸ Because of all this, we make a firm and sure written covenant, and our princes, Levites, and priests set their seal to it.

Because of all of this, the people renew their covenant with God.

2.9 Future Glory

> Romans 8:18-26 [But what of that?] For I consider that the sufferings of this present time (this present life) are not worth being compared with the glory that is about to be revealed to us and in us and for us and conferred on us! ¹⁹ For [even the whole] creation (all nature) waits expectantly and longs earnestly for God's sons to be made known [waits for the revealing, the disclosing of their sonship]. ²⁰ For the creation (nature) was subjected to frailty (to futility, condemned to frustration), not because of some intentional fault on its part, but by the will of Him Who so subjected it— [yet] with the hope ²¹ That nature (creation) itself will be set free from its bondage to

decay and corruption [and gain an entrance] into the glorious freedom of God's children. 22 We know that the whole creation [of irrational creatures] has been moaning together in the pains of labor until now. 23 And not only the creation, but we ourselves too, who have and enjoy the firstfruits of the [Holy] Spirit [a foretaste of the blissful things to come] groan inwardly as we wait for the redemption of our bodies [from sensuality and the grave, which will reveal] our adoption (our manifestation as God's sons). 24 For in [this] hope we were saved. But hope [the object of] which is seen is not hope. For how can one hope for what he already sees? 25But if we hope for what is still unseen by us, we wait for it with patience and composure. 26 So too the [Holy] Spirit comes to our aid and bears us up in our weakness; for we do not know what prayer to offer nor how to offer it worthily as we ought, but the Spirit Himself goes to meet our supplication and pleads in our behalf with unspeakable yearnings and groanings too deep for utterance.

This is talking about the future glory that is to come at the 2nd coming of Jesus Christ. If we are understanding resurrection, that He resurrected once, and is coming back again — that is the future hope. This gives me peace — and the devil cannot torment me with threats of death — he cannot touch my life. Just like in Job chapters 1 and 2, satan was given permission to test Job, but had a limitation that he could not touch the "life" of Job. We must make sure that we renew our mind to receive from the life that can't be touched — because the soulish realm can be touched — anything that is still attached and conformed to the world, he will "touch" that, he has access. This is why we are to love less those things such as parents, spouses, children, our own life (as in Luke 14), love less (hate) in comparison to God. We steward our children, they are kingdom assets that we steward, they belong to the kingdom. When this is our mindset about them, we understand the attacks that come at them differently. We should be in covenant with our spouse, which is an example of our covenant with God.

Prayer: You love us so much that You do not leave us unaware or unprepared. Seal this teaching in us with Your Holy Spirit, with Your presence – show us even more what it means to understand these scriptures, and that You are dealing with some roots in us – that we must be rooted and grounded in You so that none of the roots of deception and sin that the enemy has in this world can stay rooted in us. Renew our minds to the original intent that we were created to worship You, to praise You, to commune with You, to fellowship with You regularly, daily, all the time with no barriers or hindrances between us. God You want our utmost attention, You want our all – renew our mind, take us off of worldliness so that we truly can love You with our all. Thank You that this is not a battle, this is war! – You, the Lord of Hosts are empowering us to be in this battle. And battle after battle, we are fighting from victory (not for it or to it). Renew our mind that we would truly understand the victory – and that You get the glory. Amen.

Prayer: We study to show ourselves approved, but when we come together to pour out, You show Yourself as the true Teacher – and You allow our spiritual eyes to see, and give us spiritual ears to hear what it is that we need to better operate as kingdom citizens in the earth realm. Thank You for showing us/ identifying/ revealing to us worldliness and darkness – wrong thinking and evil thinking that is not lined up to Your word. Thank You for causing us to know the truth more and more. Your word says that You desire all men to be saved, and grow in the knowledge of Truth – thank You that daily we are growing in understanding who You are and who we are in You. Thank You for strengthening us, and equipping us for the battles that we are in. You are the Lord of Hosts in this war – as we seek You, You give us military instructions day by day, in each battle that we face. We continue to humble ourselves and remain submitted unto You, that in resisting the enemy, he flees, and You always get the glory and the victory. Amen.

Before we get into this next section on Romans 11, I want to take a brief but relevant sidebar look at why God has a "chosen people". This can be seen throughout Deuteronomy 4, His chosen people (Israel) were to portray the truth, preserve the truth, and proclaim the truth. *HOWEVER,* they were a disobedient stiff-necked and rebellious people — there are 6 recorded cycles of rebellion in the Old Testament (9 stages in each cycle). And these are our examples of how to behave and not behave in covenant with God.

Romans 11 is titled *Israel's future salvation* and *reconciliation and restoration of Israel.*

> Romans 11:11 So I ask, Have they stumbled so as to fall [to their utter spiritual ruin, irretrievably]? By no means! But through their false step and transgression salvation [has come] to the Gentiles, so as to arouse Israel [to see and feel what they forfeited] and so to make them jealous.

Salvation was for the Jews, and is now extended to the Gentiles (if you are not a Jew, you are a Gentile) — as we grow in this relationship with God, and the nations roundabout see that we have a relationship with the God that they think they have a relationship with because they know the letter of the law; but as they see God poured out on all mankind, it is supposed to make them jealous for their God and cause them to repent and accept Jesus Christ the Messiah. This is why we must grow in the Truth. Another side note is that the church does not replace Israel.

> Romans 11:12-21 Now if their stumbling (their lapse, their transgression) has so enriched the world [at large], and if [Israel's] failure means such riches for the Gentiles, think what an enrichment and greater advantage will follow their full reinstatement! 13 But now I am speaking to you who are Gentiles. Inasmuch then as I am an apostle to the Gentiles, I lay great stress on my ministry and magnify my office, 14 In the hope of making my fellow Jews jealous [in order to stir them up to

> imitate, copy, and appropriate], and thus managing to save some of them. ¹⁵ For if their rejection and exclusion from the benefits of salvation were [overruled] for the reconciliation of a world to God, what will their acceptance and admission mean? [It will be nothing short of] life from the dead! ¹⁶ Now if the first handful of dough offered as the firstfruits [Abraham and the patriarchs] is consecrated (holy), so is the whole mass [the nation of Israel]; and if the root [Abraham] is consecrated (holy), so are the branches. ¹⁷ But if some of the branches were broken off, while you, a wild olive shoot, were grafted in among them to share the richness [of the root and sap] of the olive tree, ¹⁸ Do not boast over the branches and pride yourself at their expense. If you do boast and feel superior, remember it is not you that support the root, but the root [that supports] you. ¹⁹ You will say then, Branches were broken (pruned) off so that I might be grafted in! ²⁰ That is true. But they were broken (pruned) off because of their unbelief (their lack of real faith), and you are established through faith [because you do believe]. So do not become proud and conceited, but rather stand in awe and be reverently afraid. ²¹ For if God did not spare the natural branches [because of unbelief], neither will He spare you [if you are guilty of the same offense].

Salvation was first to the Jews — yet was rejected — then extended to the Gentiles. In the plan of redemption, God already knew this would happen. His plans as in Jeremiah 29:11-13 are a promise that must not be rejected. But this text goes on to basically say don't get haughty and think you supersede Israel, because you do not; you are engrafted along with them.

> Romans 11:22-29 Then note and appreciate the gracious kindness and the severity of God: severity toward those who have fallen, but God's gracious kindness to you — provided you continue in His grace and abide in His kindness; otherwise you too will be cut off (pruned away). ²³ And even those others [the fallen branches, Jews], if they do not persist in [clinging to] their unbelief, will be grafted in, for God has the power to graft them in again. ²⁴ For if you have been cut from what is by nature a wild olive tree, and against nature grafted into a cultivated olive tree, how much easier will it be to graft these natural [branches] back on [the original parent stock of] their own olive tree. ²⁵ Lest you be self-opinionated (wise in your own conceits), I do not want you to miss this hidden truth and mystery, brethren: a hardening (insensibility) has [temporarily] befallen a part of Israel [to last] until the full number of the ingathering of the Gentiles has come in, ²⁶ And so all Israel will be saved. As it is written, The Deliverer will come from Zion, He will banish ungodliness from Jacob. ²⁷ And this will be My covenant (My agreement) with them when I shall take away their sins. ²⁸ From the point of view of the Gospel (good news), they [the Jews, at present] are enemies [of God], which is for your advantage and benefit. But from the point of view of God's choice (of election, of divine selection), they are still the beloved (dear to Him) for the sake of their forefathers. ²⁹ For God's gifts and His call are irrevocable. [He never withdraws them when once

they are given, and He does not change His mind about those to whom He gives His grace or to whom He sends His call.]

Gifts — is plural. Calling — is singular. We cannot pervert God's grace, His grace is to keep us attached to our life-Source. I also see John 15 in this section, of abiding in Him, or being pruned. People quote this out of context all the time. He is talking about the gift of salvation. This is a good response for the once saved always saved argument.

> Romans 11:30-32 Just as you were once disobedient and rebellious toward God but now have obtained [His] mercy, through their disobedience, 31 So they also now are being disobedient [when you are receiving mercy], that they in turn may one day, through the mercy you are enjoying, also receive mercy [that they may share the mercy which has been shown to you—through you as messengers of the Gospel to them]. 32 For God has consigned (penned up) all men to disobedience, only that He may have mercy on them all [alike].

God knows that His chosen people are going to be disobedient. Again, they went through 6 cycles of 9 stages of disobedience and rebellion. But He knew, and had mercy on them. Like in the wilderness when they murmured and complained, but God was still feeding them and taking care of them — they still had the cloud by day, and the pillar of fire by night — still leading them, still feeding them, still providing for them even though they were a rebellious people — that is what mercy looks like.

> Romans 11:33 Oh, the depth of the riches and wisdom and knowledge of God! How unfathomable (inscrutable, unsearchable) are His judgments (His decisions)! And how untraceable (mysterious, undiscoverable) are His ways (His methods, His paths)!

Verse 33 is a repeat of Isaiah 55:8-11. This is also why we ask for Ephesians 1:17-19 to be flooded with light so that we can know some of this stuff that is unsearchable, unfathomable, undiscoverable, mysterious — His methods/ plans/ paths — this is why we seek Him.

> Romans 11:34 - 12:3 For who has known the mind of the Lord and who has understood His thoughts, or who has [ever] been His counselor? 35 Or who has first given God anything that he might be paid back or that he could claim a recompense? 36 For from Him and through Him and to Him are all things. [For all things originate with Him and come from Him; all things live through Him, and all things center in and tend to consummate and to end in Him.] To Him be glory forever! Amen (so be it). 12:1 I appeal to you therefore, brethren, and beg of you in view of [all] the mercies of God, to make a decisive dedication of your bodies [presenting all your members and faculties] as a living sacrifice, holy (devoted, consecrated) and well pleasing to God, which is your reasonable (rational, intelligent) service and spiritual worship. 2 Do not be conformed to this world (this age), [fashioned after and

adapted to its external, superficial customs], but be transformed (changed) by the [entire] renewal of your mind [by its new ideals and its new attitude], so that you may prove [for yourselves] what is the good and acceptable and perfect will of God, even the thing which is good and acceptable and perfect [in His sight for you]. ³ For by the grace (unmerited favor of God) given to me I warn everyone among you not to estimate and think of himself more highly than he ought [not to have an exaggerated opinion of his own importance], but to rate his ability with sober judgment, each according to the degree of faith apportioned by God to him.

He was telling them that God has a chosen people, but as a result of their rebelliousness the door was opened for others, but warned to not get prideful about it because He would bring them back in, it is all part of His plan. Then He began to talk about how powerful and awesome His plan is that we do not even know. I love how at verse 36, everything is IN HIM — started in Him, will end in Him. Then it goes on to tell us to be a sacrifice, a living sacrifice. How often? Daily! We ask for His daily bread, we need to be on the altar of sacrifice daily. We see this grace again in Romans 12:3.

Putting all of this in context of what was taking place in Romans 11, to help us understand the plea to present our bodies as living sacrifices, to not think like the world, but renew our mind, then do not "think" we have arrived or have privileges over anyone else. We saw that God had a chosen people and because they began to think wrong, with haughty thoughts, they ended up being pruned away. The pruning process in John 15 that says that every branch that does not bear fruit He prunes and takes away. This pruning means to tie it up and get it out of dirty stuff—to move it to a place to be more fruitful in the future, but presently has to go through a cleansing process.

2.10 Deception

1 John 2:21-24 I write to you not because you are ignorant and do not perceive and know the Truth, but because you do perceive and know it, and [know positively] that nothing false (no deception, no lie) is of the Truth. ²² Who is [such a] liar as he who denies that Jesus is the Christ (the Messiah)? He is the antichrist (the antagonist of Christ), who [habitually] denies and refuses to acknowledge the Father and the Son. ²³ No one who [habitually] denies (disowns) the Son even has the Father. Whoever confesses (acknowledges and has) the Son has the Father also. ²⁴ As for you, keep in your hearts what you have heard from the beginning. If what you heard from the first dwells and remains in you, then you will dwell in the Son and in the Father [always].

There are a lot of people that are believing lies that are not real. People that are deep and wonderful and say things like "Jesus was an apostle, He was a good teacher, but He was not the son of God." There are a lot of people that say and believe these things, and I will not fight with them, I will just share the gospel presentation: that Jesus came through the virgin birth, lived, was crucified (but really He gave up the ghost — It Is Finished), was buried and rose again on the third, and now He ever lives to make intercession, and all you have to do is accept Him and be born again. Now if they say "that is stupid, and it doesn't make sense," then I will not fight with them — because the god of this world has blinded their eyes so that they cannot see, and I will pray to the Lord of the harvest that He would open their eyes, remove the blinders from their eyes so that they can see — but my feelings will not be hurt. Yes, it breaks my heart, just like it breaks God's heart when He sees His children living contrary and foolish, but I will not take it personal, because they are not doing it to me personally, but to God. When we know who God is and who we are in Him, we do not get caught up with this personal attack anyway.

> 1 John 2:25-26 And this is what He Himself has promised us—the life, the eternal [life]. 26 I write this to you with reference to those who would deceive you [seduce and lead you astray].

There are some people who will try to deceive you — we are renewing our mind to get back to the garden. What happened in the garden? Mankind was deceived, and then they sinned. So when we see here in the text that there are those that will try to deceive and seduce you, we know that it is the spirit that entered in the garden through a serpent — so this spirit has entered into a cunning person around you and is trying to seduce you right back to the garden trial. We have to make sure that we are not responding to people out of our own intellect or prideful, but we have to respond with the mind of Christ, we have to respond with kingdom mandates and principles, with kingdom ways of thinking, with kingdom righteousness (ways of doing and being right with God) — we CANNOT respond out of the flesh — this is why we have to renew our mind.

> 1 John 2:27 But as for you, the anointing (the sacred appointment, the unction) which you received from Him abides [permanently] in you; [so] then you have no need that anyone should instruct you. But just as His anointing teaches you concerning everything and is true and is no falsehood, so you must abide in (live in, never depart from) Him [being rooted in Him, knit to Him], just as [His anointing] has taught you [to do].

This is our instructions how to not fall prey to those that would try to deceive (as in verse 26), it is because we have the anointing. When you accepted Jesus Christ, you have Him right then, — He is the spirit of Truth, and will constantly reveal things to you. It is our responsibility to seek God, through the agent of the Holy Spirit that lives in us (the light of the world that stepped out into darkness and lives in you), if we take things to Him, instead of trying to lean to our own understanding, then we would not get off track so much, and accept the fruit of deception that the enemy has packaged for each of us.

> 1 John 2:27 MSG Christ's anointing teaches you the truth on everything you need to know about yourself and him, uncontaminated by a single lie. Live deeply in what you were taught.

But as for you — he was basically saying, "I can't tell you about anyone else, but you I know." This was John writing this letter in his old age to the elect, to people who know the Lord (see 1 John 1). He was encouraging the believers to allow the word to dwell and remain — that reminds me of John 15, of abiding in Him. There is an abiding that has to happen.

This is a good thing to meditate on and recognize that we have the spirit of truth as our teacher; and is a good response to people that try to hurl their degree or education at you...I do not even respond to those types of arguments because I know who I am, and I know Whose I am, and I know Him and what He is doing and is capable of doing, and I know that He chooses the least likely, and all I have to do is humble myself and stay humble in His presence. I am not moved by what people are saying; they can try to make you feel like less than because they have more degrees than a thermometer, it does not matter.

It is His anointing that is my Teacher; it is His anointing that destroys the yokes; His anointing abides in me — dwells in me — keeps me — strengthens me — empowers me. When I am being attacked in my thought life (or even verbally) with thoughts or accusations of thinking that I am holier than thou, and people question if they can be taught something by me; I recognize it as the spirit of deception and I will meditate on the fact that it is His anointing that is my Teacher. The Lord God Sovereign Ruler, creator of heaven and earth, His anointing teaches me and destroys yokes. That means that if there are any yokes in my thinking, or that I face in my life, it is His anointing that will destroy those yokes. Sometimes you have to tell yourself "His anointing abides in me — dwells in me — keeps me — strengthens me — empowers me!" Like David in the Psalms, he told his soul why are you downcast and tripping within? He encouraged himself in the Lord, and this 1 John 2:26-27 is a good reference to encourage ourselves, that He is our Teacher, abides in us, destroys yokes! When hope-lessness is attacking, we need to selah, pause and calmly think on this.

Look at Psalm 37:4, when you delight yourself in the Lord, He will give you what it is you are to desire — then He will fulfill it. This Psalm 37 is titled *blessings to the righteous.* It is as we delight ourselves in the Lord, that He places desires within our heart (because He has already given us the new heart that already knows His commandments, Ezekiel 36). Stop focusing on the stuff that we want, that we think He is supposed to give us because it is the desire of our heart — stop focusing on that, and focus on the Lord God Sovereign ruler, and you will realize that the stuff you were thinking about is not even half of what Ephesians 3:20 says *exceedingly abundantly above all that you can ask or think.*

Reviewing and putting the book of First John in context: it begins in chapter 1 talking about the Word of life — that is Jesus. Then it talks about the test of righteousness; then obedience and love, then love in action, next the test of belief. Testing to see if your love is genuine, is it live or is it Memorex? Do you really believe in this love that is in action? 1 John 3 in the Message bible is titled *when we practice real love* — which means there can be a fake or false love — or a worldly love. Then in 1 John 4, it discusses the source of love — so putting chapter 3 and 4 together in principles, God will test our love, but we need to know that the source of our love is not us, but Him, and that is why we are being tested.

> 1 John 3:11:12 For this is the message (the announcement) which you have heard from the first, that we should love one another, 12 [And] not be like Cain who [took his nature and got his motivation] from the evil one and slew his brother. And why did he slay him? Because his deeds (activities, works) were wicked and malicious and his brother's were righteous (virtuous).

A principle I see here is that you will be walking in uprightness, and a brother will come and swat at you for no reason, it is because you did a virtuous thing, this brother will come trying to kill you. Lord help us!

> 1 John 3:13-14 Do not be surprised and wonder, brethren, that the world detests and pursues you with hatred. 14 We know that we have passed over out of death into Life by the fact that we love the brethren (our fellow Christians). He who does not love abides (remains, is held and kept continually) in [spiritual] death.

Love God, love people. Are you really saved? Where is your love? It should be seen in action.

> 1 John 3:15 Anyone who hates (abominates, detests) his brother [in Christ] is [at heart] a murderer, and you know that no murderer has eternal life abiding (persevering) within him.

Be mindful of the worldly saying that has crept into our thinking, when someone does something irritating, to say (even within ourselves, maybe not out loud), but to say "I hate her, she gets on my nerves." We must cast down these types of thoughts — they are murderous.

> 1 John 3:16-19 By this we come to know (progressively to recognize, to perceive, to understand) the [essential] love: that He laid down His [own] life for us; and we ought to lay [our] lives down for [those who are our] brothers [in Him]. 17 But if anyone has this world's goods (resources for sustaining life) and sees his brother and fellow believer in need, yet closes his heart of compassion against him, how can the love of God live and remain in him? 18 Little children, let us not love [merely] in theory or in speech but in deed and in truth (in practice and in sincerity). 19 By this

> we shall come to know (perceive, recognize, and understand) that we are of the Truth, and can reassure (quiet, conciliate, and pacify) our hearts in His presence

The test of belief begins here at verse 18.

If your heart is having issues, just get in His presence. You may ask how? Delve into the "in Him" scriptures of Ephesians and Colossians, and even as mentioned right here in 1 John 3:16. His presence is not manufactured, it is simply acknowledging that our spirit man is created in His image, and slowing down and quieting yourself to acknowledge the US-ness of whatever situation we are facing (see Genesis 1:26-28 for the reference of US-ness, He said *let US create man in our image*). When you know the truth, is when you are able to access His presence, and as this verse says, we can reassure, quiet, conciliate, and pacify our hearts in His presence.

> 1 John 3:20 Whenever our hearts in [tormenting] self-accusation make us feel guilty and condemn us. [For we are in God's hands.] For He is above and greater than our consciences (our hearts), and He knows (perceives and understands) everything [nothing is hidden from Him].

Sounds like Jeremiah 18, but we will keep reading.

> 1 John 3:21-22 And, beloved, if our consciences (our hearts) do not accuse us [if they do not make us feel guilty and condemn us], we have confidence (complete assurance and boldness) before God, 22 And we receive from Him whatever we ask, because we [watchfully] obey His orders [observe His suggestions and injunctions, follow His plan for us] and [habitually] practice what is pleasing to Him.

This is another example of Psalm 37:4, it is because we obey Him we can ask and He will do — but it is according to His word. We must have love in action; love God and love people. Re-read that 1 John 3:22. If you are not receiving what you asked for, here is a question: what are you observing, or how is your obedience?

This section of 1 John 3 beginning at verse 19, is a repeat of 2 Corinthians chapter 4, which is titled *an honest and tried ministry*, and a *confident ministry*. We gain this confidence in Him because we have been honest and tried, and our confidence is in Him — none of these things move me. As in 2 Corinthians 4:17, these light afflictions are achieving for us. Stop looking at the stuff that you are going through, and that is going on around you, Paul calls them light momentary afflictions. As you meditate and look at His glory, that is where your boldness comes from to walk through all of these afflictions.

Jeremiah 29 is titled a *letter to the captives* – before I could even read where He sent me, He said *"You are no longer a captive to a bruised/ wounded/ tainted/ bleeding soul – but you have been set free in Me and are now captive to My abiding spirit/ anointing/ presence – free to walk out ALL of My plans in this season – so continue in Proverbs 3:4-6, and I will continue to reveal, illuminate, lead, guide, speak to your heart My daughter."* This is another good revelation that has produced a boldness and confidence in Him. Because our mind has been conformed to being bruised/ wounded/ tainted/ bleeding – so He comes in and takes away that conformity and transforms your mind to think like this "That My spirit abides in you, My anointing is in you, My presence is in you – and you are free to walk out all of the plans that I have given you." A side note is that when God speaks personal things to you, such as this note He revealed to me about Jeremiah 29, you must write it down and hold onto it because you never know there will be a day when you are grasping for air (figuratively), and God will bless you to come back across the words of comfort and encouragement He has spoken to you.

> Jeremiah 29:4-14 Thus says the Lord of hosts, the God of Israel, to all the captives whom I have caused to be carried into exile from Jerusalem to Babylon: 5 Build yourselves houses and dwell in them; plant gardens and eat the fruit of them. 6 Take wives and have sons and daughters; take wives for your sons and give your daughters in marriage, that they may bear sons and daughters; multiply there, and do not be diminished. 7 And seek (inquire for, require, and request) the peace and welfare of the city to which I have caused you to be carried away captive; and pray to the Lord for it, for in the welfare of [the city in which you live] you will have welfare. 8 For thus says the Lord of hosts, the God of Israel: Let not your [false] prophets and your diviners who are in your midst deceive you; pay no attention and attach no significance to your dreams which you dream or to theirs, For they prophesy falsely to you in My name. I have not sent them, says the Lord. 10 For thus says the Lord, When seventy years are completed for Babylon, I will visit you and keep My good promise to you, causing you to return to this place. 11 or I know the thoughts and plans that I have for you, says the Lord, thoughts and plans for welfare and peace and not for evil, to give you hope in your final outcome. 12 Then you will call upon Me, and you will come and pray to Me, and I will hear and heed you. 13 Then you will seek Me, inquire for, and require Me [as a vital necessity] and find Me when you search for Me with all your heart. 14 1 will be found by you, says the Lord, and I will release you from captivity and gather you from all the nations and all the places to which I have driven you, says the Lord, and I will bring you back to the place from which I caused you to be carried away captive.

Verse 7 here is like in 1 Timothy 2, pray for the city you live in. Verse 13 with ALL, not bits and pieces.

> Isaiah 61:1-4 The Spirit of the Lord God is upon me, because the Lord has anointed and qualified me to preach the Gospel of good tidings to the meek, the poor, and

afflicted; He has sent me to bind up and heal the brokenhearted, to proclaim liberty to the [physical and spiritual] captives and the opening of the prison and of the eyes to those who are bound, ² To proclaim the acceptable year of the Lord [the year of His favor] and the day of vengeance of our God, to comfort all who mourn, ³ To grant [consolation and joy] to those who mourn in Zion—to give them an ornament (a garland or diadem) of beauty instead of ashes, the oil of joy instead of mourning, the garment [expressive] of praise instead of a heavy, burdened, and failing spirit— that they may be called oaks of righteousness [lofty, strong, and magnificent, distinguished for uprightness, justice, and right standing with God], the planting of the Lord, that He may be glorified. ⁴ And they shall rebuild the ancient ruins; they shall raise up the former desolations and renew the ruined cities, the devastations of many generations.

This section in Isaiah 61 is titled *announce freedom to all captives* — *as* in Jeremiah 29, you are no longer a captive to all the "foolywag" going on, but to God's presence/spirit/anointing. We are free from captivity to worldly conformity, and we are in bondage to captivity to kingdom conformity. Personally, I don't mind being in bondage to the King, I do not want to be in bondage to the "foolywag" of this world.

Jesus quoted Isaiah 61:1 when He read it from the scroll in the synagogue (Luke 4:18).

At Isaiah 61:3 oil of joy, garment expressive of praise — so we have to renew our minds that if the enemy, or life, is trying to make us feel heavy, burdened, or a failing spirit, we must drop that and get our praise on!

Leviticus 26:3-4, 6, 9, 14

> ³ If you walk in My statutes and keep My commandments and do them, ⁴ I will give you rain in due season, and the land shall yield her increase and the trees of the field yield their fruit.
>
> ⁶ I will give peace in the land; you shall lie down and none shall fill you with dread or make you afraid; and I will clear ferocious (wild) beasts out of the land, and no sword shall go through your land.
>
> ⁹ For I will be leaning toward you with favor and regard for you, rendering you fruitful, multiplying you, and establishing and ratifying My covenant with you.
>
> ¹⁴ But if you will not hearken to Me and will not do all these commandments

Again, this is similar to Jeremiah 18, where God was promising provision, but it is contingent on us. We cannot just live any kind of way, then get upset and say "God's promises aren't coming to past?" His promises are contingent on obedience — He rewards faithfulness.

This Leviticus 26 is titled *the blessings for obedience* — God is trying over and over again to get us to be obedient, to walk in obedience. The blessings for obedience are seen in verses 1-14, and curses for disobedience are seen in verses 15-46; this is just like in Deuteronomy 28 — God is repeating Himself.

Verse 3 is a condition, look at it in the Message bible: *If you live by my decrees and obediently keep my commandments.*

We must do it to receive all of this; but we want to forget the "if" piece and live any kind of way, then question God with "where are You?" All of these promises of God seen in verses 4, 6, and 9 are all good, but WE MUST pay attention to the "if" of verse 3 — we can't skip over that "if" — see the reverse of "if" in verse 14. God is not an "Indian giver" or a fair weather God, there are some "ifs" attached that we have the freedom to choose: choose to live in line with verse 3 *if you walk in My statues,* or with verse 14 *but if you will not hearken to me and will not do all these commandments* — the choice is yours, which is part of the Renewal of the Mind!, to make sure that we make kingdom choices — He sets before us life and death, then instructs us to choose life — choose verse 3 over verse 14.

> Isaiah 61:7-9 Instead of your [former] shame you shall have a twofold recompense; instead of dishonor and reproach [your people] shall rejoice in their PORTION. Therefore in their land they shall possess double [what they had forfeited]; everlasting joy shall be theirs. 8 For I the Lord love justice; I hate robbery and wrong with violence or a burnt offering. And I will faithfully give them their recompense in truth, and I will make an everlasting covenant or league with them. 9 And their offspring shall be known among the nations and their descendants among the peoples. All who see them [in their prosperity] will recognize and acknowledge that they are the people whom the Lord has blessed.

I want this to be my testimony, but it will not happen if I do not do my part. Verse 7 the PORTION... we have some things that we have to be doing. When we do our part, He does His part, and even more, He does exceedingly abundantly above all we could ask or think. I was just asking for my needs to be met, not really concerned about other people seeing — but it brings glory to Him for them to see — we must make sure that we give the glory to God, not self — because that is how you end up in trouble and lose it anyway.

A few other references to this principle are found in Isaiah 7:3, Isaiah 10:20-22, Isaiah 8:18, Jeremiah 2:4-8, Jeremiah 31:31.

Sidebar on finances: We are not in the famine. God will give more than enough; our Heavenly Father; He will meet our needs and our wants — and desires. We are coming in <u>agreement</u> with what God says about our finances — that I line my will (and mind) up with what You have already said.

Prayer: Thank You for the Light that over-floods our heart. Thank You that You show us how to abide, how to remain, how to set our sights on You, how to walk upright in the IF's of Your word/ decrees/ commandments that IF we love You with our all, that IF we keep Your commandments, that IF we obey You God. The commandment that You have given unto us is LOVE. Let us be a people that love in action, not just thoughts or talk (lip service), but let us be a people that truly walk in love – let it be our walk. Let us be love epistles for You God. Help change us and transform our thinking and our mind, that even when we are wronged by people, that You would give us insight/ wisdom/ revelation/ knowledge as to how to right a wrong that was done against us – we will be the people that love and walk in forgiveness – that issue out and dispense Your forgiveness through our forgiveness of man.

We thank You that You are desiring us to be a people that are tested and tried in our belief, that if we say that You are love and that we want to walk in love, that God You will test us, like in 2 Corinthians chapter 4 and chapter 5, that we be that tried and tested, honest, confident ministry in You O Lord. Ministry meaning: meeting the needs of Your people; and our number 1 need is love from You the Creator. Give us capacity and insight and wisdom as to how to help people see and receive Your love, in a way that they can receive it. God thank You for tearing down the walls as we spend time soaking in Your word and in Your presence – that You would give us the ability to help tear down walls that we encounter in Your people that would make it difficult to love. Thank You that You allow our hearts to stay pressing hard, and to remain hot after You God; not a hard heart that doesn't seek You, but a heart that is panting hard and long after You God that our souls truly are thirsting for You, to be transformed by You, by Your word, by Jesus, by the Holy Spirit indwelling us to be broken off of worldly conformity – let us no longer think like the world thinks, but let us be transformed to think like Your Son Jesus Christ thinks – with the mind of Christ that You have left and given unto us. We will continue to glorify You, honor You, and praise You. Amen!

Chapter 3 – Repent

> Romans 12:1-3 NLT And so, dear brothers and sisters, I plead with you to give your bodies to God because of all he has done for you. Let them be a living and holy sacrifice—the kind he will find acceptable. This is truly the way to worship him. 2 Don't copy the behavior and customs of this world, but let God transform you into a new person by changing the way you think. Then you will learn to know God's will for you, which is good and pleasing and perfect. 3 Because of the privilege and authority God has given me, I give each of you this warning: Don't think you are better than you really are. Be honest in your evaluation of yourselves, measuring yourselves by the faith God has given us.

Looking at verse 3, don't think you are more...it is something about the way we are thinking.

Change your thinking, another way to say this is simply: repent. Be sober minded. Looking at Romans 12:2 change your thinking, God will not just do it for you, there is something that you have to do. Renewal of the Mind!; you have to do that.

But what does repent mean? As a new believer, I always heard people say "just repent" – but I never knew what it meant. I found that there is more to repentance than just "I'm sorry, I messed up". Without repentance we cannot be effective at Romans 12:1-2, because there is more to it than just I'm sorry. This is why we keep messing up, because we don't fully understand repentance so we have no power to stop messing up.

> Matthew 4:16-17 The people who sat (dwelt enveloped) in darkness have seen a great Light, and for those who sat in the land and shadow of death Light has dawned. 17 From that time Jesus began to preach, crying out, Repent (change your mind for the better, heartily amend your ways, with abhorrence of your past sins), for the kingdom of heaven is at hand.

This is a quote from Isaiah 9, that Jesus is the promised Messiah. But here in Matthew 4:17, the Amplified defines repentance as "change your mind for the better, heartily amend your ways, with abhorrence for your past sins." It is more than just "I'm sorry" – it is changing your mind by renewing it with the word of God, by removing it from conformity to the world. Anything that is dark in you, you need the Light turned on. Change your thinking.

John the Baptist's job was to declare "repent for the kingdom of heaven is at hand." It didn't mean say "I'm sorry for adultery, for drinking, for cussing..." that is not what it meant. It meant change your mind for the better, heartily amend your ways – and even abhorrence for your past sins (you can't believe you even did that!). The enemy will get you stuck on the mindset of "ugh, I can't believe I did that", so that he can get you in condemnation and guilt if you never fully understand what repentance is.

Now the initial repentance is being baptized into repentance by accepting the Lord Jesus Christ. And now you have the responsibility to get your mind right, transform it, every single day — and you do this with the word of God.

In Luke 15 we see 3 different parables/stories here, but all 3 of them are telling the same story, and the moral of the story is: REPENT.

> Luke 15:7 Thus, I tell you, there will be more joy in heaven over one [especially] wicked person who repents (changes his mind, abhorring his errors and misdeeds, and determines to enter upon a better course of life) than over ninety-nine righteous persons who have no need of repentance.

Parable One — the lost sheep:
Repent is really, that you change your mind, and determine to do it better. You don't do it yourself, you have the help of the Holy Spirit to do this. So yes, you are saved, the initial repentance into salvation has taken place, but your mind has to be renewed every day because the battlefield is the mind (as discussed in a previous chapter). Yet know that the enemy will try to keep you from repenting.

> Luke 15:10 Even so, I tell you, there is joy among and in the presence of the angels of God over one [especially] wicked person who repents (changes his mind for the better, heartily amending his ways, with abhorrence of his past sins).

Parable Two — the lost coin:
We see repentance a little different here.

Parable Three — the lost son:

> Luke 15:16 And he would gladly have fed on and filled his belly with the carob pods that the hogs were eating, but [they could not satisfy his hunger and] nobody gave him anything [better].

Could not satisfy — the slop of the world and religion does not satisfy!

> Luke 15:17 Then when he came to himself, he said, How many hired servants of my father have enough food, and [even food] to spare, but I am perishing (dying) here of hunger!

Came to himself — changed his mind.

> Luke 15:18 I will get up and go to my father, and I will say to him, Father, I have sinned against heaven and in your sight.

When we repent, it is not just I'm sorry because I messed up, but that we realize that what we did was an infraction of what a kingdom citizen should be doing. It is seeing that I have sinned against heaven, and man.

> Luke 15:19-20 I am no longer worthy to be called your son; [just] make me like one of your hired servants. 20 So he got up and came to his [own] father. But while he was still a long way off, his father saw him and was moved with pity and tenderness [for him]; and he ran and embraced him and kissed him [fervently].

Thank God He has pity and tenderness for us!

> Luke 15:21 And the son said to him, Father, I have sinned against heaven and in your sight; I am no longer worthy to be called your son [I no longer deserve to be recognized as a son of yours.

He humbled himself — he saw that he didn't deserve anything!

Not everyone was excited for this change of mind. The older brother got an attitude, had the wrong mindset.

> Luke 15:31-32 And the father said to him, Son, you are always with me, and all that is mine is yours. 32 But it was fitting to make merry, to revel and feast and rejoice, for this brother of yours was dead and is alive again! He was lost and is found!

This verse 32 is why we have to get our mindsets and attitudes right. There are some people who walked upright with God, they lost their mind and walked away, then they will come to themselves and come back humble. They are not asking to jump back where they were, but just let me be a servant! Ready to serve now with the broken and contrite heart as in Psalm 51:10 that God is seeking after anyway. When you humble yourself, that is when you will be exalted — that is when the Father put the robe back on him and had the party and put him back into position. But humility had to take place first.

We that are still in the house with the Father need to be mindful of, and not be like the older brother, and as in Psalm 73 looking at what someone else has going on. The prodigal son was dealt with, he did not just get off free: being in that hog pen *blessed* him big time!

Review: repent is to change your mind for the better, heartily amend your ways, with the abhorrence of past sins.

Side bar: some principles that we can see here in Luke 15, while we are here are:

- According to verse 1-7, it is okay to have people of doubtful reputation around you, just make sure that you live upright before them.
- According to verse 11-20, being undisciplined can cause us to lose our senses; and will bring us to repentance when we get back to our right mind.

Luke 17:3 Pay attention and always be on your guard [looking out for one another]. If your brother sins (misses the mark), solemnly tell him so and reprove him, and if he repents (feels sorry for having sinned), forgive him.

If he changes his mind, amends his ways, then forgive. The principle for us to see is that we are our brother's keeper. We pay attention and keep a guard for the brethren, but the purpose for this watch/guard/care for the brethren is to get them to repent. You are not there to tear them down, or step on them, or tell everybody what they did — love covers a multitude of sins. Love sees someone outside of the will of God, and lovingly approaches them and has pity and compassion and brings them back into right standing. That is what reprove is, it is correction, not beating or broadcasting.

We first have to get an understanding of repentance ourselves, then we can see when others are in error and help bring them back into repentance.

Repent — determined to enter into a better course of life; thinking about things differently.

Now when we read the latter part of Romans 12:2, let God change the way you think...be transformed by the entire renewal...now you see why we have to watch what we are thinking — change our thinking. But the first thing we have to get right, is what repentance means. It is not just "I'm sorry" — there are some actions that should be following. Repentance is a heart job, it is not just lip service without the heart attached. Just like there are some people that are saying they are saved, and that really is just lip service without the heart attached.

There is a section in Psalm 119 that is titled "God's law is a lamp to the feet" — not talking about natural feet, but the feet of your mind. Where is your mind taking you? Psalm 119 is all about the law of God, so getting a better understanding of the law of God, which is the word of God will help you have light on this journey that you are on.

This is a sample of what the mind is, and what must be renewed:

Psalm 119:113 AMP: I hate the thoughts of undecided [in religion], double-minded people, but Your law do I love.

Psalm 119:113 MSG: I hate the two-faced, but I love your clear-cut revelation.

You can see why we can't be a double-minded people, we must be of a single mind. Double-mindedness means worldliness and kingdom – your mind can't be on both, it will be on either or. So I set myself to seek the kingdom things, and as worldliness pops up, I will pull it down. He used the word hate – that is strong speech.

How do you get out of double-mindedness? One way is to get a better understanding of the law of God. It is a light to your feet and will lead you out. Keep reading this stanza of text here about His Law as our hiding place:

> Psalm 119:113-120 I hate the thoughts of undecided [in religion], double-minded people, but Your law do I love. ¹¹⁴ You are my hiding place and my shield; I hope in Your word. ¹¹⁵ Depart from me, you evildoers, that I may keep the commandments of my God [hearing, receiving, loving, and obeying them]. ¹¹⁶ Uphold me according to Your promise, that I may live; and let me not be put to shame in my hope! ¹¹⁷ Hold me up, that I may be safe and have regard for Your statutes continually! ¹¹⁸ You spurn and set at nought all those who stray from Your statutes, for their own lying deceives them and their tricks are in vain. ¹¹⁹ You put away and count as dross all the wicked of the earth [for there is no true metal in them]; therefore I love Your testimonies. ¹²⁰ *my* flesh trembles and shudders for fear and reverential, worshipful awe of You, and I am afraid and in dread of Your judgments.

This reminds me of the prodigal son, he had all those friends when he had money, but the deceitfulness of riches landed him in the pig pen! At verse 120, like with Romans 12:1, tells us what to do with the flesh: put it on the altar! Because it does not even know how to act right. We will look more in depth at Psalm 119 in the next chapter.

Part of the battle and the struggle is when you feel a major attack against you to not do something that you have on the agenda for God, if God did not blatantly say no, you better press and do it! A perfect example occurred one time with the Kingdom Business Singles ministry, I knew not many people would be there, I began to reason why I could cancel, however the Lord spoke to my reasoning and encouraged me to press on in purpose and minister as if there were thousands of people. Only 3 people showed up (besides me), but God was able to target exactly what everyone needed – it was such a powerful lesson. Even though I came in dragging, tired, sluggish, but obedient and willing – so when the anointing stepped in, we all left out of there full in Him. The lesson to learn is that you may have to fight to get going, but persevere, the enemy fights you so hard to not even start because he knows that the anointing will show up and do damage to his kingdom of darkness! So press! If you have a bible study or church event that you know you are supposed to be attending or helping with, but it seems like the heaviness won't lift? It is because the enemy knows that if you get this, it will damage his hold on you, so he fights you so hard to not keep going. He will not win the overall battle, we fight FROM victory, but the enemy thinks he is gaining ground because he has convinced you that you are too tired, or to justify why you can't do what you need to do. No! You press into purpose and fulfill what you are to do for God, and in fulfilling purpose, it brings a lightness, a lifting of the load that seemed to be pressing you to not go forward. Not only for you, but for those attached to you, those watching your Christian walk.

3.1 Worldliness

> 1 John 2:15-17 Do not love or cherish the world or the things that are in the world. If anyone loves the world, love for the Father is not in him. ¹⁶ For all that is in the world—the lust of the flesh [craving for sensual gratification] and the lust of the eyes [greedy longings of the mind] and the pride of life [assurance in one's own resources or in the stability of earthly things]—these do not come from the Father but are from the world [itself]. ¹⁷ And the world passes away and disappears, and with it the forbidden cravings (the passionate desires, the lust) of it; but he who does the will of God and carries out His purposes in his life abides (remains) forever.

Lust of the Flesh
Lust of the Eye
Pride of Life

Everything that we face in life, every temptation that we face is rooted and grounded in these 3, lust of the flesh, lust of the eye, pride of life. If we can renew our mind according to the word of God, with what these 3 things are, we can be mindful of them so we do not fall to them. A good reference item for understanding this is a mini book written by Cooper Beaty on Understanding Worldliness.

Lust of the Flesh — craving for sensual gratification. I will add craving for sex, food, stuff that makes you feel good. (If it feels good, do it). Do not love what the world loves.

Lust of the Eye — greedy longings of the mind. The mind must be renewed to make sure that pride and greed are stripped out. These things can hide, this is why Psalm 139:23-24, the warrior, the man of God David cried out to God to search his heart and find any way that is not right. He was basically saying, "see if You see any worldliness in me, any cravings for sensual gratification." Which basically that is what happened when he saw Bathsheba bathing on the rooftop. It was the lust of the flesh, which then made it to the eye with the greedy longing of the mind. Seeing her bathing was not the sin, it was when he had the desire to sleep with her, with actions following.

The mind longs for sex (contrary to the way God prescribed it: adultery, fornication, masturbation, etc.), for the short way out, to not have to suffer — but the kingdom way is "if you suffer with Me, you will reign with Me." But the mind of this world is contrary.

Pride of Life — assurance in one's own resources or in the stability of earthly things. Makes you think that you can do this; that you can be good enough to think like God on your own. This is why it is difficult for the rich man to get into heaven, because he is more reliant on his resources than on a savior, so God identifies that there is a problem in his heart — that he loves the world (his money) more than he loves God. His assurance is in his money and the stability of what he can see. It is people like this that have a shrine to their bank account.

In Luke 4 (Jesus in the wilderness being tempted), the 3 things the enemy tempted Jesus with are right here. Turn the rock into bread — "Deal with your flesh. Aren't You hungry?" Trying to get Jesus to do the right thing the wrong way. "I can give you the kingdoms of the world" — this was playing into the greedy longings of the mind. Jesus did not need him to give that to Him, it was already promised to Him that He would have to go through suffering to receive it — yet the enemy was trying to offer a short cut. There are no short cuts to pleasing God, you have to do what you have to do. Short cuts are of worldly thinking.

Look at the instruction of the tabernacle with all of the tedious sacrifices: the blood, cut the sinew, put this here, etc. — this all lets us know that it will take some work to be pleasing to the Lord. Those things alone do not please the Lord, it requires your heart right as you go through those things. That is why the enemy tries to trip people up with the desire for a bigger church, with wrong motives of money or notoriety. The right thing, the wrong way or with wrong motives is never pleasing to God. It is one thing to plan, to map out expectancy, etc. — but another thing for the outcome of funds and notoriety to be your aim and goal. Yes, you have to plan, but plan with the Great Planner. And the ideas and plans need to be of God, not for greedy gain.

There is a difference between wealth and riches. If your reliance is in your wealth, not God, there is a problem. Wealth is for the kingdom; and helps things in the kingdom flow, not for us to brag about how much money we have or status.

Looking at 1 John 2:17, we see how 1 John 2 and Romans 12 go hand in hand. That we not have these things of worldliness going on in our inner man, do not allow the lust of the flesh (craving for sensual gratification), or the lust of the eye (greedy longings of the mind), or the pride of life (assurance of anything outside of God) to go on in the mind. Example, if you were taught that you can only please God by coming to church every Sunday, then that basically is the pride of life because you thought you could please God in your own will. You can't. Even if you come to church every Sunday for the rest of your life, that alone does not please God. Especially if you are coming every Sunday, but you are not growing in knowing Him.

We have to make sure that what is going on in the soulish realm is not 1 John 2:16. That we not conform, as explained in 1 John 2:16 of the Amplified bible. The enemy is good at changing the game up and making us think it is not the same thing. Until we get the word in us and know what we know and Who we know, we will keep falling for the okey doke.

This next text will mess with some worldly thinking.

> 1 Thessalonians 5:11-12 Therefore encourage (admonish, exhort) one another and edify (strengthen and build up) one another, just as you are doing. 12 Now also we beseech you, brethren, get to know those who labor among you [recognize them for what they are, acknowledge and appreciate and respect them all] — your leaders who are over you in the Lord and those who warn and kindly reprove and exhort you.

This text has been my heart cry when I see leadership teams and ministry not going where it needs to go. It may be that we are not doing what it says right here in verse 12. If you only know the book by the cover, you do not know the book. It is not until you read the book, and some books you have to read over and over again. In doing this, getting to know whom we labor with, we fortify as the followers get to know the leader, and the leader is responsible to the follower. The follower gets to see that the leader is not perfect, and gets to see where their strength comes from — that God's strength is made perfect in their weaknesses. To see how they grew to operate past the weakness and allowed grace of God to take over. The followers need to know this about the leaders, and each other.

When we renew our mind to know those who labor among us; yes, know no man after the flesh, but after the spirit — so when you see the dead flesh that is laid on the altar, then you get to know better who you have laboring with you. To know that you have a true warrior on your side — ride or die! The world has this principle down pact, look at the gangs, they know who they have with them, they protect their leader, they are loyal. We need to do this in the kingdom. What has happened is that the cares of this world has made it hard to get to know all of the "sheep" at the same time.

The text says "those who kindly reprove and exhort" — they do not beat you over the head or mistreat you. But warn and kindly reprove, because they love you and love is patient, love is kind, love is long-suffering. So that is what your leaders should do, they should love the "hell" out of you — literally! Love the world out of you. Because of the love of God, reproof comes; instruction, correction, telling me how to please God, not please church/ religion/ traditions of man — but a God pleaser. That is what we should be being led in, lead the people into pleasing God, into growing and knowing who God is and who we are in Him. God pleasers! That is the purpose of my life — to lead people to be like Christ — to love God. I do this by sharing my love relationship, and He is not a respecter of person's.

I was saved in 1988 when I heard the gospel presentation for the first time. No one ever taught me how to love God. I was taught how to come to church. I was taught to be on

time. I was even taught the expositor bible study series. I went to new partner's orientation that taught me programs. Yet no one really taught me how to love God until around 2000. Let me take a slight
detour and share some history here. I never had someone sit down with me and teach me about the love of God. It was in the hunger for Him, that I "stumbled" across 1 John 2:20-27 about having the unction of the Holy Spirit as my teacher. I spent hours in the bible and reference materials at my kitchen table (this was before the internet was so common, and was not in my home). A Portion Ministries was birthed at that kitchen table, alone with God, being taught of the Holy Spirit. I had the Love of God sit down with me and teach me the Love of God — and I have promised God that I will not let anyone that is hungering after Him as I was, have to do it alone, that I would be here as a teacher, a leader, a guide to the love of God. Here am I, send me (see Isaiah 6), that is the call of God on my life.

Am I perfect? NO! But I know that His love is being perfected in me. I am a yielded vessel, a God-pleaser, and this has brought me much persecution with being mis-understood — but keep on keeping on and it will all come to the light, the motives of why you do what you do. I do what I do: study, teach, pray, dance, sing, administrate, whatever — because I love God! Not for title, not to be recognized, not for any other reason. It is because of the love of God that I even live. I could have, should have been dead so many times over, but His grace has kept me alive in the land of the living and continues to lead/ guide/ teach/ instruct me. For His Glory!

We have to renew the minds of the leaders that are leading the sheep: lead them in a love relationship. Even when reprove comes, it is out of love — he said kindly reprove them, and exhort them. Exhorting is simply a word of encouragement.

> 1 Thessalonians 5:13 And hold them in very high and most affectionate esteem in [intelligent and sympathetic] appreciation of their work. Be at peace among yourselves.

It almost seems like this verse 13 does not fit. He was in essence saying, love on your leaders, hold them in high esteem (as they think not more highly of themselves), appreciate their work, then it seems like he changed the subject? Be at peace among yourselves. So was there a dis-peace amongst the people and the leaders?

> 1 Thessalonians 5:14 And we earnestly beseech you, brethren, admonish (warn and seriously advise) those who are out of line [the loafers, the disorderly, and the unruly]; encourage the timid and fainthearted, help and give your support to the weak souls, [and] be very patient with everybody [always keeping your temper].

Help the weak souls renew their mind so that they will no longer be weak. Be very patient, always keeping your temper — we may be born again, but we have a weak soul when we are always losing our temper and going off on people. Ouch, or amen — whichever fits. I was talking to me!

> 1 Thessalonians 5:15-16 See that none of you repays another with evil for evil, but always aim to show kindness and seek to do good to one another and to everybody. [16] Be happy [in your faith] and rejoice and be glad-hearted continually (always);

This is truly about Renewal of the Mind!, it says stuff like "be happy in your faith." This deals with what is going on in the soulish realm — get a better understanding of your faith that brings happiness — not based on what happens, but on the fact that faith is in Him.

> 1 Thessalonians 5:17 Be unceasing in prayer [praying perseveringly]

A praying spirit, like Karen Clark Sheard said in a song. So when my mind begins to think about the situation or trial I am going through, I have been trained by the Holy Spirit to not respond, but to change the channel in my thinking, to call on that praying spirit within; unceasing in prayer.

> 1 Thessalonians 5:18-21 Thank [God] in everything [no matter what the circumstances may be, be thankful and give thanks], for this is the will of God for you [who are] in Christ Jesus [the Revealer and Mediator of that will]. [19] Do not quench (suppress or subdue) the [Holy] Spirit; [20] Do not spurn the gifts and utterances of the prophets [do not depreciate prophetic revelations nor despise inspired instruction or exhortation or warning]. [21] But test and prove all things [until you can recognize] what is good; [to that] hold fast.

Test and prove it in your thinking that has been transformed by the word of God. I try these things by the word of God. The Amplified says prove it until you can recognize what is good — not worldly good, but see what is of the tree of the knowledge of Life, not the tree of good and evil. My faith is in the knowledge of the tree of Life.

> 1 Thessalonians 5:22-24 Abstain from evil [shrink from it and keep aloof from it] in whatever form or whatever kind it may be. [23] And may the God of peace Himself sanctify you through and through [separate you from profane things, make you pure and wholly consecrated to God]; and may your spirit and soul and body be preserved sound and complete [and found] blameless at the coming of our Lord Jesus Christ (the Messiah). [24] Faithful is He Who is calling you [to Himself] and utterly trustworthy, and He will also do it [fulfill His call by hallowing and keeping you].

We see the tri-part being of man. The God of peace Himself sanctify you, so if you are not in perfect peace, are you serving the God of peace? Your mind is not on Him, do not make things more difficult than they have to be. Put your mind on Him, not the things of the world. He separates you from profane things by telling you to stop thinking on them — but put your mind on these things as in Philippians 4. You separate yourself from the profane things of this world: the lust of the flesh, the lust of the eye, and the pride of life — and you take your cues from the kingdom. In doing so, this is how your spirit and soul and body can be preserved sound and complete.

"They that hunger and thirst for righteousness shall be filled." I am no longer hungering and thirsting for the things of this world because I was trained and raised on the things of this world: the lust of the flesh, the lust of the eye, and the pride of life. God had to Genesis 12 me, move me away to get that out of my thinking, to help me set my mind on these things. Sometimes God has to take you out of your environment and put you in a rough place to get you to change your thinking so that when He does bless you into the land flowing with milk and honey, you do not blow it. So God has to deal with us in the wilderness so that we not be lazy, murmur, and complain. Like what Joseph went through, yet his testimony with naming his son Manasseh (meaning God *has made me forget all my toil and hardship **and** all my father's house* Genesis 41:51). It wasn't that Joseph said "forget them, it is their bad, not mine", but that Joseph forgot all of the toil and hardship that came from the jealousy of his brothers at his father's house. We see this when he recognized his brothers, but they did not recognize him (Genesis 42-45), yet he still allows the plan of God to be manifested strategically. We see a perfect example of Renewal of the Mind!, true repentance when we see Joseph say to his brothers "you meant evil against me, but God meant it for good, in order to bring it about as it is this day, to save many people alive" (Genesis 50:20 NKJV).

Prayer: Thank You for expanding the few verses of Romans 12:1-3 to be so much more. Thank You for getting us off of the pages of life, that we study to show ourselves approved, but when it is time to walk it out, You come in and have Your way. You lead us and expose us to what You know our spirit man needs to be exposed to for this part of the journey that we are on. Thank You for showing us how to be sensitive and understand the things of this world: the lust of the flesh, the lust of the eye, and the pride of life – that you give us easy examples that we see temptation when it comes and not take our cues from the dead flesh that is trying to get us to listen to what lives in it. But that we will take our cues from the mind of Christ because we are renewing our mind to receive from it. You told us in Matthew 6 and Luke 12 to seek First the kingdom and all that other stuff will be added – we choose to not let our minds go to fleshly thoughts/ concerns/ worries/ anxieties, but we choose to say Your kingdom come Your will be done in our lives daily. Expand our understanding, increase us even the more, give us the capacity to retain what You are exposing us to. We want to be found pleasing to You and walking it out. We do not want to be found like in the bible of those people that were always gaining knowledge but never getting the power attached to it. Amen.

Looking at various scriptures to see where the mind needs to be renewed. A lot of people are saved and told to renew their minds, but we are not being taught what it is and how to do this.

> Hebrews 4:12 For the Word that God speaks is alive and full of power [making it active, operative, energizing, and effective]; it is sharper than any two-edged sword, penetrating to the dividing line of the breath of life (soul) and [the immortal] spirit, and of joints and marrow [of the deepest parts of our nature], exposing and sifting and analyzing and judging the very thoughts and purposes of the heart.
>
> Matthew 28:20 Teaching them to observe everything that I have commanded you, and behold, I am with you all the days (perpetually, uniformly, and on every occasion), to the [very] close and consummation of the age. Amen (so let it be).
>
> 1 Peter 2:11 Beloved, I implore you as aliens and strangers and exiles [in this world] to abstain from the sensual urges (the evil desires, the passions of the flesh, your lower nature) that wage war against the soul.

Review of the tri-part being. The body is where "your father the devil" lives, or plays with the lust of the flesh, the lust of the eye, and the pride of life. The soulish realm is where our mind, will, emotions, reasoning, intellect, thoughts, memories, conscious are, and must be renewed to not think on worldliness. The spirit was born again at the acceptance of Jesus Christ.

An example are the things in our memory bank that when we think of them, they insight certain things in our soulish realm and in the flesh. Think of music, when we hear the first note, or the first sung line of "Let's get it on..." — what memories come up; or are attached to that song? We then have to go to the Lord and ask that our memories be renewed because we do not need that song insighting wrong things. We are in the world, not of it, music will be played in various places, so we must be healed in that memory, where that memory does not take us to worldliness. We must bring our mind into subjection to think like kingdom. Be mindful to not go to the far opposite extreme, and cut out all music and say people are of the devil for listening to any type of music besides gospel or Christian. As Paul said in one of the epistles, you used to do that very thing, so do not be judgmental, just renew your mind and have balance. We will look more in depth at memories in another chapter.

Maybe it is not music, but a certain smell or thing that triggers worldly thoughts of fear, shame, anger, rage. We renew our mind to change what our responses are. If we do not, we will make fleshly/ worldly decisions — basically un-wise decisions and we cannot afford to do this in this day and age.

> 1 Peter 5:8 Be well balanced (temperate, sober of mind), be vigilant and cautious at all times; for that enemy of yours, the devil, roams around like a lion roaring [in fierce hunger], seeking someone to seize upon and devour.

Sober and vigilant means that we are aware of our surrounding. Be sober of mind, don't be absorbed in wild imaginations (see 2 Corinthians 10:7). The sobriety of our minds is based on kingdom things, not worldly things.

At 1 Peter 1:5-9, your faith is in your spirit man, and the renewed mind. So be firm in your faith/ your mind/ your thinking. Be rooted in your mind — have a made up mind that when the enemy manifests in any way, shape, or form (know that he does not manifest as a red horned demon, but as an angel of light); but when he does manifest, no matter the form, we are equipped with a sober mind — the mind of Christ.

A trial that I have been going through for 17 years (the same testing), the players and key pieces
change their clothes, but when it is all said and done and I fail the test and get to go back over it
with the answer key, I see it was the same test, just worded or dressed up differently. So we have to be sober of mind so that we can see when the enemy is switching stuff up, just a little bit. That is what he did to woman in the garden, he changed it up, and it became deception.

> 1 Peter 2:11 Beloved, I implore you as aliens and strangers and exiles [in this world] to abstain from the sensual urges (the evil desires, the passions of the flesh, your lower nature) that wage war against the soul.

The alien here is your spirit man. The sensual urges are in the soulish realm — so this text is letting us know that in the soulish realm, there are evil desires, passions of the flesh, that play with your lower nature — that wars against your soul.

The word of God (according to Hebrews 4:12) is what helps us do Psalm 139:23-24. As he said in Psalm 119: *Your word is a light unto my path and a lamp unto my feet,* because the word turns the light on to any thoughts or purposes in the heart that are not right. The word causes the shifting — persecution comes because of the word — but you can be shifted so that your thoughts line up to His thoughts (that are not like ours as in Isaiah 55:8-11). Meshing these scriptures together, the word that God speaks will not return to Him void, but it is active, operative, energizing, effective. It is not that the word does not work, it is that we are not in line with the word. We may have mental agreement, but the heart is not in it.

3.2 Rest

Hebrews 4 is a text about the promise of rest. We have to renew (change) our mind about what rest means. It is not to lay down with no action/movement and sleep, or go on vacation. The promised rest that God is talking about is not that. The context of this chapter is that the children of Israel were murmuring and complaining, they did not have the capacity to renew their mind; all they could think about was the circumstances going on with them, instead of keeping their mind focused on God. They began to murmur and complain, therefore they did not enter into His promised rest.

> Hebrews 4:1 Therefore, while the promise of entering His rest still holds and is offered [today], let us be afraid [to distrust it], lest any of you should think he has come too late and has come short of [reaching] it.

Look at the language used here, this is all about the thought life.

> Hebrews 4:2 For indeed we have had the glad tidings [Gospel of God] proclaimed to us just as truly as they [the Israelites of old did when the good news of deliverance from bondage came to them]; but the message they heard did not benefit them, because it was not mixed with faith (with the leaning of the entire personality on God in absolute trust and confidence in His power, wisdom, and goodness) by those who heard it; neither were they united in faith with the ones [Joshua and Caleb] who heard (did believe).

Remember the definition of "faith": the leaning of the entire personality on God in absolute trust and confidence in His power, wisdom, and goodness. So they did not mix what they heard with believing that God said He would deliver. It was about trust. Almost every test that we go through is a trust test. You say you trust, but then you do things contrary; but when you really trust Him, you are not fretting and anxious. Do you really trust Him to meet your needs?

See Matthew 6, don't worry about those things, seek the kingdom. So we have to change our mind of what the kingdom looks like — the kingdom is not what you will eat or wear. Do not worry about the kingdom, you simply seek the kingdom. You ask for understanding, and as you get an understanding of the kingdom, and the King of the kingdom, you will realize that the King has all of your provisions.

This does not mean that you will get a check from heaven, but it means that God will make ways out of no way and you will not even know what happened. Look at the trust that Elijah exhibited when he allowed ravens to bring him bread and meat (See 1 Kings 17). Ravens are by nature stingy/selfish birds, they don't feed people. Also, where would a raven get bread from, especially in the wilderness? Not only that, but he drank water out of a muddy brook? These were the commands of God; the provisions of God — it did not make sense to natural thinking, but the man of God trusted enough to obey.

A brief nugget faith and trust is: "Trust is the eye of the newborn soul and the ear of the renewed soul" (E.M. Bounds). Mr. Bounds was basically saying that we must renew our mind by faith to truly trust God. When I read this statement, it reminded me of when Jesus would say "let him that has an ear to hear, listen" — it is a process to have that hearing ear, and trust God by faith, with not worrying and anxiety.

ஒ

We should not be dying off as the forefather's did in the wilderness, we have the help of the Holy Spirit and direct access into the Holy of Holies. They could only gain access once a year when Aaron the high priest went in — so what is our excuse? We need to get clean and access Him.

> Hebrews 4:9-10 So then, there is still awaiting a full and complete Sabbath-rest reserved for the [true] people of God; [10] For he who has once entered [God's] rest also has ceased from [the weariness and pain] of human labors, just as God rested from those labors peculiarly His own.

Renew your mind that once you enter God's rest, you do not have the weariness and pain of human labor. We must renew what rest looks like. We rest by getting in the word and letting the word that is full of power cut and deal with us.

> Matthew 11:28 Come to Me, all you who labor and are heavy-laden and overburdened, and I will cause you to rest. [I will ease and relieve and refresh your souls.]

He causes us to rest, eases, relieves, and refreshes our soul — sounds like Renewal of the Mind! because that is what a refreshed soul is. This is how you rest, by learning of Him!

> Matthew 11:29-30 Take My yoke upon you and learn of Me, for I am gentle (meek) and humble (lowly) in heart, and you will find rest (relief and ease and refreshment and recreation and blessed quiet) for your souls. [30] For My yoke is wholesome (useful, good—not harsh, hard, sharp, or pressing, but comfortable, gracious, and pleasant), and My burden is light and easy to be borne.

We must renew our mind with the word of God that cuts like a 2-edged sword. It cuts to cut stuff back, and it cuts anything that is coming at you that is wrong. His word is uprooting, and is planting.

We have heard of Jesus, we hear the Good News and are born again, now we must like a child, learn of Him. Matthew 11:25, the cleverness and learning of this world does not understand Jesus, but Jesus told us that we must enter the kingdom as a child, we come as babes in the kingdom, and it is as we learn of Him that we begin to mature. Not so much of spiritual maturity, because the spirit man has the mind of Christ, it is in the soulish realm that we are growing and maturing in our mind, will, emotions, reasoning, intellect, thoughts, memories, conscious.

3.3 Obedience

I want to look at 1 Peter 2:11, however, we have to put it in context, so we will begin at 1 Peter 1. Keep in mind that the bible was not written in chapter and verse format, each of the books were just one continuous book/ letter with no breaks in it, the chapter and verse divisions were added later. The word of God is divinely inspired by God, the canon of scripture — with all of the books that the spirit of the Lord wanted in here (there are other inspired books that are not included in the canon of the 66 books of the bible). This is why we can't just start at like chapter 2, because it is a continuation of what was being said in chapter 1.

> 1 Peter 1:21 Through Him you believe in (adhere to, rely on) God, Who raised Him up from the dead and gave Him honor and glory, so that your faith and hope are [centered and rest] in God.

Our faith and hope is in the fact that God has raised us up; believe in Him, rely on Him for that understanding. It is not our understanding. We thought that we could be good enough, some people were taught that access into heaven was gained by going to church a lot, and/or by learning all of the books of the bible but that is not access to heaven. Access to heaven is through Jesus Christ, and that is it. Your faith and hope cannot rest in you and your ability to be good enough, because you will never be good enough on your own apart from Him.

> 1 Peter 1:22 Since by your obedience to the Truth through the [Holy] Spirit you have purified your hearts for the sincere affection of the brethren, [see that you] love one another fervently from a pure heart.

Purifying of our hearts can only be done through the help of the Holy Spirit. We do not have the ability to do that. Our own self cleansing of our hearts is as filthy rags, see Isaiah 64. We need the help of the Holy Spirit, and the only way to get it is to be born again, regenerated as we will see further here in 1 Peter 1.

> 1 Peter 1:23 You have been regenerated (born again), not from a mortal origin (seed, sperm), but from one that is immortal by the ever living and lasting Word of God.

Our "regeneration" comes from the word of God, from the Truth of God, Jesus is the word, through salvation in Him comes the regeneration of our spirit. With the regeneration of our spirit being born again, we now receive the help of the Holy Spirit. And it is a Renewal of the Mind! process to learn how to receive from Him in the soulish realm, which is where your mind, will, emotion, intellect, reasoning, imaginations, memories, thoughts, conscience, etc. are — all of that must be renewed to receive from the regenerated, born again Mind of Christ.

> 1 Peter 1:24-2:1 For all flesh (mankind) is like grass, and all its glory (honor) like [the] flower of grass. The grass withers and the flower drops off, 25 But the Word of the Lord (divine instruction, the Gospel) endures forever. And this Word is the good news which was preached to you. Chp 2:1 So be done with every trace of wickedness (depravity, malignity) and all deceit and insincerity (pretense, hypocrisy) and grudges (envy, jealousy) and slander and evil speaking of every kind

First Peter 2:1 is telling us that we will be regenerated, and we will still have these things trying to be there in our soulish realm (in our mind, will, emotion, intellect, reasoning, imaginations, memories, thoughts, conscience, etc.), but we now have the help of the Holy Spirit to help us be done with them. These are the things that are in that desperately wicked heart that we do not know (Jeremiah 17:9-11), that we have to give access to and say search my heart O Lord and see if there be any way in me (Psalm 139:23-24) — for anything like this listed here in 1 Peter 2:1, and lead me in Your way everlasting — help me renew my mind to not allow these things to manifest. That is when we say "set a guard before my mouth" — it is not that He is looking at what is coming out of your mouth, but what is going on in your heart, because out of the abundance of the heart, the mouth speaks. Peter is identifying for us, that even though we have a regenerated born again spirit, as in 1 Peter 1:23, and the word of God endures forever, as in 1 Peter 1:25, now when we get into 1 Peter 2:1 he is letting us know that we do have the ability to access the mind of Christ but we must renew our soulish realm: our mind, will, emotion, intellect, reasoning, so that we are done, and no longer take our cues from wickedness, depravity, deceit, insincerity, and that whole list there — they are all still there trying to give cues, but we to have to deaden their ability, turn a deaf ear — meaning, turn our spiritual ear to be deaf to these things and to be open to the Holy Spirit that is giving us the truth.

> 1 Peter 2:2 Like newborn babies you should crave (thirst for, earnestly desire) the pure (unadulterated) spiritual milk, that by it you may be nurtured and grow unto [completed] salvation

What does this mean "grow unto completed salvation?" Salvation is in 3 tenses: justification (this happened at Calvary, and personally when you accepted Jesus Christ as Savior — when you were born again), and then we are walking through the sanctification process (we go through this while we are living as a born again spirit in this dirt suit in the process of Renewal of the Mind!). We are growing in the process of sanctification, it grows us. Spiritual growth is not the spirit realm growing, but the soulish realm growing and receiving the capacity to receive from the spirit realm; because when you are born again, you are born with the mind of Christ, that already knows how to love Him, already has the will of God, and so we are growing unto completed salvation. And then glorification will happen at the second coming of the Lord Jesus Christ.

Let me take a personal side bar here: to be absent from the body is to be present with Christ — take me on to glory now, I want to go now. I'm not saying that I am suicidal, but just longing to be with Him full-time and not have to deal with this life any more. But when you really understand the glory of God, and the purpose of God in your life — that He has placed a purpose in your life that is so much bigger than you, it gives you a longing to want to stay in this earth and fulfill purpose. I realized that when I began to say "I want to be out of here, I am tired, I can't take it anymore," that I am talking out of the flesh because God is in control of my times. Back to the text:

> 1 Peter 2:2-5 Like newborn babies you should crave (thirst for, earnestly desire) the pure (unadulterated) spiritual milk, that by it you may be nurtured and grow unto [completed] salvation, ³ Since you have [already] tasted the goodness and kindness of the Lord. ⁴ Come to Him [then, to that] Living Stone which men tried and threw away, but which is chosen [and] precious in God's sight. ⁵ [Come] and, like living stones, be yourselves built [into] a spiritual house, for a holy (dedicated, consecrated) priesthood, to offer up [those] spiritual sacrifices [that are] acceptable and pleasing to God through Jesus Christ.

That born again spirit man, living stone, is coming to be built into a spiritual house. But understand that the things of the flesh and the things of this world do not want you to be properly placed in this spiritual house — so there will constantly, and consistently be a fight against those things like listed in verse 1. But our weapons are not carnal, you do not have to deal with those thoughts alone — we have the word of God that helps us pull down these thoughts (like in verse 1), and we erect whatever is good, lovely, pure, noble, of good report, think on these things — these are the things that we need to be having our mind on.

> 1 Peter 2:6 For thus it stands in Scripture: Behold, I am laying in Zion a chosen (honored), precious chief Cornerstone, and he who believes in Him [who adheres to, trusts in, and relies on Him] shall never be disappointed or put to shame.

"He who believes in Him" — that is your thought life — you have to have your thoughts on Him. You have to adhere to, trust in, rely on Him to never be disappointed or ashamed. So if there is a situation that is going on in your life that is bringing disappointment, your hope is in the wrong thing. Because hope does not disappoint. I know this sounds contradictory, because Proverbs 13:12 says: *hope deferred makes the heart sick.* Understand, that when your hope is in things in this world, you will receive unrelenting disappointment. But when you place your hope in Christ, where no matter what comes your way: tragedy or blessing, good or bad, light or dark, no matter what comes, your hope is in Him. What is making you sick is that He has not come for the second coming. But then this makes you grateful that He has not come yet because there is still a lot of work to be done; there are still a lot of souls that have not heard the truth of the gospel. They have heard church, they have heard preachers preach cute encouraging messages (not kingdom), they have heard Christians in the media that have messed things up, but they have not heard the true gospel. Instead of being heartsick, go ahead and get your desires fulfilled in the tree of life and do what He has called us to do right here.

Again our hope is in Him.

> 1 Peter 2:7-8 To you then who believe (who adhere to, trust in, and rely on Him) is the preciousness; but for those who disbelieve [it is true], The [very] Stone which the builders rejected has become the main Cornerstone, 7 And, a stone that will cause stumbling and a Rock that will give [men] offense; they stumble because they disobey and disbelieve [God's] Word, as those [who reject Him] were destined (appointed) to do.

Understand that our job is to sow seeds of who this Chief Cornerstone is. We are living stones, and are examples that we are built on the Cornerstone. But some people will reject it, it should not disappoint you, or hinder you. I am speaking to Paulette D right here!

Let's look at what happened when Jesus was rejected in his hometown of Nazareth, (Matthew 13:52-58) and *Jesus could do no great work because of their unbelief.* So I am personally asking the Lord, for my friends, and with my family that knew me as "Pooh Bear" or "Church Lady", that He would deal with their unbelief, that He would cause them to have ears that hear and eyes that see Him, that He would deal with the areas that keep them from being good ground, deal with the shallowness, compacted, stony stuff that He would deal with the areas that are keeping them from being good ground. Deal with those areas that are causing unbelief, that they would be able to hear and receive the word of God. And it is okay if they do not receive it from me, that is fine, but receive it from the laborer that God sends across their path. That they would one day realize that God has placed me there as a tool for them, and for all.

> 1 Peter 2:9 But you are a chosen race, a royal priesthood, a dedicated nation, [God's] own purchased, special people, that you may set forth the wonderful deeds and display the virtues and perfections of Him Who called you out of darkness into His marvelous light.

You want to know how to be a part of the chosen race? Don't reject His Son! That gets you in. For years I had come to church and no one really told me what a royal priesthood or a dedicated nation looked like. They told me what church looked like, and how I should change the way I dress, and come to Sunday school, etc. — now those things are important, but they are not what my relationship with God are built on. Teach me relationship of what a royal priesthood looks like, give me the sincere milk of what a royal priesthood looks like.

Let's renew our minds, that as the body of Christ/ as the church/ as the mouthpiece and the hands and feet of the gospel, we help people grow in knowing who God is, and who they are in Him. The first part of evangelism is to catch the fish; the second part is to expose the fish to the Truth of God's word with the help of the Holy Spirit (which causes the fish to be cleaned). As it says in 1 Timothy 2:4, "*God desires all men saved and increasingly to perceive and recognize and discern and know precisely and correctly the divine Truth.*" How does this happen? First, men are born again, spiritually born fresh anew — now what they need to do is to do as 1 Peter 2:2 "*crave, thirst for, earnestly desire the pure unadulterated spiritual milk.*" God has placed an anointing on my life to help His people grow in knowing the Truth of His word.

I just keep taking these rabbit trails, but they are making the point of what God is saying. Back to the original text: "Called out of darkness" — yes we lived in darkness apart from Him when our spirit man was dead. Then, once we received Christ and were born again, we still must renew our mind to not be in darkness. It does not matter how good we were, or how much we went to church, or if we never went to church, but always did good (by giving to the poor and charity etc.) — we were still in the dark without Christ. Yet He brought us out of the dark into His marvelous light.

> 1 Peter 2:10-11 Once you were not a people [at all], but now you are God's people; once you were unpitied, but now you are pitied and have received mercy. 11 Beloved, I implore you as aliens and strangers and exiles [in this world] to abstain from the sensual urges (the evil desires, the passions of the flesh, your lower nature) that wage war against the soul.

Do you see what is going on? We have to renew our mind! First to know that we are aliens and strangers; citizens of another kingdom, so we have to seek and get a better understanding of the King and the kingdom, and the constitution (which is the word of God). We are exiles and strangers in this world, meaning our spirit man was created in His image — as in Genesis 1:26-28. Created in the image of the heavenly triune God (Father, Son, and Spirit). He created us on earth, but created us in His image which made us aliens because His image is heavenly, not earthly. Then in Genesis 2:7 and 2:22, the Lord made the dirt suit/ body for the spirit to live in as God breathed the spirit of life into them. This was the beginning of the aliens, dual citizens. Yet deception and sin came in as we see in Genesis 3, the lamb was slain to cover them — actually the Lamb was slain before the foundations of the world, but here we see it taking place in the earth realm. Now with this in mind, let's go back to 1 Peter 2:11.

Where did these sensual urges come from? They came from what happened back in Genesis 3, when man ate of the knowledge of the tree of good and evil, as the Amplified says "the difference between good and evil, blessing and calamity." Now they knew the difference, because before that, all they knew was that everything God created was good; they did not even need to know what evil or calamity was.

Here is a nugget, and something I have been pondering on for years. Look at Genesis 2:9, there were 2 trees identified by name, they were not told to leave the tree of Life alone, only the tree of knowledge? When we have a quest for knowledge, apart from the tree of Life, we will have a problem (see Genesis 3:25).

These sensual urges and the lower nature, because of the death that happened in Genesis 3, we now have 2 natures: 1) the nature of God, created in His image, and 2) the Adamic nature that came as a result of Adam committing treason and giving up his lordship over to satan/ the enemy. So we see the lower nature, and then the regenerated nature. Your regenerated nature is what should rule and dominate, but we see that the lower nature is still there — we can clearly see it in the struggle/battle of Romans 7:14-25. The lower nature gives you sensual urges, evil desires, and passions of the flesh, but 1 John 2:16 tell us to not love worldliness — those things wage war against the soul, and do not want you to have Renewal of the Mind! which is renewal of the soul. So we must, must, must set our mind — you cannot mess with a made up mind — make up our mind that we are not going to give into the lower nature, but regenerate our mind with the word of God.

> 1 Peter 2:12 Conduct yourselves properly (honorably, righteously) among the Gentiles, so that, although they may slander you as evildoers, [yet] they may by witnessing your good deeds [come to] glorify God in the day of inspection [when God shall look upon you wanderers as a pastor or shepherd looks over his flock].

If you keep reading the chapter, it goes on to talk about Christian submission, and Christ our example. We will stop here with this reference, but it was good for us to journey back to Genesis, the place (or state) that we are to renew our minds to. As a matter of fact, almost every scripture we see in the New Testament ties back to Genesis 1-3, because it is all about renewing our minds back to Genesis chapter 2; trying to get back as if deception and sin never happened, and we live in constant direct communion with God. We know that the lower nature is there, but we must renew our mind to not respond to the lower nature, but the regenerated nature.

This has been something for us to Selah — pause and calmly think on that. Chew on it. Think about it, renew our mind.

Prayer: Thank You for Your servant Paulette Denise, with all of the hurting and the pain, and the crushing, and the breaking, and the bleeding that has taken place – it is just Your servant on the Potter's wheel. You get Your glory as You find the areas that are marring the clay, mash it down, and bring it up. And I Your servant, though it hurts, I will not scream, squeel, or get off the wheel. But I will let You do what You need to do – and must do to get all of Your glory, every ounce of it. Let no flesh glory in Your sight. Kill and crucify Paulette Denise, that You O God may get what is needed. Thank You for removing the flesh. Get glory out of Your servant – get the flint knife and keep cutting back everything that is not like You that must be cut. Thank You for strengthening me in the process, thank You for those that You send alongside

to labor with me, and to grow. Like David, when you sent the 3-D brothers to him at the cave at Adullam, they had issues, were discontented, in debt, and disgruntled – yet You sent them. We are not perfect, we have our issues, but You O God are getting the glory, honor, praise out of us. Thank You Lord for changing us, for purging us, for cleansing us. Amen.

༄

3.4 Receive

Looking at the fact that we hear a lot, and say we receive it, but the way to tell if we really receive it is that it changes our behavior and actions. We should make some adjustments in our life, this is part of the duties of faith — to be doers of the word and not hearers only. We hear good word, sermons, studies, but it is not helping us through the trials and tribulations we face in life? We have to truly receive it. We will define "receive" in a moment to make sure that we understand what receive means — that could be the piece that we are missing. We say that we have faith, but what could be missing is our receptivity (our ability to receive).

> Mark 11:22-24 And Jesus, replying, said to them, Have faith in God [constantly]. 23 Truly I tell you, whoever says to this mountain, Be lifted up and thrown into the sea! and does not doubt at all in his heart but believes that what he says will take place, it will be done for him. 24 For this reason I am telling you, whatever you ask for in prayer, believe (trust and be confident) that it is granted to you, and you will [get it].

Not just any old faith, but faith in God. How often? Constantly, this does not mean sometimes, or that I had faith yesterday, or the last time — but constantly means constantly — every day that you wake up, you will have to make sure that you place your faith in God, not in situations, circumstances, finances, etc. We have to renew our mind, because we were not raised having faith in God. We were raised that God is a good God, or that God is a God of anger and will discipline you and you will get in trouble — but our faith in God, who He is, in His attributes and characteristics needs to grow daily — constantly.

It is something about being able to receive. First you have to believe; that is your faith growing. When we pray and ask God to give us revelation, illumination, insight, knowledge, wisdom into the things of God, we are asking God to expand our belief system. To actually expand the stuff in me that helps me believe whatever I am asking You according to Your word that I have taken the time to renew my mind to, help me believe these things; and when I truly believe them, I will receive them.

> Mark 11:25 And whenever you stand praying, if you have anything against anyone, forgive him and let it drop (leave it, let it go), in order that your Father Who is in

heaven may also forgive you your [own] failings and shortcomings and let them drop.

Sometimes we have people deposited and injected in our lives, and their role is to help us stay in un-forgiveness. Because the enemy knows that if people stay in un-forgiveness, they can believe and pray all they want, but if there is any un-forgiveness present, their prayers will be hindered. We have to make sure that we are a people that walk in forgiveness. Again, when we truly walk in love, we do not need forgiveness because WE do not keep account of wrong (1 Corinthians 13:5), so we are always walking in love, and do not need to forgive. We choose to let someone off the hook right when they wrong us, we do not keep account of it — easier said than done — we must renew our mind.

As I meditated on this thought of walking in love and not needing to forgive, I seriously asked the Lord "So I am supposed to just let them keep doing me dirt?" The response was, that I need to identify if this person is carnal or spiritually mature. Carnal is like a baby believer; that must grow in the mind renewal process. Babies cry, poop on themselves, make a mess, are unruly, make a bunch of noise, and really don't care who they are disturbing. So we just have to ask God for wisdom of how to deal with this grown baby standing in front of us proclaiming that it is fully grown.

Back to defining "receive", www.blueletter.org says it means *to take with the hand, lay hold of any person or thing in order to use it; to take up one's self.* Then looking to the Merriam-Webster online dictionary, it means *to come into possession of.* Once you receive something, you have to come into possession of acquire it. Additional definitions said *to permit it to enter; admit; great; welcome; to act as a receptacle or a container for (such as a cistern).* So putting this definition back in the text of Mark 11:25, take with the hand — the hand of faith that "reaches" into the unseen (in the natural) in order to make use of it — this shows true possession when we by faith, grasp and truly receive the living word of God. We cannot only mentally agree, but we must permit it to enter into our thoughts, greet and welcome it, truly believing that we have received. Be a faithful receptacle or container of the power of God to manifest in the world.

Another definition of "receive" is *to assimilate through the mind or senses.* So when you renew your mind, (which sometimes takes its cues from the senses), when you renew your mind according to the word of God, it now takes it cues or senses from there, instead of the circumstances that are going on in front of you.

The etymology (root) of the word "receive" comes from "heave" — which means *to elevate; to lift; raise, to cast; to draw* — so to receive something means to be elevated by it, it will lift you and raise you. So in the text, talking to this mountain and telling it to move, you receive that the mountain really moves, actually is elevated, is raised, is thrown, is cast into the sea.

Remember one of the definitions for receive is to acquire. Looking up what "acquire" means, it is *to seek; to obtain; to get as one's own; to come into possession or control of often by unspecified means; to come to have as a new or added characteristic, trait or ability.* Substituting this back into the text, when He said whatsoever you ask in prayer, believe that you receive — He was actually saying believe that you have come to have as a new characteristic, trait or ability. I will add on, as long as it is according to the will of God and the word of God. He wants us to see what it means to receive.

This has been us getting a better understanding of receive, and the way that we know we received the word, is that it changes us.

> Matthew 6:25-34 Therefore I tell you, stop being perpetually uneasy (anxious and worried) about your life, what you shall eat or what you shall drink; or about your body, what you shall put on. Is not life greater [in quality] than food, and the body [far above and more excellent] than clothing? 26 Look at the birds of the air; they neither sow nor reap nor gather into barns, and yet your heavenly Father keeps feeding them. Are you not worth much more than they? 27 And who of you by worrying and being anxious can add one unit of measure (cubit) to his stature or to the span of his life? 28 And why should you be anxious about clothes? Consider the lilies of the field and learn thoroughly how they grow; they neither toil nor spin. 29 Yet I tell you, even Solomon in all his magnificence (excellence, dignity, and grace) was not arrayed like one of these. 30 But if God so clothes the grass of the field, which today is alive and green and tomorrow is tossed into the furnace, will He not much more surely clothe you, O you of little faith? 31 Therefore do not worry and be anxious, saying, What are we going to have to eat? or, What are we going to have to drink? or, What are we going to have to wear? 32 For the Gentiles (heathen) wish for and crave and diligently seek all these things, and your heavenly Father knows well that you need them all. 33 But seek (aim at and strive after) first of all His kingdom and His righteousness (His way of doing and being right), and then all these things taken together will be given you besides. 34 So do not worry or be anxious about tomorrow, for tomorrow will have worries and anxieties of its own. Sufficient for each day is its own trouble.

Don't worry about these things, if you really believe and receive the word and are not worrying, then get busy seeking the kingdom. Some people say that it does not take all of that, all of that studying, reading your bible, going to church, fellowshipping with believers — but it takes that for me to renew my mind and seek the kingdom so that I don't worry about what I'm going to eat/ wear/ live/ etc. It may not take all of that for you, but it does for me. I am not you, and you are not me; we are all unique — He made us fearfully and wonderfully. Just like no one has the same thumbprint, God made us unique, and just like our thumbprints are not the same, our mind/ thinking patterns are not the same. We have been exposed to various things throughout our lives and upbringing and we are just different. Some people learn differently than others, some people learn by writing things down, some people learn by reading — it takes different things for different people. I cannot judge how you learn, but a good leader would be able to see and understand which method works for which people.

When we really understand this seeking the kingdom, not being anxious, then your behavior should be different. We are to act as a fruit inspector, not judging people but seeing the fruit on their tree (and just because fruit has bruises, does not mean it is not useful), but a sign of worrying and being anxious is trying to take short cuts, or comparing yourselves among yourselves — these are things you do when you are not really seeking first the kingdom. When you seek first the church, instead of kingdom you will have a problem understanding someone with a kingdom mindset — the kingdom will always be misunderstood. People fight the church, they fight tradition, they fight religion, but you cannot fight the kingdom — it is an established fact. Seek first the kingdom, those things will be added to you — if you are truly receiving the word, then do not be anxious. And do not promote church over kingdom (church building, organization). The more time you spend in the word, the more persecution comes your way. The bible says that persecution comes *because* of the word, so when you seek the kingdom, you get in the word; so expect the promised tribulations, trials, attacks, persecution (from without and from within).

Just sharing how I learned scripture, Matthew 6:33 was one of the scriptures that truly changed my life. When I saw that I was not to worry about what you will eat/ live/ wear — my life was completely transformed. I also came across a book by Rick Joyner titled "There were 2 trees in the garden," that really taught me the difference between kingdom and church/ tradition/ religion — it was a kairos moment in my life that happened accidentally, on purpose. I used to go to thrift stores and ask the Lord to lead me to materials to help me know Him more. This particular day, was the time that I had come into the Matthew 6:33 quest for kingdom knowledge (I believe it was around 1997 or 1998). The combined knowledge of Rick Joyner's book, and continued teaching of the Holy Spirit, prepared me for the many persecutions that accompanied being an authentic Christian. Now, everything did not change overnight, however, I did receive power to make decisions and life changes that caused me to grow closer and closer to Him — I also made even larger mistakes, but with the larger mistakes, came larger lessons learned and principles to pass on to other believers.

When you start really seeking who God is, and who you are in Him, and what it means to be found in Him; getting a better understanding of Calvary, and what "it is finished" means; and what justification means, that it was in the past; and sanctification, it is the process that I am walking through; and glorification, that it is something to take place in the future: these are all kingdom — and when you seek these things, the other things of what you will eat, what you will wear, etc.; those things will chase you down and be added to you. Meditate on His word day and night. Some will tell you it does not take all of that. They would rather quote Joshua 1:8, than really live it by meditating day and night to be prosperous and have good success — they want a Vending Machine God, instead of a relationship with a loving Father that is grown through spending time in His word.

Another sidebar principle that I learned there in Joshua 1:6-9, was that 3 times the Lord told Joshua to have courage and be strong; well, how do we be encouraged? Because we are in the word of God, and it brings courage for us to walk it out as a kingdom citizen. When people tell me it does not take all of that, I say "give me a scripture for that," because this text says meditate day and night. So for the "it doesn't take all of that people," what bible are you reading? It takes all of that for me, it may not take all of that for you, but it does for me and my God, and my relationship with my God — it is a personal relationship. It may not take all of that for you because you are more concerned with church, religion, tradition, and a program — but me myself, I am more concerned with understanding this kingdom that I am a part of, that I am supposed to be seeking — because in the kingdom is where the benefits of God are released to me. In seeking the kingdom, I don't have to be worried about what will be happening here and there.

The way of the righteous is revealed in Psalm 1.

> Psalm 1:1-2 NKJV Blessed (happy, fortunate, prosperous, and enviable) is the man who walks and lives not in the counsel of the ungodly [following their advice, their plans and purposes], nor stands [submissive and inactive] in the path where sinners walk, nor sits down [to relax and rest] where the scornful [and the mockers] gather. ² But his delight and desire are in the law of the Lord, and on His law (the precepts, the instructions, the teachings of God) he habitually meditates (ponders and studies) by day and by night.

> 1 Corinthians 2:9 But, on the contrary, as the Scripture says, What eye has not seen and ear has not heard and has not entered into the heart of man, [all that] God has prepared (made and keeps ready) for those who love Him [who hold Him in affectionate reverence, promptly obeying Him and gratefully recognizing the benefits He has bestowed].

We cannot close the text there and say that no one can know what God has in store for them — we must put it back in context so that we can receive the full council of God, so that it can operate. If you take just verse 9 and walk away, it is partial and does not help you. That is like having a front tooth that is broken, beginning the process to get the crown, but never following up, you will look funny. So if you just take verse 9 and try to build a doctrine on it without the surrounding text, that is what you have done, because the actual crown is in verse 10. But let's look back even further and begin here:

> 1 Corinthians 2:4-5 And my language and my message were not set forth in persuasive (enticing and plausible) words of wisdom, but they were in demonstration of the [Holy] Spirit and power [a proof by the Spirit and power of God, operating on me and stirring in the minds of my hearers the most holy

emotions and thus persuading them], ⁵ So that your faith might not rest in the wisdom of men (human philosophy), but in the power of God.

You can have divine assistance in the Renewal of the Mind! process. He didn't talk with worldly wisdom, if anybody could, it was Paul, but he didn't. It was the power of God operating in the minds of the hearers and persuading them — that is why certain people do not even invite me into certain things, because they have the human wisdom, and don't really want God's wisdom. Like in Ezekiel 22:23-31, the problem was in leadership, the people weren't being taught the truths of God's word — and even now, some do not want the word, but to be entertained.

> 1 Corinthians 2:6-9 Yet when we are among the full-grown (spiritually mature Christians who are ripe in understanding), we do impart a [higher] wisdom (the knowledge of the divine plan previously hidden); but it is indeed not a wisdom of this present age or of this world nor of the leaders and rulers of this age, who are being brought to nothing and are doomed to pass away. ⁷ But rather what we are setting forth is a wisdom of God once hidden [from the human understanding] and now revealed to us by God — [that wisdom] which God devised and decreed before the ages for our glorification [to lift us into the glory of His presence]. ⁸ None of the rulers of this age or world perceived and recognized and understood this, for if they had, they would never have crucified the Lord of glory. ⁹ But, on the contrary, as the Scripture says, What eye has not seen and ear has not heard and has not entered into the heart of man, [all that] God has prepared (made and keeps ready) for those who love Him [who hold Him in affectionate reverence, promptly obeying Him and gratefully recognizing the benefits He has bestowed].

Verse 9 of the Amplified bible is a love test. If you really love God, then do you hold Him in affectionate reverence? Do you promptly obey Him? Do you gratefully recognize the benefits that He has bestowed? This is why we have to grow and understand the love of God; all of His benefits; better understand all that salvation contains; the sanctification process; the characteristics of God. When we see all of this, it empowers us to promptly obey Him and have affectionate reverence for Him — not just a form of godliness without power, but here is the power.

> 1 Corinthians 2:10 Yet to us God has unveiled and revealed them by and through His Spirit, for the [Holy] Spirit searches diligently, exploring and examining everything, even sounding the profound and bottomless things of God [the divine counsels and things hidden and beyond man's scrutiny.

The Holy Spirit is the answer to knowing these things that God has prepared for us. We must understand the characteristics of the Holy Spirit — we must understand the triune God. A lot of people do not welcome the Holy Spirit in, but my favorite scripture is Psalm 139:23-24 that welcomes Him in to search me. Another scripture that goes with this is Ephesians 1:17-19 asking God to flood the eyes of my heart with light so that anything that is dark cannot hide. Also, so that I can know and understand the hope to which I am called. But some people do not want that. Why? Because they do not want to be diligently explored or examined on the inside because they have some yucky stuff in there, and they know it, and they are not ready to let it go. It is a choice to let the Holy Spirit come and examine you. He is a gentleman and will not force you or smack you across the head and tell you to let that go. Look at Psalm 139:23-24, search me, and then lead me. He can lead us, and we can choose to not follow, and we will stay right there. We must renew our mind!

> 1 Corinthians 2:11-12 For what person perceives (knows and understands) what passes through a man's thoughts except the man's own spirit within him? Just so no one discerns (comes to know and comprehend) the thoughts of God except the Spirit of God. 12 Now we have not received the spirit [that belongs to] the world, but the [Holy] Spirit Who is from God, [given to us] that we might realize and comprehend and appreciate the gifts [of divine favor and blessing so freely and lavishly] bestowed on us by God.

That worldly spirit as in 1 John 2:16, the lust of the eye, the lust of the flesh, and the pride of life — we have not received this spirit, but the Holy Spirit.

> 1 Corinthians 2:13-16 And we are setting these truths forth in words not taught by human wisdom but taught by the [Holy] Spirit, combining and interpreting spiritual truths with spiritual language [to those who possess the Holy Spirit]. 14 But the natural, nonspiritual man does not accept or welcome or admit into his heart the gifts and teachings and revelations of the Spirit of God, for they are folly (meaningless nonsense) to him; and he is incapable of knowing them [of progressively recognizing, understanding, and becoming better acquainted with them] because they are spiritually discerned and estimated and appreciated. 15 But the spiritual man tries all things [he examines, investigates, inquires into, questions, and discerns all things], yet is himself to be put on trial and judged by no one [he can read the meaning of everything, but no one can properly discern or appraise or get an insight into him]. 16 For who has known or understood the mind (the counsels and purposes) of the Lord so as to guide and instruct Him and give Him knowledge? But we have the mind of Christ (the Messiah) and do hold the thoughts (feelings and purposes) of His heart.

Verse 14 is a great example to the "it don't take all of that" people; and verse 15 will take some time and study — it is not automatic.

Yes, people want to see, but it is revealed by the Holy Spirit, but the carnal (non-spiritual man) cannot hear the Holy Spirit and will think you are crazy. Going on into chapter 3, remember the breaks were not always there:

> 1 Corinthians 3:1-3 However, brethren, I could not talk to you as to spiritual [men], but as to nonspiritual [men of the flesh, in whom the carnal nature predominates], as to mere infants [in the new life] in Christ [unable to talk yet!] 2 I fed you with milk, not solid food, for you were not yet strong enough [to be ready for it]; but even yet you are not strong enough [to be ready for it], 3 For you are still [unspiritual, having the nature] of the flesh [under the control of ordinary impulses]. For as long as [there are] envying and jealousy and wrangling and factions among you, are you not unspiritual and of the flesh, behaving yourselves after a human standard and like mere (unchanged) men?

He didn't say they were not saved, but they were behaving carnally. He addressed them as "brethren," that means that they are believers, born again into the body of Christ. But he could not talk to them because they were still immature. A piece of biblical history here is that this was 3 years after their conversion, Paul was coming back to visit and expected them to be mature — just like in the natural, at 3 years old, they should be using words and mature — but they were not. How do we know if someone is spiritual verses non-spiritual? They are born again, but controlled by the lower nature, the nature of the flesh, the ordinary impulses of the flesh that has all these things present — still envying, jealousy, wranglings and factions (fighting and bickering) — this is what the unspiritual does — this identifies which nature is operating, and that you have not matured. So we must renew our mind to mature in being able to receive from the mind of Christ that it just said we have (in 1 Corinthians 2:16).

Prayer: Thank You for causing us to truly understand what it means to receive the word of God by faith. That when we receive the word of God, our actions/ behavior/ lifestyle should change if we truly receive Your word. Therefore we give You access into our heart – thank You for growing us in what we believe. We believe in the Lord Jesus, we believe in the finished work of Calvary, we believe therefore we receive whatsoever we ask in prayer, and we ask according to Your word. Thank You for Your plans and purposes for Your people coming to pass. The things that You have revealed to us by Your Holy Spirit (as in 2 Corinthians 2:10); and as we take the time to examine our hearts, examine ourselves, search ourselves we open and lay ourselves open and plain before You God, that You continue to reveal all that needs to be worked on. That it not be an overwhelming process, but that You are here with us, You are our teacher, You are our strengthener, You are our comforter, and in the midst of the trial and tribulation that we go through, because of the persecution that only comes to try our faith and strengthen us in knowing Who You are, and who we are in You. You are strengthening us in understanding You and every name, every characteristic that You could name Yourself, strengthening us in understanding the "I AM", I AM that I AM. Whatever it is that we need, You have said that I AM, not might be, but You AM. So we thank You and glorify You for helping us transform our minds. For helping us not walk in a state of anxiety, and worry, and fret, but to have our minds stayed on You that we would be able to walk in the perfect peace that You promise. We give You glory, honor, and praise. Amen.

3.5 Salted in Fire

Prayer: We may be going through situations and trials, but we have learned contentment in the midst of them all. Our contentment and our hope is in You. We go through everything that we go through for You to get the glory. Truly help us understand what it means to have our mind renewed according to Your word O God. Do us as in Ephesians 1:17-19, flood the eyes of our heart with Light so that we can know the hope to which we have been called, and understand Your depth, Your height, and more and more about You O God. It is all about You. Amen.

When I first read Mark 9:49-50, it left a huge question mark for me, because it just didn't make sense to "be salted with fire?" So with this next section, we will get a better understanding of what it means to be salted with fire. This verse is in the "hot sauce," the red letters are the words of Jesus speaking. The book was written by Mark, but he was quoting what Jesus said. First let's read this text in 3 different versions to get a surface understanding:

Mark 9:49-50 AMP, MSG, NLT:

> AMP [49] For everyone shall be salted with fire. [50] Salt is good (beneficial), but if salt has lost its saltness, how will you restore [the saltness to] it? Have salt within yourselves, and be at peace and live in harmony with one another.

> MSG [49-50] "Everyone's going through a refining fire sooner or later, but you'll be well-preserved, protected from the eternal flames. Be preservatives yourselves. Preserve the peace."

> NLT [49] "For everyone will be seasoned with fire, and every sacrifice will be seasoned with salt. [50] Salt is good, but if the salt loses its flavor, how will you season it? Have salt in yourselves, and have peace with one another."

The word "salted" here is being interchanged for tested, or refined. So we are being salted with fire, tested with fire, and refined with fire. As in the NLT, salt is for seasoning we have to renew our mind as to what it means to be the salt of the world, the seasoning of the world.

Putting these 2 verses back in context of what was going on in Mark 9; those were the last 2 verses of what was being said, there were 48 verses before this, so putting it back into context of what was going on before He made this statement about us being salt. That we not take 2 verses and run off with them, but keep them in the entirety of context to get an even deeper message and tools to renew our mind.

Mark 9 Verses 2 - 13: *The Transfiguration*
Jesus had taken 3 disciples with Him to pray, was transfigured to look like diety. Peter got excited, but had wrong thinking, needed to be renewed.

Mark 9 Verses 14-29: *Jesus Heals a Demon-Possessed Boy* – and *There Are No Ifs*
When they came down from the mountain they encountered this young man with demons. The disciple's faith was not right so they could not cast the demon out. Jesus cast it out.

Mark 9 Verses 30-32: *Jesus Again Predicts His Death*
Jesus questioned them questioning among themselves about true discipleship, and who would be first. Jesus' response to them was telling them who the greatest in the kingdom is.

Mark 9 Verses 33-37: *The Greatest in the Kingdom* – and *So You Want First Place?*
If you want to know what true discipleship looks like, I didn't say true church membership, but discipleship. We are not called "Church-tians" we are called "Christ-ians" — Christ like, a learner of Christ. This section shows what true discipleship looks like.

Mark 9 Verses 38-50: *Using the Name of Jesus*

So this last section here is the conclusion of the matter of what real discipleship looks like. Also, the power of using the name of Jesus.

Now let's read through these last 2 sections to see why Jesus said "be salted by fire."

> Mark 9:33-42 And they arrived at Capernaum; and when [they were] in the house, He asked them, What were you discussing and arguing about on the road? [34] But they kept still, for on the road they had discussed and disputed with one another as to who was the greatest. [35] And He sat down and called the Twelve [apostles], and He said to them, If anyone desires to be first, he must be last of all, and servant of all. [36] And He took a little child and put him in the center of their group; and taking him in [His] arms, He said to them, [37] Whoever in My name and for My sake accepts and receives and welcomes one such child also accepts and receives and welcomes Me; and whoever so receives Me receives not only Me but Him Who sent Me. [38] John said to Him, Teacher, we saw a man who does not follow along with us driving out demons in Your name, and we forbade him to do it, because he is not one of our band [of Your disciples]. [39] But Jesus said, Do not restrain or hinder or forbid him; for no one who does a mighty work in My name will soon afterward be able to speak evil of Me. [40] For he who is not against us is for us. [41] For I tell you truly, whoever gives you a cup of water to drink because you belong to and bear the name of Christ will by no means fail to get his reward. [42] And whoever causes one of these little ones (these believers) who acknowledge and cleave to Me to stumble

and sin, it would be better (more profitable and wholesome) for him if a [huge] millstone were hung about his neck, and he were thrown into the sea.

This is a warning to anyone who causes a little one, (a believer who acknowledges Him) to stumble. This means that we really have to be careful of what we are saying. This is why I am very sensitive to the spirit of offense. Now the word of God sometimes is an offense, I just need it not to be Paulette that is offending people. Because if it is Paulette that is offending, and not the word of God, then Paulette has a judgment to stand before God of being an offense to one of His children. Now if the word of God offends you, you are fighting the word, not Paulette. That is why the Lord teaches us to set a guard before our mouth that we not be an offense to someone else; because we know how serious it is. This is also why He says not to put a novice (a new convert, a beginner) in position. Note, there are some people that have been saved for 20 years and are still a new convert! Their growth is stunted, they have not grown in the things of God — but they swear they are fully mature — and they try to teach everybody something they think they have, even though they really don't — it has not taken root — because if they really receive it, as mentioned earlier, there will be change/ actions following/ modified behavior/ life changes. So if they just hear it, but not receive it, then they have all of this knowledge with no power. This is why James says:

> James 3:1-2 Not many [of you] should become teachers (self-constituted censors and reprovers of others), my brethren, for you know that we [teachers] will be judged by a higher standard and with greater severity [than other people; thus we assume the greater accountability and the more condemnation]. 2 For we all often stumble and fall and offend in many things. And if anyone does not offend in speech [never says the wrong things], he is a fully developed character and a perfect man, able to control his whole body and to curb his entire nature.

We want to make sure that we are not causing people to stumble. God is calling and raising people up and doing a new thing, and a quick work so that we can share the word of God with others, but we better make sure that we are sharing the word of God, not our opinion, not some man-made stuff, not religion and traditions, but we must share the word of God, because if you do not, then you cause one of these to stumble and sin. James 3 takes it even further and warns that we should be careful that *we* do not stumble and sin. All of this will make us very humble —I will not open my mouth and talk loosely.

Back to Mark 9:42, do not cause God's people to stumble.

> Mark 9:44-48 And if your hand puts a stumbling block before you and causes you to sin, cut it off! It is more profitable and wholesome for you to go into life [that is really worthwhile] maimed than with two hands to go to hell (Gehenna), into the fire that cannot be put out. 45 And if your foot is a cause of stumbling and sin to you, cut it off! It is more profitable and wholesome for you to enter into life [that is really worthwhile] crippled than, having two feet, to be cast into hell (Gehenna). 47 And if

your eye causes you to stumble and sin, pluck it out! It is more profitable and wholesome for you to enter the kingdom of God with one eye than with two eyes to be thrown into hell (Gehenna), [48] Where their worm [which preys on the inhabitants and is a symbol of the wounds inflicted on the man himself by his sins] does not die, and the fire is not put out.

Hand — foot — eye...cut it off! Understand that if this was meant literally, we would have more people with only one hand and one foot and walking around with one eye! This is symbolic and parabolic speaking, where God speaks in parables, and those that have a kingdom mindset (heart) can hear what He is saying. And those that are still natural Looky-Lues, trying to serve God through religion, tradition, rules and regulations will get grossed out, throw up their hands, and leave.

He is not saying literally cut your hand off if you keep touching stuff — no — it is your spiritual hand. Here are a few texts to back up this thought. In Psalm 145, it says *blessed be God that teaches my hands to war* — well if the weapons of our warfare are not carnal but mighty through God for the pulling down of strongholds and IMAGINATIONS — the hand that you are cutting off is the hand of imaginations that is running off into areas that it should not be running into — touching things that ignite carnal thoughts instead of spiritual. Cut off those thoughts with the word of God, get the knife — the 2 edged sword of the word — get your flint knife and cut off those fleshly thoughts. He is teaching my hands to war, and the weapons are not carnal that I am warring with.

If your foot causes you to stumble — so if you are not spiritually walking in the ways of God, (we walk by faith and not by sight) — this is not moving right foot then left — but it is in your thinking. Faith is the evidence of things not seen, faith is seeing it in the spirit realm, and believing God to manifest it in the natural realm. Faith is leaning our entire personality in complete trust and confidence in God. So if your spiritual foot is walking you into something that is not trusting God; the enemy will try to lead you astray, yes physically, but even more to try and get the feet of your mind to walk in doubt and unbelief; to get the feet of your mind to walk outside of the will of God, outside of the word of God. Many of us have more word in us than we think we have, but we listen to the enemy talking against our faith. Faith and fear cannot reside together. We are renewing our minds. And looking at this scripture from a renewed view.

Eyes — we always ask God to flood the eyes of our heart, daily! The enemy wants to keep your eye blinded and in darkness, or contrary to the word of God. This is why we constantly pray the Ephesians 1:17-19 in our lives daily. We need to be flooded with light so that we do not walk in sin, as it says in Psalm 119 *that your word is a light to my feet and a lamp to my path.* We must understand that our spiritual hands must war in the spirit; our feet must walk the walk of faith, not doubt and fear; our eye what are we looking at, must have the light of the word.

In Isaiah 6, which is the call of God on my life to speak to His people, *who shall We send, send me:* God said go to the people with a message, but they will have eyes that do not see, and ears that do not hear; but you still must go say it. You cannot have understanding on your own, apart from Christ. Let's look at these eyes and ears as God spoke to Isaiah:

> Isaiah 6:2 Above Him stood the seraphim; each had six wings: with two [each] covered his [own] face, and with two [each] covered his feet, and with two [each] flew.

See how these go back to Mark 9 with the eyes and feet. We have to allow the wings of God to cover us — it said they covered their face, so that you do not see, smell, etc. — and your senses do not lead you the wrong way. Covered the feet, so that you do not walk where you should not walk. Then with the other 2 wings they flew — we are human beings, we do not fly — but we are to soar in the spirit realm, in the glory of God.

If something is going on that is causing you to stumble and slip, cut that off with the renewal of your mind. It all starts with taking your mind off of worldly conformity (1 John 2:16 lust of the flesh, lust of the eye, pride of life) and putting it on kingdom. When you are kingdom minded, you serve the King of the kingdom. Where ever He says turn, you go — speak to whom He says speak to — listen to His orders.

Back to Mark 9, if your hand, your foot, or your eye causes you to sin, (and anything outside of faith is sin; which faith is the leaning of your entire personality in complete trust and confidence in God): If what you see, what you touch, where you go, are causing you to sin? Put the knife to it (Hebrews 4:12)!

Refined, salted, tested with salt (Mark 9:49-50). NLT of verse 50 — *must have the qualities of salt among yourselves and live in peace* — we see that God is concerned about us living in peace.

Looking at salt a little deeper, my studies led me back to Matthew 5:13-16

> Matthew 5:13-16 You are the salt of the earth, but if salt has lost its taste (its strength, its quality), how can its saltness be restored? It is not good for anything any longer but to be thrown out and trodden underfoot by men. 14 You are the light of the world. A city set on a hill cannot be hidden. 15 Nor do men light a lamp and put it under a peck measure, but on a lampstand, and it gives light to all in the house. 16 Let your light so shine before men that they may see your moral excellence and your praiseworthy, noble, and good deeds and recognize and honor and praise and glorify your Father Who is in heaven.

The teaching on salt and light go together. To get the saltiness back, you have to live in the light — His light. In His light, do we see light (Psalm 36:9). This text gives a clue of how to get the saltiness, that we let our light shine as in verse 16. We can't be salt and be hiding —

we loose the saltiness in the dark, so put it in the light — and let your light shine before men. We let the light shine, not for personal or selfish reasons, but so that men may see your moral excellence and your praiseworthy noble good deeds and recognize and glorify our Father in heaven. Not that we be recognized, but our heavenly Father. If they keep looking at you, that is on them — you just keep looking at your Father and keep operating in moral excellence (right standing with God, His way of doing and being right). Just make sure that the deeds you are doing are pleasing unto God, not man. It is praiseworthy for you to be obedient to God.

Back to being salted, tested, and refined with fire — it means *to purify or to kindle*. See Matthew 3:11-12, as John the Baptist spoke.

> Matthew 3:11-12 I indeed baptize you in (with) water because of repentance [that is, because of your changing your minds for the better, heartily amending your ways, with abhorrence of your past sins]. But He Who is coming after me is mightier than I, Whose sandals I am not worthy or fit to take off or carry; He will baptize you with the Holy Spirit and with fire. 12 His winnowing fan (shovel, fork) is in His hand, and He will thoroughly clear out and clean His threshing floor and gather and store His wheat in His barn, but the chaff He will burn up with fire that cannot be put out.

John baptized into repentance, which is simply changing your mind. The word "abhor" here, means *be disgusted for your past sins, so much so that you will stop repeating them* — I am talking to ME if no one else! Jesus' fire will burn up the chaff, the things that do not belong to Him — the waste and non-useful stuff. John the Baptist baptized into repentance: the washing of the water of the word. Yet when Jesus comes, not only will you have to have repentance of your old ways, and receiving Jesus for salvation (the initial repentance) — this is where we get the water, but now we need the fire — the Holy Spirit fire that burns within like in Acts 2:1 as a fulfillment of Acts 1:8. The Holy Spirit was poured out on them, I am not amplifying the tongues, but amplifying the fact that the fire of the Holy Spirit hit them and they began to operate, and that is what we need. Back to the salt, if your salt has lost its saltiness, ask God to fill you and fill you again with Fire (we will discuss this in the next section, about being filled again).

Again, the fire is to purify and to kindle — to drive you. It is not for sensationalism of saying "I spoke in tongues" — but about being endued with power. You need that power because your hand, your foot, and your eye has been conditioned to worldliness, and you need the fire of God to help you not follow the worldly hand, eye, and foot — but follow the godly, the kingdom way. And you can only do it with the fire of the Holy Spirit. Salted with fire. Luke 3:15-17 is a repeat of Matthew 3. The point is, I do not want to end up in the fire that cannot be distinguished, I do not want to be chaff. How do you move from being chaff, to being wheat? Like in the parable that Jesus told of the sower that sowed seed, and at night an enemy came and sowed weed among his seed. Jesus said do not pull the weeds out, because you might harm the wheat, but let them grow together, and at the end we will be able to tell the weeds from the real wheat — the real disciples of Christ. They look alike while they are growing, but when they mature is when we can tell the difference. The weeds stay erect, proud, and propped up. But once the wheat is mature, the weight of being real wheat, will make it bow down, humble itself So we can see if we are really the wheat, because we will be walking humble before God, bowed down, low (See Matthew 13:24-30).

Looking at how this fits into the theme scripture of Romans 12:1, we are to be living sacrifices. On www.blueletter.org, it defines "sacrifice" as a *victim*. We are to be a living victim. The sacrifice is to be laid on the fire — to be consumed by the fire. **We are being salted, tested, refined by fire as a living sacrifice — DAILY.** This is why it can seem like we are going through one thing, after another, after another — each day it is something new. Well, each day you are a new sacrifice, but do not panic, if you continue with Romans 12:2 (Renewal of the Mind!), you will not have a problem with Romans 12:1 (living sacrifice) — DAILY! If we move off of conformity to the world, over to kingdom conformity, then we will understand that the fire is there only to purify us and keep us salty, not to kill us. Well, if you are weeds, not wheat, it will kill you?! But if you are wheat, if you are truly a disciple of Jesus Christ, that fire will not kill you, but humble and purify you.

Here is a biblical example of this at the call of Matthew:

> Matthew 9:13 Go and learn what this means: I desire mercy [that is, readiness to help those in trouble] and not sacrifice and sacrificial victims. For I came not to call and invite [to repentance the righteous (those who are upright and in right standing with God), but sinners (the erring ones and all those not free from sin).

It is funny how this Matthew 9:13 sounds almost contradictory to Romans 12:1, but not if you have renewed your mind. He is basically saying that He desires that we be ready to help those in trouble, over us preparing these external sacrifices. We should sacrifice in our heart to help people in trouble; it is no longer "me & my" but you are doing what the King wants you to do. We can see the fire, and the sacrifice, and the things that are needed to do this. We have to get our minds changed, we are to be salt. We are to be salt to the world — that means that we are going to bring testing and refining to the world.

Another principle I found looking at salt one www.blueletter.org, looking at the meaning of salt, it says that *salt which food is seasoned, and sacrifices are sprinkled*. They would put the salt on the sacrifice to keep it from retarding and/or spoiling. Salt was also *used to fertilize arable land (arable means used for growing crops)*. This is better understood by a quote I found "It is your prerogative to impart to mankind (likened to arable land) the influences required for a life of devotion to God." As salt, we should be imparting to mankind that they need to have a
life of devotion to God. Are we making people thirsty for Him? Like when you eat salty foods, you need some water or something to try to wash down that saltiness, so are we making people thirsty for God, for the water of the word?

I also found that salt is *a symbol of that health and vigor of soul which is essential to Christian virtue*. By us being salt, we help invigorate the soul of others. It also said salt is *symbolic of a lasting concord because it protects food from putrefaction and preserves it unchanged*. They did not have ice and refrigerators as we do now, they would salt meat to keep it from becoming putrefied, or decaying; to preserve it and keep it from changing and going bad. We should be able to salt flesh, salt people and keep them from getting worse — we should be able to get them off of fleshly thinking, and worldly thinking long enough for them to see who Jesus is, and that He desires for them to have soul help and peace.

Another nugget about salt, is that it is wisdom and grace exhibited in speech. So let your speech be seasoned with salt, means that you should have wisdom and grace in what you are saying. This is why Proverbs tells us to set a guard before our mouth.

We will be fired (as in Mark 9), let's make sure that we choose the fire of God over the fire of the enemy. Choose the God that answers by fire; the fire of purification and sanctification — to be salted by fire. Not the fire that burns because of wavering and doubt that hurts and consumes the chaff, the things not of God. We want the fire of purification and sanctification as we will see here in Malachi 3 (which is a follow up to the salted by fire we saw in Mark 9:49-50).

This section in Malachi 3 is titled *the master you have been looking for, and the coming day of judgment*. We will all have to stand individually before the judgment seat of Christ, according to our works, and the truths we have been exposed to — how much truth you are metabolizing in your life, you will be judged on that. But this reference is a different judgment.

> Malachi 3:1-3 Behold, I send My messenger, and he shall prepare the way before Me. And the Lord [the Messiah], Whom you seek, will suddenly come to His temple; the Messenger or Angel of the covenant, Whom you desire, behold, He shall come, says the Lord of hosts. ² But who can endure the day of His coming? And who can stand when He appears? For He is **like a refiner's fire and like fullers' soap**; ³ He will sit as a refiner and purifier of silver, and He will purify the priests, the sons of Levi, and refine them like gold and silver, that they may offer to the Lord offerings in righteousness.

The Message calls it "strongest lye soap" and the NLT calls it "strong soap that bleaches clothes". What is the fire that purifies, or the soap that bleaches us clean? It is the blood of Jesus. The blood of bulls and goats could only cover sin, only Jesus' blood could take it away. As in Revelation, who is able to stand; them that have washed their garments. A purification must take place. The garment referred to here is the robe of righteousness. We need to grow in knowing who God is, and who we are in Him. As we grow in knowing about the righteousness of God, what it means to be in right standing with God, with the help of the Holy Spirit that will help us walk it out. Our thinking has to be adjusted to understand what righteousness is. Offerings in righteousness, silver and gold have I not, but such as I have I give to you — it is not about money. They understood the purification process of silver and gold. Silver was a form of payment — they understood it even more in that day.

Listen and look with the eyes and ears of your heart. God is desiring to purify us and make us pure silver and gold. Gold is symbolic of redemption — so as we get a better understanding of all that redemption includes (past, present, and future — justification, sanctification, glorification); as we better understand redemption, then our offerings in righteousness are amplified.

Be encouraged — know and understand that God is testing us, He is salting us, He is refining us as the Refiner's fire. Know that the Old Testament is Jesus Christ concealed, and the New Testament is Jesus Christ revealed — there are so many things that are quoted in the New Testament that are a revelation of fulfillment of what was said and done in the Old Testament. This Malachi 3 is talking about John the Baptist coming, the forerunner; and it is talking about Jesus Christ coming — the covenant keeper — the one that came and cut covenant in His own blood. Jesus fulfilled all of that, and at new birth, we receive the mind of Christ and are in covenant with all of that. We now need to renew our mind to the fact that we are in covenant with the Creator of heaven and earth — that we are created in the image of Him — that is who our covenant partner is.

> Mark 9:50 NLT Salt is good for seasoning. But if it loses its flavor, how do you make it salty again? You must have the qualities of salt among yourselves and live in peace with each other.

Again, the qualities of salt on www.blueletter.org are defined as *salt with which food is seasoned; those kinds of saline matter used to fertilize arable land.* When you fertilize something, you help it produce more. So when you are called to be salt, to be fertilization, you should help produce more in the soil being sown into. Even this mentorship that the Lord is calling me to do, I am putting salt from me into the people that the Lord is calling me to mentor so they should produce more fruit. Not necessarily more than what I have, but they should produce more than what they have at the time they receive the salt. When you put Miracle Grow on a plant, you are fertilizing it to help it be productive — and that is what our lives should be doing for each other. Even as it says in Jude, have pity on some, those that are wavering and doubting, salt them — meaning you help them be salty. You preserve them from the fire. Help them have qualities of salt, do not let them get stuck and caught up in wavering and doubt.

How can I be salted? As I asked the Lord, He led me to Ephesians 5:18, which is by being filled with the Holy Spirit. We will look at it in several translations:

Ephesians 5:18 AMP, MSG, NLT, CJB:

> AMP And do not get drunk with wine, for that is debauchery; but ever be filled and stimulated with the [Holy] Spirit.
>
> MSG Don't drink too much wine. That cheapens your life. Drink the Spirit of God, huge draughts of him.
>
> NLT Don't be drunk with wine, because that will ruin your life. Instead, be filled with the Holy Spirit.
>
> CJB Don't get drunk with wine, because it makes you lose control. Instead, keep on being filled with the Spirit.

As in the Complete Jewish Bible, keep on being filled — it is continual. The word "keep" and the word "being" are action words. So the way to not get caught up in debauchery is to be filled with the Holy Spirit. I went to www.blueletter.org to understand this principle of "being filled with the spirit", it means to *make full; to fill up; to cause to abound; to furnish or supply liberally; to make complete in every particular; to carry through to the end, to accomplish, carry out.* So we are to be completed with the Spirit; be stimulated with the Spirit. This definition reminds me of Philippians 4:19 AMP, when Paul said my God shall fill to the full, liberally supply all of my needs, according to His riches in glory. It is the Holy Spirit that is doing these things — He is filling us. And in your mind, the soulish realm, by you asking to be flooded (filled) with light and that God would search your heart (as in Ephesians 1:17-19, and Psalm 139:23-24), that is your being filled and flushing out all of the impurities; the refining process.

This Ephesians 5:18 says to be filled with the Spirit, so of course I looked that up on www.blueletter.org. The "Spirit" is defined as *the third person of the triune God, the Holy Spirit, coequal, coeternal with the Father and the Son.* Also, the spirit is *the vital principle by which the body is animated.* The other term here that I looked up was "wine" — it said do not be drunk with wine. So one of the metaphors that I found for wine is *the fiery wine of God's wrath* — so don't be found on the fiery side of God's wrath, because as the various translations showed, it can cause you to lose control, ruin your life, and get caught up in debauchery. We are being filled with the spirit, not just any spirit, but the Holy Spirit, the Spirit of God, the Spirit of Truth, the Spirit of Christ — that is the spirit that we need filling us. That is why I tell people that have an addiction to alcohol to look on the bottle, it says "distilled spirits" — distilled means dead! I do not want dead spirits in me. And it says spirits — plural — NOT! I only want The Holy Spirit — singular — dwelling in me.

God is opening our eyes so that we can see. If we call ourselves disciples, we should be creating disciples. We cannot be on fire for God some 17-18 years and not be creating thirst in people?! No, I am salt, I should create thirst, and then I should also go back and cause healing. Another property of salt is that it heals wounds — yes it burns first, but it makes it heal speedily. The word is a 2-edged sword, it cuts, and then we come in as salt and help bring in healing — not infection.

Here is another kingdom paradox that messed me up as an immature believer; when Jesus said that we are to eat of His flesh and drink of His blood (John 6:53), this was so not a literal thing. My carnal, un-renewed mind totally rejected this! It took me to have my mind and understanding renewed, that eating of His flesh is not cannibalism, but that He is the word of God, and we must do the word (take it in, eat it, digest it, metabolize it, and walk it out). Not just taking it in, it goes through our system and passes back out with no metabolization, and we never benefit from it. And not to over eat, over indulge and be obese on the word because we are consuming more than we are walking out.

Prayer: This promised fire is not about tongues, but about the power to be a witness. Increase our understanding of what being a witness is. That we witness to the saved, and the un-saved, those that do not look like us, but that You O God send us to. Let us not be moved by appearances, but let us be moved by Your Spirit telling us what to do, what to say, and how to be who You have called us to be. Thank You for strengthening us, for giving us fortitude, that WHEN the buffeting and the persecution comes, because of the revelation that You are revealing, we are prepared and well able to persevere. That we be able to walk in Your grace, that is more than enough, that says that even in our weakness, You make us strong because we know that the persecution comes because of the word, and because our eyes have been enlightened to the depths of Your word, we can bank on the persecution coming. But You have told us to be of good cheer, You have overcome the world. You told us that persecution was going to come, and that if we have given up anything (houses, land, children, family, anything) for You, we shall receive a hundred fold in this life, WITH PERSECUTION. So we understand that persecutions are coming. Cause us to not run from the persecution, and help us change our mind and renew our mind as to understanding the role and the purpose of persecution in our life. It is not that You are trying to kill us, but that You are trying to purge us and purify us, and get us to be who You have called us to be. And it is not just about us, but about Your people – You are allowing the fire and persecution to drive us to open our mouths and proclaim who You are. And that we would make it through these tests to be able to have a testimony, because they overcame by the blood of the Lamb and the word of their testimony – and our testimony will be according to Your word, of how we got to know Your word through the help of the blood of Jesus, that by Him dying as our sacrifice, we can now present our bodies as a living sacrifice – because He lives. That we take a "blood bath" and understand that it is only in Him that we are righteous.

Thank You for dealing with our understanding and opening our minds, opening the eyes of our heart that we can see even the more, who You are and who we

are in You. To better understand Your love, and that we begin to see how all things are working together because we love You God; and then we begin to see our purpose. That we will see that our purpose is in You, it is for You to get the glory. We will not be moved when people try to glorify us, and honor us, and magnify us – we will turn it all back over to You, like in Your word when You said for us to do these things that glory and honor be given unto You and Your name, not us. All of the glory belongs to You O God – for us knowing Your word and being better epistles in this land – we give You the glory, that You be glorified, not me or anyone else but You O God – that men glorify You, not us. That it is You that shine Your light through us, that we are the lamps that are not trying to be hidden, and the salt that is going to bring seasoning/ grace/ wisdom even the more. That people would begin to know who You are through our lives.

Thank for being able to use someone so seemingly insignificant as me. As we saw in Matthew 1, if You could use 2 harlots and an idolatrous woman in the genealogy of Your Son, You can definitely use me. So we say, have Your way. We did not always choose our paths or our past, but the one thing that we are doing, we are choosing our present and our future by saying yes to Your Son Jesus Christ. So have Your way in us, teach us to be more and more like Christ. Cause us to see the areas and the ways in our lives that are not like You and not pleasing to You; and then strengthen us through the help and the fire of Your Holy Spirit to make the needed changes. Strengthen us to cut off our spiritual hand/ foot/ eye that causes us to stumble and sin. I give You the glory for this trial You have walked me through in summer 2012, that You have shown, strengthened, and empowered me to cut off stuff that would cause me and others to stumble and sin – because as a teacher, I do not want to lead anyone astray, and I do not want a millstone around my neck. According to Your word in Luke 12, I understand that to whom much is given, much is required – so I live to the requirement that You have for me and it is to be holy, for You are holy – and You are empowering me to walk in it. I give You glory, honor, and praise, in Jesus name – AMEN!

3.6 A Closer Look at the Book of Romans

A time of preparation, like gumbo — we will look at several ingredients that He will mix together.

Prayer: Thank You for blessing me to bring others into the knowledge of Who You are. That You are the Lord God Sovereign ruler. That You are in control. That You are the Creator of the heavens and the earth, and the Creator of our spirit made in Your image and likeness. Thank You, that as You O God have given me the ingredients for the gumbo, the Holy Spirit is stirring it up and applying the water, seasonings of grace, and the needed heat.

We Your servants are here, willing, listening. Thank You for massaging us in Your word, for getting the kinks out spiritually (like a natural massage), we may be a little sore, but we choose to have the right attitude, and know that once the soreness goes away, the result will be good – this all has purpose. Open these scriptures, and our eyes that we would see an even deeper level of them. Now is the set time, kairos moment in history that You desire to open these scriptures up to us. We are here, listening. Speak God, and we will do whatever it is that You call us to do and say. All the glory belongs to You. Amen

Looking at something I came across regarding Martin Luther of the Reformation regarding the
book of Romans, and why it is so important to get an understanding of the book of Romans. He experienced an "irritation" against religion and ritualistic services, without involving the heart stirred him so that he wrote the 95 Thesis that came against the Roman Catholic Church, which caused a Reformation. Not just of the Protestant church, but reformation of people reading the word. It was through his "irritation" that he stood up against the Pope and declared that the word needs to be in the hands of every believer. Sola scriptura (scripture alone), not the Pope.

Martin Luther wrote the following regarding the book of Romans:

> "It is the true masterpiece of the New Testament, and the very purest Gospel, which is well worthy and deserving that a Christian man should not only learn it by heart, word for word, but also that he should daily deal with it as the daily bread of men's souls. For it can never be too much or too well read or studied; and the more it is handled the more precious it becomes and the better it tastes."

This quote makes me want to say "How do I add the book of Romans into my daily devotional?" This book (Renewal of the Mind!) is themed on Romans 12, but the entire book of Romans is about righteousness, and the foundational verse is Romans 1:16, which we will look at in a moment.

Another quote I found regarding the book of Romans is "Romans requires all the mental makeup we have, and then it must be bathed in prayer and supplication before the Holy Spirit can teach us." We should read it and get a mental understanding, then go on in prayer with God (which is communion with Him), and supplication (which is getting your supplies met). So read it, get acquainted with it, and know that understanding is progressive. We are giving the Holy Spirit access to come and teach us.

> Romans 1:16-17 For I am not ashamed of the Gospel (good news) of Christ, for it is God's power working unto salvation [for deliverance from eternal death] to everyone who believes with a personal trust and a confident surrender and firm reliance, to the Jew first and also to the Greek, ¹⁷ For in the Gospel a righteousness which God ascribes is revealed, both springing from faith and leading to faith

[disclosed through the way of faith that arouses to more faith]. As it is written, The man who through faith is just and upright shall live and shall live by faith.

We see the initial salvation of accepting Jesus Christ here in verse 16 — God's power working unto salvation — with a personal trust and confident surrender. Then verse 17 adds on faith to faith, so that we can see that faith should be increasing. Our faith in God increases as we live by faith and walk by faith (as the NKJV of verse 17). People may hear about Jesus Christ, and receive eternity, but they do not grow in the more faith PORTION of text here; they put their human understanding on something that is spiritual and cannot be understood like that. See how in the following section, right after talking about the just shall live by faith, then it begins to show what it looks like to not do so, and be given over to a reprobate mind; that by itself does not sound good, we are supposed to be renewing our mind, not going into reprobate?

> Romans 1:18-23 For God's [holy] wrath and indignation are revealed from heaven against all ungodliness and unrighteousness of men, who in their wickedness repress and hinder the truth and make it inoperative. 19 For that which is known about God is evident to them and made plain in their inner consciousness, because God [Himself] has shown it to them. 20 For ever since the creation of the world His invisible nature and attributes, that is, His eternal power and divinity, have been made intelligible and clearly discernible in and through the things that have been made (His handiworks). So [men] are without excuse [altogether without any defense or justification], 21 Because when they knew and recognized Him as God, they did not honor and glorify Him as God or give Him thanks. But instead they became futile and godless in their thinking [with vain imaginings, foolish reasoning, and stupid speculations] and their senseless minds were darkened. 22 Claiming to be wise, they became fools [professing to be smart, they made simpletons of themselves]. 23 And by them the glory and majesty and excellence of the immortal God were exchanged for and represented by images, resembling mortal man and birds and beasts and reptiles.

Here in verse 18-23, the truth, is the truth, is the truth — whether we believe it, receive it, or suppress it and act like it doesn't exist. This section shows what suppressing the truth looks like. In verse 20 he said it is evident, not invisible. They recognized that something was going on, but they still would not give Him the credit and glory for it; and made up their own view of what they think is going on with God. See at verse 21, they think they know more than God!

> Romans 1:24-32 Therefore God gave them up in the lusts of their [own] hearts to sexual impurity, to the dishonoring of their bodies among themselves [abandoning them to the degrading power of sin], 25 Because they exchanged the truth of God for a lie and worshiped and served the creature rather than the Creator, Who is blessed forever! Amen (so be it). 26 For this reason God gave them over and abandoned them to vile affections and degrading passions. For their women exchanged their

natural function for an unnatural and abnormal one, ²⁷ And the men also turned from natural relations with women and were set ablaze (burning out, consumed) with lust for one another—men committing shameful acts with men and suffering in their own bodies and personalities the inevitable consequences and penalty of their wrong-doing and going astray, which was [their] fitting retribution. ²⁸ And so, since they did not see fit to acknowledge God or approve of Him or consider Him worth the knowing, **God gave them over to a base and condemned mind to do things not proper or decent but loathsome,** ²⁹ Until they were filled (permeated and saturated) with every kind of unrighteousness, iniquity, grasping and covetous greed, and malice. [They were] full of envy and jealousy, murder, strife, deceit and treachery, ill will and cruel ways. [They were] secret backbiters and gossipers ³⁰ Slanderers, hateful to and hating God, full of insolence, arrogance, [and] boasting; inventors of new forms of evil, disobedient and undutiful to parents. ³¹ [They were] without understanding, conscienceless and faithless, heartless and loveless [and] merciless. ³² Though they are fully aware of God's righteous decree that those who do such things deserve to die, they not only do them themselves but approve and applaud others who practice them.

Let's take a brief sidebar and define what a reprobate mind is. On www.blueletter.org it defines "reprobate" from Romans 1:28 as *not standing the test, not approved. That which does not prove itself such as it ought.* The Amplified bible makes it even clearer by saying *God gave them over to a base and condemned mind to do things not proper or decent but loathsome.* The Merriam-Webster online dictionary defines "reprobate" as *to condemn strongly as unworthy, unacceptable, or evil; to refuse to accept; to reject.* As I am typing out these definitions, I am reminded of Jeremiah 17:9 of how off the chain the heart apart from the influence of God is — to me, this is another picture of the reprobate state of man without God (either from rejecting Him, suppressing the Truth, or never acknowledging Him).

Also notice in this section about people in this state of mind, it never says they are going to hell. God did not send the children of Israel to hell for their disobedience, they just exited this realm sooner than planned, and will have to answer to God for their willful ignorance, stupidity, and rejection. This is why we have to help people grow from faith to faith and from glory to glory. Hell is real — I do not preach hell, I preach the Truth! I turn the light on and add salt. So that in accepting truth, you miss hell through obedience to the Truth.

We took the time to read this because we will have to deal with people who are in these states of mind. Also, to see why it is so important that we take the time to read the book of Romans. In Romans is where we hear that all have sinned and fallen short of the glory of God; and the wages of sin is death; and the battle going on in chapter 7; no condemnation in Christ Jesus in chapter 8, and the theme scripture for salvation; we see the future salvation in chapter 11. This book project is themed on Romans 12, so we have to look at the entire book as well, and know what God is saying.

We have to be reading the word of God over and over again. Do not listen to the enemy telling you that you read it once; read it again — and again (Romans 10:17). Meditate on the truths; that we can grow from faith to faith and glory to glory. It is a living word, we have the Holy Spirit leading/ teaching/ guiding us, so we must be reading the word to plug into even more power.

Before we go forward, let's go back and re-read the quote about why it is so important to study the book of Romans: "Romans requires all the mental make-up we have, and then it must be bathed in prayer and supplication before the Holy Spirit can teach us."

The Message bible titles Romans 12 *Place Your Life Before God* — the whole purpose of this book is showing people how to place their lives before God.

> Romans 12:1 I appeal to you therefore, brethren, and beg of you in view of [all] the mercies of God, to make a decisive dedication of your bodies [presenting all your members and faculties] as a living sacrifice, holy (devoted, consecrated) and well pleasing to God, which is your reasonable (rational, intelligent) service and spiritual worship.

This is symbolic of the sacrificial system in the Old Testament, in the book of Leviticus. We need to get a better understanding of what a blood covenant is, and how it was offered. If we do not have that understanding, we can't extract the true meaning of Romans 12:1. We need to truly know what it means to be a living sacrifice. God will not "make" us do this, He has to follow the order of what He set in the earth: YOU are to present YOUR body as a living sacrifice — that is YOUR reasonable service not God's. God did His reasonable service in sending His Son and in empowering you with the help of the Holy Spirit to strengthen you to not listen to the flesh.

> Romans 12:2 Do not be conformed to this world (this age), [fashioned after and adapted to its external, superficial customs], but be transformed (changed) by the **[entire] renewal of your mind** [by its new ideals and its new attitude], so that you may prove [for yourselves] what is the good and acceptable and perfect will of God, even the thing which is good and acceptable and perfect [in His sight for you].

The ENTIRE — not just parts. And thank You Lord for being long-suffering and patient, because some stuff is taking a little bit longer to know, but I want my entire mind renewed. I do not want to go to heaven with any of this earthly-mindedness in me. That is probably why I am still here. There are some hard-headed and rebellious people, still running from God, yet He still reminds them that they are to be a living sacrifice. He wants us to renew our entire mind, and stop making excuses for why we can't.

"Even the thing perfect for you" — me renewing my mind does not tell me what to do for you. If you want to know for you, then you have to do the same thing. But the blessed thing about this, is that God has us here as iron sharpens iron, we are here for one another to help us go through; and to help us see what it looks like to be a living sacrifice. I can help you in the Renewal of the Mind! process, but I can NOT do it for you. Even the Apostle Paul, when he wrote this letter, he said "I beg of you, I beseech you, I appeal to you..." — he did not say, "I will do it for you" — but he told them that they had to do it, the same with us.

> Romans 12:3 For by the grace (unmerited favor of God) given to me I warn everyone among you not to estimate and think of himself more highly than he ought [not to have an exaggerated opinion of his own importance], but to rate his ability with sober judgment, each according to the degree of faith apportioned by God to him.

Do not have an exaggerated opinion of self, but be confident in what you know — keeping in mind that there is even more to know.

> Romans 12:9-10 MSG Love from the center of who you are; don't fake it. Run for dear life from evil; hold on for dear life to good. Be good friends who love deeply; practice playing second fiddle.

When you say you love someone, really love them — not this worldly love, but true love, as in 1 Corinthians 13, which is patient, kind, long-suffering, doesn't keep account of wrong, rejoices with others. Right after talking about love, he switches to talking about being childish. So when it comes to loving others, we are to love them with that kind of love — not a childish love, but a Manly love — the love of God. Not the stuff that we manufacture, not according to this world — don't fake it.

He was really helping me when it says "run from evil" — he did not say "cuss evil out" — but to hate what is evil. Turn from wickedness, do not try to get as close to the edge as you can without falling off, but turn from it, run from it.

3.7 Trailblazers

Isaiah 58 is titled *right and wrong fasting,* and *your prayers won't get off the ground.* Another translation titles this section a *full life, in the emptiest of places.* I gathered from these titles that the Lord is saying in this chapter that your prayers will not get off the ground if they are done hypocritically when fasting out of hypocrisy instead of relationship. In my studies, I found that God hadn't called them to fast, but had actually given them feast days — but they were hypocritically religious, and fasted to make a big show of it. We will see at verse 5, that this was displeasing to the Lord.

> Isaiah 58:1-6 Cry aloud, spare not. Lift up your voice like a trumpet and declare to My people their transgression and to the house of Jacob their sins! ² Yet they seek, inquire for, and require Me daily and delight [externally] to know My ways, as [if

> they were in reality] a nation that did righteousness and forsook not the ordinance of their God. They ask of Me righteous judgments, they delight to draw near to God [in visible ways]. 3 Why have we fasted, they say, and You do not see it? Why have we afflicted ourselves, and You take no knowledge [of it]? Behold [O Israel], on the day of your fast [when you should be grieving for your sins], you find profit in your business, and [instead of stopping all work, as the law implies you and your workmen should do] you extort from your hired servants a full amount of labor. 4 [The facts are that] you fast only for strife and debate and to smite with the fist of wickedness. Fasting as you do today will not cause your voice to be heard on high. 5 Is such a fast as yours what I have chosen, a day for a man to humble himself with sorrow in his soul? [Is true fasting merely mechanical?] Is it only to bow down his head like a bulrush and to spread sackcloth and ashes under him [to indicate a condition of heart that he does not have]? Will you call this a fast and an acceptable day to the Lord? 6 [Rather] is not this the fast that I have chosen: to loose the bonds of wickedness, to undo the bands of the yoke, to let the oppressed go free, and that you break every [enslaving] yoke?

They were caught up with the externals and what people could see. God was calling them out and telling them that He was not concerned with all of that, but with His people being taken care of. There are a lot of people in church (not kingdom) that are concerned about titles, numbers (of people at their church, and how much money they can get from them) – but is any one going out of there loosed from the bonds of wickedness? Or bands of yokes being destroyed? It is the anointing that destroys the yokes. Jesus was anointed to destroy the yokes of oppression and bondage, and slavery – is that who you are representing with this "show of religious fasting"?

> Isaiah 58:7 Is it not to divide your bread with the hungry and bring the homeless poor into your house – when you see the naked, that you cover him, and that you hide not yourself from [the needs of] your own flesh and blood?

This is what A Portion Ministries is all about – helping those that hunger and thirst for righteousness to be filled. This ministry is called to help feed; and to help bring the bread. Evangelism is 2-fold: it is 1) catching the fish, 2) growing/maturing the fish – the discipleship piece: that is to divide the bread, to share the Bread of heaven with those who do not know Him, and help disciple/mature those who do know Him. For those that are poor and without a house, we help them access the spiritual house of Jesus for eternity. When we see someone naked, walking around lost like I once was – never really had a covenant relationship with God, never knew who Jesus was to accept Him as a real covering (not just fire insurance). To know that Jesus gives us a robe of righteousness to cover our nakedness, when we thought those fig leaves would cover us? NOT!

At verse 7, "His own flesh and blood" reminds me of how Jesus of Nazareth could do no great works because of their unbelief in His hometown. I heard a trusted bible mentor say that the answer for unbelief is to teach the Truth, giving foundations to believe in. We still have to be there for our family and friends, we still have to cry loud and spare not.

> Isaiah 58:8-10 Then shall your light break forth like the morning, and your healing (your restoration and the power of a new life) shall spring forth speedily; your righteousness (your rightness, your justice, and your right relationship with God) shall go before you [conducting you to peace and prosperity], and the glory of the Lord shall be your rear guard. ⁹ Then you shall call, and the Lord will answer; you shall cry, and He will say, Here I am. If you take away from your midst yokes of oppression [wherever you find them], the finger pointed in scorn [toward the oppressed or the godly], and every form of false, harsh, unjust, and wicked speaking, ¹⁰ And if you pour out that with which you sustain your own life for the hungry and satisfy the need of the afflicted, then shall your light rise in darkness, and your obscurity and gloom become like the noonday.

Putting this together with the Romans 12, the world is not going to do this. They are going to get all they can, can all they get, and hide the can! They are not concerned or looking at what anybody else has. But what I have is so precious, and I understand that it is precious, and it is more than enough for me, and makes me not be selfish and only think about me. We live in a sin-sick world of people who are dying, God gives us *assignments* and we must fulfill those *assignments* — that was what A Portion Volume II was about, fulfilling *assignments* — but as you fulfill those *assignments*, then shall your light rise in darkness and you come up from obscurity as the noonday.

> Isaiah 58:11 And the Lord shall guide you continually and satisfy you in drought and in dry places and make strong your bones. And you shall be like a watered garden and like a spring of water whose waters fail not.

We will have to go against the reality of this world and do and be who God has called us to do and be.

> Isaiah 58:12 And your ancient ruins shall be rebuilt; you shall raise up the foundations of [buildings that have laid waste for] many generations; and you shall be called Repairer of the Breach, Restorer of Streets to Dwell In.

It does not only require money to raise up these foundations, but it will take character, integrity, heart, spending time, the power of God, His Spirit, His grace (unmerited favor) — this is what we need to be able to operate. And this is for the generations.

Another part of the call of God on my life is this Isaiah 58:12, repairer of the breach — the trailblazer that is restoring the streets to dwell in.

This verse 12 was a prophetic word spoken to me before I left Rhema Bible Training Center in Tulsa, OK. Keep in mind that this is initially talking of the coming Servant, Jesus Christ, but He is the Greater One that lives in me, He desires to do this — and He needs a yielded vessel to operate through. A living body that has been presented as a living sacrifice, that has not conformed to this world, but has been transformed by the renewing of the mind with the word. This verse 12 is what the Lord has called me to do — in another translation verse 12 is called "trailblazing", to go off the beaten path and to make new trails for the generations to come behind. It is setting a mark; go in the way no one goes, but making trails for others to follow.

Trailblazers don't wait to see what others will do, and do not need accolades of others — only the clear instructions from God to press forward making a narrow path for others to follow. Trailblazers are leaders that don't mind laying the ground work for others (for many generations) — and are not selfish or self-minded — but their goal is to be a conduit for the Repairer of the Breach and for the Restorer to operate through.

> Isaiah 58:13-14 If you turn away your foot from [traveling unduly on] the Sabbath, from doing your own pleasure on My holy day, and call the Sabbath a [spiritual] delight, the holy day of the Lord honorable, and honor Him and it, not going your own way or seeking or finding your own pleasure or speaking with your own [idle] words, 14 Then will you delight yourself in the Lord, and I will make you to ride on the high places of the earth, and I will feed you with the heritage [promised for you] of Jacob your father; for the mouth of the Lord has spoken it.

Here is another instance of "IF" being a major role in the outcome. A lot of people read the first few things and think this does not apply to us (talking about Sabbath and Holy Day, etc.), but we must keep reading, and see that the "IF" also applied to honoring Him by not going our own way and speaking idleness. The "IF" promise is answered in verse 14 with "THEN" — the THEN promises of verse 14 are contingent on fulfilling the IF pre-requisites of verse 13. God is a promise keeper, yet we must be also. It is as we honor Him, also as we learn of His Sabbath and His holy day — learn what it means and how it applies to us today, that we get a better understanding of delighting ourselves in the Lord, and receive the ability to ride on the high places of the earth — God gets all of the glory.

This section has been true gumbo. We will put it under the fire of God. As with Paul, and the thorn given because of the many revelations; just know that fire and persecution are going to come, and when it comes, it will cook the gumbo. It will be delicious — O Taste And See that the Lord is good.

Prayer: Thank You for this time of preparation. You have given us the ingredients, we have prepped the food and put it all together, and You provide Your fire. You are the God that answers by fire. But when Your fire comes, it does not consume the sacrifice that is of You. But whatever is fleshly and worldly will be consumed. But the kingdom will remain, it will be like the burning bush, on fire, but not consumed. It is consumed with fire, but is not damaged. You are doing what You need to do: season us, salt us, turn the light on, massage us and get the kinks out spiritually. You are showing us how to

present our bodies and to renew our mind according to Your word O God, not according to tradition and religion. Yes, we do need some of that, because You are a God of order in the earth realm, but we do not let worldly order outweigh kingdom order. You are calling us to see the significance of the book of Romans, as we hunger and thirst after You, You show us the nuggets You have for us here. Continue to transform us and show us how to be here for a sin-sick world – how to help.

As in Romans 1, the list of things that happened after the reprobate mind is the same list in Galatians 5 (works of the flesh), and 2 Timothy 3 (perilous times) – so You are telling us over and over in the word of God that these things will be so, and how to escape them – by first seeking the kingdom. And as we are growing in knowing who we are in Your kingdom, not just for us, but to benefit Your kingdom. I want to be the best ambassador You have placed within me, not better than anyone else, they are not my standard, Jesus is, so thank You for showing me more and more how to be like Him.

Thank You for allowing us to truly understand what it means to be trailblazers – thank You for calling people to go down the trails that I am blazing for You. I am just a yielded servant, and You are showing me how to wield the sword of the word of Truth that chops down the obstacles in our way. Thank You for showing us what it truly means to hunger and thirst after righteousness, to be a man after Your own heart (male and female man) that we are seeking Your heart, that we are seeking the water of God. Thank You that we are recognizing and acknowledging the thirst – that we are painfully aware that there are things that we need in Your word, in the constitution of our kingdom that will refresh, support, and strengthen our souls for You O God. That You desire for us to be those trees that are planted by the rivers of living waters, to be those trees whose leaves bring healing to the nations. We are doing what we must do. We are purging, cleansing, transforming, renewing our mind – moving from worldly conformity to kingdom conformity. Thank You that Your will and Your purpose be done.

I do not want to fulfill a project, but what You have called me to be. If it never becomes a book, just that it helped transform us in the process. Strengthen us because of the many revelations that will be accompanied by the many persecutions – because we are good ground, we are not worried about the persecution because the seed is already in the broken up ground of our heart – so the bird cannot steal it. Thank You for showing us how to pull down the strongholds of the enemy that thinks he can live in our house. No! Evicted! He cannot, and will not live in us – we are a people where You O God live in us, we are Your dwelling place. Amen.

Prayer: Thank You for teaching us and training us – giving us spiritual eyes to see and spiritual ears to hear. Thank You for causing us to recognize the refiner's fire, that it is evident in our lives. That You are causing us to understand purification and sanctification even more. Thank You for removing the impurities and the falsities out of us, so that when the elements of this world get on us, we remain pure before You. We do not try to work our works of righteousness, but we walk in the imputed righteousness of Jesus Christ – all we do is renew our mind to better understand and to better walk with the robe of righteousness covering us. Thank You for showing us what it means to always be being filled (it is continual), we do not want the wine of wrath and of worldliness, which causes Your wrath – which is rejecting Your way of doing and being right. We choose to not live like that, which can cause us to live loose and ruin our lives.

But as we take the time to seek after You, growing in knowing who You are, choosing to take our mind off of worldly thinking – as we do these things, You O God pour what is needed in the sanctification process. You are working the qualities of salt within us – to be preservation, to be seasoning. That You are equipping us to walk in the word of Jude, we can be there for our brothers, be there to have mercy on those that waver and doubt – that we can cause love to cover a multitude of sin. You have us in a process and are expanding us to know better what it means to be salted, tested, and purified by You O God.

Judgment is coming, but our hope is in You because we have put on our robes of righteousness. You are teaching us to judge ourselves by conforming to the kingdom, by transforming our minds with the kingdom constitution. And because You are sending the many revelations, we do not think it strange concerning the fiery trials that have come because of the revelation because of the word that You have sown into our hearts, and we have received. Thank You that in the midst of the revelation, Your grace is amplified, Your grace that is sufficient for any and all things – that it is being made evident. That we are walking in grace, not perverting it; persecution is coming because of the abundance of revelation and Your word being advanced and exposed in our lives. Continue to give us grace and mercy, and as You give it to us, we are the examples and the containers for Your grace and mercy for Your people that are living here in the earth realm. Be glorified Lord. Amen. So be it – pause and calmly think on that! Amen.

3.8 Soul Ties

Renewal, is it a soul tie, or a wound in the soul that needs to be healed? Because scripture does not say soul ties, but it does show us areas to where people were hurt so bad, sorrowful of heart, in need of being healed in that area. Is it a soul tie that needs to be cut, or is it a wound that needs to be healed? Is it that our soul is tied to someone else's soul? I really do not think that is what it is, but that our soul is so wounded, bruised, and jacked up from the situations in the past. Not that you have to deal with that person again, or the situation, but to deal with the wounded-ness in your soul between you and the Creator of your soul — the Lover of your soul that wants to renew your soul with kingdom instead of the hurt. This is why we cannot have our eyes on who or what hurt us, but on Him to be in the perfect peace that He promised. Which is where? In the soulish realm. If you do not believe me, see Philippians 4:7 and Isaiah 26.3.

> Philippians 4:7 And God's peace [shall be yours, that tranquil state of a soul assured of its salvation through Christ, and so fearing nothing from God and being content with its earthly lot of whatever sort that is, that peace] which transcends all understanding shall garrison and mount guard over your hearts and minds in Christ Jesus.

> Isaiah 26:3 You will guard him and keep him in perfect and constant peace whose mind [both its inclination and its character] is stayed on You, because he commits himself to You, leans on You, and hopes confidently in You.

It is not about tied and untied, but healed and unhealed soulish realm to keep you out of bondage. So if you have some areas in your soul that are not healed, then you are in bondage in those areas. If every time you think about that thing, it makes you sick to your stomach? That means you need to be healed. If there is something in your thought life that is causing you to have bondage, it is not necessarily a soul tie to a person, but it is a wound in your soul from a situation or circumstance that needs to be healed. You will get to know God as Jehovah Rapha, the Lord God that healeth thee (Exodus 15:26). Lord heal me in my soul, heal me in my inner man, because when my inner man is hurt, I am stuck!

You do not need to go back to the originator of the soul tie (or wound), but the Originator of your soul! To renew and heal back to the way it was designed. To heal your soul and make it new all over again the way He created it. He doesn't patch the messed up stuff, but brings a newness that comes only from Him.

The issues that you overcome are an indication of the anointing that you are designed to walk in, because the devil no longer has anything in common with you so you can walk in the full authority and dominion to cast him out. You can then walk in the anointing, for it is the anointing that destroys the yoke — the anointing can heal the wound in that person, and can be used to destroy the yoke — the active dark power in the lives of people, and the unhealthy cycles/behaviors in our life. The active dark power has access because of the wound in the soul. Jesus Himself said in John 14:30 *"the god of this world comes and when he comes he finds nothing in common in Me."* The god of this world can't be in the spirit of God/Jesus, the test was in the soulish realm — Jesus was a man, and was tempted on every point just like us, but He did not sin. So in order for Him to be tempted like us, it was the soulish realm that was tested and tempted; Jesus was saying there is nothing in common with Me and him (the god of this world).

We have to renew our mind, that life situations/ circumstances/ trials and tribulations/ events and everything that we go through, cannot leave deposits of wounds in our soul.

When we get this understanding, it increases our ability to be conduits for the yoke destroying anointing that wants to operate through our lives.

Personally, I see a wound in my soul area that is causing me to "perceive" rejection and neglect. I need that wounded area healed so that I can walk in full authority and dominion in this area.

Sometimes you have to put yourself in remembrance. So when you are going through hellish situations, you better get in your word! Go back over the word God has already given you. Sometimes He will give you new stuff, but a lot of times, the answer is already revealed to you, you just need to meditate, chew on it to receive ALL the nutrients provided. Fresh revelation.

As a teacher of the word, I still go through attacks. Like my daughter told me once she had children of her own "Momma, you made it look easy raising children, working, and going to school. But it is NOT EASY!" So true, and we do the same in the word, people see from the outside looking in and think teachers have arrived and do not have any struggles. That is not true! We have struggles, and are held to a higher standard, so we better struggle according to the spirit, not the flesh — and the mind has to be renewed to make it through. Just being transparent. Back to my daughter, now that she is a mother herself, she sees how difficult it was, but now she has to walk it out. The same spiritually, we have made living the Christian life look easy, but we have to walk by faith, and so do those that we are training and teaching. Increase our faith in God, our trust in God, by renewing our mind constantly — Renewal of the Mind! God loves us, and whom He loves He chastens and disciplines — He will give us what we need and when we need it if we will just cry out to Him. The plan of the enemy is to keep us from crying out.

This manuscript has been tested in the laboratory of life. I could not write this without going through the attacks. Like Moses, the enemy would not take a "let my people go," it took 10 plagues to accomplish that, and even God had to intervene there — not by power nor by might. So the same with this project, the enemy is not happy about Renewal of the Mind! tactics being released to the body of Christ, so I have been fought every step along the way, but like Moses and Joshua, I will be found doing what the Lord has called and equipped me to do. It is His doing, not mine, it is called grace.

Understand that it takes the grace of God to truly help us repent. The initial repentance comes from accepting Jesus Christ as savior; this is being born again into the family of God. Regarding the "once saved, always saved" argument and being truly born again — that people can be saved, then sin and go to hell. I disagree with this argument because my daughter is my daughter, whether she sins or not — her sinning does not stop her from being my daughter — it hinders fellowship, but it does not negate relationship. The fact that I am her parent does not change because she misbehaves — it may end her natural life faster, and may keep us from having fellowship here on earth, but it does not stop the fact that she is my child. The same thing with God, we are His children, He is our God. And whom He loves, He chastens — He must really love me, because I'm always being chastened. Also, the parable of the lost son in Luke 15, the father was always the father, yet fellowship with his way-ward son was dead — only restored after his son "came to himself" and repented, and restored fellowship.

Prayer: Thank You for the many revelations that You are pouring our way. Along with the revelation, You are pouring in grace. Grace that strengthens and encourages us and lets us see that there is purpose in the madness. Help us to be a people that consistently live repentant lives, that as we see the truth of God, that we agree with the truth and fall out of agreement with the falsities that we have been exposed to. Give us boldness in this time of study, that we have boldness in You.

Strengthen us for the heightened warfare that we will go through because of the word. Trials and tribulations come because of the word. Persecution comes because of the word. The word was sown, prove us to be good ground that produces some kingdom-fold return. Through each and every trial, God deal with any stony-ness, any hardness in our hearts, any thorny places that would keep the word from getting into the good ground. Continue to search our hearts in the soulish realm and show us any wounds that You desire to work on and heal. Therefore when the enemy comes, he finds no wound in our soul and we are empowered with dominion and authority to cast out the forces of darkness that are choosing to rise up on the scene. Lord it is all about You getting glory and being glorified.

Thank You for Your empowering grace that allows us to truly repent of soulish issues that aim to keep an opening for the enemy to continue to create dead situations in our thinking. Like the prodigal son, allow us to come to ourselves when we see that we have moved out of the place of fellowship with You to walk in our own ways. Restore O Lord. Amen.

Chapter 4 – Kingdom Mindsets

4.1 Pride

Wheat grows with weed — the wheat will humble themselves as they mature. The false will be lifted in pride and not bow down, and will be cut down; it is about humility verses pride.

> Romans 12:3 For by the grace (unmerited favor of God) given to me I warn everyone among you not to estimate and think of himself more highly than he ought [not to have an exaggerated opinion of his own importance], but to rate his ability with sober judgment, each according to the degree of faith apportioned by God to him.

Verse 3 is all about humility verses pride. We must remain humble before the Lord. Allow Him to correct us, and instruct us. Some people are even prideful with the fact that they have renewed their mind; they have an attitude as if it were them — when really it was done with the help of the Holy Spirit as we heard about the need. Our *assignment* is to help others do the same, not lord it over them that you do not think like that anymore. As a matter of fact, when we see people thinking like we used to think, like in Jude, we should:

> Jude 1:20-22 But you, beloved, build yourselves up [founded] on your most holy faith make progress, rise like an edifice higher and higher], praying in the Holy Spirit; 21 Guard and keep yourselves in the love of God; expect and patiently wait for the mercy of our Lord Jesus Christ (the Messiah) — [which will bring you] unto life eternal. 22 And refute [so as to] convict some who dispute with you, and on some have mercy who waver and doubt.

Have mercy, some will waver and doubt. Do not judge them, you do not have a hell to put them in, and you cannot get them in heaven, you need to have mercy on them. Verse 23 goes on to show us how to have and show this mercy.

> Jude 1:23 [Strive to] save others, snatching [them] out of [the] fire; on others take pity [but] with fear, loathing even the garment spotted by the flesh and polluted by their sensuality.

Prayer: Thank You for causing Your people to really think about what we are thinking about. That You are causing us to powerfully and effectively change and renew our mind according to Your word. Thank You that we are dual citizens and You are helping us to see what it means to be a simultaneous

citizen of the kingdom of heaven and the kingdom of earth. Thank You God that You are increasing our understanding and knowledge. Increase us by giving us revelation, illumination, knowledge, insight, wisdom into Your kingdom, into the ways of doing and being right – and to righteousness – into all that You would have us to see. As we go forward into this section, allow us to get a healthy understanding of the word pride in our minds and know how to operate with it – to eradicate worldly thinking about pridefulness, and replace it with Your mindset of what true pride is. Our pride/ trust/ hope/ confidence are all in You, not in self or our own abilities or in the arm of man, but in You. Amen.

❧

Before we can properly talk about pride, we have to talk about where it entered. We see pride entering in Genesis 3, when satan prompted the woman to respond in pride. The initial temptation is rooted and grounded in pride. But before we can even look at this, we have to see how satan (the enemy) arrived in the garden?

We must renew our mind, and be attached to sound biblical teachers that will teach us all of the word of God. We must understand the canon of scripture, the 66 books of the bible that the Holy Spirit allowed to be here to tell the story of redemption. But we must also know that the bible is not arranged chronologically; we would think that it starts at Genesis 1, then 2, then 3 — but there is a detour in the books of prophesy (in Isaiah and Ezekiel) where it shows us where lucifer was cast out of heaven. We are about to go on a quick history lesson. You also have the Holy Spirit that will bear witness with your soul.

We are to come unto Jesus and learn of Him to experience Rest, as in Matthew 11:28 — we are learning more of Him and where the authority was given over from Adam to the ruler of this world through deception, disobedience, and sin. Jesus is the last Adam that came to restore our lost authority.

Here is a true cinematic moment in Ezekiel 28:13-19 and in Isaiah 14:11-17, where the prophet goes back and tells of the fall of satan. Where he was the angel of worship — this is why the enemy does not want us to praise and worship, because he once did that — God did not create us because He was lonely, but He created us to worship Him.

> Ezekiel 28:11-19 Moreover, the word of the Lord came to me, saying, ¹² Son of man, take up a lamentation over the king of Tyre and say to him, Thus says the Lord God: You are the full measure and pattern of exactness [giving the finishing touch to all that constitutes completeness], full of wisdom and perfect in beauty. ¹³ You were in Eden, the garden of God; every precious stone was your covering, the carnelian, topaz, jasper, chrysolite, beryl, onyx, sapphire, carbuncle, and emerald; and your settings and your sockets and engravings were wrought in gold. On the day that you were created they were prepared. ¹⁴ You were the **anointed cherub** that covers

with overshadowing [wings], and I set you so. You were upon the holy mountain of God; you walked up and down in the midst of the stones of fire [like the paved work of gleaming sapphire stone upon which the God of Israel walked on Mount Sinai]. ¹⁵ You were blameless in your ways from the day you were created until **iniquity and guilt** were found in you. ¹⁶ Through the abundance of your commerce you were filled with lawlessness and violence, and you sinned; therefore I cast you out as a profane thing from the mountain of God and the guardian cherub drove you out from the midst of the stones of fire. ¹⁷ Your heart was proud and lifted up because of your beauty; you corrupted your wisdom for the sake of your splendor. I cast you to the ground; I lay you before kings, that they might gaze at you. ¹⁸ You have profaned your sanctuaries by the multitude of your iniquities and the enormity of your guilt, by the unrighteousness of your trade. Therefore I have brought forth a fire from your midst; it has consumed you, and I have reduced you to ashes upon the earth in the sight of all who looked at you. ¹⁹ All who know you among the people are astonished and appalled at you; you have come to a horrible end and shall never return to being.

Isaiah 14:11-17 Your pomp and magnificence are brought down to Sheol (the underworld), along with the sound of your harps; the maggots [which prey upon dead bodies] are spread out under you and worms cover you [O Babylonian rulers]. ¹² **How have you fallen from heaven, O light-bringer** and daystar, son of the morning! How you have been cut down to the ground, you who weakened and laid low the nations [O blasphemous, satanic king of Babylon!] ¹³ And you said in your heart, I will ascend to heaven; I will exalt my throne above the stars of God; I will sit upon the mount of assembly in the uttermost north. ¹⁴ I will ascend above the heights of the clouds; I will make myself like the Most High. ¹⁵ Yet you shall be brought down to Sheol (Hades), to the innermost recesses of the pit (the region of the dead). ¹⁶ Those who see you will gaze at you and consider you, saying, Is this the man who made the earth tremble, who shook kingdoms? ¹⁷ Who made the world like a wilderness and overthrew its cities, who would not permit his prisoners to return home?

We are exposing the root of pride — now bringing this back into the Romans 12 Renewal of the Mind! and the pride piece — we have to make sure that we eradicate worldly pride from our vocabulary. It must be uprooted, we cannot deal with pride from a worldly viewpoint.

Looking at a few scriptures to illustrate worldly pride:

Job 33:15-17 [One may hear God's voice] in a dream, in a vision of the night, when deep sleep falls on men while slumbering upon the bed, ¹⁶ Then He opens the ears of men and seals their instruction [terrifying them with warnings], ¹⁷ That He may withdraw man from his purpose and cut off pride from him [disgusting him with his own disappointing self-sufficiency].

From this Job 33 reference, I see that God reveals His will, yet we do not listen half the time. So He does as with verse 15, He approaches in a dream, in a vision, to open the ears of men — this explains God waking us up at the 3am times, He is trying to get us to see as in verse 17 to cut off our pride — as the Amplified says "to disgust us with our own disappointing self-sufficiency". There should be no pride in self, in me, in man — but only in God.

> Proverbs 11:2 When swelling and pride come, then emptiness and shame come also, but with the humble (those who are lowly, who have been pruned or chiseled by trial, and renounce self) are skillful and godly Wisdom and soundness.

No swelling, or as I say in reference to Romans 12:3, don't get the "big head". The opposite of pride is humility — and we can see here that my pride is in Him which makes me lowly because I have been pruned and chiseled so I now renounce self. I have learned how to be self-less in His righteousness. It is as we truly grasp this principle of humility (not having worldly pride), that the wisdom and soundness operate in our life.

> Proverbs 21:24 The proud and haughty man—Scoffer is his name—deals and acts with overbearing pride.

> Proverbs 29:23 A man's pride will bring him low, but he who is of a humble spirit will obtain honor.

Our pride is in God, and that will make us humble. Either way it goes, we will get low. Either we will humble ourselves, prostate ourselves in the presence of God — get low. Or we will get lifted up in pride and get knocked down — get low. I would rather just humble myself and not get knocked down.

> Matthew 23:12 Whoever exalts himself [with haughtiness and empty pride] shall be humbled (brought low), and whoever humbles himself [whoever has a modest opinion of himself and behaves accordingly] shall be raised to honor.

This goes back to James, let's look at it:

> James 4:6-8 But He gives us more and more grace (power of the Holy Spirit, to meet this evil tendency and all others fully). That is why He says, God sets Himself against the proud and haughty, but gives grace [continually] to the lowly (those who are humble enough to receive it). 7 So be subject to God. Resist the devil [stand firm against him], and he will flee from you. 8 Come close to God and He will come close to you. [Recognize that you are] sinners, get your soiled hands clean; [realize that you have been disloyal] wavering individuals with divided interests, and purify your hearts [of your spiritual adultery.

We must do verse 6 thoroughly to be able to do verse 7. We MUST not operate proud or haughty, or have our pride in anything else but God. The devil has fooled many people to think that their pride is in God, when really it is not – since we are not humble before God, we are resisting the devil, but he is not fleeing, but riding our back. It is as we are thoroughly humbled and submitted to God that we can resist the devil. NOTE it says resist the devil, not talk to him, or rebuke him, or cast him out – but resist him through the grace and power gained through being submitted unto God. This is another component in the Renewal of the Mind! process of how to defeat the works of the enemy in our lives.

I found a definition of pride in Mark 7:22 that says *pride (the sin of an uplifted heart against God and man)*. This comes from the section where Jesus was teaching and talking about what defiles a man in Mark 7:19-23. Jesus identifies these as originating in the thought life – the stuff that must be renewed with the help of the Holy Spirit and our efforts of renewal.

The help of the Holy Spirit – He is our "Helper", not our "Do-er" – He will help us renew our mind, but we must put effort to it. This entire manuscript is a tool to help us be DO-ers of the word, not hearers only. We must be doing what He has instructed us to do, for the Holy Spirit to Help us with.

> 1 Corinthians 15:30-31 [For that matter], why do I live [dangerously as I do, running such risks that I am] in peril every hour? ³¹ [I assure you] by the pride which I have in you in [your fellowship and union with] Christ Jesus our Lord, that I die daily [I face death every day and die to self.

How many of us can say this? Paul was saying that his pride was in the people's fellowship with Christ – not in flesh. As a mentor and teacher, I want to be able to have the pride in the mentees that they are fellowshipping with Christ Jesus. That they spend time on their own, not just when we get together, but they take what we share together and commune with Christ directly, and share the additional revelation of what they discover on their own.

> Philippians 3:3 For we [Christians] are the true circumcision, who worship God in spirit and by the Spirit of God and exult and glory and pride ourselves in Jesus Christ, and put no confidence or dependence [on what we are] in the flesh and on outward privileges and physical advantages and external appearances –

No confidence, or pride, in the flesh, but in Jesus Christ! Not in the church, religion, tradition, not regulations, not in following rules or coming every Sunday and Wednesday – but our pride is in Jesus Christ. This Philippians 3:3 is good healthy godly pride. This is also part of why I minister as Paulette Denise with no last name, because the Lord told me, that flesh and blood had nothing to do with the anointing that is in my life – it is all for His glory.

Another definition of pride is found here in this section on the qualifications of leaders:

> 1 Timothy 3:6 He must not be a new convert, or he may [develop a beclouded and stupid state of mind] as the result of pride [be blinded by conceit, and] fall into the condemnation that the devil [once] did.

This verse has a footnote to see Isaiah 14. So it is imperative that new converts truly learn about the kingdom, and not be thrust into leadership too fast to keep them from being blinded by deceit or falling into condemnation — as the devil will try to have them get inflated/ swelling/ the big head/ thinking of themselves more highly than they ought. Which 1 Timothy 6:4 says *"He is puffed up with pride and stupefied with conceit, [although he is] woefully ignorant"* — stupefied — that is an actual word! But yes, any pride other than godly pride opens the door for deceit; welcomes it in. So we must only have confidence in God, through Jesus Christ.

> 1 Peter 5:5-10 Likewise, you who are younger and of lesser rank, be subject to the elders (the ministers and spiritual guides of the church)—[giving them due respect and yielding to their counsel]. Clothe (apron) yourselves, all of you, with humility [as the garb of a servant, so that its covering cannot possibly be stripped from you, with freedom from pride and arrogance] toward one another. For God sets Himself against the proud (the insolent, the overbearing, the disdainful, the presumptuous, the boastful)—[and He opposes, frustrates, and defeats them], but gives grace (favor, blessing) to the humble. ⁶ Therefore humble yourselves [demote, lower yourselves in your own estimation] under the mighty hand of God, that in due time He may exalt you, ⁷ Casting the whole of your care [all your anxieties, all your worries, all your concerns, once and for all] on Him, for He cares for you affectionately and cares about you watchfully. ⁸ Be well balanced (temperate, sober of mind), be vigilant and cautious at all times; for that enemy of yours, the devil, roams around like a lion roaring [in fierce hunger], seeking someone to seize upon and devour. ⁹ Withstand him; be firm in faith [against his onset—rooted, established, strong, immovable, and determined], knowing that the same (identical) sufferings are appointed to your brotherhood (the whole body of Christians) throughout the world. ¹⁰ And after you have suffered a little while, the God of all grace [Who imparts all blessing and favor], Who has called you to His [own] eternal glory in Christ Jesus, will Himself complete and make you what you ought to be, establish and ground you securely, and strengthen, and settle you.

Again, the opposite of pride is humility. So we should check ourselves daily to make sure that we are operating in humility. Also, this text is similar to the earlier text in James, and shows the connection between being humble to God (under His hand), to be exalted in His due season — but even more than the exaltation part, being humble will equip us to be able to live worry free because we are able to cast all of our cares/ concerns/ worries/ anxieties on God with the confidence (godly pride) that He cares for us and is able to take care of them all; and empower us even further with the ability to be sober of mind because our pride is in Him, we have dropped off the things that try to coax us into worldly pride, therefore we see the plan of the enemy in verse 8 being LIKE A LION, not a lion, but LIKE a lion, that we are able to withstand because we are firm in the faith in Jesus Christ — our pride is in Him, so we defeat the enemy at his tricks/ schemes/ wiles/ plans/ strategies because we have the godly strategy of humility.

> 1 John 2:16 For all that is in the world — the lust of the flesh [craving for sensual gratification] and the lust of the eyes [greedy longings of the mind] and the pride of life [assurance in one's own resources-or-in-the-stability of earthly things] — these do not come from the Father but are from the world [itself].

We renew our mind to not think like the world as identified here in this text. The pride of life puts our confidence in stuff (or self), which can be here today, and gone tomorrow.

Prayer: Thank You for causing us to be a people that do not operate in the pride of this world, but to be a pride-less people. We hold no pride in self, no pride in flesh (the arm of man). But our hope, our trust, our confidence, our assurance is in You. We better understand the pride that comes from being in Jesus Christ – that it has nothing to do with the earthly realm. Thank You for A Portion Ministries, that You have called for such a time as this.

We will rise up and seek You, and hear from You; then You allow us to chronicle what it is that You are saying. Thank You for feeding Your people and for loving Your people so much – and for those that You have hidden in places, but they are yet studying/ meditating/ eating and metabolizing Your word – thank You for the remnant that is yet seeking after You and studying – for You to get the glory.

Thank You for the plans and purposes that You have for Your people. Thank You for showing us that we must eradicate pride out of our lives, and we must truly be resting in You God. Thank You that in the promised sifting process, You are just allowing us to kill self more and more. And that we are presenting our bodies as living sacrifices, we are killing our ability to think worldly thoughts, but to think highly of You – to think on those things above, whatever is good and pure and lovely. Amen.

Prayer: Thank You for the right mind, the sound mind that desires to seek You and be renewed by You. Thank You for calling us for such a time as this for the Renewal of the Mind! project. We know that there is true warfare attached with renewing our mind – so thank You for continually and consistently teaching our hands to war, and to use the weapons of our warfare which are not carnal, but they are mighty through You O God, that pulls down strongholds, imaginations and high things that try and exalt themselves against

You O God. We thank You for helping us renew our mind, to not be conformed to the world, or try to squeeze into the world's way of thinking – but to be transformed to be who You have created us to be. Thank You for renewing us back to Eden thinking – that we think like in the Garden of Eden.

Thank You that as we study, You will give clarity, revelation, illumination, insight, wisdom as to what it means to truly be a kingdom citizen with a renewed mind. Operating as a dual citizen – as an ambassador of the kingdom of heaven, living away from home in this place called earth. We are decreeing and declaring seeing eyes and hearing ears as we go forward. Speak Lord speak, Your servants are listening. Lead Lord lead, and we will follow. Guide/ instruct/ correct/ rebuke/ reproof/ chasten/ discipline – we welcome it all. Thank You for wisdom rising up in us, that You give us ways in which to handle life situations and circumstances/ people/ and things that arise – Your wisdom arises. Just like with Abigail, there was a time she could've approached Nabal when he was drunk and told him what was going on, but she used wisdom and Your timing – so thank You for showing us Your kairos, Your timing for things – Your set time – Your appointed time for things to come to past. Thank You that gifts within are not dormant, but being sharpened and strengthened in the wait process. Amen.

<u>4.2 Memories</u>

The mind is the soulish realm; where the mind, will, emotions, intellect, reasoning, imaginations, memories, thoughts, conscience, etc. are — we will take a closer look at memories in this section. The Merriam-Webster online dictionary defines "memory" as *the power or process of reproducing or recalling what has been learned and retained especially through associative mechanisms.*

We need to learn of Him, as in Matthew 11:28-30, and Paul also said several times in the epistles "I have learned" — so we need to recall what we have learned. We have learned some things according to the flesh and according to the world, but we have to learn it according to the kingdom. Learn to be patient in suffering and trials, because the world does not think like that. The world will tell you to give someone a piece of your mind; and if they do you, then you need to do them; these are the ways of the world, not of the kingdom. God is dealing with our memory bank, that we recall the lessons learned in Him (with the help of the Holy Spirit).

"Memory" is also defined as *a device (as a chip) or a component of a device in which information especially for a computer can be inserted and stored and from which it may be extracted when wanted.* Understand that our mind is similar to a computer, and has to be programmed and have the right things according to the kingdom — deprogram bad thinking (bugs that will cause your system to crash), and get programmed according to the word of God with what God says. As in Isaiah 55 which says His thoughts are not our thoughts and His ways are not our ways, they are higher and greater than ours. And in Ephesians 3:20, He can do exceedingly abundantly above all that we can ask or think. So it is something about getting our memories plugged into His, so that we can be expanded and do what we are supposed to be doing.

Some synonyms for memory are mind; recollection, remembrance; reminiscence; total recall; contemplation; meditation; musing; reflection; awareness; consciousness; apprehension; comprehension; perception. All of these have to be renewed according to the word of God — we cannot let stuff stay in our memory, in our remembrance — we cannot reminiscence on stuff that is not scripturally or biblically sound.

Even looking a step further at some antonyms (the opposite) of memory, and making sure that we do not have these operating when it comes to principles of the kingdom: *amnesia; repression; forgetfulness.* The enemy wants us to operate with spiritual amnesia, that we do not think properly, that we access the wrong thoughts and memories as we are going through trials — when all we have to remember is that God is a deliverer, and that He has delivered me out of so many things, and will deliver me out of whatever it is I face — this is not the time to get spiritual amnesia!

At the time of this note, I had been teaching the Firm Foundation new believer and new partner discipleship class at my church for over 5 years; I did not mind re-teaching the same curriculum because God would change me each and every time. I would find new truths in the existing texts over and over again — it also depended on the students sitting before me, their hunger level, their existing levels of understanding.

But in October 2010, I was teaching the prayer class, and when discussing the 5 levels of communication, the Holy Spirit had me tell of a healing process that I was going through with our pastor. It wasn't that Pastor Lorenzo had done anything wrong, but that I had some areas in me that needed to be healed by the power of God.

Going back a little further, I had sensed God dealing with me to heal the broken father syndrome (I will discuss this further), and Pastor refers to himself as my spiritual father, but every time he would say it, it would vex me. God showed me that it was a past gaping wound that had to be healed before I could go forward. I would read the word and pray, asking God to reveal the issue to me; but He never did. He would just give me the next set of instructions, and I would have to follow them. It is no coincident that the book project I was working on at that time was titled "Christians on *assignment* — talking about obedience." So I was obedient to the spirit of the Lord and scheduled a counseling meeting with my pastor.

What was discovered was that I had a deep soul wound, that the root went so far back, and only God could heal it. This was discovered because in the teaching of the 5 levels of communication in the Firm Foundation discipleship class, the lowest level is clichés, yet the highest level is complete honesty. Pastor asked me if I trust him. My first response was "yes", but then I changed it to "no with an explanation". Yes, I trust him as my pastor, I trust the anointing of God that he operates with, I trust him to live with character and integrity because that is what he always taught us, and that is what the anointing had revealed to me. But I did not trust him as a father figure, or personally as a man – and it had nothing to do with anything that he had done to me, but we both realized that this wound was deep and would require either God or counseling to deal with. Honestly, I was hurt, but also spiritual hunger and thirst heightened and sent me deeper into God for healing of my soul. I had received the title of the 3rd book already (Renewal of The Mind!), and knew that I was in for a journey with God to be qualified to write this time again, like the last 2 volumes required.

Then, to show the orchestrating hand of God in it all, the mentorship program that I was a part of would be beginning a soul healing class the first week of January. That first class helped me see the entry point of the wound. Then at a retreat I attended that January, the Lord showed Himself even clearer, and gave me individual specifics.

But before I begin to share the scripture that the Lord showed me to lead me along the paths of Renewal of the Mind!, I have to go back and address what I once called the "broken father syndrome". I had a session with my counselor, she is a spirit filled certified marriage and family counselor that I saw in previous years, but it had been about 2 years sense my last visit. I went to see her about this "broken father syndrome" – but as I told her this, she told me that was the problem. To quote her, she said "stop referring to it as broken father syndrome. Because when you name it that, and refer to it as that, then that is what you will have. It is not that your pastor is not doing something, he doesn't even know you feel this way or what you are going through...know that he has a lot on his plate, and you have a lot on your plate, and you can't expect him to know all of that. If you stop looking at it like that, as broken, then the hurt will not be that deep." So simple, yet so profound, and changed my focus. So her advice was "do not say you have a broken father syndrome because you don't. You do not know how to operate with an earthly father. That is fine. But you do know how to operate with the heavenly Father, and that is all that counts. Stop trying to force it in the natural, God did not design you to have fulfillment that way, your fulfillment comes from Him."

This is renewal of the Mind! – change the way you are thinking, change the way you are looking at it. Many of us do not know how to operate with a father figure – and just like a young man I heard on television say "I couldn't be a father to you, because I didn't know how to be a father." This is what a lot of us are going through. And in the personal situation with my pastor as a father figure, he has a great father figure in his natural father raising him, but as far as the strong father figure in fathering grown people in the church, not so. And/or, he has not gotten to that part of his training with God, so it will take some patience. He is not trying to make me suffer — if he knew how much I hurt, it would hurt him to know that I hurt like this. So we must be patient and let the Holy Spirit deal with us. We are a body fitly joined together.

And just like God, He sent another confirmation that I was viewing this situation from the wrong side. I was at church the following Sunday and was sitting speaking with about 3 married women and discussing the mental attacks that we have all been experiencing. It was amazing to me that they all have similar attacks, and they are married — and the enemy has been lying to me and telling me that I am going through these attacks because I am single — not so! Even married women go through the mental attacks of the enemy, and even the more, because they have someone there, and you'd think that having someone there would make that loneliness go away, but it does not, but amplifies the situation because she cannot explain/describe to him what is going on — it is a void that only God can fill, not man or a husband, or work, or ministry, or children, or anything else, BUT GOD!

Psalm 62:1 For God alone my soul waits in silence; from Him comes my salvation.

Sometimes your soul has to get quiet and wait on Him. Stop longing for other people and other things to come in a fill the void. We must learn to wait on God.

We have to get our minds renewed to understand what it means to carry our cross, figuratively speaking. No, we are not walking around with trees on our back, carrying a literal crucifixion cross. So we have to be renewed in our mind to understand the figure that it is referring to.

> Luke 14:27-33 Whoever does not persevere and carry his own cross and come after (follow) Me cannot be My disciple. 28 For which of you, wishing to build a farm building, does not first sit down and calculate the cost [to see] whether he has sufficient means to finish it? 29 Otherwise, when he has laid the foundation and is unable to complete [the building], all who see it will begin to mock and jeer at him, 30 Saying, This man began to build and was not able (worth enough) to finish. 31 Or what king, going out to engage in conflict with another king, will not first sit down and consider and take counsel whether he is able with ten thousand [men] to meet him who comes against him with twenty thousand? 32 And if he cannot [do so], when the other king is still a great way off, he sends an envoy and asks the terms of peace. 33 So then, any of you who does not forsake (renounce, surrender claim to, give up, say good-bye to) all that he has cannot be My disciple.

This is why we have a problem, because we are being taught to be loyal and faithful to the church (the building, the organization, the people), but not what the cost of discipleship is: it means surrender everything. Teach me how to love God more than I love my mother, my father, my husband, my wife, my children, even my own self! This is what we should be teaching people.

> Luke 14:34-35 Salt is good [an excellent thing], but if salt has lost its strength and has become saltless (insipid, flat), how shall its saltness be restored? 35 It is fit neither for the land nor for the manure heap; men throw it away. He who has ears to hear, let him listen and consider and comprehend by hearing!

Loss of saltiness, this is a mouthful, but if it is not right, just throw it out. Lord give us an "ear to hear/listen comprehend" — this is talking about the mindset.

One day I was walking on the Galveston beach, just meditating on the word and spending some quality time with God, and I heard the Lord say *"You see this vast sea — just a tiny glimpse of Me — the wound locked in the pit of your soul will act larger than this if not dealt with."* The Lord was showing me that there was something going on in my soulish realm that needed to be healed/ renewed/ refreshed/ strengthened/ supported. The healing process that the Lord was walking me through, He related to an outpatient surgery that I had back in December 2010, I went to sleep and woke up without any knowledge of the pain — never felt a pain — so too with this spiritual surgery — God was basically saying "Receive My anesthesia, lay down and let Me operate and remove the cancerous cells from your soul." In this procedure, the doctor found some pre-cancerous cells that had to be removed; he also removed some of the good cells around the contaminated area to make sure everything was good; then he used dissolvable stitches. I never felt anything! The procedure was serious enough for me to be admitted in the hospital for them to do the procedure, but not too serious because I was able to go home that same day — but the fact that you can have a surgery and have someone cut on you and stitch you up, with no pain — that is God! Then this day, the Lord was showing me that He was dealing with some things in my soulish realm, as with Psalm 139:23-24, searching the heart of my soul and dealing with it.

This next excerpt from that healing walk with the Lord still amazes me, He went on to say *"Paulette you don't know what the incision looks like, but you know and trust that it is gone — and just like you took it easy the few days afterward to recover, I need you to do so this year — take it easy — slowdown in Me — rest."* I also found Psalm 24 to assist in this healing and Renewal of the Mind!, which refers to the great seas — He sent me to walk on them and for Him to operate on me in private.

The attack on my reproductive process in the natural is a carbon copy of what has been taking place over the same time frame in the spirit realm — the Great Physician has removed unhealthy matter to empower me to live and move and have my being in Him. Healed for such a time as this. Called for such a time as this. Ready with purpose for such a time as this.

Psalm 24:1-2 The earth is the Lord's, and the fullness of it, the world and they who dwell in it. 2 For He has founded it upon the seas and established it upon the currents and the rivers.

Genesis 1:1-4 In the beginning God (prepared, formed, fashioned, and) created the heavens and the earth. 2 The earth was without form and an empty waste, and darkness was upon the face of the very great deep. The Spirit of God was moving (hovering, brooding) over the face of the waters. 3 And God said, Let there be light; and there was light. 4 And God saw that the light was good (suitable, pleasant) and He approved it; and God separated the light from the darkness.

Psalm 24:1-2 is like what is being said at Genesis 1:1-4 — I struggled with including this nugget, but the Lord showed me that the enemy would love for people to not recognize the "beginning" moments in their life, to not truly recognize God as the Sovereign ruler and Creator of everything.

2 Corinthians 4:6-7 For God Who said, Let light shine out of darkness, has shone in our hearts so as [to beam forth] the Light for the illumination of the knowledge of the majesty *and* glory of God [as it is manifest in the Person and is revealed] in the face of *Jesus* Christ (the Messiah). 7 However, we possess this precious treasure [the divine Light of the Gospel] in [frail, human] vessels of earth, that the grandeur *and* exceeding greatness of the power may be shown to be from God and not from ourselves.

Genesis 1:2 is similar to 2 Corinthians 4:6-7. I meditated on these texts for the year 2011. It is so important that we understand that we have this precious treasure inside of our frail human body (dirt suit that we live in), and this precious treasure is the divine light of the gospel — that same light from back in Genesis 1 is in us. The enemy would like to lie to us and make us think it is this LITTLE light of mine — but NO! that light is not little! So when we are dealing with tearing down strongholds and wrong thoughts, we should practice trust in God and break the stronghold! Allow Genesis 1:1-4 to have the light shine in the dark places that keep us bound.

The progression of 2 Corinthians 4 is wow! Getting this "chain" of revelation makes it now possible to do verse 17 and see this stuff as light and momentary afflictions — You O God have expounded my thinking. 2 Corinthians 4 is titled *an honest and tried ministry;* and 2 Corinthians 5 is titled a *confident ministry;* so we have to be tested and tried, pass that test, to be confident.

Wow God — every place that I look in Your word I see "knewness" in You — stuff that I have read before, yet now You have illuminated so much to me that I want/need to read it all over again! "Knewness" is a made up word. Knew, because I thought I knew the word, but as He increases my understanding through the Renewal of the Mind! process, I see new in Him, so it is double: new, knew = knewness.

Genesis 1:2 — the earth — me — the vessel that Your Light is now in — WAS — (past tense) without form. Yet You O God formed me in Psalm 139 & Jeremiah 1:5.

Also the word had to be hidden that these mature spiritual connections could be made — just as division tables in elementary school — the foundation to go forward in understanding mathematical things — the Lord had given me my Teacher in 1 John 2:27 and helped me to study that I pass the test of 2 Corinthians 4, and become confident as 2 Corinthians 5.

"Here is a nugget for you My daughter — to understand that you are not broken, it is My doing that you can emotionally connect, but not physically weaken — to be the strong vessel I need for each task." This was the Lord showing me that I am not broken just because I do not express emotions like everyone else, but I am able to be strong for other people while they are going through.

God loves us, and He does still speak. Not just to the pastor or the ministers, but to anyone of His beloved that will take the time, seek His face, seek His presence, He will speak — He will speak and He will not lie. He will speak and lead and guide; and it will be according to His word, and it will be an empowerment for you direct, and also an empowerment for those connected with you.

Prayer: Thank You for teaching us what it means to present our ALL, according to Romans 12:1, present our bodies/ faculties/ all unto You as a living sacrifice. That we go ahead and renew ALL of our mind, to not think like the world, but have our entire mind renewed to think like and after You O God. Thank You for showing us what a memory looks like, and what it truly is, and that all of that stuff must be renewed. Yes, bad things have happened to us in the past, but we do not dwell on those things. What we remember are the lessons learned and see Your saving hand, Your protecting hand, Your leading and guiding hand through the midst of it all. Even the things that were the attacks of the enemy

that were meant to take us out, we can yet see You, and You still get the glory out of those situations.

Thank You for calling us to bask in Your presence, to sit in silence and allow Your spirit to sweep over us and show us what it is that we need to know from You, about You, and in You in this time and season. Thank You that in those times of soaking in Your presence, You give us revelation and show us things in Your word that we never knew before. We may have known the words, but You begin to connect it and put it together and make it make sense – and we will give You all the glory/ honor/ praise – because apart from You, we couldn't learn these principles or carry them out. Renewal of the Mind! Amen.

Prayer: Thank You for Your love that is overflowing in our hearts. Thank You for Your people – we love You, and we love Your people. Thank You for breaking our hearts to really understand Your people; those that are called by Your name, those who have accepted Your Son Jesus Christ. Allow us to walk in love with all of Your people; even when the people are unlovely, give us the ability to walk in love – to turn the other cheek – to give our enemy something to eat or drink – give us the ability to be used as instruments for Your kingdom to be advanced. We will not take any credit for it, but You will get all of the glory.

As we go forward into this PORTION *of* bible study and delve into what the Lord has exposed to me during the time of soaking in 2011, as I walked on the Gulf Coast; we ask You to bring freshness, newness, revelation, illumination, insight, wisdom into the things that You have already revealed, but even the more. Thank You for Your living word that is spoken to each of us, Your servants. Our response is Sir, yes Sir. Yes to Your will, and yes to Your way. We thank You that when our will comes up against Your will, You empower us to say "never the less, Your will be done" with the right attitude and right heart. That we are not murmuring and complaining, saying one thing, but acting another way in our heart – but that they will line up, and You get the glory, and the honor and the praise. Amen, so be it.

1 John 1 begins talking about *the Word of life,* then on to *the test of righteousness* and all the way through chapter 2 it is discussing this test of righteousness, then into chapter 3 which is about *obedience and love.* God is letting us know that we have a relationship with the word of Life, Jesus; and that our righteousness will be tested through trials, tribulations, situations, circumstances, opportunities to not act as the righteousness of God in Christ, opportunities to act like the world instead of the kingdom. God is testing us; not to see if we are going to fail, because we already have the mind of Christ, our job is to renew the soulish realm of our mind so that we can receive from the mind of Christ in the spiritual realm.

1 John 2:20 But you have been anointed by [you hold a sacred appointment from, you have been given an unction from] the Holy One, and you all know [the Truth] or you know all things

Sometimes we need to Selah: pause and calmly think on the fact that we have the unction, we have the anointing, and we know the Truth. The enemy will try to make you think that you do not know anything, and that what you do know no one wants to hear or cares about — but when you really Selah: pause and calmly think on that, fall in love with the Truth of this, and fall out of agreement with the lies that the enemy has hurled at us all of these years in our life — O my goodness, the power that is available!

4.3 Healing

"Thy word have I hidden in my heart that I might not sin against You" — has a greater meaning — we have to deposit the word, overflow, overload, even hide it so that when we are away from the 'physical' book, we have no excuse for wrong thoughts — unchecked thoughts. This is Renewal of the Mind!, when we go through and deposit the word in the overflow, that even when we can't open the bible to read, we can SELAH — pause and calmly think on the word that we have hidden in our heart that is to deal with those wrong thoughts that the enemy will bombard us with, especially on a sick bed! The enemy will try to taunt you with the doctor's report, but whose report will you believe!? Personally, as I was going through this trial, the enemy tried to harass me saying stuff like "Ha, you have cancer." But I just laughed and said "Even if it was cancer, God is the healer, He is the Lord God Jehovah Rapha, and He will heal me anyway — these people in the doctor's office and the hospital just needed to touch this glory (His glory) so He sent me here!" I began to taunt the enemy with his own words.

We have to get to where we expect the un-common things to happen. They are uncommon to the world, but they are common according to faith and a kingdom citizen that understands that in the kingdom realm nothing is missing, nothing is broken, all of our needs are met and supplied far above anything that we could ever ask or think — that is uncommon in the world, but it is common to us.

Formed weapon of sickness and disease, there may be symptoms that have manifested, but that will not prosper. I may have felt under the weather, but I know Jesus as my Healer! I am not just quoting a book, or singing a song, I KNOW YOU AS MY HEALER! Several

times have these weapons of sickness and disease formed against me, and You have healed out of each one of them because I am yet in the land of the living. Sometimes it has felt really heavy, and in the natural, felt like it was prospering, but I said like Job "God You have a hedge of protection around me" — the enemy can't touch me, he is just touching the dirt suit that I live in. As we continue to understand the separation of the tri-part being: that we are a spirit, we possess a soul, and we live in a body (Hebrews 4:12 shows those divisions) when we truly understand it, then we will understand what the attack is. The attack of this formed weapon of sickness and disease that is coming against my body is only to kill, steal, and destroy my faith in Jesus Christ the Healer. But I know You as my Healer, my trust is in You, my confidence is in You.

Now I will not be an idiot and not go to the doctor, and I will take the prescriptions, etc., along with prayer. It is just a formed weapon that will not prosper! This is about Renewal of the Mind! — as I was going through a terrible sinus infection, the enemy began to taunt me, saying things like, "Here you are supposed to have healing in your hands, and you can't even get this little thing healed?" I immediately shut him up with the word, it is only a formed weapon that is not going to prosper, or stop anything. I began to exhort myself saying stuff like, "If it has to be; then strengthen me. He is the One that allowed the test, and He knows that I have in me what I need to pass the test. I am here to serve You God, and this formed weapon is causing hindrances in my ability to do what I need to do for You, as well as tarnishing Your reputation — Lord, You must be allowing this because either You need me to get to someone along the way, that our paths would cross no other way (such as a nurse, a doctor, someone in a waiting room or pharmacy); or, You are trying to get me to see something."

The first thing to do when you find yourself dealing with this is to shut the enemy up; do not let him talk to you and tell you all of that foolishness. The word, is the word, is the word — He has healed us! By the stripes of Jesus Christ, we are healed. My spirit man walks in complete health and wholeness; my soulish realm walks in complete health and wholeness; but this dirt suit, this body — we have to take authority over it, and enforce that authority over the enemy. We have to press and go forward — do not let formed weapons stop you from being who God has called you to be. This dirt suit acting stupid; that is all it is, a dirt suit acting stupid — don't let it get you to change your "mind" as to Who you trust, and Who you serve, and Who He is. I know Him as healer, that is who He is, He is healer — the fact that these formed weapons of sickness and disease are here, does not mean that I do not know Him as healer. He is watching this entire trial. I will not even complain, God teaches in demonstration.

A young lady called me for prayer (James 5:16), it was at a time when I was dealing with a formed weapon of a severe sinus infection. It was almost embarrassing that I could not even get a sentence out without coughing. I had confidence that the Lord saw it all, I had to get quiet and sit still, talk to this dirt suit, and then yield my soulish man over to my spirit man, with God leading us, and pray for this person — the prayer spoke directly to her spirit, bringing healing to her. I told the Lord Thank You, because in my weakness is His strength made perfect — because I truly felt like I could not do anything for this young lady, the room was spinning and I just wanted to go home and get in my bed — physically, I was having a hard time. It is at times like these that we begin to say "Well God, how can I help them...how can the sick help the sick?" The Lord's response to me was "If you identify yourself as *the sick,* then you can't help anybody else." I do not identify myself as sick, but as walking in divine health and wholeness in my spirit man, but this dirt suit is under attack. When I understand this, then I can still be in the warfare — this is not a battle, this is war! — I can still be in the warfare even though I am under attack.

We have to renew our mind as to what healing is. We have to tap into the mind of Christ in the spirit realm, renew the mind in the soulish realm, and take authority over the dirt suit we live in that has the formed weapons coming against it that will not prosper.

Prayer for healing: Thank You for healing and wholeness in the dirt suits of myself and all attached to this ministry – that You have me praying over, and in joint prayer over their souls. I thank You God that their souls be renewed to not be moved by the formed weapons of sickness and disease, by the symptoms that are forming in their dirt suit, their spouses, their children. Give us the understanding of the believer's authority – to truly rise up and understand the authority in the soulish realm, as we are rising in it in the spirit realm, and take authority and walk it out in the natural realm. First in the dirt suit that we live in, then on behalf of others. Thank You God that You renew our mind to truly understand this battle and attack. Thank You for Your word in Hebrews 4:12, that You are giving us the ability to see which realm we need to tap into and operate as a tri-part being. Just as You O God are a tri-part being (Father, Son, Spirit) that operates as One, You are showing us how to do that and get all parts to line up (spirit, soul, body) and operate in unity as one. Give us the capacity, as the tri-part being, created in Your image, that we be truly empowered to do Romans 12:1-2, lay the dirt suit/ the body/ the natural man on the altar; then to take the soulish realm and renew it according to Your word, to be transformed by the renewing of Your word in our mind. We thank You for even taking us into Romans 12:3, that we not get puffed up and misunderstand what is going on, because we understand authority – it actually causes us to be more humble, and gives us a new charge to make sure that we walk in the believer's authority, and we share it with others without a cockiness – yes with boldness, and with the power of the Holy Spirit, but not with natural cockiness and pride. Because people can fight with me, but they cannot fight with Your word and the truth. So thank You for empowering us for such a time as this. Amen!

> Romans 12:2 MSG Embracing what God does for you is the best thing you can do for him. Don't become so well-adjusted to your culture that you fit into it without even thinking. <u>**Instead, fix your attention on God.**</u> You'll be changed from the inside out. Readily recognize what he wants from you, and quickly respond to it. Unlike the culture around you, always dragging you down to its level of immaturity, God brings the best out of you, develops well-formed maturity in you.

Fix your eyes on God, not the formed weapons of sickness and disease, or your husband acting silly, or escalating bills, or anything else, but on God. This PORTION that says *readily recognize what He wants from you and quickly respond to it* – is one of the results of what happens when we ask God to search our heart (Psalm 139:23-24), and to flood the eyes of our heart (Ephesians 1:17-19), our response should be to quickly respond to it – we have the empowerment of the Holy Spirit to make it all possible.

Truly understanding this Renewal of the Mind! process – will mature and develop us.

> Romans 12:2 NLT Don't copy the behavior and customs of this world, but let God transform you into a new person by changing the way you think. Then you will learn to know God's will for you, which is good and pleasing and perfect.

We are born again anew in the spirit realm at the new birth, we receive the mind of Christ (the new heart that has His laws and knows and wants to obey Him) but we are hindered in our ability to receive from it based on how we are thinking. This is why this verse in the NLT says *do not copy the behavior and customs of this world* – behaviors and customs come from the thought life – the belief system. Your belief system can't be after the ways of this world; but must be after the kingdom.

> Romans 12:3 MSG I'm speaking to you out of deep gratitude for all that God has given me, and especially as I have responsibilities in relation to you. Living then, as every one of you does, in pure grace, it's important that you not misinterpret yourselves as people who are bringing this goodness to God. No, God brings it all to you. **The only accurate way to understand ourselves is by what God is and by what he does for us**, not by what we are and what we do for him.

The last part of verse 3 in the Message bible shows a problem that is going on right now, because a lot of people know what church is, what religion is, all of these rules and regulations, but they do not know what or who God is, therefore, they are not able to rightfully look at themselves to see the contrariness to the word of God.

Someone else may mis-interpret your actions, and think that you are acting prideful, or with impure motives – you just make sure that you are not guilty of that before God – another reason why we constantly ask God to flood the eyes of our heart, and to search our heart regularly. Self-examination and self-judgment according to the standard of the word of God is a healthy practice to keep us from the prideful side of Romans 12:3.

Again, we cannot look at other people for understanding ourselves, but look to God and who He is and what He does for us. The problem at times is that other people look at you and misinterpret your actions, then we turn around and believe their lies. No! I know that I am nothing without Him — and apart from Him I can do no good thing — and apart from Him I can do NO-thing — and that nothing good dwells in the flesh. I do not know them pridefully, but I know them humbly — which makes me stand in awe and shocked that God can still use me in spite of all that I know about me! Because the more you know about Him, the more un-done you will appear in light of who He is — the closer you get to God, the more un-done you see that you really are — and that should create humility; and make you want to get even closer to Him, because you know how un-done you are without Him. You should be 100% dependent upon God every day, "I can't live a day without You. If You are not going to be with me, go ahead and take me to glory, because I can't do this without You." A lot of people really do not have this mindset — they say they do, but they don't — they say it with their mouth, but it is not really their mindset. These warped mindsets can stand as roadblocks to healing — we must continue in Renewal Of The Mind!

The enemy does not know any new tricks, and is using the formed weapons of sickness and disease. Therefore we must inundate our mind with the word of God — we must decree and declare the word of God over our life. Again, we are looking at the fact that there is no weapon formed against us that can prosper — we can't stop the weapons from forming, but we are to stand on the word of God that those weapons not prosper, or come to past, or yield the fruit that they are designed to yield. We are lifting up a standard against the enemy that is trying to come in — and the standard is the word of God; and is putting our trust and confidence in the word of God. Sometimes these formed weapons of sickness and disease can get us so off; and we get so busy looking at the symptoms because they are actual symptoms. We do not deny the facts, pain is pain — your body hurting is real and can distract us and keep us from focusing on God. We need to do what the word of God says, stay focused on the Lord, and He will keep us in perfect peace. These formed weapons of sickness and disease with the attached symptoms, come to make us take our mind off of Him — that we lose the peace of God that passes all understanding that is supposed to guard our hearts and minds. We want to put our complete trust and confidence in God.

We may not understand why some of these weapons form or are coming at us, I am not trying to solve that problem, or figure that out — I am not amplifying the sickness and disease or formed weapons, but I am amplifying the word of God. We will look at several scriptures to empower us to be able to live and walk upright and continue to go forward in this battle.

Just know that the devil is a liar, and will try to get you to focus on the symptoms and formed weapons — but do not focus on him and the lies, but on God and the truth of the word of God. Know this, you can't stop the weapons from forming, but your attitude while you are going through the trial is all about what is your confession? Is it "He is still my savior! He is still my healer! He is still the Lord God, Elohim, I love Him with my all!" As you are going through these trials, let them be reminders to put your mind on Him.

> Mark 9:25-29 But when Jesus noticed that a crowd [of people] came running together, He rebuked the unclean spirit, saying to it, You dumb and deaf spirit, I charge you to come out of him and never go into him again. ²⁶ And after giving a [hoarse, clamoring, fear-stricken] shriek of anguish and convulsing him terribly, it came out; and the boy lay [pale and motionless] like a corpse, so that many of them said, He is dead. ²⁷ But Jesus took [a strong grip of] his hand and began lifting him up, and he stood. ²⁸ And when He had gone indoors, His disciples asked Him privately, Why could not we drive it out? ²⁹ And He replied to them, This kind cannot be driven out by anything but prayer and fasting

Something the Lord showed me about this scripture, is that when the demon manifests, you do not have time to stop and fast. You must be living a fasted lifestyle, and a lifestyle of prayer. Yes, fast from food and deny the flesh, but also fast worldliness and pray the word of God. What we are doing right now in this section on healing, we are taking our mind off of the worldly views of sickness and disease — and are renewing our mind that sickness and disease is not of God, and He is not trying to teach you a lesson with the sickness it itself — I know that sounds contradictory, but the only lesson He is trying to teach you is to trust Him through it all. You would not dare put sickness and disease on your own children to discipline them; sickness and disease is a result of the fall of mankind due to sin in the garden — it is not God being mean to us — He is not a mean and cruel God — but as we change our thinking as to what is going on; and as we fast looking at the way that the world looks at it; and as we pray the word of God concerning the weapons of sickness and disease that have formed against us, and stand on the word, then we get to see a manifestation of spiritual things taking place.

We will next look at Isaiah 53 in several versions:

> Isaiah 53:3-5 NLT He was despised and rejected—a man of sorrows, acquainted with deepest grief. We turned our backs on him and looked the other way. He was despised, and we did not care. ⁴ Yet it was our weaknesses he carried; it was our sorrows that weighed him down. And we thought his troubles were a punishment from God, a punishment for his own sins! ⁵ But he was pierced for our rebellion, crushed for our sins. He was beaten so we could be whole. He was whipped so we could be healed.

> Isaiah 53:3-5 MSG We looked down on him, thought he was scum. But the fact is, it was our pains he carried— our disfigurements, all the things wrong with us. We thought he brought it on himself, that God was punishing him for his own failures. But it was our sins that did that to him, that ripped and tore and crushed him—our sins! He took the punishment, and that made us whole. Through his bruises we get healed.

> Isaiah 53:3-5 AMP He was despised and rejected and forsaken by men, a Man of sorrows and pains, and acquainted with grief and sickness; and like One from Whom men hide their faces He was despised, and we did not appreciate His worth or have any esteem for Him. ⁴Surely He has borne our griefs (sicknesses, weaknesses, and distresses) and carried our sorrows and pains [of punishment], yet we [ignorantly] considered Him stricken, smitten, and afflicted by God [as if with leprosy]. ⁵But He was wounded for our transgressions, He was bruised for our guilt and iniquities; the chastisement [needful to obtain] peace and well-being for us was upon Him, and with the stripes [that wounded] Him we are healed and made whole.

The number one sin that God healed through Jesus Christ, is being separated from Him, which occurred in Genesis 3. It is when we accept the plan of redemption through Jesus Christ, His shed blood, that we receive salvation. We then must grow in knowing all that salvation entails, it is 3-parts: 1) justification (this took place at Calvary); 2) sanctification (we are walking through this from the day we said yes to Jesus, until the day that our spirit man leaves this dirt suit that we live in — one of the roles of the sanctification process is preparation for glorification, which is part 3). We see all three of these stages of salvation summarized here in this Isaiah 53; when we transform our thinking to believe and understand what salvation is, this is getting in agreement with the truth of God's word. Many have been exposed to bad doctrine or theories regarding salvation and healing, but we must fall out of agreement with the lie, and get in agreement with the truth to be made whole. Let's look at a repeat of this text in the New Testament:

> 1 Peter 2:22-25 He was guilty of no sin, neither was deceit (guile) ever found on His lips. ²³When He was reviled and insulted, He did not revile or offer insult in return; [when] He was abused and suffered, He made no threats [of vengeance]; but he trusted [Himself and everything] to Him Who judges fairly. ²⁴He personally bore our sins in His [own] body on the tree [as on an altar and offered Himself on it], that we might die (cease to exist) to sin and live to righteousness. By His wounds you have been healed. ²⁵For you were going astray like [so many] sheep, but now you have come back to the Shepherd and Guardian (the Bishop) of your souls.

The Message bible says *His wounds became your healing* — and the New Living Translation says *by His wounds, you are healed*, we must meditate and change our thinking for what salvation includes. Look at verse 24 again, this is showing that we are dead to sin; and anything outside of faith is sin — our faith is not to acquire things, but our faith is trusting

Jesus for salvation; and is trusting God in complete confidence through Jesus. Therefore we see that we are dead to sin, and alive to righteousness — which is right standing with God that is imputed to us through accepting Jesus Christ. It is as we change our thinking to understand what righteousness is — because the enemy is lying to a lot of us and telling us we are not righteous, and giving us all these excuses and reasons for the sickness to be there in our life — but the devil is a liar! Accept forgiveness of your sin, and understand that it is not any of your past actions that have you going through this, or your present actions. Sickness and disease is from the devil; and is a result of the fall of mankind.

> Luke 6:17-19 And Jesus came down with them and took His stand on a level spot, with a great crowd of His disciples and a vast throng of people from all over Judea and Jerusalem and the seacoast of Tyre and Sidon, who came to listen to Him and to be cured of their diseases— 18 Even those who were disturbed and troubled with unclean spirits, and they were being healed [also]. 19 And all the multitude were seeking to touch Him, for healing power was all the while going forth from Him and curing them all [saving them from severe illnesses or calamities].

The Lord is in our midst today (as in verse 16), and His healing power is going to drive out any illnesses, calamity, sickness or diseases, or unclean spirits that are attacking our bodies. If you read on in this Luke 6, it begins to talk about *the Beatitudes* of being in the kingdom (verses 20-23), then it talks about *give away your life* (verses 24-26). Understand that God is going to keep you, be reminded of these: with long life He will satisfy me, and while I am in the land of the living, while I have life and breath in my body. He is going to bless you, then you are to give your life away.

Jeremiah 33 is titled *things you could never figure out on your own* — trying to figure out what is going on is difficult to do, so we will trust God for true healing. It began talking about a prophetic word that Jeremiah received; verse 6 is the key, but we will keep it in context:

> Jeremiah 33:2-9 MSG "This is GOD's Message, the God who made earth, made it livable and lasting, known everywhere as GOD: 'Call to me and I will answer you. I'll tell you marvelous and wondrous things that you could never figure out on your own.' 4-5 "This is what GOD, the God of Israel, has to say about what's going on in this city, about the homes of both people and kings that have been demolished, about all the ravages of war and the killing by the Chaldeans, and about the streets littered with the dead bodies of those killed because of my raging anger—about all that's happened because the evil actions in this city have turned my stomach in disgust. 6-9 But now take another look. I'm going to give this city a thorough renovation, working a true healing inside and out. I'm going to show them life

whole, life brimming with blessings. I'll restore everything that was lost to Judah and Jerusalem. I'll build everything back as good as new. I'll scrub them clean from the dirt they've done against me. I'll forgive everything they've done wrong, forgive all their rebellions. And Jerusalem will be a center of joy and praise and glory for all the countries on earth. They'll get reports on all the good I'm doing for her. They'll be in awe of the blessings I am pouring on her.

This is a promise to us, when we understand and accept Jesus Christ and become a part of God's beloved, He says that He is going to cure us, and lay health and healing on us, and will reveal to us an abundance of peace, prosperity, security, stability and truth (as the Amplified bible says it). If you read on in the chapter to verse 9, God is basically saying "Yes, there was some sin in the camp, but I have promised to bring and restore health and healing, prosperity, stability, security. Not only that, but then the people round-about will see it and I will get the glory." There are people around us that are seeing us go through this formed weapon of sickness and disease (family, friends, coworkers, etc.), but when they see us walk in complete healing — total, upright, healed...the glory that He will receive.

Sickness and disease are not allowed in the Lord's presence, and this next section of scripture is titled: *A Promise of The Lord's Presence* — it is as we renew our mind to the word of God, and His presence that we see that there is healing attached.

> Exodus 23:20-25 Behold, I send an Angel before you to keep and guard you on the way and to bring you to the place I have prepared. ²¹ Give heed to Him, listen to and obey His voice; be not rebellious before Him or provoke Him, for He will not pardon your transgression; for My Name is in Him. ²² But if you will indeed listen to and obey His voice and all that I speak, then I will be an enemy to your enemies and an adversary to your adversaries. ²³ When My Angel goes before you and brings you to the Amorites, the Hittites, the Perizzites, the Canaanites, the Hivites, and the Jebusites, and I reject them and blot them out, ²⁴ You shall not bow down to their gods or serve them or do after their works; but you shall utterly overthrow them and break down their pillars and images. ²⁵ You shall serve the Lord your God; He shall bless your bread and water, and I will take sickness from your midst.

Drive out all of the "ites" before you — that means get your mind off of worldliness, all of those things that were in the world — when you get your mind off of that... do not bow down to the idols of the world (i.e. spouse, children, money, success, etc.) — those are the idols of this world — we create idols. We say things like "I have to live", then we put our job before God... we cannot do that. Yes, use wisdom and you do have to work, but God must be first in your heart. When you have Him first, not bowing down to the idols that are in front of you with worldliness, but blot them out and do not do what they did — when you serve the Lord your God, He will bless your bread and your water, and He will take away sickness from your midst. Yes, the "ites" are before us, but He has sent the angel of the Lord before us to prepare the way — this battle is not yours, it is the Lords. And just like with Elisha prayed "Lord help my servant see that they that are with us are more than they that are with them" — so yes, there are some "ites" in the land, but the angel of the Lord has gone before you to prepare the way, just make sure that when you show up on the scene that you do not bow down to their idols and start doing things the way they did things. The promise here is that when you get in alignment with this word, and serve the Lord God, He will bless your bread and your water and will take sickness from your midst.

The children of Israel went through several cycles of idolatry and deliverance (6 times in the Old Testament do we see this 9-stage cycle that they went through) — who are we to think that we would be free from the same thing? Actually, we can be free when we seek God and ask for the help of the Holy Spirit to keep from doing that; but a lot of us are ignorant to the fact that we are doing things displeasing to the Lord. Ignorance is not bliss, it will hurt you — to be ignorant of the covenant of God, ignorant to what it means to walk as the righteousness of God in Christ Jesus (in right standing).

But before we get into this Deuteronomy 30, let me take a sidebar and address one of these lies of the enemy that he always tries to trip the children of God up with: YOU ARE ONLY HUMAN. I may be a human, but I am empowered with the Holy Spirit; the Greater One, the Light of the world who created the heavens and the earth lives in me! I want the Light to rule me, not the human side of me. People will try to talk you into believing this lie and say things like: "You are only human. You have needs. God knows your heart." But Jeremiah 17:9 tells us yes, He knows our heart, it is desperately wicked and deceiving — who could know it? No one but the Holy Spirit! So do not fall prey to the "you are only human" thinking; people will tell you that "some of the battles you are going through are because you are only human." No! These battles that we are going through are a result of the fall of mankind. So we will get aligned with word of God, and stop believing the lies of the enemy! It doesn't matter if you have believed this way (in a lie — that you are only human) all of your life — that is only a part of the fact, but the truth of the matter is that the Light of the world lives in you and empowers you to live above this type of thinking. Know that you are a spirit, you possess a soul, and you live in a body — and you are not lead by your soulish realm: where the mind, will, emotion, imagination, intellect, reasoning, thoughts, personality; conscious, memory are and needs to be renewed to the word of God — renewed to the mind of Christ that you received on the day that you said yes to Jesus. It is in the spirit realm, but you have to renew your thinking to act on it and accept what He is trying to reveal to you. We have truth being revealed to us daily, but we do not accept it because it is encountering the falsehood that has been in us. We must renew our mind. This was a sidebar for us to know that in order to walk in health and healing, we have to keep our minds stayed on Him.

Deuteronomy 30:16-20 [If you obey the commandments of the Lord your God which] I command you today, to love the Lord your God, to walk in His ways, and to keep His commandments and His statutes and His ordinances, then you shall live and multiply, and the Lord your God will bless you in the land into which you go to possess. 17 But if your [mind and] heart turn away and you will not hear, but are drawn away to worship other gods and serve them, 18 I declare to you today that you shall surely perish, and you shall not live long in the land which you pass over the Jordan to enter and possess. 19 I call heaven and earth to witness this day against you that **I have set before you life and death, the blessings and the curses; therefore choose life**, that you and your descendants may live 20 And may love the Lord your God, obey His voice, and cling to Him. For He is your life and the length of your days, that you may dwell in the land which the Lord swore to give to your fathers, to Abraham, Isaac, and Jacob.

Know and understand that God has promised to bless us, and just as the blessing and the curses are detailed in Deuteronomy 28 and Leviticus 26, here in Deuteronomy 30:19 we have a choice to make to walk in the life. Some of these things may "seem" hard to do, but that is because our mind is set on worldly thinking. We have the empowerment of the Holy Spirit as in 1 John 2:27 our unction and teacher that teaches us concerning everything and is true — but the devil does not want you to know that. The devil doesn't mind you having a bible, or going to church, or watching church on the television, he just doesn't want you to get in agreement with the truth of the word of God. As in 1 Timothy 2:4, God desires all men saved, but the second part of that text is that He wants us saved and to understand the truth. Many people are getting saved, the first part of this text, but are missing it when it comes to getting an understanding of the truth. Yes, the spirit man is born perfect and whole, with the mind of Christ, from the day of New Birth, but what must grow in understanding is the mind, the soulish realm to be able to access and to yield to the spirit and the mind of Christ — which can take some time.

Psalm 103:1-5 Bless (affectionately, gratefully praise) the Lord, O my soul; and all that is [deepest] within me, bless His holy name! 2 Bless (affectionately, gratefully praise) the Lord, O my soul, and forget not [one of] all His benefits — 3 Who forgives [every one of] all your iniquities, Who heals [each one of] all your diseases, 4 Who redeems your life from the pit and corruption, Who beautifies, dignifies, and crowns you with loving-kindness and tender mercy; 5 Who satisfies your mouth [your necessity and desire at your personal age and situation] with good so that your youth, renewed, is like the eagle's [strong, overcoming, soaring]!

O my soul — this must be renewed, it is where the mind, will, emotion, imagination, intellect, reasoning, thoughts, personality; conscious, memory — all of this MUST be renewed. Whatever has gone on in your past — good, bad, ugly — whatever, you have to look to the Lord and allow Him to cause the "all things" to work together for the good

(Romans 8:28) — change your thinking. Get out of victim mentality that gets caught up in "why does stuff always happen to me?" Don't let the pain be wasted pain, but press into God and allow Him to cause all things to work together for the good — because you love Him. If some painful things are going on, meditate on the love of God; get you something on the love of God, better understand the attributes of the love of God so that you can understand and see the purpose for all of those things that took place in your life.

This next text is titled *a psalm of praise and trust*, Psalm 34. We must renew our mind to trust God. When you get a moment, read the entire Psalm 34.

> Psalm 34:15-22 The eyes of the Lord are toward the [uncompromisingly] righteous and His ears are open to their cry. 16 The face of the Lord is against those who do evil, to cut off the remembrance of them from the earth. 17 When the righteous cry for help, the Lord hears, and delivers them out of all their distress and troubles. 18 The Lord is close to those who are of a broken heart and saves such as are crushed with sorrow for sin and are humbly and thoroughly penitent. 19 Many evils confront the [consistently] righteous, but the Lord delivers him out of them all. 20 He keeps all his bones; not one of them is broken. 21 Evil shall cause the death of the wicked; and they who hate the just and righteous shall be held guilty and shall be condemned. 22 The Lord redeems the lives of His servants, and none of those who take refuge and trust in Him shall be condemned or held guilty.

Be encouraged to know that trials and tribulations are going to come, but you have to praise God and trust Him in the midst of it all.

> Jeremiah 30:16-17 Therefore all who devour you will be devoured; and all your adversaries, every one of them, will go into captivity. And they who despoil you will become a spoil, and all who prey upon you will I give for a prey. 17 For I will restore health to you, and I will heal your wounds, says the Lord, because they have called you an outcast, saying, This is Zion, whom no one seeks after and for whom no one cares!

The children of Israel were being disciplined because of their disobedience; but when they cried out to God, He heard them and healed them and brought restoration of their wounds. It is through the blood of Jesus Christ that we access this today.

We referred earlier to the text and the fact that "this kind go not out but by fasting and praying" — this next scripture reference is in a section that is addressing *right and wrong fasting*. We see here that fasting isn't about make a big show about denying the flesh; but is about this:

> Isaiah 58:6-14 [Rather] is not this the fast that I have chosen: to loose the bonds of wickedness, to undo the bands of the yoke, to let the oppressed go free, and that you break every [enslaving] yoke? ⁷Is it not to divide your bread with the hungry and bring the homeless poor into your house—when you see the naked, that you cover him, and that you hide not yourself from [the needs of] your own flesh and blood? ⁸**Then shall your light break forth like the morning, and your healing (your restoration and the power of a new life) shall spring forth speedily**; your righteousness (your rightness, your justice, and your right relationship with God) shall go before you [conducting you to peace and prosperity], and the glory of the Lord shall be your rear guard. ⁹Then you shall call, and the Lord will answer; you shall cry, and He will say, Here I am. If you take away from your midst yokes of oppression [wherever you find them], the finger pointed in scorn [toward the oppressed or the godly], and every form of false, harsh, unjust, and wicked speaking, ¹⁰And if you pour out that with which you sustain your own life for the hungry and satisfy the need of the afflicted, then shall your light rise in darkness, and your obscurity and gloom become like the noonday. ¹¹And the Lord shall guide you continually and satisfy you in drought and in dry places and make strong your bones. And you shall be like a watered garden and like a spring of water whose waters fail not. ¹²And your ancient ruins shall be rebuilt; you shall raise up the foundations of [buildings that have laid waste for] many generations; and you shall be called Repairer of the Breach, Restorer of Streets to Dwell In. ¹³If you turn away your foot from [traveling unduly on] the Sabbath, from doing your own pleasure on My holy day, and call the Sabbath a [spiritual] delight, the holy day of the Lord honorable, and honor Him and it, not going your own way or seeking or finding your own pleasure or speaking with your own [idle] words, ¹⁴Then will you delight yourself in the Lord, and I will make you to ride on the high places of the earth, and I will feed you with the heritage [promised for you] of Jacob your father; for the mouth of the Lord has spoken it.

Understand that there is healing here — see verse 8 again! And at verse 13, when it refers to the Sabbath — Jesus is the Sabbath, and when you rest in Him, and stop trying to do things on your own, is when you will have this promised peace and prosperity. Do not speak of worldly things, but speak of what Jesus speaks of — so we must renew our mind to understand who Jesus is and how He operated (Matthew 11:29). We call ourselves a Christian, that means Christ-like, and we have to renew our mind to truly know what this means. It does not mean that we go to church every Sunday, or that we have the entire bible memorized (because memorizing it, and knowing it are two different things), but we must grow in knowing who God is, and who we are in Him — our "in Him" is in Jesus.

We will just hone in on a few verses of this last text, but in your own time, read and meditate on the entire Psalm 107. We will look at verse 20, but this psalm is talking about some disobedience that took place in the camp, and then God sends forth healing.

> Psalm 107:1 O give thanks to the Lord, for He is good; for His mercy and loving-kindness endure forever!

If you are sitting there in pain, this is a good meditation verse. We do not give thanks because of the pain, but because He is good, and a good God will not let you sit there in pain and suffering like that for long. So meditate on the fact that His mercy and loving-kindness is good, and He is keeping you alive in the land of the living — in the midst of the pain, change your thinking and your focus to be on Him.

> Psalm 107:19-24 Then they cry to the Lord in their trouble, and He delivers them out of their distresses. ²⁰ **He sends forth His word and heals them and rescues them from the pit and destruction.** ²¹ Oh, that men would praise [and confess to] the Lord for His goodness and loving-kindness and His wonderful works to the children of men! ²² And let them sacrifice the sacrifices of thanksgiving and rehearse His deeds with shouts of joy and singing! ²³ Some go down to the sea and travel over it in ships to do business in great waters; ²⁴ These see the works of the Lord and His wonders in the deep.

Prayer: God I thank You and praise You for this time in Your word. For the time that You are training us and allowing us to fast worldliness and pray Your word O God. You are equipping us by exposing our spirit man to Your word – we receive it and accept it, we believe Your word. Thank You that by the stripes of Jesus Christ are we healed. Thank You for Mark 11, that we receive what we believe when we pray. Thank You for manifested healing, health, wholeness. Thank You that in spite of the formed weapons of sickness and disease that have come against me, and those that are attached to me in my sphere of influence, I pause from the norm of life and pour out my life to get in this word and pray it back to You and over their lives, that Your word is powerful and effective, and will not return to You void.

Thank You for equipping me to help others grow in understanding Your will and word concerning wholeness, healing, life, health, strength. We magnify and amplify You O God, we set our mind on You, and we think on these things: whatever is pure, lovely, holy, of above – we think on these things and thank You in the midst of all that is going on. We can't stop anything from happening, we do not understand why some of these things are coming our way, but the

one thing we do know is that You are in control. Our trust is in You, we will yet praise You in the midst of every formed weapon, storm, sickness and disease, situation, circumstance, trial, tribulation – none of these things move us from believing and trusting Jesus for salvation, and trusting You as the Lord God Jehovah Rapha, the Healer. You empower us with Your Holy Spirit that leads, guides, and directs Your people – we are Your people, You are our God and we thank You for being a covenant keeping God. Help us grow and understand what it means to be in covenant with You, the God of the Universe. Thank You for the praise reports that will come in as a result of us renewing our mind with Your life changing word. Whatever the formed weapons of sickness and disease, or the doctor's report, they are names that can be named, and You are above them all. You are the God of healing, wholeness, restoration. Our redeemer – and the redeemed of the Lord will say so! We trust You, we give You praise, glory and honor. Amen, and amen!

4.4 Like Psalm 23

Renewal of the Mind! is like the Psalm 23 renewal.

> Psalm 23:1-6 The Lord is my Shepherd [to feed, guide, and shield me], I shall not lack. ² He makes me lie down in [fresh, tender] green pastures; He leads me beside the still and restful waters. ³ **He refreshes and restores my life (my self);** He leads me in the paths of righteousness [uprightness and right standing with Him—not but for my earning it, but] for His name's sake. ⁴ Yes, though I walk through the [deep, sunless] valley of the shadow of death, I will fear or dread no evil, for You are with me; Your rod [to protect] and Your staff [to guide], they comfort me. ⁵ You prepare a table before me in the presence of my enemies. You anoint my head with oil; my [brimming] cup runs over. Surely or only goodness, mercy, and unfailing love shall follow me all the days of my life, and through the length of my days the house of the Lord [and His presence] shall be my dwelling place.

In Romans 12:2, we are asking Him to renew our mind (the soul); then in Psalm 23:3, He refreshes and restores my soul. We will be looking at the process a little more, but first let's look at a few other scripture references of "renew" that I found to tie it all together.

> Psalm 51:10 Create in me a clean heart, O God, and renew a right, persevering, and steadfast spirit within me.

If the spirit man is born again, this is not what is being referred to here, that is done within the new birth. We talked earlier about how the heart lies in both the spirit realm and the soulish realm. It is the soulish part where He is creating this clean, renewed, heart, it is within the soul.

> Psalm 51:12 Restore to me the joy of Your salvation and uphold me with a willing spirit.

Psalm 51 was written after David sinned with Bathsheba, and murdered Uriah (her husband). Sometimes in life, situations can cause you to feel like there is no joy — this is when we cry out to God for the restoration of the soulish realm, because the spirit man was the same all along.

The next scripture reference is another of my favorite texts that completely revolutionized my walk with Christ.

> Revelation 22:17 The [Holy] Spirit and the bride (the church, the true Christians) say, Come! And let him who is listening say, Come! And let everyone come who is thirsty **[who is painfully conscious of his need of those things by which the soul is refreshed supported, and strengthened]**; and whoever [earnestly] desires to do it, let him come, take, appropriate, and drink the water of Life without cost.

When I saw that there were things for my soul to be *refreshed, supported, and strengthened*, I became even more eager to find out what this was all about.

Now to the definitions I discovered as I compared these references of "renew". At Romans 12:2, this renew means *a renewal; a renovation; a complete change for the better*. If we are asking God to renew our mind, we are asking Him to completely change it for the better. And this Renewal of the Mind! can only be done by the Holy Spirit:

> Titus 3:5 He saved us, not because of any works of righteousness that we had done, but because of His own pity and mercy, by [the] cleansing [bath] of the new birth (regeneration) and renewing of the Holy Spirit

This renewal comes through salvation; that is why we said earlier: restore to me the joy of salvation. So the renewal comes through salvation, and it is to bring a change for the better. The devil will lie to you, yet remember Jesus comes to bring His Abundant Life, it is through His Abundant Life that we have salvation of our soul (eternity — that is abundance). Then we have access to God's mercy and grace in the earth realm, but the enemy came to kill, steal, and destroy — and will lie to you and tell you things in your soulish realm that do not cause a change for the better. So you have to listen and watch what is happening in the battleground of your soul (your mind): God speaks to edify, the enemy speaks to kill, steal, and destroy.

A few of the definitions I found for the word "mind" found in Romans 12:2 are *the mind, comprising alike the faculties of perceiving and understanding and those of feeling, judging, determining. The intellectual faculty, the understanding. A particular mode of thinking and judging, i.e. thoughts, feelings, purposes, desires.*

We have to renew our mind to the constitution of the kingdom (the word of God), that it would help us reason and have understanding. That it would give us the type of intellectualism that we need, and it is only in Him. Human intellect will take you to a dead end place every time, as in Proverbs 16:1, 9; and Proverbs 19:21 — the plans of man seem good until God comes in and shows the truth. I do not lean to my own understanding, but His understanding, as in Proverbs 3, and His word is a lamp to my feet and a light to my path. We MUST get to where we get the word in us, to do all of these things.

> Psalm 23:1 The Lord is my Shepherd [to feed, guide, and shield me], I shall not lack.

The world will to tell you that you are in lack, example "Oh, you do not have school supplies for your children — or enough money to put gas in your car — or the holidays are coming up, you aren't working, what are y'all going to do?" But you have to set your mind to say: You O God are my Shepherd — and continue right on in this verse 1. Do not fixate on the voices from the outside telling you that you lack, when the truth says that you do not lack. Then you have to ask God for wisdom, sit still, and if and when God tells you to do something, do it. Don't get caught up in these prosperity gospels of name it and claim it, blab it and grab it — God is not Santa Claus where you give Him a wish list and He just does it. No. There is a part on our behalf to be done: we first have to believe Him as our Shepherd, we also have to contend for the faith (stand and fight for what you believe, the enemy will fight you every step of the way).

> Psalm 23:1-3 MSG 1-3 GOD, my shepherd! I don't need a thing. You have bedded me down in lush meadows, you find me quiet pools to drink from. True to your word, you let me catch my breath and send me in the right direction.

Telling God thank You for renewing and restoring my soul, is letting me catch my breath. I can come in Your presence, bask in Your presence, and breathe — as the song we sing "this is the air I breathe, Your very word spoken to me."

Understand that God is doing this for His name's sake. Also, understand that this psalm is identifying us as sheep — sheep have no pride whatsoever — sheep are actually dumb. He has to lead them beside the still water because rushing water scares them, and because they are scared of the water, they will not drink, and will get dehydrated and cause a lot of other problems. But my Shepherd loves me so much, that He will not take me by scary stuff, but will calm it down and take me to it and let me drink of Him (as in Revelation 22:17, thirsty soul drinking).

This "soul" here in Psalm 23:3 is a different word than in Romans 12:2, but it is still very relevant. It means *soul, self, life, creature, person, appetite, mind, living being, desire, emotion, passion.* Have you ever gone through some situations in life that just killed your desire, your passion, and/or destroyed your appetite? The enemy has come with all these attempts at killing, stealing, and destroying stuff — and it makes you not be passionate for the things of God because you begin to look at other's that seem to be getting away with not living right — but get into Psalm 73 and in Psalm 37 and see that no one is getting away with anything — and that it is best to walk the way of the renewed mind that brings glory to God, than the ways of the world that only glorify the carnal side of worldly thinking.

Basically what Psalm 23 is telling me, as the definition of soul says, He is restoring my appetite to eat the things that will make me not have to need anything.

Relating this to Romans 12:2 change your thinking, renew the soulish realm, as the definition here says: renew your life, renew your appetites, renew your emotions, renew your passions, renew your reasonings, renew your activities of the mind (with the word of God, not the world) because the world will have you really thinking you are coo-coo for cocoa puffs.

The word "restore" in Psalm 23:3, is the same word that is in Psalm 51:12 and it means *to return, turn back*. Understand, there is a restoration that can go the wrong direction — and that is called apostasy, when you restore your thinking back to the way this world thinks, and not thinking like God. It is when you willingfully say "I hear what you are saying God, but I like the way the world says/does it" — that is called apostasy — and is turning back from God. If you are not for God, you are against Him, there is no in between. "Restore" is also defined as *the turning back to God*, which means to repent. This verse is in essence saying He causes my soul to repent for His name sake.

Another thing I noticed in reviewing this word restore, were all of the other uses of the word in the bible that have the same meaning: bring; render; answer; recompense; recover; deliver; put; withdraw; requite — all of these He is doing for my soul! Recompense — means He has paid the price for me to have soul peace and soul prosperity.

Even to implore the law of first mention, He is restoring us back to the state in Genesis because it was lost when deception and sin entered in. Genesis 3:19, the word "return" is used to explain that this dirt suit (body) will return to dirt; be restored to that which it is was made out of. The spirit-man will be "restored" also to its place of eternity based on the decision the soul-man (which was awakened to good and evil) chooses while it resides in the body (dirt suit). Also, in Genesis 8:3, 7, 9, the waters returned, the raven, and the dove returned (or did not return), but it is the same word for restore. A side nugget I gleaned about the raven and the dove — we get to see the example of coming back into the ark of safety — so He restores my soul, brings me into a safe place where no matter what is going on, I am safe in Him. He allows the waters of life to come in, to arise, but I am in the ark, the safety of Him — we are to come in and close the door.

Part of Psalm 51 is, if we find ourselves in sin, then we must repent; which means to change our thinking — not just say I'm sorry, but to have actions following that show true repentance. Here in Psalm 51:4 we have a good example of repentance when he says *against You and You only have I sinned and done that which is evil*. Not only that, but to go on and offer allocution of the details of what was going on in the sin. Psalm 51:6 is David telling the

Lord, "I know who You are" — and asking for wisdom, as we always do with Ephesians 1:17-19, flood us with light so that we can have this wisdom — which is a repeat of Psalm 23:3, asking for the inner self to be restored — the Lord does this when we are open and honest before Him, broken and contrite. The enemy wants us to keep things hidden, because if it is hidden it festers and has the ability to trip us up, but we must expose it to God — as in a heart cry I once made to the Lord to "expose the wounds, so that You can extract the poison out of me, so that I can go on."

> Psalm 51:10 MSG God, make a fresh start in me, shape a Genesis week from the chaos of my life.

My life was in all kinds of chaos, as in Genesis 1, the world was in darkness (which comes from the root word for chaos) — but then He spoke and it was alright. So this verse 10 in the Message bible is saying God make me new just like that — as in the New Living Translation, renew a loyal spirit within me. Because we can become disloyal to God, we know who He is, we know all of His characteristics, but continue to do things that are not right. Again, Psalm 51:10 is after David sinned with Bathsheba and murdered her husband and tried to cover it up; but when we attach Psalm 51:12 to this chain of events, it says: *restore to me the joy of Your salvation and uphold me with a willing spirit*. A willing spirit — take the will that was in me that got me in trouble, and give me a willingness to be in right standing with You, because I have messed up, and I need You to renew me.

Side bar: in order for David to commit adultery, and murder of her husband, he first had to commit idolatry in his heart because he began to covet and idolize another man's wife (he already had several wives and concubines! This was sheer idolatry.)

Our mind needs to be renewed to the obedience of walking before God. Another definition of this word "renew" here in this text is *that of cutting or polishing; of newness appears to proceed for that of a sharp polished splendid sword* — which brings to mind Hebrews 4:12, the word that is sharp, and it is for the renewing of our mind. And in Psalm 119 which says before I knew Your word I went astray, but now I keep Your word, hearing, receiving, loving and obeying it — and Your word have I hid in my heart that I might not sin against You. If we are to be epistles, we are to be sharp and cutting some things that people can see God's goodness in our life. That even if you do mess up, you go to Him in the renewal process — we should live this Psalm 51 everyday of our life.

This word renew is also a military term (this is not a battle, this is war!) as in 1 Samuel 11:14, when the kingdom was being renewed. Again in 2 Chronicles 15:8, the altars were renewed by military force — and when God steps on the scene, His people will put away their idols and renew the altar to the Lord.

> 2 Chronicles 24:4 KJV And it came to pass after this, that Joash was minded to repair the house of the Lord.

Here is a good example of a person's heart being minded to bring repair to the place of God. God is always behind the scene, and if we will obey and yield to Him telling us to do things, it will be accredited to us, but if not, we will be dealt with. Like Pharaoh — God was trying to work with his heart, but he just kept being hard-headed, so God let his heart get harder. Or even Jonah, he had a prophetic message that God had given him to deliver to the people of Nineveh, but in is mind (his own thinking), he did not want to go — God taught him a quick object lesson involving a storm, a big fish, and purpose — yet Jonah still had a bad attitude, then God rebuked him again, and we do not hear anything else from Jonah's life.

༄

4.5 Thirsts

> Psalm 103:5 Who satisfies your mouth [your necessity and desire at your personal age and situation] with good so that your youth, renewed, is like the eagle's [strong, overcoming, soaring]!

We may be going through some things, but we need to recognize who God is — He satisfies my mouth with good things, just like in Psalm 23, He is my Shepherd and I don't want — there is no lack. We must renew our mind to know this. It is as I know this, He gives me wisdom, insight, and favor to cause these things to manifest in the natural realm that are needed.

> Revelation 22:16-17 I, Jesus, have sent My messenger (angel) to you to witness and to give you assurance of these things for the churches (assemblies). I am the Root (the Source) and the Offspring of David, the radiant and brilliant Morning Star. 17 The [Holy] Spirit and the bride (the church, the true Christians) say, Come! And let him who is listening say, Come! And **let everyone come who is thirsty** [who is painfully conscious of his need of those things by which the soul is refreshed, supported, and strengthened]; and whoever [earnestly] desires to do it, let him come, take, appropriate, and drink the water of Life without cost.

There is something that we are to drink in — we are to drink this living water that Jesus supplies and have wells of living water bubbling up on the inside (as in John 4:14). And because you are a part of the bride/ the church/ the true Christians, people are going to come and drink of the water from your well. So think it not strange why you are ministering to someone else when it appears you are under attack, and feel like you can be of no use to God — it is because you have the Living Water. This reminds me of when Jesus told His disciples to go back and they responded with "where else are we going to go? You have the word!" There are other people that are connected to you, they may get on your last nerve, but you have the word and must be patient and have compassion that they can get past whatever they are going through and realize that you have the living word.

When you term yourself Christian, you are basically calling yourself the Bride of Christ. To quote my pastor "how are you going to date Jesus, but you do not like His bride?" That is just crazy — you must be connected to a church, to a body of Christ. The body has many members, each joint supplying the need — you cannot be disconnected and function properly. Whoever is really thirsty will connect, and come and drink — whoever is not, will pitty pat and act like they understand.

Drilling down on the word "thirst" here, the Amplified offers the explanation of thirst as *are painfully conscious of his need of those things by which the soul is refreshed, supported, and strengthened* — but how am I aware of that? One way is that my Shepherd keeps giving me what I need because He restores my soul. I found the following on www.blueletter.org *figuratively, those who are said to thirst who painfully feel their want of and eagerly long for those things by which the soul is refreshed, supported, strengthened.* So we have to press into God for this understanding, as in Matthew 5:6, when we are aware of this thirst, we will be satisfied in Him, not in anything from the world.

In Matthew 25:35-44, Jesus was referencing when we do for others, we do it for Him — and we are the living wells that others are able to come and drink of the living well, and to eat of the Bread of Life that we have in our life (not molded or maggot infested bread, but fresh daily manna) — and are able to share it with others: your children, your husband, your parents, your cousin, those that are around you. Live the gospel, share the gospel, and if you have to, use words. But they must see it operating in your life — you are an epistle read by men. Because you are hungry and thirsting, they may see you down and out, they see the formed weapons of sickness and disease, but they see you yet praising God, and yielding to God.

Also in John 4:13-15, is about the wells of living water unto everlasting life that Jesus promises us. My first real encounter with the presence of God was similar to this woman at the well, I experienced God's presence and the refreshing of the soul happened, then He gave me instructions on how to correct some things in my life that were out of order — but in society right now, a lot of people do not want to be corrected — but when you have the Living God correcting you, it empowers you to be able to go and help other people that are standing at the same well that you used to stand at, and help them out of that. Renewal of the Mind! He has allowed me to renew my mind, and has empowered me to be able to help others.

We renew our mind by recognizing that He is our Shepherd; He restores our soul — and when we do miss it and sin, we can repent, like Psalm 51, we can change our mind and ask Him for the newness that comes in and from Him. And then we need to always stay hungering and thirsting for Him, because as we hunger and thirst, we shall be filled. But we will not be filled to sit on it, but to be a water supply and living well to others.

We are to preach the gospel, and if we must, use words! This call is not to a pulpit, but a call to preach the gospel with our life. The gospel is HIS-story in our life of the transforming power of the saving grace of Jesus Christ.

Prayer: Thank You that apart from You we can do NO-thing. Thank You for calling us to Romans 12:1-3 everyday of our lives. Thank You that we would crucify the flesh, and not lean to our own understanding – not give into the fleshly passions, appetites, emotions, and desires. But our mind is being renewed in the word to who You are God, that we could live pleasing unto You. We do not do it apart from You, we do not estimate ourselves to be anything apart from You – You do not do it for us, but for Your name's sake in the first place. So we get in Your name, we run into Your name – You are our refuge, our stronghold, our high tower. We Your people humble ourselves before You. We choose to renew our mind – to violently take our mind off of worldly thinking and place it back onto the things of the kingdom. Thank You for causing us to be aware of our soul needs every day – that we get in the river of living water, that we drink, we eat, we wash, we cleanse, we get strengthened and restored to go into battle. Thank You for restoring us to eat of the tree of life as if we never ate of the tree of the knowledge of good and evil; this is the Renewal of the Mind! process, to take our mind off of good and evil, right and wrong, being pleasing and not being pleasing – but to keep our minds with Jesus at the center of it all. We do not want to be self-centered, as the tree of the knowledge of good and evil produces, but Christ-centered. That we be compassionate to Your people – able to help hurting people in this sin-sick dying world. It is all about You, Your plans, Your purposes, Your goals. Thank You for getting Your glory out of each and every one of Your servants.

As in Ecclesiastes, You make everything beautiful in its time, so in the midst of the breaking process, You are beautifying me – and You get the glory. Thank You for continually speaking peace into my heart, causing my longing heart to rest in You and to be confident in You. Thank You for each and every servant and person You send my way for me to minister to and to sow the knowledge of Your word and prayer into. Thank You that we would turn our hearts to truly developing and understanding the knowledge of who You are and who we are in You – that You get the glory and honor out of Your servants. Amen, so be it!

4.6 Worship

A plain definition of "worship" is *man's response to the revelation of who God is* — so as we grow in knowing who God is and who we are in Him, our worship experience should deepen and heighten. This is when it no longer takes a church building or a cheerleader to tell us to worship God, because we are growing and knowing who God is.

Looking at worship and the fear of the Lord in Psalm 119. Fear God — this doesn't mean I am scared to get in trouble; but the closer you get to God, and the more of His glory that you see, you will begin to see that you are un-done and the more you begin to understand what the fear of God is. As Psalm 119 is all about the fear of the Lord, we must renew our mind to know that Jesus fulfills the law. Therefore this entire Psalm is talking about knowing and obeying the laws, precepts, ordinances, commands, word, testimonies of the Lord Jesus Christ.

A good example of this type of fear is seen in Isaiah 6:5. The fear of God literally means reverence Him — and you can't truly worship Him if you do not reverence Him. We must mature and grow up in understanding the fear of God, to develop into true worshipers in spirit and in truth (John 4:24).

"Hearing, receiving, loving, obeying" is mentioned 13 times in Psalm 119 of the Amplified bible; and the opposite of it is mentioned 3 times — which means it must be something important for us to apply these verses, hearing/ receiving/ loving/ and obeying them. We can see that this principle really has something to do with worship.

- Verse 5 — Oh, that my ways were directed and established to observe Your statutes ... HEARING, RECEIVING, LOVING, AND OBEYING
- Verse 17 — Deal bountifully with Your servant, that I may live; and I will observe Your word... HEARING, RECEIVING, LOVING, AND OBEYING
- Verse 44 — I will keep Your law continually, forever and ever... HEARING, RECEIVING, LOVING, AND OBEYING
- Verse 56 — This I have had [as a gift of Your grace and as my reward]: that I have kept Your precepts... HEARING, RECEIVING, LOVING, AND OBEYING
- Verse 67 — Before I was afflicted I went astray, but now Your word do I keep... HEARING, RECEIVING, LOVING, AND OBEYING
- Verse 88 — According to Your steadfast love give life to me: then I will keep the testimony of Your mouth... HEARING, RECEIVING, LOVING, AND OBEYING
- Verse 100 — I understand more than the aged, because I keep Your precepts... HEARING, RECEIVING, LOVING, AND OBEYING
- Verse 101 — I have restrained my feet from every evil way, that I might keep Your word... HEARING, RECEIVING, LOVING, AND OBEYING
- Verse 106 — I have sworn [an oath] and have confirmed it, that I will keep Your righteous ordinances... HEARING, RECEIVING, LOVING, AND OBEYING
- Verse 115 — Depart from me, you evildoers, that I may keep the commandments of my God... HEARING, RECEIVING, LOVING, AND OBEYING
- Verse 129 — Your testimonies are wonderful [far exceeding anything conceived by man]; therefore my [penitent] self keeps them... HEARING, RECEIVING, LOVING, AND OBEYING

- Verse 134 – Deliver me from the oppression of man; so will I keep Your precepts... HEARING, RECEIVING, LOVING, AND OBEYING
- Verse 146 – I cried to You; save me, that I may keep Your testimonies... HEARING, RECEIVING, LOVING, AND OBEYING

We see that the principle of hearing, receiving, loving, and obeying has to do with worship because according to verse 17, God will correct and instruct me, and the more He does, the more I learn and know of Him, the more I hear, receive, love, and obey Him.

At verse 44, sometimes you have to tell yourself you will keep the law (keep in communion with Jesus), I mean talk to yourself like David did in Psalm 42:5 when he said "why are you downcast O my soul" – he was talking to himself, then he followed it up with "I will yet hope in the Lord". And sometimes you have to tell yourself, "I will keep the law – me, myself, and I – my mind, will, emotions, intellect. I will keep the law." Tell yourself, decree and declare a thing (Job 22:28).

According to verse 56, God graces us to keep His precepts, to receive it, to love it, to obey it.

According to verse 67, there is a purpose in why God allows us to go astray. Also, note that there is a process here:

- You hear it; you can't just hear it, you have to listen.
- Then you receive it.
- Then you have to fall in love with it.
- And finally, you have to obey it.

Like the saying "I hear what you are saying, but your actions are speaking so loud I can't hear what you are saying" – so if we really are hearing, receiving, and loving the law of God (Jesus); then we ought to be obeying – it should be seen, with the evidence of fruit of what you are saying you hear.

Affliction causes us to get in line with the word. I can be painfully transparent and share that I learned about the significance of abstaining from pre-marital sex (fornication) through actually doing it, and now I truly understand His word. Now, because I was afflicted as a result of sinful behavior that God did not agree with, living outside of the will of God – now His word do I keep. He has strengthened me to now where I can hear that sex is reserved for marriage; I receive it, and am in love with it. And that love relationship (worship), causes me to be able to obey it. Where I will not give into the flesh that screams and hollers, and the old un-regenerated mind that only knows sex and how good it feels, and "the world does it like this, so why can't I? Or, it's yo thang do what you want to do!" NO! I am in love with this word, and because I love it so, I am going to obey it. I didn't just hear it and receive it, but I fell in love with it, and when you love like that, it should be demonstrated by obeying the word – and Jesus is the Word. I am not just talking about words on a paper, or a set of rules, but Jesus, my savior, Who became flesh and dwelt among us, JESUS!

Not for my sake, but because Your love is demonstrative, You will give life to me (as in Psalm 119:88). And life to me represents Jesus Christ — the Tree of Life. So the more that we grow in knowing and understanding salvation and all of its benefits (past — justification, present — sanctification; and future — glorification), it is as we grow in these areas, that is where our life comes from. As in Matthew 11:28-30, He gives the rest and promised Life as we learn of His steadfast love. And with this life that we receive, we are now enabled and empowered to keep His testimony hearing them, receiving them, loving them, and obeying them.

At verse 100, just being older in the natural does not make us mature. We can be old naturally, and childish spiritually — it is the word that will expose us and make us confess the childishness. God exposes our spiritual childishness, so that we can grow, and He will give us the wisdom and capability to understand more than the aged. This hearing, receiving, loving, and obeying of His precepts will give you wisdom that age and years cannot give you. So do not let the enemy minimize you, and do not despise small beginnings, but allow the Lord to use that to His advantage.

At verse 101, notice the progression here: before God was directing and establishing me, and dealing with me bountifully, He gave me a grace and a gift to keep His word, then affliction caused me to keep His word, then when I recognized His steadfast love — that caused me to keep His word. And now He is giving me more understanding than the aged, which has empowered me to restrain my feet from every evil way! This reminds me of the Lord's prayer (or model of prayer) in Matthew 6 and Luke 12 when it says "deliver us from evil" — God is giving us deliverance from temptation and He is keeping us from the evil, giving us a way of escape and a way out. It is as we grow in understanding that God has always given us a way of escape, so we stop falling to the "I'm only human" lie! It is when we realize that this is a lie, and God has given deliverance from every temptation (1 Corinthians 10:13), then we restrain our own feet. I have heard too many people say "when God wants me to stop IT, He will take IT away from me" — whatever the IT is, whatever issue they are dealing with i.e. smoking, fornication, lying, etc. — no, in Romans 12:1-2, there are too many "you's" in there, meaning that God has empowered us to do what the text says: it is as YOU present YOUR body as a living sacrifice which is YOUR reasonable service, and YOU not be conformed to this world, but YOU be transformed by the renewing of YOUR mind — so YOU have to restrain YOUR feet! You have the help of the Holy Spirit to help you, but you do not need to think that God is going to just do it all because He doesn't.

He gave the children of Israel the Promised Land, but they had to go and possess the land, they had to go and drive out the "—ites" that were in the land. He empowered them to do it. We have some "—ites" that are in our land, some thoughts, some doctrines and theologies of this world, that we need to drive out — and we need to say "I have restrained my feet from every evil way" — because there are evil thoughts that come at us, the enemy fires his fiery darts at us regularly, everyday — so what we need to do is quench them with faith in the Word of God as Ephesians 6:16 says to do — the saving shield of faith. It is when you quench these thoughts, or darts from the enemy, then you keep your way.

This is no different than what took place in the Garden of Eden with woman, the enemy gave a suggestion that sounded really good — but we do not want to operate out of the knowledge of the tree of good and evil, but out of the tree of Life, which is Jesus. Woman should never have listened and given in to the promise of good, because there was an evil attached to it. It is not about being good, everything God made until that point He declared to be good, so what was this? It was the trickery and beguilement of God's enemy trying to make her think that God didn't want her to be as good as He was — a pure lie! We have to learn to restrain our feet, do not think it is all up to God. Yes, He has a part to play in it, but you have a part to play also: YOU present YOUR body as a living sacrifice — and you cannot come and say "well, if God wants me to be a living sacrifice, then He will tie me up and lay me down." No. That is not the way it goes, you have to prepare your own sacrifice. Just like with Abraham and Isaac, when he took Isaac up on the mountain as a teenager and "bound" him up and laid him on the altar — God didn't do it, Abraham had to do it (Genesis 22:9). God was testing Abraham's heart to see if he loved Isaac more than Him, and Abraham passed the test and an Angel called out to him to stop and told him "now I see that you fear and love Me more." God already knows what He is going to do, He is just testing you to see what the motives of your heart are: is it worship? Is it true worship? Or is it a form without power?

How many of us make an oath to God, but do not keep it completely? See verse 106. Then we wonder why things seem to be going wrong? It is when His righteous ordinances come up against your flesh feeling good, or you being in worldly peace (I call it worldly peace, because God gives you the peace that passes understanding, that even in the midst of a trial, you may have shaky knees naturally, but you choose to keep the decrees of God knowing that He has empowered you to do it — brings that peace that passes understanding, not this pseudo-peace of thinking we have everything figured out). This reminds me as in Job 22:28, *You shall also decide and decree a thing, and it shall be established for you, and the light [of God's favor] shall shine upon your ways* — so if we decree and declare that we will keep His righteous ordinances, that we will hear them, receive them, love and obey, when I hear them and they do not feel good to me, I choose to go ahead and receive it, fall in love with it, and obey it. But we hear traditions of man, church regulations and rules, and are trying feverishly to keep that, instead of paying attention to what the Law/Word says. Remember, Jesus fulfills the law, so everywhere here in Psalm 119 (and the bible, especially Old Testament), He came to fulfill the law, not do away with it.

Verse 115 — there will be some evil doers that are around you, and what you are to do is to decree and declare that you will keep the commandments of your God — because bad company corrupts good habits (1 Corinthians 15:33), so there is a separation that must take place.

Verse 129 – we have to keep the testimonies of God and understand that His testimony far exceeds anything conceived by man. We may have a testimony, but understand that in Revelation it says we overcome by the blood of the Lamb and the word of our testimony, so you can't have a testimony apart from the blood. A testimony is giving an account of the blood of Jesus (or the hand of God – His miraculous works) in your life.

"My penitent self' – means I am ever living a life of repentance, and asking God daily to change my thinking – repent means to change your thinking; to heartily amend your ways with abhorrence for past sins.

Verse 134 – when it appears that man is oppressing you, it is then that you look to God; look to the Word that was flesh and dwelt among us; look to Jesus for deliverance. Like in Isaiah 61 and Luke 4:18 when Jesus said the spirit of the Lord is upon Me and He has anointed Me to deliver the down-trodden. You look to Him, because man will try to keep you down and degrade you and say you will never be nobody, or that you are single, or not married to the right person, or do not have the right education – just oppression of man through words – maybe not literal bondage, but oppression to the ill words spoken over you that you have falsely believed.

In order to be delivered from depression of man, you have to hear God over man. What voice are you listening to more? The voice of man, or the voice of God? And the voice of God will not scream and holler or do aerobics to be heard, it is usually a still small voice that speaks to you; so when you listen to it, you hear it, then you receive it, then fall in love with it, and obey it – obey the voice of God and the word of God.

In conclusion, getting these principles of hearing, receiving, loving and obeying – it is as we take His statutes, observe His word, keep His law/ precepts/ word, as we know His word, as we keep the testimony of His mouth, as we keep His righteous ordinances, as we keep His commandments as we do this our worship life and experience is heightened and enhanced.

> Luke 2:25-29 Now there was a man in Jerusalem whose name was Simeon, and this man was righteous and devout [cautiously and carefully observing the divine Law], and looking for the Consolation of Israel; and the Holy Spirit was upon him. 26 And it had been divinely revealed (communicated) to him by the Holy Spirit that he would not see death before he had seen the Lord's Christ (the Messiah, the Anointed One). 27 And prompted by the [Holy] Spirit, he came into the temple [enclosure]; and when the parents brought in the little child Jesus to do for Him what was customary according to the Law, 28 [Simeon] took Him up in his arms and praised and thanked God and said, 29 And now, Lord, You are releasing Your servant to depart (leave this world) in peace, according to Your word.

Simeon was not just praying for himself here — all of the references to "You" are in capital, so God is releasing His servant, Jesus, in the baby... yes, Simeon is talking, but you must have a spiritual ear to hear and spiritual eyes to see, and not miss, that this is the declaration as in Isaiah 9:6 — Simeon was saying so much more than we can see. As it said in verse 25, he was serious, he was devout, cautiously and carefully observing the divine law — so he saw with spiritual eyes what was going on — not just religiously memorizing the law, but the ability to recognize that it was being manifested in his presence — also in response to the prophetic word that God had given him that he would not die until he saw this fulfilled it was the "set time". Scripture is multi-dimensional — this is God talking to Himself about Jesus; but this is also Simeon seeing that what he was waiting on was fulfilled.

> Luke 2:30 For with my [own] eyes I have seen Your Salvation

Simeon was telling God that he saw His salvation, the plan of salvation in the child.

> Luke 2:31-35 Which You have ordained and prepared before (in the presence of) all peoples, 32 A Light for revelation to the Gentiles [to disclose what was before unknown] and [to bring] praise and honor and glory to Your people Israel. 33 And His [legal] father and [His] mother were marveling at what was said about Him. 34 And Simeon blessed them and said to Mary His mother, Behold, this Child is appointed and destined for the fall and rising of many in Israel, and for a sign that is spoken against 35 And a sword will pierce through your own soul also—that the secret thoughts and purposes of many hearts may be brought out and disclosed.

Simeon was basically telling her that her son had a great destiny / purpose — and that she would go through a lot of distress of soul, and that many people would be brought out. Telling her that raising this child would bring suffering and sorrow. Also at verse 34, he spoke to Mary, not Joseph, why?

> Luke 2:36-40 And there was also a prophetess, Anna, the daughter of Phanuel, of the tribe of Asher. She was very old, having lived with her husband seven years from her maidenhood, 37 And as a widow even for eighty-four years. She did not go out from the temple enclosure, but was worshiping night and day with fasting and prayer. 38 And she too came up at that same hour, and she returned thanks to God and talked of [Jesus] to all who were looking for the redemption (deliverance) of Jerusalem. 39 And when they had done everything according to the Law of the Lord, they went back into Galilee to their own town, Nazareth. 40 And the Child grew and became strong in spirit, **filled with wisdom; and the grace** (favor and spiritual blessing) of God was upon Him.

Verse 40 and verse 52 show us what we should be increasing in as we renew our mind: WISDOM, FAVOR, AND GRACE. As we saw in Titus 2:11, grace helps us reject heresy and the falseness of this day.

Luke 2:52 And Jesus increased in wisdom (in broad and full understanding) and in stature and years, and **in favor with God and man.**

Prayer: Thank You for wisdom and stature increasing in us – thank You that we are being increased and enlarged in our spirits to have understanding and knowledge and wisdom of Who You are, and who we are in You – that we be the kingdom ambassadors and representatives in the earth realm for such a time as this. Amen.

Romans 7:24 - 8:2 O unhappy and pitiable and wretched man that I am! Who will release and deliver me from [the shackles of] this body of death ²⁵ O thank God! [He will!] through Jesus Christ (the Anointed One) our Lord! So then indeed I, of myself with the mind and heart, serve the Law of God, but with the flesh the law of sin. Chp 8:1 Therefore, [there is] now no condemnation (no adjudging guilty of wrong) for those who are in Christ Jesus, who live [and] walk not after the dictates of the flesh, but after the dictates of the Spirit. ² For the law of the Spirit of life [which is] in Christ Jesus [the law of our new being] has freed me from the law of sin and of death.

Looking again at the fact that Jesus fulfills the law. In Romans 7 is where we have a battle going on between the soulish realm and the spirit realm — of doing the things I don't want to do. We see the law of sin at work, but God through Jesus Christ delivers. Then Romans 8:1-2, in Christ we have no condemnation, because the law of the spirit of life (sounds like the tree of life from Genesis and Revelation), is the law of our new being. It is IN HIM, since He fulfilled the law, our new being is in Christ which frees me from the law of sin and death.

Now this is not a permit to pervert grace just because we are in the age of grace where Jesus is ruling and reigning. Grace is there if you miss it, but we cannot live any kind of way, grace is there to catch us if we fall, not to commit sin boldly and attempt to pervert grace (as if you could?!). Grace is like the safety net; that as we walk the walk if (or when) we fall, grace is there to catch us. But we do not intentionally jump off — it is a fall/ stumble/ overtaken. But here in Romans chapter 8, we see that Jesus sets us free from the law of sin that was warring with us in Romans chapter 7.

It is as we grow, that we will truly understand the freeing power of Jesus Christ, that He frees us from the battle that is going on within, so that instead of trying to fight on our own with the very thing that we keep doing (which actually only highlights and heightens the battle within — NO) — we must change our focus (change the channel). So instead of looking at the law of sin, and the flesh, and the very thing that you desire not to do anymore (whatever IT is), look to Jesus, He is the Author and the Finisher of your faith. As in the book of Numbers when the Children of Israel were being bitten by fiery serpents (sent by God because of the sinfulness of His people; as the Amplified says at Numbers 21:4, they became *impatient, depressed, much discouraged and many died*.) Moses cried out to God and received instructions to make a serpent of brass to be raised on a pole for the Israelites to look to and live. Look to Jesus, the brazen serpent of the Old Testament type and shadow, that was fulfilled in Jesus being raised on the cross, and raised from the dead.

Look to the "In HIM's" as found in the book of Ephesians and throughout the New Testament, that in Him we have redemption, that in Him we are adopted, in Him we have our righteousness, in Him we have forgiveness of sins. Refocus what you are looking at, do not keep saying to yourself over and over again "I really need to stop IT", if you really want to stop doing IT, stop focusing on IT and focus on Him!

> Galatians 2:13-16 And the rest of the Jews along with him also concealed their true convictions and acted insincerely, with the result that even Barnabas was carried away by their hypocrisy (their example of insincerity and pretense). 14 But as soon as I saw that they were not straightforward and were not living up to the truth of the Gospel, I said to Cephas (Peter) before everybody present, If you, though born a Jew, can live [as you have been living] like a Gentile and not like a Jew, how do you dare now to urge and practically force the Gentiles to [comply with the ritual of Judaism and] live like Jews? 15 [I went on to say] Although we ourselves (you and I) are Jews by birth and not Gentile (heathen) sinners, 16 Yet we know that a man is justified or reckoned righteous and in right standing with God not by works of the Law, but [only] through faith and [absolute] reliance on and adherence to and trust in Jesus Christ (the Messiah, the Anointed One). [Therefore] even we [ourselves] have believed on Christ Jesus, in order to be justified by faith in Christ and not by works of the Law [for we cannot be justified by any observance of the ritual of the Law given by Moses], because by keeping legal rituals and by works no human being can ever be justified (declared righteous and put in right standing with God).

I wanted to include Galatians 2:11-21, but that is a large section to quote — when you get a moment, read the entire Galatians 2. But at verse 13 we are talking about the heart of worship, and here they were acting insincerely v13; they did it then, they will do it now.

Basically, this Galatians 2 is showing that Jesus fulfills the law and Paul was saying "Stop trying to make people get under these rituals to be saved" — these rituals were a type and a shadow, but now Jesus is here to fulfill those, we no longer have to do those rituals, we just need to get IN HIM. The circumcision is not of the flesh (actual body parts), but of the heart (soulish realm) — cutting off the foreskin of your heart which is where your thoughts are, which is basically saying Romans 12:2 — be renewed so that you can receive from the mind of Christ instead of a worldly mindset.

When we look at worship through God's law, and Jesus fulfills the law then worship becomes more evident that it is not about music, or a program, or keeping rituals; hence

Psalm 119 being about the law is a good place for us to meditate to truly understand worship.

A sidenote regarding Psalm 119: I keep referring to Psalm 119 because I had an additional project that is titled "Growing In Knowing God, A Daily Devotional Based on Psalm 119" that I was working on at the time of this project. It is part of the Renewal of The Mind! process, that combines Romans 12:1-2, with Joshua 1:8, and the entire Psalm 119, which is broken up into 22 stanzas of 8 verses each — and can be used as a daily devotional to meditate on "this book of the Law day and night" to get a better understanding of the law and how the meditation process can be enhanced with this knowledge. You are to read a stanza of 8 verses in the morning, and the same 8 verses again at night — and meditate throughout the day — do this for the 22 days, one stanza of 8 verses per day, and see how you Grow In Knowing Who God Is.

> Day 1 – Keepers of God's law, verses 1-8
> Day 2 – Purity, the fruit of the law, verses 9-16
> Day 3 – Eyes to see God's law, verse 17-24
> Day 4 – Prayer for understanding the law, verses 25-32
> Day 5 – Living the Lord's way, verses 33-40
> Day 6 – Salvation through God's law, verses 41-48
> Day 7 – Comfort in God's law, verses 49-56
> Day 8 – The Lord our portion, verses 57-64
> Day 9 – God's law taught by affliction, verses 65-72
> Day 10 – Confidence in the law, verses 73-80
> Day 11 – A longing for comfort, verses 81-88
> Day 12 – God's unchangeable law, verses 88-96
> Day 13 – The love of God's law, verses 97-104
> Day 14 – God's law a lamp to the feet, verses 105-112
> Day 15 – God's law a hiding place, verses 113-120
> Day 16 – The psalmist loves God's law, verses 121-128
> Day 17 – The psalmist keeps God's law, verses 129-136
> Day 18 – God's law is true, verses 137-144
> Day 19 – A cry for salvation, verses 145-152
> Day 20 – Keeping God's law in adversity, verses 153-160
> Day 21 – Peace in keeping God's law, verses 161-168
> Day 22 – A Prayer for understanding, verses 169-176

4.7 The Role of Affliction

As I took the challenge of meditating on Psalm 119, I found another recurring theme, which is the role of affliction. We have 7 references in Psalm 119 regarding the idea of affliction; each revealing the role affliction plays in us *"Growing In Knowing God"* — which is important to our worship life because worship is us responding to God revealing to us who He is; so that we can now see how affliction in our lives (that seems like cruel and unusual punishment) really is not that at all. It is not that God is angry with us, or punishing us, but teaching us Himself (His law). Read and ponder these 7 references together from Psalm 119:

- Verse 50: This is my comfort and consolation in my **affliction:** that Your word has revived me and given me life.
- Verse 67: Before I was **afflicted** I went astray, but now Your word do I keep [hearing, receiving, loving, and obeying it].
- Verse 71: It is good for me that I have been **afflicted,** that I might learn Your statutes.
- Verse 75: I know, O Lord, that Your judgments are right and righteous, and that in faithfulness You have **afflicted** me.
- Verse 92: Unless Your law had been my delight, I would have perished in my **affliction.**
- Verse 107: I am sorely **afflicted;** renew and quicken me [give me life], O Lord, according to Your word!
- Verse 153: Consider my **affliction** and deliver me, for I do not forget Your law.

Affliction is a teacher to teach us God statutes, His word. Really, just re-read these 7 verses about 3 or 4 times and truly see that the role of affliction in our lives has been a part of Romans 8:28, all things working together for the good, and for His glory. Personally, I am dealing with a situation with my youngest daughter right now, she believes that I am upset with her because she has not made wise choices in some areas. However, I am not upset about the past, it cannot be changed, I am just learning the patience that God has with His children as I am patient for her to see the lessons learned through affliction as a result of bad decisions. I am faithful to meet her basic needs and fulfill my parental role in her life, but until she cries out like David did here in the Psalm, I have to allow the Romans 8:28, and the afflictions she faces to occur. Very tough job on my part, but she thinks she is the only one hurting — we do God like this all the time. Even as I just typed this paragraph, I heard the Holy Spirit whisper Proverbs 22:6 to me *Train up a child in the way he should go [and in keeping with his individual gift or bent], and when he is old he will not depart from it.* As I re-read the verses above, this Proverbs 22:6 is a partner scripture to Psalm 119:67 that we all must walk out. Whether we received the word as a natural child, or an adult child (spiritually), we will all have to learn His word through afflictions. Add on Psalm 34:19 about the many afflictions that the Lord delivers the righteous out of. I am also standing on Mark 10:28-30 for my family restoration, but notice the highlighted word:

Mark 10:28-30 Peter started to say to Him, Behold, we have yielded up and abandoned everything [once and for all and joined You as Your disciples, siding with Your party] and accompanied You [walking the same road that You walk]. 29 Jesus said, Truly I tell you, there is no one who has given up and left house or brothers or sisters or mother or father or children or lands for My sake and for the Gospel's ³⁰ Who will not receive a hundred times as much now in this time – houses and brothers and sisters and mothers and children and lands, <u>WITH PERSECUTIONS</u> – and in the age to come, eternal life.

Another way of saying afflictions is persecution. So there is a promised restoration, but there are also promised persecutions. We must renew our mind to endure.

Back to these Psalm 119 afflictions, at verse 92, you have to keep the law even in afflictions, because without the law (Jesus), you perish. Also, at verse 107, in the midst of affliction, God's law gives life — we know that is not talking about a list of rules and do's and dont's, but the law of Christ, as mentioned in Romans chapters 7 and 8, that delivers us from the struggles within, and without. At the conclusion of these 7 verses above, affliction helps me to not forget His law; do not focus on the affliction, but the law (Jesus) — seek Him. Allow afflictions to drive you into the arms of Jesus, not the world and sin.

Prayer: Thank You for purpose being made manifest and evident in our lives, and in the hearts and the lives of Your people. Thank You for Your prophetic power and fire turning within my heart that I could pull out Your mind/ will/ emotions and put it in words to be able to deliver it to Your people. Thank You that I decrease and You increase with the knowledge and the meditation, the Selah of the word going forward. Thank You for what You are doing, and thank You for the lives of those whom You have attached to me. Thank You for causing us to grow in knowing who You are and who we are in You – and for causing us to grow in knowing Your sovereignty – that You are the sovereign God, and we can understand this closer look at worship through the law (Psalm 119) which is Jesus Christ. Thank You that we can see Your sovereign hand in our lives and those around us – give us the ability to be able to speak on behalf of Your sovereignty – that You are in control of all things; even when things do not look like You are in control, You still will yet get the glory out of it. Thank You for making Yourself more and more evident, and for making Romans 8:26 evident in our lives, that even when we do not know how to pray, Your Holy Spirit comes and intercedes on our behalf. Thank You God that You are causing all things to work together on our behalf because we love You and we are called according to Your purpose. Thank You God that nothing can separate us from Your love – NOTHING – not height, nor depth, nor perils, nor sword, nor principalities, nor things pending, nor things seen or unseen – nothing shall be able to separate us from Your love.

Thank You that as we hear Your word, we hear it/ receive it/ love it/ and obey it because You have given us the best example of Love whereby You so loved the world that You gave Your only begotten Son. Thank You for causing us to grow in understanding Calvary and salvation. Thank You that we do not let one day go by that we remain in a stagnated state, but that we be ever growing, and not be backslidden – as Smith Wigglesworth said, "one day that we have not grown in You is to be backslidden" and we do not want to be backsliders. We understand Your word that says You are married to the backslider, but we are

making a conscious effort to be ever moving forward, to be ever growing, to be ever producing for You. We are created to produce, to produce kingdom mindsets, to produce true worshippers that worship You in spirit and in truth. Enough of church, tradition, religion, and doctrines of man – but God let us really understand Your precepts, Your commands, Your laws, Your testimonies, and what it truly means to fear You, to reverence You, to stand in awe of You.

Thank You that as we draw closer to You, You draw closer to us. It is as we get closer to You, that we see how un-done we truly are; and our response should be worship, that we see that You are worthy; worth-ship. Another word for worship is service; it should be service unto You. Love God, love people. And because we love You, we love Your people – and we are the hands that show people Your love in this earth realm in this time and in this season. Thank You for continually expanding our understanding of who You are and who we are in You. That our worship experience heightens and grows deeper and deeper in You, that You get the glory, the honor, and the praise from Your servants. Have Your way in the lives of Your people. Amen.

Before I close this section on worship and this chapter on kingdom mindsets, I would like to share a life-changing powerful reference on worship. My entire band, praise team, and praise dancers read this book together, and discussed the principles before rehearsals. This totally transformed our praise and worship at my church. The book is titled "Worship – The Ultimate Priority" by John MacArthur. Thank you Pastor Michael Ewing and the House of Simon Band at The Fellowship of Love Church in Richmond TX – this really heightened my worship experience and I just had to share. Be blessed.

Chapter 5 – Kingdom Finances

5.1 Rich Verses Wealthy

We are renewing our mind on the role of riches and wealth. Rich is about money, wealth is about supplies for the kingdom, they both have a different focus.

Definitions:
> Wealth: wealth; riches; substance; a high value; enough; sufficiency. Riches: wealth and riches.

Like in the parable, it will be difficult for a rich man to inherit the kingdom, because the focus is on money, not God (Deuteronomy 8:18, Matthew 19:23-24). When Jesus told him to sell everything and come, it was not that it costs to get into heaven, but that Jesus perceived and saw that people's hearts were more attached to money, than to God. Therefore we want to change our thinking and our understanding. This was a heart check.

One of the age old taboos in the church is to talk about money. People do not want to hear it. Personally, my family was severely burned by a church that had wrong motives and bad doctrine regarding money – this had left me with a bad view of riches and wealth and the leadership in the church. Even myself personally, I have experienced some pretty "interesting" teaching and practices with churches and finances – this is another reason I want to renew my mind according to the word of God, not all of this bad representation. I do not want passed on thoughts, or an illustration I like to use when sharing the principle of studying it for myself, "I don't want someone else to chew up my food and put it in my mouth. No, I am mature enough and have learned to make my own meals. We come to church to get the recipes and examples, but then we must put action to what we receive." So I want to get my own understanding of the kingdom ingredients concerning rich verses wealth.

Let me share a testimony from when I went to a women's retreat back in 1998. I had pre-registered for the event, the group had prayed over the names of the attendees, and prepared laminated bookmarks with a personalized scripture on it for each of us. Side note: this is also why it is important to pre-register, not just for the group to have a headcount, but for special preparations such as this – that was a bonus principle, as I am involved in putting on different conferences, retreats, and workshops. But the scripture that We Care

Ministries selected for me is Psalm 112:3, and it reads "Paulette — God's Chosen Vessel. Wealth and riches shall be in her house and her righteousness endureth forever." I still use this bookmark to this day, I use it as the check divider for my duplicates in my checkbook. There have been times that I would go to the checkbook and see it, then question the Lord saying "You said riches and wealth will be in my house, but this is not what it is looking like?" Well, God's word works — what needs to change is our view of His word.

God's word is true, the thing we must do is get in line with it. It requires God's timing as well as us being willing and obedient. There is the set time, the time of harvest, and God is the only one that turns the hand of time.

We can see here in Psalm 112:3 that the Lord desires the righteous to have both riches and wealth. Let's put it in context and begin at verse 1.

> Psalm 112:1-3 Praise the Lord! (Hallelujah!) Blessed (happy, fortunate, to be envied) is the man who fears (reveres and worships) the Lord, who delights greatly in His commandments. ² His [spiritual] offspring shall be mighty upon earth; the generation of the upright shall be blessed. ³ Prosperity and welfare are in his house, and his righteousness endures forever.

So prosperity and welfare are in their house, also wealth and generosity. Riches and wealth are not for us to be stingy, or braggadocios; as a righteous person, we will not be a hoarder. You will give stuff away. It will blow some people's mind and they won't understand why you are so generously giving, especially of good stuff, but we should be givers.

We can see that riches and wealth are not about us.

> Psalm 112:4 Light arises in the darkness for the upright, gracious, compassionate, and just [who are in right standing with God].

Before we even look at the money, riches and wealth, we have to go back up to verse 1 and see that it says you are blessed when you fear God. Again, God's word works. We must work on our understanding. This prosperity and wealth in my house forever may not happen right away as far as the finances side is going. We also need to understand that in 3 John 2, He said "beloved I would that you prosper and be in good health, even as your soul prospers" — so your soul prospering (meaning you are renewing your mind), causes good wealth and prosperity; but prosperity is not just about money, it is an endowment of power from God. He says "I give you the power to get wealth" (Deuteronomy 8:18).

In Psalm 112:2, it talks about our offspring being mighty, so we have to make sure that we are training up, not just natural children, but spiritual children as well. We renew our minds together, we help younger believers believe and grow. Then at verse 3, in order for the righteousness to endure forever, it must be rooted and grounded in Jesus Christ — no self-righteousness.

❦

Sidebar: When you have spiritual ears to hear, you will hear other things that the person is speaking. Because Jesus says when 2 or 3 are gathered together, there I am in the midst. So the spirit of truth is here, and He is speaking to our hearts. It may not be from the pulpit, or the teacher, or the words on the page, but He speaks heart to heart.

Back to the text at hand, if you are in a dark place, as long as your righteousness is in Him, the light is going to arise. As you seek Him, as you give Him access — the light will arise and come in. Anything dark, the light will arise. Light always overpowers dark.

> Psalm 112:5-7 It is well with the man who deals generously and lends, who conducts his affairs with justice. ⁶ He will not be moved forever; the [uncompromisingly] righteous (the upright, in right standing with God) shall be in everlasting remembrance. ⁷ He shall not be afraid of evil tidings; his heart is firmly fixed, trusting (leaning on and being confident) in the Lord.

Psalm 112:5-7 is another part the enemy comes after, he will try to steal your confidence in the Lord to not be firmly fixed in the Lord regarding riches and wealth. Your heart can be firmly fixed that you are saved, and that God loves you, so why can't your heart be firmly fixed that God desires riches and wealth, prosperity, generosity and welfare to be in your house forever?! The enemy's tactic here is to get you to major on the minor things. But you will not be afraid of evil tidings because Psalm 91 says *they that abide in the shadow of the Most High,* we will not even be ruffled, knowing that He will protect us and take care of us. My confidence is in God, I trust You God — trust/ lean on/ and am confident in the Lord, not in this world, not in money.

There are times that I am facing a situation that I have no idea how it will work out — no comprehension of how it will happen. But the one thing that I know, is that God will take care of me and make provisions. He always comes through and makes a way out of no way. Our confidence is in Him, not in people or a system. Because I trust and fear God, I will praise Him in the midst of the trial, knowing that He is in control. These times make me stand on Psalm 139:23-24 even more, allowing the Lord to search my heart and expose and remove any darkness, like we just talked about at Psalm 112:4, let the light arise in darkness because I am choosing to stand as the righteousness in Christ Jesus.

We are renewing our mind, know that you will not get to the riches and wealth part if you do not understand that your confidence MUST be in Him — you must understand the trust part. Or, you may get to the riches and wealth, but it will be like in Hosea when they put their money in purses with holes in it; or as in Isaiah 55, when God asked His people "why do you spend your money for that which does not satisfy?" You can get money, but know that riches and wealth do not make people happy — look at Michael Jackson, or Michael Vick who had money and still got caught up in foolishness. There are so many people with a lot of money, and they still do not have that happiness the world promises with money. Understand this, you may come into money, and even acknowledge that God blessed you with it, but if your heart is not right, if you are not fearing God, and calling for the light to constantly expose the darkness, if you are not walking upright, if your trust and confidence (which is your heart) is not fixed in Him — that money will just fly away and take wings. When you leave this earth realm, the money is not going with you — it is an inheritance to the next generation.

> Psalm 112:8-9 His heart is established and steady, he will not be afraid while he waits to see his desire established upon his adversaries. ⁹ He has distributed freely [he has given to the poor and needy]; his righteousness (uprightness and right standing with God) endures forever; his horn shall be exalted in honor.

In Psalm 112:8-9 the riches and the wealth that you obtain through the fear of the Lord and the light of God, and the righteousness of God being in your life — it is all for you to do verse 9: distribute freely. Not for you to hoard all on yourself. The poor and the needy referred to here is not just talking about money, but as in Isaiah 58 about true fasting that says that you give to the poor and the needy. Matthew 5 says blessed are the poor in spirit. We help those that are needy and poor in spirit — we distribute freely to them of the knowledge that God has given us, as well as the finances that have come our way.

We went through all of Psalm 112, to keep verse 3 in context. We are not going to force scripture to support the idea that God will make us rich and wealthy. No! But I know that I have seen the spiritual abundance and supply of God that the Lord wants to get to and through me, but was at a loss of the "how to" access it. I found that we have to be ready WHEN the finances come — we must not have a poverty mentality, but truly have renewed our mind to the purpose and role of riches and wealth. It is better to have a plan, and no opportunity; that we not get caught like those who have won the natural lottery and then said it ruined their life — it was because their eyes were focused on the money and what it could do for them. They were not seeking the Lord and what He wanted done, and how to handle all of the pressure of things and people coming up out of nowhere. No, I have sat with the Lord and planned out some "what next" type things for the funds that will come in. First and foremost, to be a covenant keeper, then to know the estate of my affairs, how much is needed to be a debt free steward. Then to have plans of where to sow seed for the kingdom, first in my church home and personal ministry, then the list of where I have prayed about.

I said something above that I want to bring up again: poverty mentality! This is like a slavery mentality; like the children of Israel with the manna, their thinking was off, they got tired of the manna and complained that they had it better back in bondage to Egypt, at least they had what they wanted to eat. What!?! Their needs were being met, yet they still complained. Does that not sound like some modern day believers? God is keeping a roof over our head, it may not be where we want it, or as fancy as we want it, but we have a place to sleep, clothes to wear (the same thing, but not outgrowing it — like the Israelites), we have substance (maybe we don't like it or just tired of the same old thing). Is life in the kingdom more than what you will eat, wear and were you will live?!?! We must change and get rid of these warped mentalities.

We have to get to where we say, the things that I have been through may not have all been good, but thank You God that it is all working together for good! What I am to do now is renew my mind with the word of God to properly view riches and wealth. What is it that You want me to do Lord? I have a list of places that I want to sow seed, because His word says He gives seed to the sower; so I remind God that I am a sower, and when He sends the seed my way, I will strategically scatter it in good ground of the kingdom — not just for me, myself and I. Prepare yourself to be a sower, by having a plan — it is better to have a plan with no opportunity, than an opportunity with no plan. Part of the plan for seed that I have is supporting missions — some local (here in the United States), some global (around the world). I heard a phrase while at Rhema Bible Training Center "Some go, some pray, some pay" — I endeavor to be part of the going, the praying, and the paying.

We are renewing our minds back to Eden, back when God first created man to commune with Him in the garden. But because of the entrance of deception and sin into the world, our communication was severed and we now have to commune with Him through the tree of Life that we were put out from in Genesis 3:25. See section 1.4 regarding the "Two Trees" in the garden. So let's go back and see in Genesis 2 of what we have to renew our mind to. Understand that enough is never enough to the carnal nature, to the Adamic nature — because they had access to everything in the garden, except for one tree; and enough was not enough! The enemy was able to deceive them with "God is just trying to keep stuff from you..." type thoughts to get them to disobey the instructions. Today, the enemy says stuff to us like "He doesn't mind you having the best, or quality stuff — and He will provide" — I am referring to a time a few years ago that the Lord allowed me to purchase a car for my oldest daughter. I had received spirit to spirit detailed instructions on the proposed budget for the car. But my daughter really wanted something outside of the budget and outside of the specific details for the car. My instructions were to purchase a reliable 4 door vehicle, with a payment of no more than $250 per month — but her heart was set on a Volkswagen Bug, that only comes in a 2 door.

Also, the monthly payment would be $330 instead of $250 — I rationalized and reasoned that it was not *that* much. I listened to the lies of the enemy about how God will provide, and He doesn't mind you having nice things. Just disobedient — but it seemed good. Just like the woman in the garden. We are not to talk to the devil; we should not be holding conversations with him. The one thing that we should do is to say the word. When the enemy came as an angel of light with the thoughts to disobey the instructions of God, I should have reminded him of the instructions from God, and the word of God that I was standing on. Sometimes that is our problem, it sounds good, and leans toward our carnal nature – but is not 100% obedience – and I am sorry, 99.5% just will not do! We must be 100% obedient to the word of God, the will of God, and the instructions of God. This trial that I went through with this vehicle took me 2 years to be delivered from! I had to be delivered from the foolish decision that I made to disobey the instructions of God. God is not a God of confusion, when He gives specific instructions, that is what He means.

We have to be careful, I was guilty of listening to the voice of my child, over the voice of the Lord that spoke to my spirit and gave me instructions. That disobedience messed with the riches that were in my possession, and caused major problems. You do know that when we miss it, and mess up, there are some consequences that have to be dealt with. By me missing it, and being disobedient, God graced me through 2 years of paying 2 car notes (because 3 months after she got the car, she lost her job and was pregnant – the additional expenses for the pregnancy were around $80 per month! $330 - $250 = $80. Not to mention, having an infant in a 2 door car). But He graced me to be able to handle her car note, my car note, insurance, and the additional $80 per month – for 2 years! Not to mention, the way in which I was delivered from the 2nd car note was no walk in the park, nothing like I would ever have expected, the car caught on fire one day while my daughter was driving it, with my grandson in the backseat! The insurance paid the car off, and I had enough funds left over to purchase that 4 door car with no car note! I learned my lesson – it was extremely financially tight for me for 2 years. And you just never know what other opportunities were blocked.

Another consequence or repercussion that I have had to deal with as a result of that bad decision 5 years ago, is that neither my daughter nor myself have been to the dentist in 5 years – because the funds in my possession have been tied up waiting on things to get back in line. The consequences are so far out reaching what we know they are. We cannot afford to be disobedient to the known will of God, we must listen to the details of instructions.

> Genesis 2:7-17 Then the Lord God formed man from the dust of the ground and breathed into his nostrils the breath or spirit of life, and man became a living being. 8 And the Lord God planted a garden toward the east, in Eden [delight]; and there He put the man whom He had formed (framed, constituted). 9 And out of the ground the Lord God made to grow every tree that is pleasant to the sight or to be desired – good (suitable, pleasant) for food; the tree of life also in the center of the garden, and the tree of the knowledge of [the difference between] good and evil and blessing and calamity. 10 Now a river went out of Eden to water the garden; and from there it divided and became four [river] heads. 11 The first is named Pishon; it is the one flowing around the whole land of Havilah, where there is gold. 12 The gold of that land is of high quality; bdellium (pearl?) and onyx stone are there. 13 The second river is named Gihon; it is the one flowing around the whole land of Cush. 14 The third river is named Hiddekel [the Tigris]; it is the one flowing east of Assyria. And the fourth river is the Euphrates. 15 And the Lord God took the man and put him in the Garden of Eden to tend and guard and keep it. 16 And the Lord

God commanded the man, saying, You may freely eat of every tree of the garden; 17 But of the tree of the knowledge of good and evil and blessing and calamity you shall not eat, for in the day that you eat of it you shall surely die.

Look at verse 7, we see the tri-part being — we see spirit, soul, and body. Spirit of Life, is the tree of Life, is Jesus, the spirit that is created in His image. Became a living being — that is the soulish realm, the part that now must be renewed. The dirt suit is the body.

Question, in view of verse 7 in comparison to verse 17, what was it that died? It was the spirit man that was born of the breath of life. There was still human breath in the body, that is the soulish realm, but the ability to communicate with the spirit that was created in His image is what died, and that is the part that must be born again (which will contain the mind of Christ) — it is the soulish realm that lived on and must be renewed from thinking that relies on the knowledge of good and evil instead of the tree of life — the Adamic nature.

> Genesis 2:18-25 Now the Lord God said, It is not good (sufficient, satisfactory) that the man should be alone; I will make him a helper (suitable, adapted, complementary) for him. 19 And out of the ground the Lord God formed every [wild] beast and living creature of the field and every bird of the air and brought them to Adam to see what he would call them; and whatever Adam called every living creature, that was its name. 20 And Adam gave names to all the livestock and to the birds of the air and to every [wild] beast of the field; but for Adam there was not found a helper meet (suitable, adapted, complementary) for him. 21 And the Lord God caused a deep sleep to fall upon Adam; and while he slept, He took one of his ribs or a part of his side and closed up the [place with] flesh. 22 And the rib or part of his side which the Lord God had taken from the man He **built up** and made into a woman, and He brought her to the man. 23 Then Adam said, This [creature] is now bone of my bones and flesh of my flesh; she shall be called Woman, because she was taken out of a man. 24 Therefore a man shall leave his father and his mother and shall become united and cleave to his wife, and they shall become one flesh. 25 And the man and his wife were both naked and were not embarrassed or ashamed in each other's presence.

It is funny how in verse 18 the Lord said it is not good that man be alone, but did not make the
companion right away? See verses 19-20, He created the animal kingdom and had Adam name them all; then at verse 21 God began the process of "building" the companion for man.

The "naked" referred to in verse 25 is not what they tried to cover up after the fall. It did not have anything to do with them being physically naked — they hadn't realized any difference, the animals did not have on clothes? They had never witnessed death before. No, this nakedness is talking about the soulish realm, their understanding that came once their eyes were opened to see good and evil, blessing and calamity. They were able to see into the soulish realm, what God did not want them to see. He wanted them to see the tree of life in the soulish realm, there were 2 trees in the center of the garden. After deception came in at Genesis 3:1, (the woman was not supposed to conversate with the enemy) sin happened, God's wrath happened, curses happened (to the serpent, to woman, and to man), yet His mercy happened as He killed an animal and covered them (instituting the first sacrificial system, even though the Law had not yet been instituted – the Lamb slain), all of this took place between Genesis 3:1-21. Our goal is to renew our mind back to before deception and sin came in; this means that we have to study to show ourselves approved.

This is a chapter on finances, rich verses wealth, but our minds must be renewed to the time when communion (communication) flowed freely between God and mankind to better understand riches and wealth. To properly transform our mind to His ways of provision, and not be conformed and locked into the world's ways of viewing riches and wealth (mammon).

These are the things that are promised to be in the house of the upright. We have to make sure that we are doing things that are righteous and upright; our behavior/ lifestyle.

> Righteousness is defined as: *justice; of God's attributes; truthfulness; ethically right; vindicated; justification; salvation of God, and prosperity of His people.*

We have a lot to change our thinking about to have these things operating and flowing in our house. We will look at several scripture references to give us something to change our thinking on, and to align our minds with.

> Deuteronomy 29:29 The secret things belong unto the Lord our God, but the things which are revealed belong to us and to our children forever, that we may do all of the words of this law.

We see that the prosperity of the righteous is contingent upon us walking righteous, we can't just live any type of way. As in Psalm 112:6, our trust is in Him, the same in Proverbs 3:4-6, it is all about trusting God. But if we read on in Proverbs 3, we see the Lord saying that He chastens/ instructs/ corrects those whom He loves. He is trying to get us equipped for the prosperity that He desires to operate in our house and endure forever – we have to be instructed/ equipped/ and have to learn biblical definitions in understanding riches and wealth according to His word. Because Deuteronomy 29 is based on covenant – God is a covenant keeping God. If you put Deuteronomy 29 in context, go back one chapter to Deuteronomy 28, it speaks of blessings and curses – we must be listening and watchful to do the word, because IF we do not, the curse will be our PORTION, not the blessing. God will not bless a mess! The number one commandment Jesus promoted is love. If we are not living a life of love, promoting God's love, being an epistle of love in this sin-sick world, then what do we expect? We must get educated on the word, get a true understanding of it for the riches and wealth to flow in our lives. If they aren't flowing, sometimes we need to check and make sure we are not out of order as in Deuteronomy 28:15-68. No man can keep the law apart from Christ; Christ fulfills the law, He came that we would be able to walk upright in the law. The blood of Jesus is what covers us and empowers us to be able to now walk under the law of grace.

When we change our thinking about finances, riches and wealth, about blessings — we open the way to be true covenant keepers.

Prayer: Let us not be a thick hearted, non-covenant people, but let us be pleasing to You. We throw our thoughts down, and receive Yours, and we walk in them. Show us Your paths, and let us not lead others astray.

Thank You for everything that has taken place in my life up until now. Thank You for the kairos moment You are bringing together. Thank You for the set time, thank You for every "there" that You have designated for my life. Amen.

> 2 Chronicles 22:13 Then you will prosper if you are careful to keep and fulfill the statutes and ordinances with which the Lord charged Moses concerning Israel. Be strong and of good courage. Dread not and fear not; be not dismayed.

We see the need to trust God, and not be fearful. God did not give us a spirit of fear, but power love and a sound mind. Love! One of the assaults of the enemy is to get people to doubt and think that they do not have to do ALL of the word — because he knows that to what degree you compromise the truth, you will not be able to walk in the full blessings that are rightfully yours. It is not that the devil is busy, people always say that, but the true problem is ignorance of the word of God — on the "it is written" that will shut the enemy down! The Greater One is in you, that is who you serve. You serve the Abundant Life giver, so why are you magnifying the one that came to kill, steal, and destroy? No! Magnify the Abundant Life giver, magnify the "it is written" of the word that you are trusting in. Not just for finances, but marriage, singleness, upright children that are trained in the way to go and not depart — and that they shall be taught of the Lord. Do not be moved by what you see — stand on the "it is written."

> Psalm 1:3 And he shall be like a tree firmly planted [and tended] by the streams of water, ready to bring forth its fruit in its season; its leaf also shall not fade or wither; and everything he does shall prosper [and come to maturity].

Here we see the prosperous righteous man. But it will only prosper when you are obedient to God. A lot of people want to teach about riches and wealth (name it and claim it; blab it and grab it; money cometh now; standing on the promises of God that says He desires you to be the head and not the tail) but also need to teach on the fact that He desires for you to "be holy, for I am holy;" and for you to be obedient to the word of God; to be a true Christian, a disciple, a learner of Christ (as in Matthew 11:28-30, learn of Him). Too many of us are trying to "come" to Him, but do not want to "learn" anything — we would rather someone give us already processed food, instead of studying it out and preparing it for ourselves — studying to show ourselves approved. The devil is a lie! We will get in the word for ourselves, we are the generation that will study it out for ourselves. It begins right here with me, I am called for such a time as this to assist in evangelism — the part that says God desires all to be saved AND *grow in the knowledge of the truth.* I will help to get people saved, and assist to help grow the saved in the knowledge of the truth.

Even going back to Psalm 112, I have been standing and believing to see the manifestation of verse 3 of the riches and wealth in my house. But it would not be possible without the verse 4, the light that arises — the Lord has called me to be a light that arises in darkness, to help those in darkness turn the light on and drive out darkness — we do this with truth! I will amplify and magnify the light of God (the Lord Jesus Christ). I will not even listen to the enemy trying to discourage and say it is foolishness and will not work. No! The enemy is a liar and just trying to keep us from standing on the word, because he knows that if we really get it, we will do damage to his kingdom of darkness, turning lights on for people and bringing them out of his domain. This is why we do not talk to the enemy, but to God. We speak the word of God with a confidence and boldness.

Not only does God desire us to be prosperous, but He desires for us to have abundance. Yet there is obedience attached to this abundance. See Psalm 132:15, Isaiah 30:23, it is God that gives the increase and the divine supplies.

Another part of renewing our mind is to stop focusing on what was lost, and focus on what it is we need to get back to the original intent of God for man in Genesis chapters 1 and 2. Let us amplify and magnify the tree of life — we have spent too much time looking at the forbidden fruit of the knowledge of good and evil — ENOUGH! Let's get to know more and more and more about the tree of life that God desires us to have for eternity! Get to know Jesus Christ even the more.

Exodus 30, the offerings at the altar of incense and the tabernacle. A ransom was to be paid by every male over 20 years old, the atonement money that should be used for the temple. A warning I found in my research *"That all are saved by the price, the precious blood of Christ. There is no respect of persons with God. The rich and the poor must come through the same door, helpless, hopeless and penniless, trusting only in the Savior of men, Christ Jesus, who paid the price at Calvary"* [A Dictionary of Bible Types]. The only price that we can pay for the atonement of sins, we cannot even pay — only Jesus can. So when we recognize that it is not even about money; when He said to give to the poor and the needy, what are we giving them? We are giving them Jesus. They are poor in spirit because they are not rich in the abundant grace that Jesus came to give us. When we get our thinking right with this, the other stuff will come.

Think about it, we are dual citizens of earth and heaven, and in heaven the streets are paved with gold — it has a low value there in heaven — it is like cement. So if we are living here in the earth realm, we should have access to some heavenly cement! Gold! But we will not get that if we do not take the time to renew our mind to what it means to be a heavenly representative here in the earth. If you do not feel that you can "be holy, for I am holy," then you will have a problem understanding how the kingdom operates, and you will not have access to the heavenly "cement" — riches and wealth.

We are renewing our mind, getting a better understanding of riches and wealth being in our house — but we will not take the scripture out of context. We must fear the Lord, we must live upright, we must grow in knowing who God is, we must have the light arising in dark places in our life — and it does not happen automatically — we must give Him access, and we must study to show ourselves approved, and we have to put on the robe of righteousness. Contrary to popular belief, there are some things that we have to do. God is not going to do it all for us.

Prayer: Thank You for being the illuminator of our hearts and understanding. You have covered many things here, Holy Spirit take it and cause it to all work together for the good, cause us to have a better understanding, cause us to see better who You have called us to be. Cause us to walk away from error, and to be a people that always walk upright before You. Cause us to have a better understanding of the fear of the Lord that we would truly fear You O God. Thank You that the blessing of the Lord makes us rich and adds no sorrow to it – let us get our thinking and our minds right that we not be sorrowful when the riches and the wealth of this world come our way, they are yet for the kingdom. You want our hearts to be set on You. Thank You that our hearts are being transformed from worldly conformity that understands money that pays bills, to riches that are of the nature of the kingdom. Thank You for supplying all of our needs, filling them to the full. As in Exodus 3, the children of Israel did not leave empty handed; they left with riches and wealth; with what was needed to fund the next phase of life that You were walking them into. Help us change our understanding to better know what it is that You are doing in us. Amen.

5.2 Stewardship

Prayer: God we give you access with the shovel of the Holy Spirit to dig up and uproot any bad doctrine, bad thinking, or bad theology that we have been exposed to. Any lies of the enemy, any deception that we have received. According to Jeremiah 1:10, up root, tear down and break – then lay foundations... that we be conformed to Your word to walk it out as our first nature, not second nature. But that it will be what we know. We will also do as the word says and not get high minded and puffed up and think that it had anything to do with us – for we know that everything that we do is because of Your Son Jesus Christ that died for us. It is in Him that we live, move, and have our being. It is in Him that we can have this sound mind not the spirit of fear – but of love, joy, peace. Thank You that Your plans and purposes are coming to pass for us, that You reveal to us even the more Your plans that are higher than ours, Your thoughts, that are higher than ours – as we spend time seeking after You and rightly dividing Your word. As we spend time taking our mind and setting it on the things above, of whatever is good, pure, noble, lovely – as we think on these things. As we spend time in Your constitution, getting to know it better – for we are ambassadors of this constitution, and how can we enforce this constitution of the kingdom, except we know it? So thank You God for the training, that You are growing us to walk in the perfection and the maturity of Jesus Christ. That You continue to get the glory, the honor, and the praise. Amen.

Looking at stewardship — getting a better understanding of it in relation to riches and wealth. We are to be stewards of the wealth and riches that are in our house (Psalm 112:3). As we are experiencing these wealth and riches, we must make sure that we are good stewards to keep them flowing. We are stewards, called to manage our life and affairs — we manage the domestic concerns.

Looking in the [Holman Illustrated Bible Dictionary] at this word "stewardship". It is defined as *responsibility to manage all the resources of life for the glory of God; acknowledging God as provider*. Every time I see God as my provider, I see Him as Jireh (Genesis 22:14 NKJV). He provided the offering for Abraham when he was tested to sacrifice Isaac. This text when Abraham learned of the Lord as Jehovah Jireh, it was not talking about money, but that the Lord will provide His own offering. The ram caught in the thicket, was symbolic of the Lamb that was to be slain instead of his resource of his son Isaac. He was to steward his son, and here he had gotten a word from God to sacrifice his son. God was testing Abraham's heart to see if he would give up the very thing that He had given him — the promised son. God was testing to see if he loved the gift more than the Giver. Yet Abraham proved his trust in God, he knew that the promise was that his posterity was in Isaac, so if God was telling Him to sacrifice Isaac, Abraham knew God was up to something, and proved that he trusted God even though he didn't know all of the details, he was obedient to the part that he did have. That is part of our problem sometimes, we are not obedient to what God has revealed, and we are crying out to God to reveal His will and plans, yet we must get in line with what He has already said — until we prove our trust in Him — it is our reasonable service to be these living sacrifices.

The word "steward" was looking at a house steward. A steward is *one in charge of household operations*. Also steward is *the one who will inherit an estate, or the heir of the house*. Stewardship, we are God's family, we are in His house, and we have an inheritance in Jesus Christ. The expression stewardship literally means *son of acquisition*. These have all been Old Testament definitions, that were before Jesus Christ was on the scene. The steward had the responsibility of doing it all, but the head of the household was responsible for it all. With our families, there is order in the house — in marriage, the husband and the wife steward together. The wife is the help meet, we are to help him take care of the house. Society today has it all messed up — we must renew our mind. We are still talking about being a steward in a household, the man is the head of the house, the woman is the helper of the head of the house — so technically, the man is responsible for it all, and the woman is there to help him and make sure that he fulfills it all. And one of their responsibilities is to steward children and bring them up in the fear and admonition of the Lord. The definition that says we have a responsibility to manage ALL the resources of life, well one of the resources of life are the fruit of the womb — our children — and then yes, we have our finances, our credit, our reputation (because sometimes your reputation can open doors when favor lights upon you — or shut them).

While we are on this sidebar about stewardship and families, I do not want to neglect to bring up single parent households. A simple prayer that the Lord gave me to pray (and keep order in my house, as well to cover my children) is **Lord, anoint me to stand in the gap on behalf of the head of my household. Amen.** And then the Lord began to show me how to pray and cover my house, my children, my finances, even myself as the head of the household is responsible to do.

Now looking at the word "steward" in the [Holman Illustrated Bible Dictionary] in the New Testament, looking at Matthew 20:8, hiring laborers in the vineyard — at the end of the day, everyone got the same pay. The word "manager" here in Matthew 20:8 means steward. The principle is that there is one wage, and it is always Jesus. First, the wages of sin is death, but Jesus redeemed us and paid the price. There is no other price to be paid for salvation: which is justification (past tense), sanctification (we are now in the process of), and glorification (in the future) — there is no other price, and there should be no other foundation laid except Jesus and Him crucified and risen again. As stewards, we are to be managers of the manifold glory of God, of the gospel of God — that is what we should be giving people, not our opinions, but give the word of God, the full counsel of God.

Back to the definitions of stewardship, in Matthew the reference is to a lord who speaks to his steward. Another term that deals with the person, or the task, or the place of stewardship that appears in Luke 12:42 (the parable of the watching servant):

> Luke 12:42 And the Lord said, Who then is that faithful steward, the wise man whom his master will set over those in his household service to supply them their allowance of food at the appointed time?

This is a favorite verse to me, because the "supply them their allowance" in the NKJV actually says "their portion" — this is A Portion Ministries — the Lord spoke to me and said *"Paulette you are to steward the truths of My word that I place in you and expose to you. You are to give them out to others."* I am that steward, I see me — and you have to personally see yourself; you are a mother; you are a wife; you are a husband, you are a father, you are a good friend; you are a church worker (teacher, singer, greeter, dancer, pray-ER, etc.) — you are to steward the truths of God that He has placed in you, that you place in others.

Again, this text says this faithful steward supplies the allowance of food — that is spiritual food. Proverbs 31:15 AMP, the founding text for A Portion Ministries reads: *She rises while it is yet night and gets [spiritual] food for her household and assigns her maids their tasks.* This ministry the Lord has called me to is about stewarding the gospel of the Lord Jesus Christ, of the kingdom of God; this book that you hold in your hand is an extension of that, and an inheritance to the generations to come.

My life purpose is about helping people grow in knowing who God is, and who they are in Him — which simply put is stewarding. I am stewarding all these talents and gifts that He has given to me, and it has multiplied. I will be diligent to put it to use, that it multiplies. What I want to hear at the end as a steward is "well done good and faithful servant" — another word for stewardship is servant.

More on the definition of "steward" is *faithful and wise servant;* which focuses on the person, not the task. The word that is translated to stewardship highlights the tasks or responsibility granted to such a person. We see that the person (the steward) has responsibility to do something, and then there is the term stewardship. Luke 16 verse 1, 3, and 8 are all examples of stewardship — contrasting the unrighteous steward. Here is a list of a few more examples: 1 Corinthians 4:1-2; Titus 1:7; 1 Peter 4:10.

Each of these texts shines more light on the meaning of stewardship and gives the New Testament picture of the believer as a house-manager for God in this world. We are in the world, but not of this world — and while we are in this world, we are to be a house manager. We are managing the manifold glory, the gospel of Jesus Christ. We are to be making sure that it is being sown, and we are to do what we can do to help the Lord build and establish His kingdom — to be a mouthpiece that cries loud and spares not.

> 1 Corinthians 4:1-2 So then, let us [apostles] be looked upon as ministering servants of Christ and **stewards (trustees) of the mysteries (the secret purposes) of God.** 2 Moreover, it is [essentially] required of stewards that a man should be found faithful [proving himself worthy of trust].

As house managers in this world, there is a faithfulness that we have to walk in. This letter Paul wrote to the Corinthians was addressing religious people; he was basically telling them that he recognized that God had called him to be a steward of the mysteries and secret purposes of God. This is what we steward: the mysteries and secret purposes of God. Yes, we may be gatekeepers as an usher, or working in children's ministry, or a deacon – there are many responsibilities that we have (which that is part of the definition, to manage all the responsibilities of life for the glory of God) – but this is the number one thing that I am called to steward: the mysteries and secret purposes of God. You may not be an apostle to the nations, but you are a mouthpiece to your house and your circle of influence – your children/ husband/ wife needs to know the goodness of God. Not that you preach at them all the time, but they need to hear out of your mouth the goodness of God, and they need to see you walking in it, and not talking contrary to the goodness of God.

> Titus 1:7 For the bishop (an overseer) as God's steward must be blameless, not self-willed or arrogant or presumptuous; he must not be quick-tempered or given to drink or pugnacious (brawling, violent); he must not be grasping and greedy for filthy lucre (financial gain).

Yes, this is talking about leadership in the body of Christ – but strong families make strong churches. As the leadership in our individual homes (the overseer of our houses) that are looking over our children/ wife/ and the affairs of our homes; in this role we should make sure that we are as this text says, blameless, not self-willed or quick tempered, etc. We need to allow the Lord to help us deal with these qualities of stewardship in the home. Personally, when I was younger in the things of God, I had a sharp mouth and a quick temper – the Lord dealt with me to set a guard before my mouth, and stop those fits of rage (grown folk temper tantrums) in my home, in front of my children, before I was ever given the opportunity to operate publicly with the body of Christ. These are things that we need to make sure, that as we are stewards in our home, we will have to give an account. Some may have been called to the nations, but when you stand before God, the first thing you will be called on is what took place in your house; where you had responsibility and authority. I do not have authority in another person's house, I have authority to teach you how to walk in the authority God has given you, and I will have to answer if I do not do that right – huge responsibilities!

This is still the section on understanding Psalm 112:3 about wealth and riches shall be in the house of the righteous and endure forever, but in order for that to happen, we have to work on being stewards right where we are. Because when the wealth and the riches come, we must be rooted and grounded that this is God's money, and I am to steward it; this will help us with tithes and offering. We bring the tithe, the tenth of our income to God (if you do not have an income, do not get anxious, just bring of any increase the Lord sends your way), then we ask God to show us how to be a good steward of the 90% that is left in our possession. Ask God to give you wisdom and favor as to how to properly allot the 90% to cover all that it must cover, including giving more of it as seed (an offering).

> 1 Peter 4:10 As each of you has received a **gift** (a particular spiritual talent, a gracious divine endowment), employ it for one another as [befits] good trustees of God's manysided grace [faithful stewards of the extremely diverse powers and gifts granted to Christians by unmerited favor].

When we see the word "gift" it is defined here as *a gracious divine* endowment; we must LEARN how to steward the gift, as in 2 Timothy 2:15, we have to study to show ourselves approved, rightly dividing the word of God so that we can know how to put this gift of being a carrier of the gospel to use. What is amazing about the next section of 1 Peter 4, is that it is titled *the Christian and suffering* — so we see in verse 10 that we receive a gift from God (a gracious divine endowment — to be able to do what He has called us to do), but that it is accompanied with suffering.

> 1 Peter 4:12-14 Beloved, do not be amazed and bewildered at the fiery ordeal which is taking place to test your quality, as though something strange (unusual and alien to you and your position) were befalling you. 13 But insofar as you are sharing Christ's sufferings, rejoice, so that when His glory [full of radiance and splendor] is revealed, you may also rejoice with triumph [exultantly]. 14 If you are censured and suffer abuse [because you bear] the name of Christ, blessed [are you—happy, fortunate, to be envied, with life-joy, and satisfaction in God's favor and salvation, regardless of your outward condition], because the Spirit of glory, the Spirit of God, is resting upon you. On their part He is blasphemed, but on your part He is glorified.

So even when they are persecuting me, I am to be envied?! Yes. This is why worldly minded people are jealous and causing problems for you because you are doing something they are not doing.

> 1 Peter 4:19 Therefore, those who are ill-treated and suffer in accordance with God's will must do right and commit their souls [in charge as a deposit] to the One Who created [them] and will never fail [them].

These definitions and scripture examples have helped us see what it means to be stewards. We will be persecuted in the process as a result of the sin nature in the world. The biblical concept of stewardship, beginning with Adam and Eve and developed more fully in the New Testament, is that God is owner and provider of all that we possess; since all belongs to Him, it is important that all be used for His purpose and glory. In Genesis, a collective responsibility was given to mankind to have dominion over the earth, to care for it and manage it for His glory, and we are to seek the mind and will of God for every decision. God expects us to use all that we have to bring glory and honor to Him — and that we exercise responsible stewardship on His behalf of every day that we live — we are responsible for the kingdom every day that there is breath in our body. Stewardship!

A summary definition is that we are to manage all that God gives. Whether it is financial resources, time, influence, or opportunity — the believer is to seek the mind and will of God for every decision concerning these things. I pose this hypothetical question, are we seeking the Lord with decisions? Yes, we seek Him about finances, especially when we do not have enough in our possession to pay what is due out. But now let's talk about other valuable items such as your time, your influence, and your opportunities. Will you set aside time to grow in knowing and understanding the constitution of the kingdom, and what it is that you are supposed to be doing)? When you take the challenge, when you do spend time with the things of God, you will see increase, as with the parable of the talents — knowledge doubles.

⁂

Looking at some types and shadows of riches in the bible — all of which bring us right back to Jesus.

> Proverbs 8:18 Riches and honor are with me, enduring wealth and righteousness (uprightness in every area and relation, and right standing with God.)

This is similar to the Psalm 112:3, riches and wealth shall be in the righteous household — it even adds on "honor". The righteousness — this is referring to the wisdom that we now receive because of the death, burial, and resurrection of the Lord Jesus Christ who is now our Savior — and we have the Holy Spirit as our teacher, He gives us this wisdom. We must stop and listen.

This word "riches" at Proverbs 8:18 in the [A Dictionary of Bible Types] says: *here we see a type of all the virtues and graces given by the Lord to His children to adorn society, bless the church, and bring honor and glory to God.* These graces through Jesus Christ are not just for us, but for society, the church, and to bring Him honor and glory — this fits in with what a steward does, and shows what we are to do with these riches, we are to bring honor and glory to God.

> Proverbs 10:22 The blessing of the Lord—it makes [truly] rich, and He adds no sorrow with it [neither does toiling increase it].

When God blesses us, endows us with power with these spiritual gifts, as we saw earlier — it is His blessing/endowment that makes us rich. Not rich according to the world's standards, but truly rich. Favor will take you further than a miracle because a miracle is a one-time thing, but favor opens doors.

Neither does toiling increase it — "toil" means *work; sweat of the brow.* So you cannot work to increase money. But here we are killing ourselves, working 2 jobs to try to make enough money to pay bills — when that will not increase the favor or blessings of God — we must make sure that we are in the word to cause these to increase through the revelation, illumination, knowledge, insight wisdom we receive as we study it out.

This word rich at Proverbs 10:22 in the [A Dictionary of Bible Types] says: *in this is described those who are filled with faith, zeal, earnestness, vision, as well as the graces of the Spirit of God.* This is an extended definition of riches: faith, zeal, earnestness, vision, and the grace of the Spirit of God — these things are where the riches come from. But you have to be a person that operates in wisdom in order for them to operate in your life as well.

> Proverbs 11:4 Riches provide no security in any day of wrath and judgment, but righteousness (uprightness and right standing with God) delivers from death.

When God sends the riches your way, you can't be relying on self or anything else, this is not pleasing to Him; we cannot put our security in the wealth, it must always be in God. [A Dictionary of Bible Types] for this text says: *this is quite significant in that it typifies all manner of human effort to put away sin, and obtain favor with God. This passage denounces all human efforts to save one's self, or to save another...Only the living Christ and His shed blood do avail to meet God's requirements.* It is Jesus' righteousness that saves our soul, not works, or the riches of this world. The "riches" of the kingdom is Jesus. We will have to give an account of what we did with the riches, with Jesus, did we proclaim Him to the world?

Prayer: Thank You for causing us to look at and get better understanding as to what it means to be like Psalm 112:3 and have riches and wealth in our houses that endure forever. We renew our mind to get a better understanding of riches and wealth and being good stewards of those possessions that You are sending our way. You see what we have need of, and You have already set provisions forward for us, You are working things out. We Your servants submit and humble ourselves to You, that we be able to resist the devil and he flee. Thank You that we are able to walk upright and in communion with You O God. Amen.

> Luke 19:12-15 He therefore said, A certain nobleman went into a distant country to obtain for himself a kingdom and then to return. 13 Calling ten of his [own] bond servants, he gave them ten minas [each equal to about one hundred days' wages or nearly twenty dollars] and said to them, Buy and sell with these while I go and then return. 14 But his citizens detested him and sent an embassy after him to say, We do not want this man to become ruler over us. 15 When he returned after having received the kingdom, he ordered these bond servants to whom he had given the money to be called to him, that he might know how much each one had made by buying and selling.

Notice that He gave all 10 of them the same amount of minas — there were expectations on all of them.

The nobleman in verse 12, is a type of Jesus Christ, He receives the kingdom from the Father (John 17:4-10). Jesus gave us all the same thing: Himself. This is similar to the parable where the owner gave everyone the same pay, no matter how long they were there, the pay was the same.

At verse 14, the people rebelled against Jesus, but it did not stop Him. We may have some loved ones and friends that are rebelling against the nobleman (Jesus) right now; they have the minas, but are not doing what they are supposed to be doing with them due to hardness of heart (Isaiah 30:15). The hardness of heart can be caused by tradition, religion, and just life circumstances — where people do not trust God, but have a mixture of these other things going on. This is why we must guard our heart against hardness, and must remain teachable and sensitive to our purpose as stewards.

> Proverbs 4:23 NLT Guard your heart above all else, for it determines the course of your life.

We have all been given deposits to be stewards of. We can see this clearer in the same parable given in a different gospel. We will be looking at both accounts in Matthew 25 and Luke 19.
> Matthew 25:14-18 For it is like a man who was about to take a long journey, and he called his servants together and entrusted them with his property. ¹⁵ To one he gave five talents [probably about $5,000], to another two, to another one — to each in proportion to his own personal ability. Then he departed and left the country. ¹⁶ He who had received the five talents went at once and traded with them, and he gained five talents more. ¹⁷ And likewise he who had received the two talents — he also gained two talents more. ¹⁸ But he who had received the one talent went and dug a hole in the ground and hid his master's money.

We see here in Matthew 25 that they all received *something,* and in Luke 19, we see that they all got the same amount of *something.*

In the parable of talents/mina — the steward given one talent, hid it, and was called a wicked steward for not properly handling what he was given. He hid it in the ground, which is symbolic of worldliness — so we can say that he was saying "I was scared to step out on kingdom, I was scared to expand, I was scared to tell HIS-story in my life. The good news, the gospel". So what this wicked steward had was taken from him and given to the person that had already increased. The principle is: be found faithful with the little, to receive even more — be faithful in the few things, to be made ruler over many (or have authority over much). The additional principle is that when God gives you something (a gift, purpose, a talent, wealth and riches, prosperity, possessions), when He gives us these things, we have to steward them. We do not usually look at the stewardship of raising our children; we are to train them up in the way to go. We have covenant with our spouse for life, but we are to steward our children. Steward them until they are grown and old enough to make their decision to live the right way. Our job is to train them in the things of God so that when they grow up, they will not depart. Now, I know personally, there may be times that it looks like they are departing, but do not be moved by what you see — continue to pray for them and believe the word that you have sown, believe that God is in control, and that they are just "working on their testimony" for the goodness of God!

Song "take my life mold it/ conform it/ transform it to Yours" — do we really mean this? If we do, we should be good stewards of it, and found doing things that are pleasing unto God. As we have read in Romans 12:1, we do this as a reasonable service to be a living sacrifice, to be pleasing and acceptable unto God — and that is what we do with the stewardship of our lives.

> 1 Corinthians 4:2-4 NLT Now, a person who is put in charge as a manager must be faithful. 3 As for me, it matters very little how I might be evaluated by you or by any human authority. I don't even trust my own judgment on this point. 4 My conscience is clear, but that doesn't prove I'm right. It is the Lord himself who will examine me and decide.

Are we being good stewards of our time, talents, resources, opportunities, abilities, influences? We have to make sure that we are. And then not just to judge ourselves, but God will judge. This is why I personally live by Psalm 139:23-24 where I ask the Lord to search my heart, meaning judge it according to Your word, and lead me in Your ways in the areas that are not right.

> 1 Peter 4:10 As each of you has received a gift (a particular spiritual talent, a gracious divine endowment), employ it for one another as [befits] good trustees of God's many sided grace [faithful stewards of the extremely diverse powers and gifts granted to Christians by unmerited favor].

As Apostle Ida B. Ullrich's school motto, "the gift is free, the call is by grace, but the mantle will cost." Meaning, as we see in this text, we all have a gift given to us by grace, but the mantle, the ability to walk in this gift by grace (not perverting it, but empowered by it) will cost us everything — our very life as we know it. We must be the living sacrifice that is continually not being conformed to this world, and being transformed by the renewing of our mind according to the word of God — and then not thinking more highly of ourselves.

> Revelation 3:8 I know your [record of] works and what you are doing. See! I have set before you a door wide open which no one is able to shut; I know that you have

but little power, and yet you have kept My Word and guarded My message and have not renounced or denied My name.

God sees that we are being persecuted and going through several trials, but we should not deny His name in the midst of it all. There is power in His name, run into His name and receive the help we need in the midst of it all.

> Romans 14:12 And so each of us shall give an account of himself [give an answer in reference to judgment] to God.

We give an account to God, not just to man. We must make sure that our conscious is clear. This is why we have to regularly and continually deal with our heart. As above, guard your heart above all because it determines the course of our life. We have to make sure that we are dealing with what is going on in our hearts. Renewal of the Mind!

We are accountable as a steward. Because God will be judging every man according to his ability. Yes, we have to answer to authority in the earth realm, but also understand that we live by a higher authority at the same time.

Keep in mind that God rewards us according to faithfulness — so will you be found faithful? Let's jump back into Luke 19.

> Luke 19:16-20 The first one came before him, and he said, Lord, your mina has made ten [additional] minas. 17 And he said to him, Well done, excellent bond servant! Because you have been faithful and trustworthy in a very little [thing], you shall have authority over ten cities. 18 The second one also came and said, Lord, your mina has made five more minas. 19 And he said also to him, And you will take charge over five cities. 20 Then another came and said, Lord, here is your mina, which I have kept laid up in a handkerchief.

He was faithful with money, and received authority over cities. We see that everyone had the same amount from the beginning, they were all given 10; we see one person produced 10 more, the other 5 more, and the final person just hid it. The question to us today is: will you be found faithful?

The same account in Matthew 25 says "faithful over few, ruler over many, enter into the joy of the Lord." See Matthew 25:19-25.

They all doubled what they had: the 5 talent person had 10; the 2 talent person had 4; but the 1 talent person — well?

Notice the different rewards of faithfulness in the same parable in 2 different gospels. In Luke 19 they were given authority for being faithful stewards, in Matthew 25 they were given to be rulers (have authority) over many and also promised to share in the joy of the

Lord. Money is the test, this is also why the enemy wants our thinking (our mindsets) off about money, so that we do not walk in, or with the authority that is appointed to us — and that we do not have the joy of the Lord. This is why the enemy tries to get so many people trapped by not properly handling money, or being faithful with money. At the same time, God is testing us, and like He said to Peter "I have prayed that your faith fail you not," we will have faith and believe God to be the provider of riches and wealth in our household and that His righteousness endures forever.

Observation / question: in Luke 19, He gave them 10 minas (the number 10 is symbolic of the supernatural); yet we only hear the report of 3 of them (the number 3 is symbolic of the Trinity); question, what happened to the other 7? The number 7 is symbolic of the church, completion, perfection.

Also, in verse 13 He gave all 10 bond servants 10 minas (plural), but when they reported out (verse 16 and 18), they said "Thy pound" in the singular. As I meditated on this asking God for clarity, and why I was allowed to notice this, the Holy Spirit showed me that He expected a return of a tenth of what He had given them — a tithe! They did not give the report on the other nine they had, but on the one, the singular. This is the answer to the age old saying when it comes to tithing, "well, I have to live" — He gave them more than enough to live on, and still support the kingdom with their time, talent, resources, opportunities, and abilities.

To those that are not working right now and do not have the tangible finances to sow: just make sure you do sow of whatever finances you do receive, but in the meantime, what are you doing with your time, talent, resources, opportunities, and abilities? Are you spending time in the word, laying a stronger foundation of understanding the King and the kingdom to which you are called? The same with the knowledge and truths that you have been exposed to, spend this time increasing in that, that you be able to give an account of increased understanding.

Back to Luke 19:20, he hid it in a handkerchief — we can say in a man-made wrapping, or a thing — striving for things like tradition and religion instead of relationship. How many people are hiding their "talent" in the fact that they have a perfect church attendance, but have not taken the opportunity to grow in knowing who God is and who they are in Him? That is a hidden talent. We have to be able to grow in understanding the word, be able to tell me how you know Jesus loves me, not just because it was a song, but be able to back it up with scripture — there should be expansion and increase on the basics that we receive. If you have been saved for over 6 months to a year, you should be able to expound on what you have heard in the word. Man-made handkerchief — working for a living, instead of working for the kingdom.

Another side note about seeking a job, we always say "God, you know I need to pay my bills, You know how much money I need, etc." — but do we ever stop and ask "God, where do You want this anointing that resides in me to be employed? To be shared? Etc. Because wherever the anointing goes comes the blessing, the endowment of power, the bills and even more will be handled, You will put the seed back into the kingdom through me." We have to change our mindset and the way we view working.

In Matthew 6:33, and in Luke 12, it talks about getting your priorities straight and seek first the kingdom. Stop toiling over what you will eat, where you will live, how you will get around (transportation — it didn't say it in the text, but it is a major toil now a days). Seek His kingdom is another way of saying grow in understanding Jesus, the "learn of Me" of Matthew 11:28-30. When we do this, learn of Him, we will stop worrying about all of that stuff, because believers believe — and as a true believer, the blessings of God will chase you down, you don't have to beg for them — they will overtake you. But you must get your priorities right. There are a lot of people that cannot get past where they are because they are wrapped up in tradition and religion and never get their priorities straight. Be a good steward of the few that God has given you, whether time, talent, resources, opportunities, and abilities — this prepares you to be faithful of the many.

In Matthew 25:18, he hid the one talent in the ground; hid it in worldliness. How many people do we see singing in the world, but started in the church, and should be bringing glory to God's kingdom? Just a thought.

Now let's make this personal: will YOU hear well done, or a rebuke? This is personal between you and God. See verse 17 and 19, they heard well done, but at verse 21 it shifts:

> Luke 19:17-26 And he said to him, Well done, excellent bond servant! Because you have been faithful and trustworthy in a very little [thing], you shall have authority over ten cities. 18 The second one also came and said, Lord, your mina has made five more minas. 19 And he said also to him, And you will take charge over five cities. 20 Then another came and said, Lord, here is your mina, which I have kept laid up in a handkerchief. 21 For I was [constantly] afraid of you, because you are a stern (hard, severe) man; you pick up what you did not lay down, and you reap what you did not sow. 22 He said to the servant, I will judge and condemn you out of your own mouth, you wicked slave! You knew [did you] that I was a stern (hard, severe) man, picking up what I did not lay down, and reaping what I did not sow? 23 Then why did you not put my money in a bank, so that on my return, I might have collected it with interest? 24 And he said to the bystanders, Take the mina away from him and give it to him who has the ten minas. 25 And they said to him, Lord, he has ten minas [already]! 26 And [said Jesus,] I tell you that to everyone who gets and has will more be given, but from the man who does not get and does not have, even what he has will be taken away.

Will we hear well done; that we took what God gave us and expanded on it? Or will we hide it in a handkerchief or in worldliness instead of placing it where it can at least gain interest. It may not double, like the others, but at least gain interest. That means there should be some type of expansion and increase of the riches of the kingdom sown into you. You should be able to expand on your understanding of salvation.

Will what you have received be taken away from you and passed on to someone else? No. Be like the 2 people here in Luke that were found faithful and heard well done. We want to walk in authority and the joy of the Lord, to be found faithful stewards, not found in neglect of duty, or unfruitfulness, or slothfulness, or unfaithfulness — this is what happens when you hide your talent in the ground or in worldliness.

The challenge is if you have been lacking in faithfulness with your stewardship of your time, talent, resources, opportunities, abilities and influence — maybe you have hidden it in a handkerchief (man-made things) or the ground (worldliness 1 John 2:16, which is actually an attitude or a mindset) — today is your opportunity to make up for those lost opportunities. Rededicate your life to the Lord, honor your commitment, or even make a commitment. Again, we should not just get caught up on the money part (especially since a lot of us don't have enough of it anyway), but we must be faithful with our time, talent, resources, opportunities, and abilities. Why do we have influence that we use for the secular world, but do not use for the
kingdom? All of your time, talent, resources, opportunities, and abilities are needed for the body of Christ to be fitly joined together. Will you be found faithful?

Share Jesus — who you love is who you talk about. Share His goodness with people and let them know that no matter where they are, God loves them. A nugget that I received from a bible teacher is that we need to meditate on the fact that God loves us, not that we love Him. Because our love is fickle and changes, but His love never changes. And to quote my pastor "anything past salvation is a bonus" — meaning that if God does anything else, besides save our soul, that is bonus. So when we take time to get to know more about Him and His love and His characteristics and attributes, and how we are to be Christ-like, and walk as disciples and learn more of Him — that is us expanding our mina/talent. It is not just about money. A lot of people get caught up wanting more money, but remember the parable that said it will be hard for a rich man to make it into heaven — because their heart is attached to the money.

Remember, God already knows what we have need of before we ask, but He wants to hear your understanding and your revelation. As in Ephesians 3:20, He will do above all we ask or think. But we have to "think on these things," and then ask. So when we tell God that we know that He already knows what we have need of, then we are to come with supplication,

He just wants to hear it out of our mouth that speaks from the abundant things within. It is an examination of the heart.

> Proverbs 20:5 Counsel in the heart of man is like water in a deep well, but a man of understanding draws it out.

Share it with God, when God sees your understanding, He can give you the ability to draw the understanding out of your own well. It was already there, but you have to come into the understanding of it. And when you have this understanding, you will now give voice to it in prayer. Prayer is a dialogue, a 2-way conversation.

> Proverbs 18:4 The words of a [discreet and wise] man's mouth are like deep waters [plenteous and difficult to fathom], and the fountain of skillful and godly Wisdom is like a gushing stream [sparkling, fresh, pure, and life-giving].

Sometimes God hears you and sees, but is just developing you in the processes. Developing long-suffering, character, integrity, confidence etc. in the midst of the wait. And when it happens, everyone will know it was the hand of God, and no one else can get the glory but Him.

Prayer: Thank You for this time of showing us how to really understand stewardship and how to be found faithful. Thank You for the peace that You place within our hearts as we are seeking after You and learning more of You. Thank You for giving us time, talent, resources, opportunities, abilities, and influences and we will be found faithful in them. If You say study, we will study. If You say rest, we will rest – because that is taking care of the resource of this dirt suit You have us living in – that is pressing the re-set button in our mind, that You come in and give us renewal and refreshing. Thank You for calling us to get in line with our time, talents, resources, opportunities, abilities, and influences – thank You for continually delivering us from procrastination. That we will have the "Just do it" mentality. Thank You God that when we read, it is not about quantity (how much), but quality – that the Holy Spirit our Teacher will be right there with us opening the word up to us. Flood the eyes of our heart that we can know You and Your purposes and plans even more.

Deal with Your people O Lord, to not hide what You have given us in worldliness, in a man-made thing, in tradition, or religion – but that we would expand our understanding of Jesus Christ, the Kingdom of God, and You O God. That we would expand our role in the body of Christ and the church (the called out) that we would be fitly joined together, meeting all of the needs. Amen!

Isaiah 55:8-13 For My thoughts are not your thoughts, neither are your ways My ways, says the Lord. ⁹ For as the heavens are higher than the earth, so are My ways higher than your ways and My thoughts than your thoughts. ¹⁰ For as the rain and snow come down from the heavens, and return not there again, but water the earth and make it bring forth and sprout, that it may give seed to the sower and bread to the eater, ¹¹ So shall My word be that goes forth out of My mouth: it shall not return to Me void [without producing any effect, useless], but it shall accomplish that which I please and purpose, and it shall prosper in the thing for which I sent it. ¹² For you shall go out [from the spiritual exile caused by sin and evil into the homeland] with joy and be led forth [by your Leader, the Lord Himself, and His word] with peace; the mountains and the hills shall break forth before you into singing, and all the trees of the field shall clap their hands. ¹³ Instead of the thorn shall come up the cypress tree, and instead of the brier shall come up the myrtle tree; and it shall be to the Lord for a name of renown, for an everlasting sign [of jubilant exaltation] and memorial [to His praise], which shall not be cut off.

As we are in the Renewal of the Mind! process, being removed from worldly conformity, and being transformed by the word of God, but then staying humble in the midst of it all — we need to keep in mind that our thoughts are not like His, and that is why we are seeking Him for His thoughts (Isaiah 55:8-13).

Prayer: Thank You for Your word and for doing what it is that we asked according to Your word – You are helping us crucify the flesh and lay self down on the altar. You are empowering us to think about our thoughts, that our thoughts not be of the world, but of You – as You said in Isaiah 55:8, our thoughts are not like Yours anyway, so we are looking to You and setting our mind on You. You said You would keep him in perfect peace whose mind is stayed on You; You are empowering us to keep our mind on You – to take it off of worldly thinking and be transformed, even conformed to kingdom thinking; thinking like You cause us to think. Thank You that You O God are giving us revelation, illumination, knowledge, insight, wisdom into the things of Jesus Christ that we would be a people that walk upright and pleasing unto You. Help us see You even the more in Your word. Help us change our thought process and our thinking patterns to line up with Your word and be pleasing unto You. In Jesus name, Amen – so be it.

When it comes to identifying scripture, I may not know the address, but tell me the scripture, I may know the people in the house. Keep this in mind, you may not know my address, but have come to my house several times. You do not know the address, but you know who lives there. So when it comes to scripture, do not get caught up on the fact that you do not know the address, but you know the people in the house. The same thing with phone numbers, technology has messed us up because we do not know anyone's phone number, we just put it in the phone — so if we lose the phone, we have lost all contact. We need to make sure that when we are committing the word to memory, "Your word have I hidden in my heart that I might sin against You", we need to make sure that as we hide it in our heart, we also learn the address by recall, by pulling it back up.

Let's not let technology be a crutch, or in reference to the word, always quoting what pastor said, or a devotional, or a book — we should be quoting what the word says, then sharing what others said about it — do not be so reliant on someone else's knowledge, study it out for yourself. Commit it to memory, address (phone number) included — I am talking about the word of God. It is okay if you do not remember it right away, but after repetition, you should learn to know these addresses. And again, you may not know the address, but to know the people in the house is just as much, if not more important. Know them, for real tho! Not adding stuff, or leaving stuff out, but really know it — and in order to get to that point, you will remember the address too! Also, make sure that it is the address, the house you want to be at, not someone else's opinion, but what the word says. Renew our mind with the word, supplemental books are good, but be sure to renew your mind and put it back in the word for yourselves. Keep the word in context to make sure that what is being said is really being said. Take the time to do this.

Parable of the servant that hid his one talent/mina... he had wrong thoughts and wrong thinking, because he KNEW that the master was a harsh man, but he needed to know that the master rewards faithfulness. He knew the master from a worldly aspect, where he was scared of the master; instead of from a kingdom aspect that says "I am responsible to the King of the kingdom, so I want to be pleasing unto Him". Know that even if I do something with it and it gets lost, He will provide as I go. We have to make sure that we do not have a worldly mindset that says "I am scared of God; or I am scared to walk out on faith; or to try this scripture because it might not work for me" — that is operating out of fear, instead of kingdom. Your mind has to be renewed to believe the word. Miracles, signs, and wonders follow them who believe — you have to believe the word and walk the word out and the miracles, signs, and wonders follow you — the blessings chase you down when you are walking in the word. We need to change our mindsets that we are to be stewards and God-pleasers with what He gives us. Do not go and hide what He has given you with the excuse that "I can't do it". These are incorrect mindsets.

5.3 Original Design

We want to be restored to the original riches and wealth to mankind that was given in Genesis chapter 2. In Genesis chapter 1, God created the spirit man; then in Genesis chapter 2, He created all of this other stuff:

> Genesis 2:9-15 And out of the ground the Lord God made to grow every tree that is pleasant to the sight or to be desired — good (suitable, pleasant) for food; the tree of life also in the center of the garden, and the tree of the knowledge of [the difference between] good and evil and blessing and calamity. 10 Now a river went out of Eden to water the garden; and from there it divided and became four [river] heads. 11 The first is named Pishon; it is the one flowing around the whole land of Havilah, where there is gold. 12 The gold of that land is of high quality; bdellium (pearl?) and onyx stone are there. 13 The second river is named Gihon; it is the one flowing around the whole land of Cush. 14 The third river is named Hiddekel [the Tigris]; it is the one flowing east of Assyria. And the fourth river is the Euphrates. 15 And the Lord God took the man and put him in the Garden of Eden to tend and guard and keep it.

Here in this garden, man had all the material riches and wealth needed. Everything that he needed was supplied for him right there in that garden. Just reading these verses on the surface, we miss some of what was being said, but looking deeper at the meaning of these names will take us a little deeper in our understanding. Stay with me through the lengthy definitions, I promise it will all tie together afterwards.

At verse 10 "Eden" means *a flat land or a wilderness; delight or pleasure.* It appears 20 times in the Old Testament, but never in the New Testament. Joel 2:3, compares Judah's condition before its destruction with Eden. Also, in Ezekiel 36:35 and Isaiah 51:3, Eden is used as an illustration of the great prosperity God would bestow on Judah. We see the prosperity God sows to His people as Eden. Reminds me of the song by Donald Lawrence "Let's get back to Eden, live on top of the world!" Getting an understanding that Eden is a pleasurable and delightful place where all of the needs are met. The footnote in my bible dictionary said "see paradise" — with that in mind, we see Eden in the New Testament when Jesus told the thief hanging next to Him that he would be with Him in Paradise (Luke 23:43). Also in Revelation 2:7, paradise is promised to the hearers and overcomers that will be granted *to eat of the fruit of the tree of life, which is in the paradise of God.*

Now looking at the names of the four river heads here in Eden:

Verse 11, "River Pishon" means *free flowing.* It was a canal connecting the Tigres and the Eupratates in the Persian Gulf. It flows around the city called Havilah, and the city Havilah means *a sandy stretch of land. The biblical name of the sand dominated region to the south, covering what we call Arabia without necessarily designating a particular geographical or political area.* In Havilah, there is gold, bedellium, and onyx stone. I looked up the definition of "bedullium" and it means *a fragrant or a bitter tasting gum from Arabia and is used in perfume and medicine.* It is bitter, but used in perfume — as people of God, we will have to go through some bitter situations, but it will leave a good fragrance. Kind of like the prayers of the saints are like incense, a sweet fragrance (Revelation 8:3-4). As we pray, and operate as intended, we will perfume some things — be used as perfume and medicine

Verse 13, "River Gihon" means *gushing fountain.* Is the primary water supply for Jerusalem. In Hebrew, means *a bursting forth*; it does not produce a steady flow, but gushes out at irregular intervals — twice a day in the dry season, to 4 or 5 times a day in the rainy season. The river Gihon is the one flowing around the land of Cush — is a city in Egypt.

Verse 14, "River Hiddekel (Tigres)" means *flows East of Assyria.* "Shows that the dependence of the important areas of subsequent world history owe their fertility to God's original garden of creation." So we go back to Eden looking at being fertile and able to produce and reproduce.

Sidenote — Assyria is a very prominent city in biblical history. It is attached to Babylon.

Verse 14, "River Euphrates" — it is the *longest, largest, and most important river in Western Asia. Many significant cities were located on the Euphrates, Babylon being the most important* [Holman Illustrated Bible Dictionary].

Tying it all together now: Eden is a flat land, a pleasant place, a wilderness place, and restored covenant with God and His chosen people. With the Renewal of the Mind! process, we are looking at getting our mind renewed on riches and wealth, prosperity and righteousness — we are renewing our mind that God desires for us to be in a pleasant place, a delightful place, a place of prosperity where all of our needs are met. Where we are in wholeness — where we have Pishon flowing out of us, a free flowing of the riches and wealth of the kingdom are flowing out of us even in a sandy stretch of area — and we are going to go through bitter tasting situations, but we are to give off a perfumed, or a medicine effect. During the process of all of this, there will be gushing fountains bursting forth — now it won't be a continual flow, but around 2 times a day in the dry seasons, and sometimes multiple times in the good harvest season. As we are doing these things, the land and the area begins to increase — the land of Cush was a huge area in Egypt — the land of Hiddekel were the Tigres and the Euphrates go is known for fertility and also a prominent water supply.

We have looked at all of these meanings and definitions to expand our thinking of the principle that I heard a teacher say that we should have more than one stream of provision flowing in our life; this made me want to study it out for myself (I heard it about 13 years ago, but I am just now following up on it — it is never too late). For a lot of us, the only stream is our paycheck, or some type of financial assistance — but as kingdom citizens, we should have at least 4 different streams flowing out and flowing in. I think it took me so long to follow up on it because I did not want to get caught up in fanatical prosperity teaching — but know that financial prosperity is not what I am aiming to draw attention to, but the fact that we renew our mind back to the garden of Eden — finances and provision were no problem there — they were evident and residue of the regular communion with God! We must get our minds right.

> Exodus 3:21 And I will give this people favor and respect in the sight of the Egyptians; and it shall be that when you go, you shall not go empty-handed.

This is a promise of actual, physical riches and wealth which comes as a result of favor and respect from the Lord. You cannot make people respect you or give you favor — favor comes from the Lord. This Exodus 3:21 was a verse that I meditated on for a long time, someone had given me this scripture and told me "Girl, God is sending you out, and when you go out, ALL of your needs will be met." Well, I had a hard time with this, and I knew I had to renew my mind to truly understand this scripture. It is funny, because all of my needs were met, according to Him, but I needed to do some changing in my thinking to recognize Him meeting my needs, and to qualify to be a steward over the more. So journey with me as we put this back in context.

The beginning of Exodus 3 is the burning bush experience of Moses. This takes place after Moses was 40 years old, raised in the king's palace, receives his call, acts prematurely and kills an Egyptian, then runs away and is hiding in the wilderness, now married and with his father-in-law Jethro taking care of the sheep, then he has this encounter with God at age 80! The first 40 years of his life were preparation, then the next 40 years of his life were another preparation — so why do we trip that we are getting up there in age!? The point of the matter is we need to make sure that we are seeking God, pleasing God, and when we miss it, run to Him and let Him bring us forward — and in DUE season, we will have our burning bush experience. Sorry, that last sentence was for me!

The recap of chapter 3 is God giving Moses instructions about delivering the people out of Egypt, and that he (Moses) will be the deliverer to these people; then in chapter 4, God equips Moses to do this very thing. So this statement in Exodus 3:21, is God speaking to Moses and letting him know His desires for the people of Israel and building up confidence in Moses to be the deliverer for the people. We must understand that we need our confidence built up in God so that we can be the deliverer. He gives seed to the sower, you are to deliver the seed. We need confidence in being a seed receiver, so that we can be a seed sower.

Riches and wealth shall be in their house — we are tying this all together and putting this statement of favor in context where He said He would give them *favor and respect in the sight of the Egyptians* — because the Egyptians had no respect for the Hebrews, but were treating them harshly — that is how Moses ended up in exile in the first place. This is a good place to address the fact that some of us are in a place of isolation, yes, we are around people (Moses was married and worked with Jethro) but he was a shepherd, which is a lonely job. He was around people but was processing what had happened the first half of his life (40 years in the palace), then the second half of his life (now there in the wilderness for 40 years), he probably had a lot going on inside, spending that time in isolation.

> Exodus 3:16-22 Go, gather the elders of Israel together [the mature teachers and tribal leaders], and say to them, The Lord God of your fathers, the God of Abraham, of Isaac, and of Jacob, appeared to me, saying, I have surely visited you and seen that which is done to you in Egypt; 17 And I have declared that I will bring you up out of the affliction of Egypt to the land of the Canaanite, the Hittite, the Amorite, the Perizzite, the Hivite, and the Jebusite, to a land flowing with milk and honey. 18 And [the elders] shall believe and obey your voice; and you shall go, you and the elders of Israel, to the king of Egypt and you shall say to him, The Lord, the God of the Hebrews, has met with us; and now let us go, we beseech you, three days' journey into the wilderness, that we may sacrifice to the Lord our God. 19 And I know that the king of Egypt will not let you go [unless forced to do so], no, not by a mighty hand. 20 So I will stretch out My hand and smite Egypt with all My wonders which I will do in it; and after that he will let you go. 21 And I will give this people favor and respect in the sight of the Egyptians; and it shall be that when you go, you shall not go empty-handed. 22 But every woman shall [insistently] solicit of her neighbor and of her that may be residing at her house jewels and articles of silver and gold, and garments, which you shall put on your sons and daughters; and you shall strip the Egyptians [of belongings due to you].

These were instructions to Moses telling him that it is time to go, he was to go to the elders of Israel, and go to the king of Egypt and tell him to let My people go — but the king will be hardheaded and will not do it of his own accord, but God will do it by His mighty hand, and there was a warning that he would have to go through some things. Yet understand that God will deal with the enemy, no need to worry about the enemy, but you will have to go through the process — and in going through the right way, you will come out with favor and respect from the people that oppressed you. This is not because of you, as in Ezekiel 36, but for His name sake — when the people roundabout see what happens, God will get the glory. This is all part of prophecy, they were in this captivity in the first place because of the murmuring, the complaining, and the hard-headedness of the forefathers, yet there would be a deliverance.

God knew He had to build confidence in Moses for the tasks, see verses 16 and 18 above, He told Moses to go to the Elders and assured him that they would listen — God knew He had to tell Moses this because these were some hard-headed people that did not want to hear anything (sounds like some of the *assignments* He has given me).

We need to understand that God's desire is for us to have favor with the people, and He will meet all of our needs. Verse 22 above were specific instructions of the plan for the women. Wow, I wondered why? As I am typing this manuscript, I heard "Because if the men did the gathering, the Egyptians would have known something was up. But since the women were looked at as not equal anyway, no one would pay attention. They received an important part in the plan of deliverance. So we women have a role to play, but just because God calls on us, and uses us does not mean that we usurp authority and try to take over! Just do what the Lord asks you to do." The instructions were *to receive of their neighbors* (the world), *these things and put them on their sons and daughters,* so we are to take the useful things for the kingdom and make sure that we are passing them on to our sons and daughters. He did NOT tell them to put these items on themselves, but on their children.

God was supplying their need, He gave them the *power to get wealth* in this exit strategy. He gave them the creative insight as to how they were to have this wealth in exiting. This had to be God giving them favor, because to have the Egyptians pay for you to leave them? That does not make sense! But we later find out that they received so much in leaving, that once they were delivered and went on to possess the Promised Land, and temple worship was instituted, the people began to bring these items to the temple — it was so much that Moses had to tell them to stop bringing it! That is the type of favor He wants us to have — and they had no problem letting go of it and using it for what they had it for — it was for God's use in the first place. This is a lesson we need to learn with what we do have possession of!

5.4 Content

> Philippians 4:19 And my God will liberally supply (fill to the full) your every need according to His riches in glory in Christ Jesus.

This section is titled *content whatever the circumstances* in the Message bible. Now we need to put this scripture in context and see that we must learn, to be content where we are. A lot of people take this text out of context and only share a part of what is being said.

> Philippians 4:10 I was made very happy in the Lord that now you have revived your interest in my welfare after so long a time; you were indeed thinking of me, but you had no opportunity to show it.

"Were thinking of me" — your mind was on me — Paul was calling attention to their thought patterns. Then added that they *"had no opportunity to show it"* — talents, resources, influence, opportunities — to show it.

> Philippians 4:11 Not that I am implying that I was in any personal want, for **I have learned how to be content (satisfied to the point where I am not disturbed or disquieted)** in whatever state I am.

This verse shows us that we truly need to be content, and defines what it looks like. Re-read this verse 11. See how the Amplified explains content as satisfied to the point where I am not disturbed or disquieted. Basically I have learned to not be disturbed or disquieted by the trials and life situations faced.

> Philippians 4:12 I know how to be abased and live humbly in straightened circumstances, and I know also how to enjoy plenty and live in abundance. I have learned in any and all circumstances the secret of facing every situation, whether well-fed or going hungry, having a sufficiency and enough to spare or going without and being in want.

We see that this is a process, he says "*I have learned*" several times in this book.

> Philippians 4:13 I have strength for all things in Christ Who empowers me [I am ready for anything and equal to anything through Him Who infuses inner strength into me; I am self-sufficient in Christ's sufficiency].

We always quote this *I can do all things through Christ who gives me strength*, but we need to keep it in context — this is essentially saying "I have learned to be content" — have we? This is basically saying, "I am ready for anything and everything that comes my way. Whether the bills are paid, or not. Whether food is on the table, or not. I'm good because He is empowering me and infusing me with inner strength in the midst of it all. My sufficiency comes in Him, not me."

> Philippians 4:14-17 But it was right and commendable and noble of you to contribute for my needs and to share my difficulties with me. 15 And you Philippians yourselves well know that in the early days of the Gospel ministry, when I left Macedonia, no church (assembly) entered into partnership with me and opened up [a debit and credit] account in giving and receiving except you only. 16 For even in Thessalonica you sent [me contributions] for my needs, not only once but a second time. 17 Not that I seek or am eager for [your] gift, but I do seek and am eager for the fruit which increases to your credit [the harvest of blessing that is accumulating to your account].

A brief summary of what was going on here: Paul was travelling, and the church at Philippi was helping him financially. They were sowing money for him to go do the work of the kingdom. They did it not just once, but twice. Paul was also saying, "It's not that you sent me the money, but the fact that I know there is fruit that is increasing to your credit because you sowed seed in me — which brings an increase that comes to you" — because Paul understood the harvest. This is kind of like the parables earlier where the servants sowed the seed and it doubled, Paul was highlighting this principle here — that it was a set up for them to be able to receive in the future because they were helping Paul (by sowing seed that was used in the harvest).

> Philippians 4:18 But I have [your full payment] and more; I have everything I need and am amply supplied, now that I have received from Epaphroditus the gifts you sent me. [They are the] fragrant odor of an offering and sacrifice which God welcomes and in which He delights.

Remember how in the Garden of Eden in Genesis 2, one of the cities was Bedullum — which is a bitter gum that is used for perfume or medicine. So here he says, "You gave something to me, it may have been bitter tasting to you, but God is receiving it as a fragrant odor, offering and sacrifice which God welcomes."

At verse 14-17, it isn't just about money, but that he knows the increase that they will receive as a result of having a right mindset about money — by being kingdom conduits for the finances to flow. Then at verse 18, this is talking about an offering and a sacrifice. Yes, we are talking about money, but our theme scripture (Romans 12:2) is talking about present our body as a living sacrifice — it is an offering unto God that is supposed to be holy and acceptable. Personally, I get blessed when I see His people increasing in grace and mercy, when I see His people realizing what it means to present your body as a living sacrifice — no longer living to please flesh, but beginning to see and think with the mind of Christ. That is when the blessing comes. Also as we do this, we begin to understand that a kingdom runs on finances — so we are just moving the finances around in the kingdom — so do what He tells you to do.

> Philippians 4:19 And my God will liberally supply (fill to the full) your every need according to His riches in glory in Christ Jesus.

Why will God do this? It is in response to the fact that you sowed seed — and were taking care of the gospel. We have to change our thinking on money and its purpose. We do not get money just for ourselves, but we get money to sow. We must change our thinking and see that there is more to money than meets the eye. We cannot think of money like the world thinks of it, but from a kingdom mindset. The liberally supply and fill to the full comes as a result of you doing what you were supposed to be doing. My God does it according to His riches in glory, not mine, or ours, but His — He has that under control.

5.5 Riches of Grace

Looking at the riches of grace — the fact that your riches come from His kingdom. People do not look at grace as part of being rich, but as we spoke early about favor, part of favor is grace. Grace leads people to repent.

> Ephesians 1:7 In Him we have redemption (deliverance and salvation) through His blood, the remission (forgiveness) of our offenses (shortcomings and trespasses), in accordance with the riches and the generosity of His gracious favor.

Our spiritual richness comes because we were redeemed with the blood of Jesus Christ. Redemption means bought with a price. The price is not dollar signs, when you are in Him, money is no big thing to you; you are now an ambassador. But you have to grow and mature in understanding what an ambassador does.

> Ephesians 2:7 He did this that He might clearly demonstrate through the ages to come the immeasurable (limitless, surpassing) riches of His free grace (His unmerited favor) in [His] kindness and goodness of heart toward us in Christ Jesus.

> 1 Timothy 1:14 And the grace (unmerited favor and blessing) of our Lord [actually] flowed out superabundantly and beyond measure for me, accompanied by faith and love that are [to be realized] in Christ Jesus.

It is as we get a better understanding of Christ Jesus, that we get a better understanding of grace; and money should not be an issue as we grow in this understanding. Caution, I am not saying to get an understanding of Him for the goal of getting money, it is as you grow in Him, that is part of the things that follow you, as in Matthew 6:33, you do not have to worry about things, but be kingdom minded.

A general reference to spiritual riches is that they are enduring:

> Proverbs 8:18 Riches and honor are with me, enduring wealth and righteousness (uprightness in every area and relation, and right standing with God).

God's blessing is the source of the spiritual riches:

> Proverbs 10:22 The blessing of the Lord—it makes [truly] rich, and He adds no sorrow with it [neither does toiling increase it].

A paradox of God's riches:

> Proverbs 13:7 One man considers himself rich, yet has nothing [to keep permanently]; another man considers himself poor, yet has great [and indestructible] riches.

Poor in spirit brings great riches in spirit, and the natural will follow.

The spiritual riches of God are unsearchable:

> Ephesians 3:8 To me, though I am the very least of all the saints (God's consecrated people), this grace (favor, privilege) was granted and graciously entrusted: to proclaim to the Gentiles the unending (boundless, fathomless, incalculable, and exhaustless) riches of Christ [wealth which no human being could have searched out]

They are unsearchable by the natural mind, you can only search them spiritually, by the Spirit. So a person must be born again; have received Jesus Christ in order to do this.

Spiritual riches are more precious than earthly riches:

> Hebrew 11:26 He considered the contempt and abuse and shame [borne for] the Christ (the Messiah Who was to come) to be greater wealth than all the treasures of Egypt, for he looked forward and away to the reward (recompense).

This was speaking of Moses, during his first 40 years of life he was raised in a palace, he had access to earthly riches, he had the best of education, clothing, food, etc., but when he realized that the riches of this world did not compare to being with his people and God, he walked away from it all.

The inheritance of God's elect:

> James 2:5 Listen, my beloved brethren: Has not God chosen those who are poor in the eyes of the world to be rich in faith and in their position as believers and to inherit the kingdom which He has promised to those who love Him?

The poor of this world are those that are rich in faith. So we must get our priorities right by seeking first the kingdom, which is faith in Jesus Christ as the Amplified bible defines faith as the leaning of your entire personality in complete trust and confidence in Him and the finished work of Calvary.

Prayer: Thank You for allowing us to renew our minds to truly understand riches, wealth, stewardship, and the kingdom in which we are called to live in as dual citizens of heaven and earth. Thank You for helping us transform our mind according to Your word that we would have a better understanding of the constitution of our kingdom. Thank You for moving us from thinking about finances from a worldly standpoint, that we realize that our poorness is

in spirit, and without you, we are nothing. Psalm 112:3 – our right standing (righteousness) only comes from You – as our own self-righteousness is as filthy rags – it is the righteousness that is imputed to us through Jesus Christ that You are looking for. Thank You for seeing us as blood bought, and seeing us through the blood. Thank You for causing us to be the bedullum, the gold, yes, it has a bitter taste, but you are bringing out of it a fragrance and an aroma to perfume and medicate – to help heal. Is there not a balm in Gilead? You are in us O God.

Thank You for changing our mind and our thinking that we would really know You – do not let us be like the servant that said "I knew You to be harsh" – but that we know You as the King of the kingdom, and You have empowered us to bring increase unto You. That You are the One that came up with reciprocity, and reaping and sowing – and we do not serve You just for stuff, but because we love You. And as we do as You have instructed us to do, You bring the increase. And as we do as in Philippians 4 and learn contentment in any and every situation, You O God see, know, and provide for all of our needs according to Your riches in glory. Your way is best – and in the process, teach us contentment – not to be murmuring and complaining along the way; but that we would be found upright in You. You know what we have need of before we even need it, You just want us to voice it to You. We see that You desire riches and wealth to be in our house, and we say yes to Your will and Your way – we give You access to move our thinking and our understanding out of the way, that You be glorified in us.

As in Exodus 3, allow us to see that You are desiring for us to leave the land of bondage, and that You are making a way, and You will give us the strategy to leave, and not leave empty handed, but have all of our needs met. You do it, You plan it, You work it out – and when You give us the instructions, our heart's cry will be "Yes to Your will! Sir, yes Sir! " Thank You for restoring us to a spiritual place of Eden, of pleasantness and delight – as we are walking in covenant rights with You. Thank You for free-flowing places in our lives, even in standing areas. Thank You for gushing fountains bursting forth in us that will happen because You are blessing us. Thank You for the fertility to give birth and produce spiritually – that You get the glory, honor, praise. Amen, so be it!

Chapter 6 – Conclusion

6.1 After all of this...

I would like to conclude this project with an exhortation from the word of God, and draw a few principles for us to live by:

> Ecclesiastes 12:11-14 The words of the wise are like prodding goads, and firmly fixed [in the mind] like nails are the collected sayings which are given [as proceeding] from one Shepherd. 12 But about going further [than the words given by one Shepherd], my son, be warned. Of making many books there is no end [so do not believe everything you read], and much study is a weariness of the flesh. 13 **All has been heard; the end of the matter is: Fear God** [revere and worship Him, knowing that He is] and keep His commandments, for this is the whole of man [the full, original purpose of his creation, the object of God's providence, the root of character, the foundation of all happiness, the adjustment to all inharmonious circumstances and conditions under the sun] and the whole [duty] for every man. 14 For God shall bring every work into judgment, with every secret thing, whether it is good or evil.

Life principles gleaned from Ecclesiastes 12:
1. Words of wisdom
2. Warning of much study in the flesh
3. Fear God
4. Every work into judgment
5. Secrets revealed (good or bad)

Listen to the word of the wise:

> Isaiah 50:4 [The Servant of God says] The Lord God has given Me the tongue of a disciple and of one who is taught, that I should know how to speak a word in season to him who is weary. He wakens Me morning by morning, He wakens My ear to hear as a disciple [as one who is taught].

Know that godly wisdom brings authority, so do not look at being outnumbered, or the least of.

> Ecclesiastes 7:19 [True] wisdom is a strength to the wise man more than ten rulers or valiant generals who are in the city.

Fearing the Lord is actually a commandment:

> 1 Peter 1:17 And if you call upon Him as [your] Father Who judges each one impartially according to what he does, [then] you should conduct yourselves with

true reverence throughout the time of your temporary residence [on the earth, whether long or short].

True religion...it will take mercy for you to be a sacrifice (Romans 12:1)

> Hosea 6:6 For I desire and delight in dutiful steadfast love and goodness, not sacrifice, and the knowledge of and acquaintance with God more than burnt offerings.

> Micah 6:8 He has showed you, O man, what is good. And what does the Lord require of you but to do justly, and **to love kindness and mercy**, and to humble yourself and walk humbly with your God?

> James 1:27 External religious worship [religion as it is expressed in outward acts] that is pure and unblemished in the sight of God the Father is this: to visit and help and care for the orphans and widows in their affliction and need, and to keep oneself unspotted and uncontaminated from the world.

Teach me how to prepare for this judgment:

> 2 Corinthians 5:10 For we must all appear and be revealed as we are before the judgment seat of Christ, so that each one may receive [his pay] according to what he has done in the body, whether good or evil [considering what his purpose and motive have been, and what he has achieved, been busy with, and given himself and his attention to accomplishing].

It is inevitable that sin will be exposed; therefore we must preach repentance to expose and correct sin:

> 1 Corinthians 4:5 So do not make any hasty or premature judgments before the time when the Lord comes [again], for He will both bring to light the secret things that are [now hidden] in darkness and disclose and expose the [secret] aims (motives and purposes) of hearts. Then every man will receive his [due] commendation from God.

6.2 Think on these things

Be encouraged to "think on these things" and do not entertain bad/wrong thoughts/things:

> Philippians 4:8-9 For the rest, brethren, whatever is true, whatever is worthy of reverence and is honorable and seemly, whatever is just, whatever is pure, whatever is lovely and lovable, whatever is kind and winsome and gracious, if

there is any virtue and excellence, if there is anything worthy of praise, think on and weigh and take account of these things [fix your minds on them]. ⁹Practice what you have learned and received and heard and seen in me, and model your way of living on it, and the God of peace (of untroubled, undisturbed well-being) will be with you.

6.3 Kingdom Ready, Thy Kingdom Come – Volume Four

A brief preview of what to expect in the fourth volume. What He is preparing us all for, and what we should be found doing. Chapters will be similar and delve deeper into:

- Great Commission
- Great Commandment
- Kingdom suffers violence
- Believer's authority
- Mercy
- Prioritize kingdom
- Angels and the kingdom
- Ambassadors of the kingdom
- From faith to faith, and glory to glory
- The role of parables and the kingdom
- Kingdom paradoxes
- Kingdom paradigm
- Kingdom covenant
- Sovereignty

I know, this is a lot of information, so I close volume three, and begin the journey for volume four — continue to pray with your now renewed mind for the Lord's will to be made manifest through A Portion Ministries to the generations present, and those to come. Lord be pleased. Blessings
~P~

Notes

Notes

Notes

Notes

Notes

Notes

Notes

Notes

Notes

Notes

Notes

Notes

Notes

Notes

Notes

Notes

Notes

Notes

Notes

Notes

References

Internet Websites:

www.biblegateway.com

www.blueletter.org

www.merriam-webster.com

Books Referenced:

Holman Illustrated Bible Dictionary
ISBN 0-80542-836-4, © 2003

A Dictionary of Bible Types, by Walter L. Wilson, Hendrickson Publishers, Inc.
ISBN 1-56563-418-7, © 1999

The Necessity of prayer, by E.M. Bounds
ISBN 0-55.68-139-0, © 1984

Suggested Reading, Books Referred to:

What Is Worldliness? By Cooper Beaty
ISBN 0-9656489-0-7, © 1997

Rejection – Its Fruits and Its Roots, by Dr. William G. Null
ISBN 0-89228-164-2, © 2005

There Were Two Trees In The Garden, by Rick Joyner
ISBN 0-88368-497-7, © 1986

Worship – The Ultimate Priority, by John F. MacArthur
ISBN 0-80240-215-1 © 2012

Other Books By Paulette Denise

Volume One — Single Women

A Portion, Volume I is directed to single women. However, everyone can benefit from this book. Paulette has written this book from where she is at this time in her life and felt compelled to share with an audience she so avidly works with, single women. This book will benefit anyone who will take the time to read it:

Single Women — Read and apply this knowledge and become whole.
Married Women — You may have entered your marriage bond with excess baggage, this book may help you to get it right. In Titus chapter 2 there is a command that says that mature women are to teach and train the younger, this book can aid you with this and it is a perfect gift for those whom you are training.
Single Men - This book offers basic points to help you in your quest of fulfilling the scripture, "He who finds a good wife." This book also talks about the preparation a young woman who is going through the process of becoming whole and a qualified "help meet" for you.
Married Men — This book talks about biblical etiquette for women in general and can shed light or understanding in your life, whether you are married or single.

Volume Two — Christians On Assignment - Talking About Obedience

One common denominator of all the assignments you will face in your Christian walk is OBEDIENCE. A Portion Volume II, Christians On Assignment, Talking About Obedience is not meant to be a how-to book, but rather a self-help tool that can be used during your preparation process. The purpose of this book is to act as a guide, making you aware of potential obstacles that you may encounter in your Christian walk and providing tools to help you navigate around them.

Some of the topics addressed are: * Defining obedience * Defining faith * The preparation process * Dealing with the heart * Prayer and fasting * Just to name a few.

If you are called of God, not just as a minister, but to be a Christian (a disciple, a learner of God) this book is for you. Written as a reference document to be used throughout your Christian walk fulfilling assignment after assignment for the Lord.

Journals: Dreams & Visions, Spiritual Growth, Sermon Notes

These journals are notebooks for you to chronicle and grow from the dreams the Lord is revealing in the last day; to track spiritual growth periodically; and to apply the sermons that you experience to actual life events — be a DOer of the word.

About The Author

Paulette Denise — No frills — just sold out love for Jesus Christ and His people.

Although she was not raised in the church, her parents instilled godly qualities within her. She received the call to ministry the day she received salvation in 1988 (just 2 days before entering the United States Air Force); however she did not answer the call until almost 7 years later in 1995. She has served in ministry at Acts Full Gospel COGIC (1998, Oakland, CA — Dr. Bob Jackson), and Greater Love Ministries (2001, San Leandro, CA — Pastors Tommy and Sheryll Gilbert); then relocated to attend Rhema Bible Training College (2002, Broken Arrow, OK, Pastor Kenneth and Lynette Hagin) where she graduated in 2004. She has been faithfully serving at The Fellowship of Love Church (2005, Houston, TX — Pastor Lorenzo & Lady Kandice Ewing) — as well as assisting as a vital part of several ministries to fulfill their mission/vision: Woman Rise Up Ministries — Apostle Ida B. Ulrich; Cassandra Scott Ministries International Prayer Line — Dr. Cassandra Scott; Visual Arts Productions, Stacy J & Unified Praise Dance Company — Minister Stacy Johnson-Harrell.

Paulette is a prayer pioneer at heart, giving the word of God entrance into the lives of God's people through intercession. She also knows that preparation time is never wasted time. An evangelistic revivalist equipped to train the body of Christ, one life at a time, she is anointed to teach and open the truths of God's word in fulfillment of 1 Timothy 2:4 KJV: *God wishes all men to be saved and come into the knowledge of the truth.*

A true "Ram in the bush" worshipper at heart — whatever the need be for worship: teach, preach, pray, dance, sing, administrate, WHATEVER the need — a true servant of the Lord, with the proper heart perspective that it is all done unto the Lord, not man, or for recognition (Colossians 3:23).

Please visit the website at: **www.aportionpaulettedenise.com**, or contact us via Facebook (Paulette Denise) or email **paulettex7@gmail.com** for booking information or more details regarding Minister Paulette Denise.

www.ingramcontent.com/pod-product-compliance
Lightning Source LLC
Chambersburg PA
CBHW051816290426
44109CB00021BA/2382